THE I TATTI
RENAISSANCE LIBRARY

James Hankins, General Editor

FICINO
PLATONIC THEOLOGY

VOLUME 4

ITRL 13

MARSILIO FICINO

PLATONIC THEOLOGY

VOLUME 4 • BOOKS XII–XIV

ENGLISH TRANSLATION BY

MICHAEL J. B. ALLEN

LATIN TEXT EDITED BY

JAMES HANKINS

with William Bowen

THE I TATTI RENAISSANCE LIBRARY
HARVARD UNIVERSITY PRESS
CAMBRIDGE, MASSACHUSETTS
LONDON, ENGLAND
2004

Printed in the United States of America

Series design by Dean Bornstein

Library of Congress Cataloging-in-Publication Data
Ficino, Marsilio, 1433–1499.
[Theologia Platonica. English & Latin]
Platonic theology / Marsilio Ficino ; English translation by Michael J.B. Allen with John Warden ; Latin text edited by James Hankins with William Bowen.
p. cm. — (The I Tatti Renaissance library ; 2)
Includes bibliographical references (v. 1, p.) and index.
Contents: v. 1. Books I–IV. v. 2. Books V–VIII.
v. 3. Books IX–XI. v. 4. Books XII–XIV.
ISBN 0-674-00345-4 (v. 1 : alk. paper)
ISBN 0-674-00764-6 (v. 2 : alk. paper)
ISBN 0-674-01065-5 (v. 3 : alk. paper)
ISBN 0-674-01482-0 (v. 4 : alk. paper)
1. Plato. 2. Soul. 3. Immortality. I. Allen, Michael J. B.
II. Warden, John, 1936– III. Hankins, James.
IV. Bowen, William R. V. Title. VI. Series.
B785.F433 T53 2001
186′.4—dc21 00-053491

Contents

Prefatory Note

This is the fourth volume in what will be a six-volume edition of the *Platonic Theology*. Once again Michael Allen is responsible for the translation and notes and James Hankins for the text and critical apparatus, though each has gone over the other's work. We would like to thank John Warden for a preliminary draft of Book XII and Ada Palmer for checking many of the references. As in the previous volumes, William Bowen has kindly provided a scanned text of the Marcel edition, which has been used as a copytext for a fresh collation of the principle witnesses.

Volume 5 will contain the huge fifteenth and sixteenth books; and Volume 6, will contain, besides the seventeenth and eighteenth books and other related texts, corrigenda, concordances and various indices.

We would be delighted to hear from scholars who have corrections or further source suggestions, particularly since, in an undertaking as huge and exacting as this, some nodding will have occurred.

M.A. and J.H.

THEOLOGIA PLATONICA DE IMMORTALITATE ANIMORUM

Capitula librorum Theologiae
de immortalitate animorum
Marsilii Ficini Florentini
divisae in libros XVIII

Duodecimus liber. Quod sit immortalis quia formatur divina mente.

Tertius decimus liber. Quod sit immortalis per quattuor signa, scilicet a phantasiae affectibus, rationis effectibus, artibus, miraculis.

The Theology on the Immortality of Souls
by Marsilio Ficino the Florentine
Divided into Eighteen Books:
Chapter Headings

Cap. II Signum secundum: ab effectibus rationis et vaticinatio.[2]

Cap. III Tertium signum: ab artium et gubernationis industria.

Cap. IV Signum quartum:[3] ab effectu miraculorum.

Cap. V Quaestiones sex de miraculis et solutiones.

Quartus decimus liber. Quod sit immortalis secundum duodecim dei dotes quas anima imitatur.

Cap. I Quod anima nitatur deus fieri, ostendimus signis duodecim secundum duodecim dei dotes.

Cap. II Quintum immortalitatis signum ab eo quod anima appetit primum verum et primum bonum.

Cap. III Sextum signum: quia animus conatur omnia fieri.

Cap. IV Septimum signum et octavum: quoniam animus conatur facere omnia atque item omnia superare.

Cap. V Nonum signum et decimum: quod homo affectat ubique esse atque item esse semper.

Cap. VI Signum XI, XII, XIII, XIV: quod cupimus quattuor dei virtutes assequi.

Cap. VII XV signum: quod animus summam expetit opulentiam et voluptatem.

Cap. VIII XVI signum: quod colimus nos ipsos ac deum.

DUODECIMUS LIBER[1]

: I :

Rationes multae et signa. Mens humana intellegendo mente divina formatur.

1 Plato, philosophorum pater, in epistola ad Syracusanos de comparanda sapientia disputans, quinque inquit potissimum ad rei cuiusque scientiam concurrere oportere: nomen, descriptionem, idolum, formulam et ideam. Exemplum de circulo sicut ipse ponamus, ut idem de ceteris omnibus arbitremur. Animus noster ad scientiam circuli commonetur saepenumero per auditum, quando audit tum nomen hoc 'circulus,' tum circuli descriptionem huiusmodi: 'Circulus est figura reflexa quae aequis intervallis undique distat a medio'. Admonetur quoque per visum, quando circulum vel torno factum ex ligno videt vel in pariete signatum, qui non verus est circulus, quoniam non perfectus, sed veri idolum et simulacrum. Per haec tria commonitus animus, avidus veritatis, eruit in actum ingenitam sibi circuli formulam. Per quam velut characterem ad ipsam circuli ideam in mente divina vigentem aciem dirigit, quae quidem directio est scientia circuli. Ostendit autem in ea epistola Plato animum corpore clausum non posse ad ideam absque quatuor illis gradibus surgere, quia oportet illum iam diu infra se lapsum primum per illa tria in se reverti, deinde per for-

BOOK XII

: I :

Many arguments and witnesses proving that the human mind is formed in understanding by the divine mind.

Plato, the father of philosophers, when he is discussing how to obtain wisdom in his letter to the Syracusans, says that for us to know each thing we mainly need a combination of these five items: name, description, image, formula, and idea.[1] Let us use the example of the circle as he did to suppose the same of all the rest. Our rational soul is often reminded of its knowledge of a circle through hearing when it hears the name "circle" or the following description of a circle: "a circle is a figure that bends back upon itself and is everywhere equidistant from its center." It is reminded too through vision when it sees a circle made out of wood on a lathe, or painted on a wall: this is not a true circle, as it is not perfect, but an image or copy of the true. So the rational soul (hungry for truth and roused by the name, description, and image) summons into act the innate formula of a circle from within itself. This formula is like a seal or character that the soul uses to direct its gaze towards the idea itself of the circle blossoming within the divine mind, and this directing is knowledge of the circle. In the letter Plato shows that a rational soul which is enclosed in the body cannot rise to the idea without ascending these four steps, since, having fallen below its own level long ago, to return to itself it has first take the initial three steps, and then use the formula which it has within to rise above itself to the idea.[2] For just as the forms of things are cast forth from the divine mind into matter by means of the soul's lowest power, that is, via the seeds of forms implanted in I

mulam quam in se habet supra se ipsum ascendere ad ideam. Sicut enim formae rerum a mente divina in materiam per infimam animae virtutem traiiciuntur, id est per semina formarum virtuti huic infusa, ita a formarum corporalium perceptione non fit transitus in divinae mentis ideas nisi per summam animae partem, id est per innatas formulas idearum, ut a formis corporis, quae omnino temporales sunt quia tam essentia quam affectione mutantur, transcendatur in formas divinae mentis, aeternas omnino quia nulla ex parte mutantur, per mentis humanae formas partim aeternas, partim etiam temporales, quia per essentiam manent, per affectionem vero ex habitu vertuntur in actum atque contra.

2 Merito enim faber qui materiam formaturus est ipse disponit. Idcirco mens illa sublimis, mentem nostram[2] per ideas quotidie formatura, ad hanc formationem olim disposuit eam per characteres idearum signavitque, quemadmodum Propheta canit: 'Super nos vultus sui lumen, ut lumen in suo lumine videremus'. Videlicet ut per formulam opportune excitatam idea non aliter accenderetur in mente quam aut ignis per sulphur in ligno aut per naturam perspicuam serenamque in aere lumen. Et quia sicut natura ad suam se habet materiam, ita paene deus ad suam, natura vero caelestem, ut quidam putant, materiam semel cunctis formis ornavit, elementalem singulis momentis exornat, ideo probabile est deum quoque materiam, ut ita loquar, angelicam semel ideis omnibus implevisse, animalem implere quotidie. Huic autem Platonicorum mysterio similis ex quadam parte videtur esse Avicennae Algantelisque opinio. Opinantur enim materiam tum elementalem tum intellectualem sub luna divinae cuidam menti tamquam formatrici subesse, cuius instrumenta sint ad elementalem materiam disponendam formae corporeae, sed ipsa tandem praeparatae materiae substantiales imprimat formas. Similiter humanam mentem

the power, so the passage from the perception of bodily forms to the ideas of the divine mind does not take place except via the highest part of the soul, that is, via the innate formulae of the ideas. The passage is such that the ascent from the body's forms, which are entirely temporal because they change both in essence and affective condition, to the forms of the divine mind, which are entirely eternal because no aspect of them changes, is made via the forms of the human mind, which are partly eternal and partly temporal; and this is because via their essence they are unchanging but via their affective condition they are turned from habit into act and back again.

It behooves the craftsman who is going to give form to matter 2
to prepare it himself. Thus the sublime mind, when it is about to give form to our mind daily via the ideas, has prepared our mind earlier for this forming, and imprinted it with the characters of the ideas. As the Prophet [David] sings, "The light of His countenance is upon us, so that we might see the light in His light."[3] By this he means that the idea catches fire in our mind through the formula struck at the right moment, just as fire is ignited in wood through sulfur, or light illuminates the air thanks to the air's clear and cloudless nature. And because nature's relationship to matter is analogous almost to that of God to His matter, but nature has adorned celestial matter, as some believe, with all the forms only once whereas it is adorning elemental matter at every single moment, so God probably filled angelic matter, if I may call it that, with all the ideas only once too, but fills ensouled matter daily. The opinion of Avicenna and Algazel seems to be somewhat similar to this mystery of the Platonists.[4] For they think that sublunar elemental and intellectual matter is subject to some divine mind as the form-giver, whose instruments for preparing elemental matter are the corporeal forms; but when matter is eventually prepared, this divine mind itself imprints the substantial forms [in it]. Likewise, they think, the human mind, having received images of bod-

per imagines corporum per sensus phantasiamque acceptas ita saepe disponi, ut in divinam illam intellegentiam se convertat atque ab illa, quatenus convertitur, eatenus formari quotidie. Neque aliud quicquam esse quod intellegere dicimus quam ab intellegentia divina formari. Quod autem dicimus meminisse, id esse videlicet habitum iam contraxisse, quo facile ad divinam mentem pro arbitrio convertamur. Sed mittamus Arabes in praesentia, quamvis Platoni satis amicos. Ad Platonica redeamus.

3 Quod autem res vere cognoscere nequeamus, nisi formemur ideis, his rationibus Plato sibi persuasisse videtur. Prima. Nomen circuli mutabile est. Potest enim usu linguae variato aliter appellari. Si est ita, descriptio quoque mutabilis est quae componitur ex nominibus. Idolum quoque mutabile. Potest enim ligneus circulus destrui et qui pictus est aboleri. Formula quoque ex eo mutabilis quod ex potentia sive habitu migrat in actum deque actu rursus in habitum. Illud autem quod per scientiam circuli comprehenditur est penitus immutabile, quoniam et universale est et non potest aliter se habere. Quapropter idea immutabili opus est ad rationem circuli immutabilem comprehendendam.

4 Secunda. Circulus, qui vel torno fit vel pingitur, non est purus, quia nonnihil rectae figurae habet admixtum. Similiter phantasia, quae sequitur illius aspectum, puram rationem circuli non assequitur, quae est a figura eius opposita penitus segregata. Ratio quoque si phantasiae auscultaverit, fallitur. Oportet ergo ut ad puram ideam recurrat qua cernat purum.

5 Tertia. Scientia vera circuli in eo consistit ut quid sit circulus cognoscatur. Quatuor vero illa qualitatem potius significant quam substantiam, quia et ipsa sunt qualitates.

6 Quarta. Verus perfectusque cognoscendi modus modum sequitur essendi. Itaque sicut tam circulus quam reliquae rerum species a mente divina per earum ideas concipiuntur et pariuntur, sic a se-

ies through the senses and the phantasy, is so prepared that it can turn towards the divine understanding, and insofar as it is turned, it is daily formed. What we call understanding is nothing other than being formed by the divine understanding; and what we call remembering is to have already contracted the habit by which we are turned towards the divine mind easily and at will. But let us dismiss the Arabs for the present, though they are quite good friends to Plato, and return to Plato's teachings.

Plato seems to have persuaded himself that we cannot know 3
anything truly, unless we are formed by the ideas, for the following reasons. First. The word for circle changes. In a different language it can be called differently. If so, the description changes too, because it is compounded of words. The image also changes; for a circle made of wood can be destroyed, and a painted circle erased. The formula too changes in that it passes from habit into act, and from act back again into habit. But what is comprehended via knowledge of the circle is completely unchangeable, both because it is universal, and because it cannot be otherwise. Therefore, in order to comprehend the unchangeable reason of a circle, we need an immutable idea.

Second. A circle produced on a lathe, or painted, is not pure, 4
because it has a certain element of straightness mingled with it. Likewise the picture in the phantasy, which is the result of looking at the visible circle, does not attain the pure rational principle of a circle, which is totally separate from and opposite to its figure. If the reason listens to the phantasy, it too errs. To see the pure circle it must therefore have recourse to the pure idea.

Third. True knowledge of a circle consists in knowing what a 5
circle is. The four steps we are talking about signify quality rather than substance, because they themselves are qualities.[5]

Fourth. The true and perfect mode of knowing follows the 6
mode of existing. Just as a circle and the other kinds of object are conceived and brought to birth from the divine mind by means of

quentibus mentibus per easdem cognoscendae videntur, ut omnes scientiae primam pro viribus scientiam imitentur. Veritas rei creatae in hoc versatur ut ideae suae respondeat undique; scientia vero in hoc praecipue ut mens congruat veritati. Non potest autem rei ipsius veritati quadrare, nisi ideae quoque quadret, in cuius congruitate sita est veritas, ut ita per ideam, quae rei causa est, rem cognoscat, siquidem vera scientia est per causam. Ideo Ioannis evangelistae theologia, quae ideam appellat rationem divinam, eam ipsam rationem vocat veritatem, quia per eam res et vere subsistant et cognoscantur vere.

7 Quinta. Intellectus quaelibet creata in ipsorum rationibus absolutis intellegit et diiudicat. Et sicut plerumque eadem sensibilia natura sua omnibus sentientibus praesto adsunt neque mutatis istis illa inde mutantur, ita eaedem intellegibiles rationes ubique et semper cunctis ratiocinantibus sese monstrant manentque stabiles in se ipsis, dum ratiocinantium animi magis minusve ad illas accedunt. Rationes huiusmodi creatis omnibus praestantiores sunt, non[3] ob id solum quod per ipsas tamquam regulas creata quaeque probantur reprobanturve, sed ob hoc insuper quod tum propter amplitudinem, tum propter simplicitatem sunt priores. Quapropter in ipso sunt deo, per quas ipse et discernit singula et disponit. Quando igitur intellectus apprehendit rationes huiusmodi, tunc apprehendit quodammodo tam deum in quo sunt, quam res quarum illae sunt exemplaria. Prius tamen secundum naturalem originem quandam quodammodo apprehendit deum, in quo illae sunt, quam res, quibus non insunt, quamvis adsint. Neque incredibile videri cuiquam debet per incorporalia exemplaria corporalia quae-

their ideas, so they appear to be known by subsequent minds through the same ideas; and the result is that all kinds of knowledge will imitate prime knowledge as much as possible. The truth of a created object consists in its corresponding in every respect with its idea. But knowledge mainly consists in the mind being in harmony with the truth. Yet it cannot square with the object's truth, unless it also squares with the idea in whose harmony the truth consists, such that the mind knows the object through the idea that is its cause (since true knowledge is via the cause). Hence the theology of John the Evangelist, which calls the idea the divine reason, also calls this reason the truth, because through it things truly exist and are truly known.[6]

Fifth. The intellect understands and judges all created objects 7
in terms of their absolute rational principles. And just as most sensible objects readily and naturally present themselves as the same to all those perceiving them and do not change when the perceivers change, so the intelligible principles always and everywhere present themselves as the same to those using their reasons, and remain unchanging in themselves, even as the rational souls of those doing the reasoning may be closer to them or farther away. Such principles are superior to all created things not only because through them, as through rules, all created objects are accepted or rejected, but also because they are prior in their amplitude and simplicity. Hence they are in God Himself, who uses them to distinguish and arrange individual entities. So when the intellect apprehends such principles, then it apprehends in a way both God in whom they exist and the objects whose paradigms they are. For in accordance with its particular natural origin, the intellect in a way apprehends God (in whom dwell the principles) before it apprehends objects (in which the principles do not dwell, though they are present to them). It should not appear unbelievable to anyone that all corporeal objects are known through their incorporeal paradigms rather than the reverse. For it

libet cognosci potius quam converso.[4] Nam per imagines sensibilium spiritales, sive in sensibus sive in speculis illae sint, sensibilia corpora, non contra sentimus. Quod autem ita hac in re decipiamur, ut dum spiritalia rerum exemplaria intuemur, saepe intueri solum naturas rerum corporeas arbitremur, quid mirum, cum et infantes quando in speculis vident simulacra corporum incorporea, et somniantes quando cogitant imagines spiritales corpora videre se credant? Sed de hoc planius in sequentibus.

8 Adde his rationibus signa duo, alterum per intellectum, alterum per voluntatem. Per intellectum hoc pacto. In speciei naturalis ceu pulchritudinis cognitione, primo quidem descriptionem pulchritudinis aliquam singulis rebus pulchris communem excogitamus. Addimus statim proprietates aliquas pulchritudinis a descriptione deductas. Has notiones forsitan concedemus posse per formulam pulchritudinis menti innatam excogitari. Sed quando in hac ipsa consideratione diutius immoramur, invenimus eam naturam pulchritudinis quam definivimus, quia mera sit, esse infinitam, et quia infinita sit, esse deum. Nullus autem sanae mentis concesserit per formulam terminatam et infra deum intervallo longissimo, immo incomparabili, existentem apprehendi naturam infinitam ipsumque deum. Igitur mens, per formulam suam ex habitu eductam in actum, ideae divinae quadam praeparatione subnectitur; cui subnexa supra se surgit. Nulla enim res supra se umquam attollitur, nisi a superiore trahatur. Quo enim pacto aqua volat in aerem, nisi calore aeris elevetur? Facile autem et naturali quodam instinctu ipsa formula, cum sit ideae radius, resilit in ideam, secumque attollit mentem, cui est infusus hic radius. Qui cum reducitur in ideam, refluit in eam sicut fontem, ceu radius repercussus in solem. Perque nodum huiusmodi unum aliquid ex mente et deo conficitur. Hinc Paulus divinus theologus inquit: 'Qui adhaeret deo unus fit spiritus'.

is through the spiritual images of sensible objects, whether they are in the senses or in mirrors, that we perceive sensible bodies, not vice versa. And is it surprising we are so deceived in this matter that when we look at things' spiritual paradigms we often think we are gazing only at their corporeal natures? For children when they see the bodiless images of bodies in mirrors, and dreamers, when they peruse spiritual images, both believe they are seeing actual bodies. I will go into this in more detail later.

To these reasons add two further signs, one from the intellect, the other from the will. [First] from the intellect. In acquiring knowledge of a natural species like beauty, we first think about a description of beauty common to all beautiful objects; then we immediately add certain properties of beauty derived from the description. We will concede that we could perhaps ponder these notions by way of a formula of beauty innate in the mind. But when we spend more time in this consideration, we find that the nature of beauty, which we have defined, is infinite because it is pure, and, being infinite, is God. Now nobody of right mind would concede that an infinite nature and God Himself are apprehensible through a finite formula existing at an immense, yea an immeasurable, distance beneath God. So the mind, using its own formula brought from habit into act, is linked to the divine idea in a preparatory way; and thus linked, it rises above itself. For nothing can ever elevate itself above itself, unless it is lifted up by something higher. How does water, for instance, rise into the air unless it is being lifted by the air's heat? Since it is the ray of the idea, the formula itself rebounds to the idea by a natural instinct and with ease, and carries with it the mind into which this ray has been irradiated. Since it is led back to the idea, the ray flows back into it as into a fountain, as a ray is reflected into the sun. And by way of a knot of this kind a single entity is compounded from the mind and from God. Hence Paul, the divine theologian, declares, "He who is joined to God becomes one spirit."[7] 8

9 Signum per voluntatem hoc est. Mens in clara veritatis cognitione tam mirabili voluptate perfunditur, ut omnem humanae voluptatis excedat modum. Talem quoque vitae statum voluntas propter se ipsum appetit solum, alia propter illum, quasi status[5] eiusmodi in summa sit arce naturae, ultra quem nihil supersit optandum.

10 His rationibus et aliis paene similibus Plato sibi persuasisse videtur nihil revera disci posse, nisi docente deo. Ideo in eadem epistola inquit: 'Divina mysteria verbis doceri non possunt. At si quis diutissime cum divinis versetur similemque illis agat vitam, subito tandem tamquam ab igne scintillante lumen veritatis effulget in animo seque ipsum iam alit'. Quod sibi scribit accidisse. Merito, quia etiam in epistola ad Dionysium regem scripserat omnem suae mentis curam in divinorum investigatione versari. Quam quidem investigationem Socrates tandem purgatione mentis assecuturam, quicquid cupit, existimat. Ideo praetermissa quandoque solita inquisitionis solicitudine ad moralem confugit philosophiam, ut mens eius beneficio corporeis discussis nubibus facta serenior, divini solis lumen semper et ubique lucens subito caperet. Quod quidem et Socrates ipse prius, deinde Plato imitatione Socratis assecutus fuisse videtur. Sed ad institutum ordinem redeamus.

11 Plato in septimo libro *De republica*, cum deum bonitatem ipsam appellavisset, adiunxit vix quidem eam percipi posse, sed hac ignorata nihil aut vere cognosci aut recte agi vel publice vel privatim. Quod quidem ab Indis philosophis Socratem et Platonem didicisse Aristoxenus affirmat. Idque Socrates Theagi apertissime declaravit, videlicet a solo deo tam haec quam alia disci, quemadmo-

[Now] a sign from the will. The mind in clear knowledge of the truth is suffused with such a wonderful pleasure that it exceeds every measure of human pleasure. The will too desires this state of life for itself alone, and everything else for its sake, as if this state dwelt on the summit of nature and nothing desirable existed beyond it. 9

With these arguments and others much like them Plato seems to have convinced himself that nothing can truly be learned unless God is the teacher. Thus he says, in the same letter: "Divine mysteries cannot be taught by words. But if someone spends all his time with things divine and tries to live his life in conformity with theirs, suddenly, as from a sparking fire, the light of truth will blaze up in his soul at last and thereafter nourish itself."[8] This, he writes, had happened to himself: and properly so, since in a letter too to King Dionysius he had written that he was devoting all his mind's energy to the study of things divine.[9] Socrates thought that such a study would at length purge the mind and enable it to achieve whatever it desired.[10] Accordingly, having set aside at some point his usual preoccupation with asking questions, he sought refuge in moral philosophy, with the result that with its aid, having dispelled the clouds of the body, his mind became clearer and was filled suddenly with the light of the divine sun that shines forever and everywhere. Socrates achieved this first himself, and then Plato seems to have done so too by imitating Socrates. But let us return to our topic. 10

In the seventh book of the *Republic,* since he had called God goodness itself, Plato adds that this goodness can scarcely be perceived, but unless it is known nothing is truly known or rightly performed, publicly or privately.[11] Aristoxenus maintains that Socrates and Plato learned this from Indian philosophers.[12] And Socrates put the same notion to Theages in the clearest terms: only from God can we learn about this or any other matter (as we discussed in the previous book).[13] But in the sixth book of the *Repub-* 11

dum in libro superiore narravimus. In sexto autem *De republica* Plato deum comparat soli, ut in libro *De amore* exposuimus, ut quemadmodum summum in genere sensibilium se habet ad sensus et sensibilia, ita summum in genere intellegibilium se ad intellectus et intellegibilia habeat. Sol oculos visuros et colores visibiles procreat. Tribuit oculis generationem, vim videndi et videndi actum, quia sine lumine nihil actu videmus. Dat rursus coloribus generationem, ac vim qua oculos possint movere, et actum per quem moveant. Sic deus, ut scribit Plato, mentibus essentiam tribuit, deinde intellegendi virtutem, postremo ipsam infundit intellegentiam. Rebus quoque intellegibilibus praestat essentiam, vim qua mentem movere queant, et actum per quem moveant. Itaque mentis actum deus cum intellegibilium actu coniungit, sicut solis lumen oculi actum cum actu colorum. Et sicut in videndo triplex est actus, motus scilicet coloris, aspectus oculi, fulgor luminis connectens actus reliquos invicem, sic in intellegendo, ubi actus intellegibilium veritas a Platone vocatur, actus mentis scientia, actus utrorumque nodus apud Platonem est deus, qui efficit ut et mens scienter intellegat et res vere intellegantur, immo facit ut ipse intellegatur.

12 Idcirco Ioannes evangelista inquit dei mentem esse viam veritatemque et vitam, ac neminem ad deum proficisci nisi per ipsam. Est enim veritas rerum intellegendarum, vita mentis intellegentis, via per quam res ipsae menti influunt et in qua mens rebus fit obvia. Quare et alibi dixit eos solos veritatis spiritum videre posse, apud quos et in quibus est deus. Nam si res bonae sub bonitatis ratione voluntatem movent atque ideo bonitas ipsa voluntatem movet per bonitatem ad bonitatem, neque aliud quicquam nisi bonitatem ipsam in singulis exoptamus, sequitur ut quia res verae

lic,[14] Plato compares God to the sun (as we explained in the *De amore*).[15] He says that the highest in the class of sensibles is related to our senses and to sensible objects in the same way that the highest in the class of intelligibles is related to our intellects and to intelligible objects. The sun procreates eyes to see and colors to be seen. To eyes it gives their generated essence,[16] their power to see, and the act of seeing (since without light we see nothing in act). To colors again it gives their generated essence,[17] and the power by which they can move the eyes, and the act through which they do move them. In the same way, writes Plato, God provides essence to minds, then the power of understanding, and finally pours in understanding itself. To intelligible objects too He gives essence, the power whereby they can move the mind, and the act through which they move it. Thus God unites the act of mind and the act of intelligible objects, as the sunlight unites the act of the eye and the act of colors. And just as in seeing the act is threefold—the motion of color, the looking of the eye, the brilliance of the light joining the other two acts together—so in understanding the act of intelligible objects is called truth by Plato and the act of mind, knowledge; and the act that knots them together for Plato is God, who ensures both that the mind knowingly understands and that the objects are truly understood. Rather, God brings it about that He Himself is understood.

As John the Evangelist says, the mind of God is "the way, the 12
truth, and the life," and no one comes to God except through it.[18] For it is the truth of the objects to be understood; it is the life of the mind that understands; and it is the way by which the objects flow into the mind and the mind comes into contact with them. Thus he said elsewhere that they alone with whom and in whom God abides can see the spirit of truth.[19] For if good things move the will by reason of goodness, and therefore goodness itself moves the will through goodness to goodness, and we yearn for nothing else but goodness in particular objects, then it follows, be-

sub ratione veritatis intellectum movent, idcirco veritas ipsa per veritatem ad ipsam veritatem moveat intellectum, neque aliud quicquam quam veritatem ipsam intellectus intellegat. Ipsam vero bonitatem et veritatem esse deum ambigit nemo.

13 Lucentes oculi luce communi lucentia vident, aures aereae[6] communi aere aerea audiunt. Veridicae mentes veritate communi vera intellegunt et pronuntiant. Voluntates quoque bonae ipsa bonitate communi afficiuntur ad bona. Et sicut oculus, solis lumine illustratus, in eo corporum colores intuetur atque figuras, neque aliud quicquam revera nisi lumen ipsum videt, licet videatur varia intueri (quia lumen ipsi infusum variis fulget splendoribus, prout a variis corporibus in visum reflectitur atque hoc quidem lumen in corporibus reflexum oculus percipit, ipsam vero in fonte suo lucem minime sustinet), ita mens nostra, dei radio illustrata, in eo ipso intellegit rerum omnium rationes, quarum fons est deus, et quae deus ipsae sunt; ideo et per dei lumen intellegit et ipsum divinum dumtaxat lumen cognoscit. Diversa tamen videtur cognoscere, quia sub diversis rerum inde manantium ideis et rationibus ipsum intellegit. Quamvis autem per dei lumen quotidie omnia cognoscamus et ipsum quoque lumen sub tali aut tali rerum figura refulgens gradatim percipiamus, puram tamen dei lucem[7] ab ideis omnibus absolutam et in suo fonte penitus infinitam non prius videbimus quam eum mentis purissimae statum adipiscamur, in quo lumen ipsum unico intuitu cunctarum simul idearum splendore refulgens contueamur. Tunc, ut inquit praeco ille veritatis insignis Ioannes evangelista, videbimus deum sicuti est, quia deum cognoscemus ut deum. Nunc enim formati hac idea vel illa videmus eum ut speciem hanc rerum aut illam, quamvis et in hac vita secundum Ioannem theologi filii dei sint, quia per divinas ideas

cause things true move the intellect by reason of truth, that the truth itself moves the intellect through truth to truth itself, and that the intellect understands nothing else but the truth itself. But nobody doubts that this goodness and truth are God.

Eyes shining with light see objects shining with light by means 13
of a common light; ears of an airy nature hear airy objects by means of a common air. Truth-telling minds understand and proclaim things true by means of a common truth. Wills that are good long for things good by means of a common goodness. The eye, illuminated by the light of the sun, sees the colors and shapes of bodies in that light, in fact sees nothing but the light itself even though it seems to see different things (since the light pouring into the eye is refulgent with various splendors insofar as it is reflected into the vision from different bodies, and the eye perceives this light reflected in bodies, but it does not receive the light at its source). Similarly our mind, illuminated by God's ray, understands in that ray the rational principles of all things whose source is God and which themselves are God; and hence through God's light it understands and knows only the divine light itself. Yet the mind seems to know different things, because it understands the light in terms of the different ideas and principles of things emanating from it. But although we know everything from day to day through God's light and by degrees also perceive the light shining under this or that figure in objects, yet we will not see the pure light of God, independent of all ideas and utterly infinite at its source, until we attain that state of mental purity wherein, in a single glance, we gaze upon that very light refulgent in the splendor of all the ideas together. It is then, says that glorious messenger of truth, John the Evangelist, that we shall see God as He is, because we shall know God as God.[20] But now, formed as we are by this or that idea, we see Him as one species or another, although even in this life, according to John, theologians are children of God because they are reformed daily through the divine

quotidie reformantur. Quarum idearum series ab eo vocatur ratio dei, vita rerum omnium, lumen mentium, non angelicarum modo, sed etiam humanarum. Humanarum, inquam, omnium, quia ita 'illuminat omnem hominem venientem in hunc mundum,' ut quicquid intellegit quisque, in ipso intellegat et per ipsum, licet tenebrosae mentes ipsum non comprehendant, quia non agnoscunt se omnia videre per ipsum. Istae quidem vocem divini spiritus ubicumque vult spirantis audiunt, nesciunt autem unde vox illa veniat quove tendat.

14 Cum haec theologi prisci cognoscerent, philosophiae studium semper cum religiosa pietate iunxerunt. Principio Zoroastris philosophia (ut testatur Plato) nihil erat aliud quam sapiens pietas cultusque divinus. Mercurii quoque Trismegisti disputationes omnes a votis incipiunt et in sacrificia desinunt. Orphei etiam Aglaophemique philosophia in divinis laudibus tota versatur. Pythagoras a matutino hymnorum sacrorum cantu philosophiae studia incohabat. Plato non in dicendo solum, sed etiam in cogitando exordiri a deo praecipiebat in singulis atque ipse semper exordiebatur a deo. Se redeo parumper ad Pythagoram. Hic cum invenisset latus[8] longius trianguli illius quem rectangulum nominant,[9] tantum posse quantum duo reliqua simul iuncta, hecatomben deo suppliciter[10] immolavit, utpote qui intellegebat nihil usquam veri sine summae veritatis lumine posse videri. Hinc denique fingitur Minerva, sapientiae dea, solo Iovis capite nata. Hinc et illud:

Ab Iove principium Musae, Iovis omnia plena.

ideas. This series of ideas is called by him the reason of God, the life of all things, the light of minds and not only of angelic minds, but of human minds too—of all human minds I say, because it so "lighteth every man that cometh into this world"[21] that whatever each of us understands he understands in and through that light, although our benighted minds do not comprehend it because they do not realize they see everything through it. They hear the voice of the divine spirit breathing where it will, but they do not know whence that voice arrives or whither it is departing.

Since the ancient theologians understood these things, they al- 14
ways combined the study of philosophy with religious piety. To start with, the philosophy of Zoroaster (as Plato testifies) was nothing other than wise piety and divine worship.[22] The disputations of Mercury Trismegistus too all begin with prayers and end with sacrifices.[23] The philosophy of Orpheus and Aglaophemus is also entirely concerned with praise of the divine. Pythagoras used to start his studies of philosophy with the morning singing of sacred hymns.[24] Not only in speaking but in thinking too Plato taught us in every single matter to begin with God; and he himself always began with God.[25] But to return to Pythagoras for a moment. When he discovered that the longer side of the triangle he called the right-angled triangle has the same value[26] as that of the other two sides added together, he sacrificed a hecatomb in gratitude to God, because he understood that nowhere could anything true be seen except in the light of the highest truth.[27] Hence—a final point—Minerva, goddess of wisdom, is imagined as having been born from Jupiter's head alone; and hence too the verse

Begin from Jupiter, o Muses: all things are full of Jupiter.[28]

: II :

Quaestio prima. De ascensu ad deum. Quomodo mens in divinam elevatur ideam.

1 Tres hic quaestiones suboriuntur. Prima, quo pacto mens in divinam elevetur ideam. Secunda, quam ob causam in eo statu deum nos videre nequaquam animadvertamus. Tertia, quo pacto hanc ipsam intellegentiam deus nobis infundat assidue, quod Plato in superioribus affirmavit.

2 Ad primam ita in praesentia respondemus. Quando phantasia, excitata per hominis alicuius figuram visu haustam, simulacro formatur humano,[11] tunc humanae speciei formula, quae latebat in mentis arcanis, instigata coruscat et mentis sive rationis aciem actu format, quam formaverat habitu. Formatio talis vel intellegentia quaedam ambigua est vel ortus intellegentiae. Postquam ita satis formata est, hominis idea formatur, id est ratione illa per quam deus hominem generat. Ita vero mens per formulam hominis ideae quadrat humanae, sicut cera quae ab annulo figurata est, quando diligenter annulo admovetur, suo congruit exemplari. Illa ipsa quadratio vera et distincta hominis intellegentia est. Ideo Plato in *Convivio* inquit animum, divinae pulchritudinis amatorem, quando divinas rationes attingit, tunc non amplius simulacra rerum, sed res veras parere; in se ipso partasque nutrire; familiarem deo fieri ac prae ceteris immortalem.

3 Sed nullus hoc arcanum lucidius quam Ioannes evangelista revelasse videtur. Qui mentem hominis, quando verum aliquid attingit, non dicit, ut solent alii, videre rem aliquam veram, sed facere

: II :

First question: On the ascent to God. How the mind is raised to the divine idea.

At this juncture three further questions arise. First, how can the mind be raised to the divine idea? Second, why, being in that elevated state, do we not realize that we are seeing God? Third, how does God keep pouring this understanding itself into us, as Plato claims in the above? 1

For the present let me answer the first question thus. When the phantasy, aroused by some man's shape derived from the sight, is formed by this human image, then the formula of the species man, which was lying concealed in the secret parts of the mind, having received this spark, blazes up; and now it forms in act the mind (or reason's acuity) which it had already formed in habit. This giving of form is a sort of ambiguous understanding or the onset of understanding. But when the mind has been sufficiently formed, it is then formed by the idea of man, that is, by the rational principle through which God generates man. Thus the mind through the formula of man adapts itself to the idea of man, just as wax which has been shaped by a signet ring when it is carefully fitted to the ring is congruent with its model. This fitting is man's true and distinct understanding. Hence Plato in his *Symposium* says that the rational soul, the lover of divine beauty, when it attains the divine principles, is no longer giving birth in itself to things' images but to things true: it is nourishing its children and becoming a friend to God, and preeminently becoming immortal.[29] 2

No one seems to reveal this mystery more lucidly than John the Evangelist. He does not say, as others are wont to say, that the human mind when it attains something true sees some true thing but rather that it "does truth,"[30] because in actuality it turns out that 3

veritatem, quia scilicet re ipsa assequitur, ut deus, qui ipsa veritas est, quasi forma eius efficiatur. Tunc enim mens, ideam induta, fit ipsa veritas rei illius quae per talem est ideam creata. Quod omnes faciunt contemplantes, quos inquit Ioannes de plenitudine divinae rationis accipere, quia scilicet quisquis vere contemplatur speciem aliquam rerum, accepit iam in se aliquam ex numero idearum, quarum plenitudo est ipsa divina ratio. Consummati vero theologi mentem aurum appellat ignitum, quia sicut aurum formam induitur ignis per quam calefit, rarescit et fulget, sic illa mens, induta divinae mentis ideas, per illas tum veritatis lumine claret, tum bonitatis fomite flagrat. Paulus quoque apostolus mentem divinorum contemplatricem affirmat tum quotidie renovari, tum in eandem cum deo imaginem transformari, tum unum cum ipso spiritum fieri. Trismegistus similiter ait ex mente pura et divinitate quodammodo unum spiritum coalescere, et Platonici omnes probant in rationibus contemplandis divinam rationem tactu quodam mentis substantiali potius quam imaginario tangi, unitatemque mentis propriam deo rerum omnium unitati modo quodam inaestimabili copulari. Quod Plato in *Phaedro* et in *Epinomide* et alibi saepe confirmat, praesertim quando in *Phaedro* divinorum ait contemplatorem a reliquis segregari, purgari prorsus, haerere deo, impleri deo et in *Epinomide* animum contemplatione perfectum penes divinam unitatem unum prorsus evadere. Idem in libris *De republica* censet.

God, who is the truth, is made as it were the form of the mind. For the mind, having put on the idea, then becomes the truth itself of the thing which has been created by that idea. All those who contemplate do this. As John says, they receive from the fullness of the divine reason,[31] because anyone who truly contemplates the species of an object has already received in himself some one of the ideas whose fullness is the divine reason itself. The mind of the complete theologian he describes as "gold refined by fire."[32] For just as gold is clad with the form of fire, and through it grows hot and becomes more refined and lustrous, so the mind clad in the ideas of the divine mind, through them waxes bright with the light of truth and blazes up with the fuel of goodness. Paul the Apostle too tells us that the mind that contemplates things divine is renewed every day,[33] and is changed into the same likeness with God, and becomes one spirit with Him.[34] Trismegistus similarly says that from pure mind and divinity there coalesces in a way one spirit.[35] And all Platonists support the view that, in the contemplation of rational principles, the divine reason is "touched"[36] by a substantial, not just by an imaginary, touching of the mind; and that the unity proper to the mind is joined to God, the unity of all things, in a manner beyond our conception. Plato often confirms this in the *Phaedrus* and the *Epinomis* and elsewhere, and particularly when he says in the *Phaedrus* that the contemplator of things divine is set apart from other men and totally purified, and that he cleaves to God and is filled with God; and in the *Epinomis*, that the rational soul, made perfect by contemplation, emerges wholly unified in the presence of the divine unity.[37] He expresses the same view in the *Republic*.

: III :

Quaestio secunda. Quam ob causam in eo statu deum nos videre nequaquam animadvertimus.

1 Ad questionem secundam ita possumus respondere. Sicut oculus per speciem coloris formatus videt colorem, speciem vero per quam videt non cernit, sic forsitan intellectus quodammodo formatus idea, per hanc statim speciem ipsam naturalem intellegit, quae per talem facta fuit ideam; ideam tamen ipsam nondum perspicue intuetur, immo non agnoscit, licet intueatur. Forte vero sic accidit in contemplationis quadrationisque initio. Sed quando pergit in contemplando congruitque magis, ipsam quoque ideam suspicit clarius agnoscitque, sed ubi eam suspiciat nondum discernit. Sicuti enim pueri dum figuras suas in eo solis fulgore qui ambit superficiem aquae prospiciunt, eas non in extrinseco lumine, sed in aquae fundo se putant videre, ita mens adhuc rudis, dum rationes rerum in sublimi videt deo, in se aut in rebus aliis videre se putat. Praesertim cum ratio rei naturalis in deo, verbi causa, ratio aeris, non deum referat prorsus ut deum et ut principium universi solutum ac liberum, sed ut exemplar aeris. Quo fit ut mens quando ratione ipsa divini aeris circumfunditur, deum intellegat non tamquam deum sed tamquam aerem; deum namque videt aereum, id est ad naturam aeris circumscriptum. Angeli vero, qui cunctis simul formantur ideis per ipsam idearum omnium congregationem fontem universae naturae conspiciunt. Sic enim divinae substantiae, non ex quadam ipsius parte ut nos, sed toti ferme se ipsos insinuant. Idcirco ubi illas videant, animadvertunt.

: III :

Second question: Why in this state we do not realize that we are seeing God.

We can respond to the second question in the following way. Just 1
as the eye, given form by the species of color, sees color, but does not perceive the species through which it sees, so perhaps the intellect, formed in a way by the idea, immediately understands via the idea a natural species that was created through the idea. Nevertheless it does not yet intuit the idea clearly, or rather, it does not recognize it although it intuits it. This may be what happens in the early stages of contemplating and matching itself to the idea. But when the intellect pursues its contemplation and becomes more and more like the idea, it also receives and recognizes it more clearly; but in receiving it it still does not see it distinctly. For just as children, when they see their shapes in the sunlight on the surface of water, suppose they are looking at them in the water's depths, not in the light above, so the still untutored mind, when it sees things' rational principles in God on high, supposes that it is looking at them in itself or in other things. This is especially since the principle of a natural element in God—say the principle of air—does not refer to God simply as God, that is, as the free and absolute principle of the universe, but as the paradigm of air. Consequently the mind, when it is overwhelmed by the rational principle of divine air, understands God not as God but as air; for it sees God as air-like, that is, as circumscribed by the nature of air. But angels, who are formed by all the ideas simultaneously, perceive the fount of universal nature through the assembling itself of all the ideas. Thus they insinuate themselves into the divine substance, not just into a part of it as we do, but virtually into the whole of it. Accordingly, when they see the ideas, they recognize them.

2 Idem continget et nobis quando in deum penitus reformabimur. Nunc vero non aliter in hac re paene omnes decipimur quam plebeii, qui cum multa nocte ad lunam videant, aiunt se in lumine lunae videre, cum tamen illud sit solis lumen, quo etiam nocte vident. Sic ingrati homines in lumine proprio et[12] naturali vera se affirmant inspicere, quae in lumine communi divinoque inspiciunt. Quod si globus ipse solis aut non exoriretur atque occideret, aut a nobis in sua illa figura nequaquam suspiceretur, ita nemo sciret unde lumen hoc mittatur in aerem quo cuncta videmus, sicut modo scit nemo unde lux demittatur in mentem qua cuncta discernimus, quia occultus est deus, unde illa descendit. Descendit autem ita ut sit intellegentiae nostrae principium, medium atque finis. Principium, quia sicut ipsius oculi visio a lumine externo fit tamquam universali causa ac etiam a scintilla quadam interiore inde accensa tamquam causa particulari, ita in nobis actus intellegendi ab ampla dei mente pendet et nostra. Medium vero, quia in ipsa aeternas discernimus rationes quae in aeternitate sunt solum. Finis denique, quia ipsam dumtaxat cognoscimus. Nam aeterna cuiusque rei ratio in ipsa aeternitate nihil est aliud secundum essentiam quam aeternitas.

3 Hic revelatur divinum illud Platonis nostri mysterium, quod in septimo *De republica* legitur. Inquit enim theologum idoneis demonstrationis fundamentis et gradibus ascendere usque ad principium universi, tangere ipsum atque tenere, adhaerentem semper his quae adhaerent principio, quippe qui nullis sensibilium rerum corporeis gradibus ad id contendat, sed ipsis speciebus per ipsas ad ipsas potius innitatur, quousque ad speciem finem universi perveniat. Brevis horum verborum explanatio erit huiusmodi.

This will happen to us too when we have been completely reformed in God. The mistake we are making is almost that of ordinary folk, who look at the moon in the middle of the night and declare that they are seeing by the moon's light when in fact they are seeing by the sun's light even at night. Like them, ungrateful men claim that they see things true by their own natural light when they are seeing them by a light that is universal and divine. If the sun's circle never rose and set, or we never looked up at it and saw its shape, no one would know whence the light by which we see all things is dispatched into the air, just as nobody now knows whence the light by which we distinguish all things is sent into the mind, because God from whom the light descends is hidden from us. It descends in such a way that it is the beginning, middle, and end of our understanding. The divine light is the beginning, because just as the eye's vision is caused by an external light as by a universal cause and by an inner spark ignited by that light as by a particular cause, so the act of understanding in us depends both on God's mind in all its amplitude and on our mind. The light is the middle or mean, because in it we descry the eternal principles that exist only in eternity. And it is the end, because we know only it; for each thing's eternal principle in that eternity is in its essence nothing but that eternity. 2

Here is revealed that sacred mystery which our Plato writes about in the seventh book of the *Republic*.[38] The theologian, he says, ascends by way of the appropriate fundamental principles and steps of demonstration up to the universe's first principle, touches it, and clings to it, always cleaving to those things which cleave to the first principle. For he does not climb towards it on the corporeal rungs of sensible bodies, but rather depends on forms themselves to ascend through forms towards forms, until he reaches the form that is the goal of the universe. The following is a brief interpretation of these words. 3

4 Theologus tum agendo tum disputando purgat a corporeis affectibus animum, segregat rationem a fallacibus rerum sensibilium coniecturis, invitat mentem ut ad veritatem huiusmodi se gradibus conferat: speciebus, id est insitis ab origine formulis; per species, id est per formationem quae nobis provenit ab ideis; ad species, id est ad ipsas ideas et rerum naturalium species considerandas. Quas species adhaerere inquit deo universi principio; ipse enim fons est idearum. Theologi vero mentem illis adhaerere, id est illis se formandam[13] insinuare, per quam insinuationem inquit deum tangere, id est divina mente formari. Adiunxit et tenere deum duabus, ut puto, de causis. Tum quia mens, ubi semel ita coepit, forte numquam talis vitae statum penitus intermittit, tum quia postquam mente divina multis ex partibus iam mens nostra formata est diutius contemplando, incipit usque adeo supra hominem sapere, ut se et per deum, et deum, et in deo contemplari non nesciat.

5 Vocat autem hic deum nominibus pluribus: principium, finem, speciem. Principium, quia ab ipso omnia et quia ab ipso exordium sumit intellegentia. Finem, quia ad ipsum et intellegentia et omnia terminantur. Speciem, tum quia ipse est actus qui res omnes dum ab ipso tamquam principio procedunt, format et facit, atque easdem dum ad eundem tamquam finem convertuntur, reformat et perficit, tum quia ⟨ab⟩ ipso mens quaeque formatur dum intellegit veritatem. Addidit deo nomen quartum, scilicet ipsum bonum vel bonitatem ipsam. Proprium boni est quod se diffundat, quod res

By action and discussion the theologian purges the rational soul from bodily affections, separates the reason from the deceptive conjectures [occasioned by] sensible things, and invites the mind to climb by such steps towards the truth: to climb a) on forms, that is, on the formulae inherent in the mind from its origin; b) through forms, that is, through the forming which comes to us from the ideas; and c) towards forms, that is, towards the ideas themselves and the forms for considering natural entities. These forms cleave to God, Plato says, the first principle of the universe; for God is the source of the ideas. The theologian's mind cleaves to them, that is, insinuates itself into them in order to be formed by them; and through this insinuation, he says, it touches God, is formed in other words by the divine mind. Plato added that it also holds on to God. For two reasons in my opinion. First because once it has thus started, the theologian's mind never perhaps completely abandons the state of such a life; and second because, after our mind has already been formed by the divine mind after long contemplation and in many respects, it begins to know superhumanly to the extent it is no longer unaware that it is itself contemplating God through God and in God. 4

Plato calls God by many names: first principle, end, and form: first principle, because everything comes from Him, and because understanding takes its origin from Him; end, because understanding and everything else reach their end in reaching Him; and form, a) because God Himself is the act which both forms and produces all things as they proceed from Him as their first principle, and reforms and perfects these same things as they turn back towards Him as their end; and b) because each mind is formed by Him when it understands the truth. Plato added a fourth name for God: the good itself, or goodness itself. The property of the good is to diffuse itself, to attract things, and to perfect them. God diffuses Himself in creating things, attracts them in converting them [to Himself], and perfects them by forming them as they is- 5

alliciat, quod perficiat. Deus se diffundit res producendo, allicit convertendo, perficit formando procedentia, reformando conversa. Ponit autem ipsum bonum supra mentem et super essentiam. Super mentem scilicet eam quae est invisibilis oculus veritatis capax, avidus bonitatis, nam deus non capax veritatis dicitur, non cupidus bonitatis, sed est ipsa veritas atque bonitas. Potest autem secundum excellentiorem sensum vocari mens, tum quia divina veritas sui ipsius non est ignara, tum quia exuberantia quadam divinae bonitatis mentes inde effluunt plurimae. Super essentiam quoque eam locatur deus quae est ipsius esse subiectum. Quinetiam locatur super esse illud quod est actus essentiae Talis enim actus, quia potentiae passivae miscetur, impurus est et finitus. Vocatur tamen a Peripateticis esse, quantum ipse est purus et absolutus actus per quem omnes essentiae actum essendi suscipiunt.

6 Plotinus autem et Proclus ipsum unum bonumque[14] super ens his rationibus collocant. Unius bonique ipsius influxus latius sese propagat quam entis influxus, materia siquidem informisque potentia magis unius bonique particeps est dicenda quam entis. Siquidem esse fit per formam, materia vero est informis, una tamen materia dicitur et avida boni. Atque hanc argumentationem a Dionysio Areopagita accepisse videntur. Praeterea, quemadmodum non idem est multitudo atque nihilum, ita non est idem ens ipsum atque unum. Neque tamen pariter disposita sunt ens quidem hinc et inde unum, ne duo rerum principia stulte ponantur. Neque rursus ens super unum, siquidem unum particeps fieret entis, neque amplius unum, sed duo, id est unum simul ensque foret. Sequitur igitur ut super ens sit unum. Denique quanto simplicius quiddam

sue forth, and by reforming them when they have been converted. Plato puts the good itself above mind and essence. He puts it above mind, that is, above what exists as the invisible eye receptive of truth and hungry for goodness; for God cannot be said to be receptive of truth or desirous of goodness. Rather He is truth and goodness itself, although He can be called mind in a more exalted sense, both because the divine truth is not ignorant of itself, and because minds issue in multitudes from an overflowing of the divine goodness. God is also set above that essence which is the subject of being, and, moreover, He is set above that being which is the act of essence. For such an act, since it is mixed with passive potentiality, is impure and finite. Yet God is called "being" by the Peripatetics insofar as He is that pure and absolute act via which all essences receive the act of being.

Plotinus[39] and Proclus,[40] however, offer the following reasons 6
for setting the one itself and the good above being. The influence of the one and the good extends far beyond that of being, because matter and unformed potency must be said to participate more in the one and the good than in being. For being comes about through form, but matter is without form, yet is said to be one and desirous of the good. (They appear to have accepted this argument from Dionysius the Areopagite.[41]) Furthermore, just as the many and nothingness are not the same, so being and the one are not the same. And you cannot arrange them side-by-side, putting being here and the one there, otherwise you would be foolishly positing two universal principles. Nor can you put being above the one, since the one would then participate in being, and not become a bigger one but two, that is, become the one and being simultaneously. It follows, then that the one is above being. Lastly, insofar as unity signifies something simpler than being which embraces both essence and existence, it accords that much more with the universal first principle. Plotinus and Proclus do not allow existence and essence to be separated anywhere lest a

significat unitas quam ens, in quo essentia et esse clauduntur, tanto magis primo rerum principio congruit. Neque segregari permittunt esse alicubi ab essentia, ne proprius actus usquam a propria potentia segregetur. Neque mirum cuiquam videri volunt quod principium rerum nominent unitatem. Sic enim distinguunt. Aut nominandum est unitas aut multitudo aut ex utrisque compositum. Sed non compositum, ne ab illo dependere cogatur, qui diversa in unum conciliavit. Non multitudo unitatis expers, quia et ipsum omni virtute et universum omni unione careret. Rursus, in principio omnium omnis esse debet potentia. Ergo si ipsum multitudo ipsa sit, quatenus in multitudinem quaelibet laberentur, eatenus potentiora evaderent. Quoniam vero quatenus ad unitatem accedunt, eatenus valentiora sunt atque contra, sequitur ut principium rerum proprie sit unitas appellandum. Denique cum unione quadam proprie singula fiant serventurque, quis non viderit unitatem ipsam esse causam omnia facientem atque servantem?

7 Item, bonum omnia simpliciter appetunt; esse vero non simpliciter, sed bene esse dumtaxat. Forte etiam si bene esse omnino nequeant, esse non appetant,[15] ut probat Olympiodorus, utpote quae esse appetent gratia boni. Bonum igitur, cum finis sit ultimus, nimirum primum omnium est principium. Si super ens existit, multo magis super vitam atque mentem. Quando vero unum bonumque dicunt, idem semper intellegunt. Sicut enim in ordine rerum bene esse in unione consistit, quoniam malum dissensione et divisione contingit, sic et super ordinem universi idem est unum ipsum atque bonum, cuius splendor est pulchritudo, quae nihil est aliud quam multarum rationalis ordo formarum in mente, anima, natura, materia inde refulgens. Supra quam pulchritudinem esse unum probant, quia illa composita sit. Rursus, super eam esse bonum, quia omnia et semper bonum appetunt; pulchritudinem vero sola quae cognoscunt eam et postquam eam noverint. Item pul-

proper act should ever be separated from its proper potentiality. They do not want it to appear odd to anyone that they call the universal principle unity. For they distinguish thus. It must be called either unity, or multiplicity, or a composite of the two. It cannot be a composite lest what makes different things one harmony be forced to depend on that composite. It cannot be a multiplicity without unity, because it would lack omnipotency and the universe would lack all unity. But omnipotency must be present in the universal first principle. So, if this were multiplicity itself, then the more things declined into multiplicity, the more powerful they would turn out to be. But since things become more powerful the closer they approach to unity, and the reverse, it follows that the universal first principle has to be called, properly speaking, unity. Finally, since individual objects are properly created and preserved by a certain unity, isn't it obvious that unity itself is the cause that creates and preserves all things?

Again, all things seek the good absolutely but not being abso- 7
lutely, just well-being. It may even be the case that if they cannot have well-being completely, they do not want being at all, as Olympiodorus maintains,[42] in that what wants being wants it for the sake of the good. The good then, since it is the ultimate end, is certainly the universal first principle. If it exists above being, *a fortiori* it exists above life and mind. But when they speak of the one and the good, they always mean the same thing. For as well-being in the order of things consists of unity, since evil is contingent on dissension and division, so above the universal order the one itself and the good are identical. Its splendor is beauty, which is nothing other than the refulgence of the rational order of the many forms in the mind, the soul, nature, and matter. But above this beauty, they contend, is the one, since beauty is composite. Above beauty too is the good, because all things always desire the good, but only those things that know beauty desire beauty, and only after they have known it. Again, we desire beauty for the sake

chritudinem gratia boni desideramus, sperantes videlicet profuturam. Postremo, bonum revera habere volumus, saepe tamen nobis satis est factum si palam pulchritudinem videamur habere.

8 Beati nimium quos universi pulchritudo, boni ipsius splendor, in ipsum bonum amore transformat, praesertim quia dum transformat in bonum, pariter reformat in unum, ideoque ipsi bono coniungit in unum. Siquidem ipsum unum bonumque tamquam idem et per omnia et super et infra pariter dilatantur, pariterque ab omnibus etiam sine cognitione naturali desiderio appetuntur. Neque differre inter se tamquam duo quaedam aequaliter disposita possunt, ne duo rerum principia sint. Neque unum super bonum esse potest, ne quid melius optabiliusque bono esse dicatur. Neque rursus bonum super unum, ne quod bonum dicitur, desinat esse bonum. Unum ergo bonumque sunt penitus idem, quando aequaliter appetuntur, quemadmodum divisio atque malum, tamquam idem, aequaliter fugiuntur.

9 Beatus qui bono prorsus unitur. Unitur autem non intellectuali virtute proprie. Haec enim cum sit multiplex atque infra intellegibile collocetur, neque congruit unitati neque quod intellegibile, id est ens universum supereminet, attingere potest. Adde quod cum unum bonumque instinctu quodam antecedente intellegentiam appetatur, consequens est ut tactu quodam super intellegentiam attingatur, tactu, ut ita loquar, unifico, per unitatem videlicet nostram, quae intellegentiam superat animamque ipsam ipsi rerum omnium unitati bonitatique non imaginaria intellegentiae copula, sed vera substantiae ipsius unione coniungit. Unde non levis quaedam et extrinseca particularisque laetitia sequitur quasi videntis

of the good, hoping it will profit us. Finally, we desire truly to possess the good, yet it suffices for us often if we just appear to possess beauty.

Happy indeed are those whom the universe's beauty, that is, the splendor of the good itself, transforms by love into the good itself, especially since in transforming them into the good, this beauty reforms them equally into the one, and in the one unites them to the good itself. For the one itself and the good are identical: they extend alike through and above and below all things, and they are sought alike by all things through a natural desire even if they lack cognition. They cannot differ among themselves like two particular things equally disposed, lest there be two first principles. Nor can the one be superior to the good, lest something were said to be better and more desirable than the good. Nor again is the good above the one, lest what is called the good were to cease being the good. Therefore the one and the good are completely identical, since they are equally desired; similarly disunity and evil, being identical, are equally shunned. 8

Happy is the man who is totally united to the good. But properly speaking he is not united by the intellect's power. For this power, since it is multiple and located beneath the intelligible, does not accord with unity, nor can it attain to what towers over the intelligible, that is, to universal being. Moreover, since the one and good is desired by an instinct prior to understanding, so is it achieved by a kind of touching superior to understanding, a unifying contact if I may call it such. This comes about through our own unity, which is superior to understanding and which links the soul itself to the universal unity and goodness, not with the image-linked bond of understanding, but with the true substantial union itself. And the result is not a trivial or external or particular delight, as of someone [merely] watching or hearing the good, but rather a vehement, inner, and universal pleasure, as of a taste or touch superior to the intellect, of someone already fully tasting 9

bonum vel audientis, sed vehemens intrinseca universalis voluptas efficitur, quasi gustus tactusque intellectu superioris suavitatem ipsam intellegibili superiorem gustantis iam penitus atque tangentis. Profecto naturalis sitis liquorem appetit prius quam sensu sitire nos agnoscamus, ac postquam agnovimus, rursus appetimus. Appetitus qui sensum sequitur imaginarius est et a substantia nostra remotior; antecedens vero, substantiae intimus. Quamobrem cum liquorem gustu consequimur, non sequentis proprie, sed antecedentis appetitus virtute complectimur et in substantiam nostram perfecte transferimus. Similiter non tam appetitio quae mentis actionem sequitur quam quae praecedit, tamquam principium motus, motionis fine perfruitur, dum substantialem conficit copulam, ideoque votum sola penitus implet.

: IV :

Quaestio tertia. Quo pacto deus nobis intellegentiam infundit assidue.

1 Sed hinc iam ad quaestionem tertiam descendamus. Hunc esse Platonis nostri sensum arbitror, quando scribit et intellectui scientiam et intellegibilibus veritatem ab ipso bono infundi, quod videlicet beneficus ille et vivificus actus omnium, qui deus est, ambit opera sua semper ac se inserit universis. Potissimum vero lucens in mentis arcanis, tum eius aciem purgat, acuit, illustrat, accendit assidue, tum formulas insitas menti vivificat, ita ut quotiens[16] curis vacui animum ad veritatis indaginem applicamus, formulae illae deo vivificante vivaciores effectae promptius palam erumpant, ac mentis acies deo irradiante succensa lucidius ardentiusque inspi-

and touching the sweetness that is superior to the intelligible. Our natural thirst desires [this] liquor before we recognize through the sense that we are thirsty; and after we have recognized it, we desire it again. The appetite consequent on the sense is image-linked and far distant from our substance, but the appetite preceding it is deep within our substance. Thus when we succeed in tasting the liquor, we do so properly by virtue not of the later [post-cognitive] appetite but of the earlier [pre-cognitive] one, and we are transformed perfectly into our substance. Similarly, it is not so much the succeeding appetite as the appetite preceding the action of the mind, which, as the motion's principle, enjoys the motion's end as long as it effects the substantial bond and so alone wholly satisfies the yearning.

: IV :

Third question: How God continually pours understanding into us.

Let us now proceed to the third question. To my mind, what 1
Plato means when he says that knowledge is poured into the intellect and truth into intelligible objects by the good itself is that the beneficent and life-giving act of all things, which is God, always encircles its works, implanting itself in them all. But principally, it shines in the secret parts of the mind: it continually purifies, sharpens, illuminates, and sets fire to the mind's vision. It also gives life to the formulae innate in the mind such that whenever we apply our soul to the search for truth, having emptied ourselves of cares, the formulae, made more alive by the life-giving God, sally forth into the open with greater eagerness; and the mind at its most acute and fired by the rays that stream from God regards

ciat. Ubi ad ipsum intellegendi actum deus se habet tamquam agens primum atque commune, formula tamquam agens proprium atque secundum, simulacrum tamquam incitamentum, mens tenet materiae locum.

2 Sed hanc rem exemplo consideremus, ut planius videamus qua ratione actus intellegendi in nos descendit ex deo. Si deus ad creandae mentis ideam in se vigentem mentem nostram temperat procreando et secum maxime configurat, atque ex lyra in lyram similiter temperatam motus sonusque transit, quid mirum[17] sonante divina mente intellegendo mentem hominis consonare? Efficit faber aliquis specula mille. His factis dispositisque in ordinem sese obiicit. In mille speculis mille fabri resultant imagines. Movet quandoque faber se ipsum hunc in modum, ut oculum suum ad reliqua membra sua circumspicienda convertat et membra pro viribus convertat ad oculum. Hos motus imagines in speculis imitantur. Ad motum viventis oculi, oculi imaginarii cuncti moventur; ad motum membrorum viventium imaginaria membra. Similiter deus animas procreat, deinde his sese obiicit tamquam speculis, per quam obiectionem in singulis imagines fiunt dei. Quae quidem imagines mentes ipsae sunt animarum, ita ut mentes[18] tum multae sint, quia multae sunt animae in quibus sunt, tum una cunctae, quia unus est deus quem referunt. Mens autem quaeque per vim intellegendi vim dei refert ideas concipientem; per formulas autem refert ideas. Hinc etiam propheticum illud, quod supra tetigimus, aperitur: 'Signatum est super nos lumen vultus tui, Domine,' et 'In lumine tuo videbimus lumen'.

3 Nempe deus per vim suam fecundam[19] qua ideas concipit discernendo, vim praestat servatque menti per quam ideas attingat in-

the formulae with greater clarity and ardor. In the act of understanding, God acts as the prime and universal agent, the formula as the particular and secondary agent, and the image as the stimulant; the mind plays the role of matter.

Let us consider this by turning to an example, so we may see 2
more clearly how the act of understanding descends to us from God. If God in creating attunes our mind to the idea of the creating mind flourishing within Him and models it very closely on Himself, and if from a lyre the motion and sound pass over to another lyre similarly tuned, why is it surprising that in understanding the mind of man is in tune with the sound of the divine mind? A craftsman makes a thousand mirrors. Having made and arranged them in order he stands in front of them. A thousand images of the craftsman are reflected in the thousand mirrors. The craftsman moves himself at a particular moment in such a way as to turn his eye towards the rest of his body's parts so that he can examine them, and to turn the parts, as well as he can, towards his eye. Reflections copy these movements in the mirrors. All the reflected eyes move to the motion of the living eye, the reflected parts to the motion of the living parts. Similarly God creates souls, then places Himself in front of them, as though they were mirrors: in this way reflections of God are formed in individuals. These reflections are souls' minds such that they are both many, because the souls are many in which they dwell, and yet collectively one since it is one God to whom they refer. But through its power of understanding each mind refers to the power of God that conceives the ideas, but through its formulae it refers to the ideas themselves. Hence the prophetic saying we mentioned above, "The light of thy countenance, O Lord, is stamped upon us" and "In thy light shall we see light."[43]

Through His creative power with which by distinguishing be- 3
tween them He conceives the ideas, God gives the mind enduring power to attain the ideas in understanding. Again, God uses the

tellegendo. Iterum deus per ideas ipsas iam conceptas et ratione discretas imprimit et servat menti formulas idearum. Ad dei motum, id est ad actum dei, continuus fit motus in mentibus. Quonam pacto? Vis quae in deo est, ideas concipiens, ad ipsas quodammodo se flectit ideas; ideae ad eam vim mutuo se reflectunt. Interea concordi quadam temperatione contingit ut vis intellegendi in hominis mente[20] si expedita sit in deumque erecta, se vertat ad formulas, et formulae ad vim convertantur intellegendi. Atque ita mentis actus mirabili consonantia dei actus perpetuo imitantur. Quoniam vero vultus in speculo, quando videtur aspicere vultum unde manat, revera potius aspiciatur quam aspiciat, ideo Paulus apostolus ait: 'Cum deum cognoveritis, immo cogniti sitis a deo'. Sic igitur superior animae nostrae vultus divini vultus imitatio a Platonicis nominatur. Usque adeo ut Plotinus Theodorusque Asinius et Iamblichus censuerint illam hominis mentem, quae non humana est, sed divina, in mundo intellegibili vivere et operari continue per continuum intuitum idearum. Moverunt autem Plotinum Theodorumque et Iamblichum ad hoc duae potissimum rationes.

4 Prima. Animae suprema mens, quia secundum se intellectualis essentia est, ideo intellegit per essentiam, sicut per essentiam ignis calet et aqua friget, licet potentia animae mente inferior per essentiam non intellegat. Itaque sicut ignis semper calet, ita mens semper intellegit. Obiecta vero intellegentiae sunt species ipsae rerum aeternae. Ac intellectus intellegendo non obiectorum simulacris fallacibus haeret, sed ut vere intellegat ipsis unitur obiectis. Ergo mens semper est aeternis speciebus unita, quo fit ut sedulo aedem colat aeternitatis. Huc illud Iamblichi tendit: 'Intellectus nostri

ideas, once they have been conceived and are rationally distinct, to impress the ideas' formulae enduringly on the mind. To God's movement — to God's act, that is — corresponds a continuous movement in the minds. How? The power in God that conceives the ideas turns in a way towards the ideas themselves and in return the ideas turn towards this power. Meanwhile, because of a particular accord and attuning, it happens that the power of understanding in man's mind, if it has been freed and raised towards God, turns itself towards the formulae, and the formulae are turned towards the power of understanding. Thus the acts of the mind continually imitate the acts of God in a marvelous accord. But since the face in the mirror, when it appears to see the face whose reflection it is, does not really see but is being seen, so Paul the Apostle says: "After that ye have known God, or rather are known of God."[44] Thus the higher countenance of our soul is called by the Platonists an imitation of the divine countenance. Plotinus, Theodore of Asine, and Iamblichus[45] go so far as to claim that the mind of man, which is not human but divine, lives in the intelligible world and operates unceasingly through the unceasing contemplation of the ideas. Two main reasons led Plotinus, Theodore, and Iamblichus to this conclusion.

First. The soul's highest mind, being in itself an intellectual es- 4
sence, understands through its essence, just as fire heats through its essence or water chills, though the soul's power inferior to the mind does not understand through its essence. Just as fire always heats, therefore, so mind always understands. But the objects of understanding are things' eternal species. In understanding, the intellect does not attach itself to the deceptive images of objects, but to understand truly it is united with the objects themselves. So the mind is always united with the eternal species, whence it eagerly dwells in the house of eternity. That is the point of Iamblichus' remark: "The being of our intellect is nothing other than the understanding of powers divine."[46] He supposes that just as the sun

esse non est aliud quam intellegere numina'. Putat enim sicut idem actus est quo et sol lunam illuminat et luna inde illuminatur respicitque luminis similitudine solem, ita eundem esse actum quo et divina mens creat illuminatque mentem nostram, et nostra creatur illuminaturque inde et intuitu illuc quodam naturali convertitur. Similiter imago in speculo eodem actu vultum respicit quo a vultu aspicitur, et sicut aspiciendo fit, ita respiciendo servatur. Eadem est animae ad deum similitudo.

5 Secunda ratio talis. Rationalis anima a mente divina fit et iungitur corpori atque inter mentem et corpus obtinet medium. Si solum haereret menti vitam corpori non tribueret. Si solum haereret corpori intellegeret utique nihil. Ergo haeret menti simul et corpori, sicut linea quae centrum tangit simul atque circumferentiam, sicut solis lumen soli coniunctum est simul diffusumque per aerem. Atque ut anima rationalis se habet ad corpus, sic mens ad animam se habet rationalem. Sed vita ipsa corporalis nihil aliud est quam actus continuus animae transfusus in corporis huius complexionem, ab anima non recedens. Igitur intellectualis animae vita nihil est aliud quam intellectus divini perennis actus, annexus animae, non solutus a deo. Et sicut anima vitae corporali semina inserit rerum generandarum, ita deus animae cognoscendarum accendit igniculos. Vita corporalis est animae rationalis simulacrum; intellectualis animae vita simulacrum est vitae mentisque divinae. Corporali vitae praesidet infima pars animae quae est potentia nutriendi. Si haec infima pars quae corpori iungitur agit semper et ipso suo esse quodammodo operatur, multo magis suprema potentia quae validior est quia suo fonti[21] haeret propinquior, operatur

illuminates the moon in the same act whereby the moon is illuminated and with the likeness of light looks to the sun, so the divine mind creates and illuminates our mind in the same act whereby our mind is created and illuminated by it and converted with a natural gaze towards it. Similarly, in a mirror the reflection gazes back at the face in the same act as the face gazes at it: as it is made by gazing, so is it preserved by gazing back. The soul is an image of God in the same way.

The second reason is this. The rational soul is created by the 5
divine mind and joined to the body and occupies the mean between mind and body. If it were only attached to mind, it would not give life to body. If it were only attached to body, it would understand nothing. Therefore it must be attached to mind and body together, as a line that simultaneously touches both center and circumference, or as the sunlight that is united with the sun but at the same time diffused through the air. Mind stands in the same relationship to the rational soul as the rational soul to body. But the corporeal life is nothing other than the continuous act of the soul transmitted to this body's temperament without departing from the soul. So the intellectual life of the soul is nothing other than the everlasting act of the divine intellect attached to the soul but not separated from God. As the soul plants seeds for generating things in the corporeal life, so God lights the sparks for understanding in the soul. The corporeal life is the image of the rational soul, but the soul's intellectual life is the image of the divine life and mind. The soul's lowest part, which is the power of nourishment, presides over the corporeal life. If this lowest part which is joined to the body is always active, and acts in a way through its own being, then *a fortiori* the highest power, which is the more powerful since it cleaves the more closely to its source, is always active and acts in a way through its own being. It acts with regard to mind from which it immediately issues. For only mind flows from mind. But mind, which is above us, being pure intellect, feeds on

semper et per esse suum quodammodo operatur. Agit autem circa mentem, unde effluit proxime. A mente enim solum mens effluit. Mens autem quae supra nos est, quia purus intellectus est, puro intellegibili pascitur, id est pura fruitur veritate. Eadem nostra mens assidue vescitur, si epulis superioris mentis accumbit. Nec iniuria intellegentiam in anima essentialem perpetuamque locamus, quia ex eo est in anima, quod convenit cum perpetuis eius essentiae causis. Et sicut animae ingenitus est appetitus boni perpetuus atque essentialis, ita et ipsius veri naturalis essentialisque intuitus sive tactus aliquis potius, ut Iamblici verbis utar. Tactus, inquam, omni cognitione discursuque prior atque praestantior. Eiusmodi sententiam hac insuper ratione divinus Iamblicus confirmavit, quod quemadmodum temporalia contingentiaque per temporalem contingentemque cognitionem attingimus, ita oportet necessaria et aeterna per essentialem et perpetuam attingere notionem, quae non aliter inquisitionem nostram antecedit quam status motum. Temporalis vero cognitio ita inquisitionem sequitur, ut contingens effectus motum sequitur ac tempus. Putant[22] autem divinum ipsum mentis actum, qui quodam intuitu et quasi tactu divinorum fit, propter actiones inferiores non intermitti quidem in se ipso, quamvis quoad animadversionem pertinet, in viribus inferioribus intermittatur, atque actus intellectus rationalis vel rationis intellectualis, qui discursione fiunt, propter operationes inferiores soleant intermitti atque converso.

6 Verum cur non animadvertimus tam mirabile nostrae illius divinae mentis spectaculum? Forsitan quia propter continuam spectandi consuetudinem admirari et animadvertere desuevimus, aut quia mediae vires animae, ratio videlicet et phantasia, cum sint ut plurimum ad negotia vitae procliviores, mentis illius opera non

the pure intelligible, that is, takes delight in the pure truth. Our mind eagerly shares the same feast if it reclines at the banqueting table of the higher mind. And we have good reason to locate essential and everlasting understanding in the soul. For it dwells in the soul, because it is in harmony with the everlasting causes of its essence. Just as an everlasting and essential desire for good is innate in the soul, so too is a natural and everlasting vision of the truth, or rather a kind of touching, to use Iamblichus' words,[47] a touching which is prior to and more outstanding than all knowledge and argumentation. The divine Iamblichus supported this view with the additional argument that, just as we reach things temporal and contingent through knowledge which is temporal and contingent, so we have to attain things necessary and everlasting through a knowing which is necessary and everlasting, and this precedes our inquiring just as rest precedes motion. But temporal knowledge succeeds inquiring just as a contingent effect succeeds motion and time.[48] But they [the Platonists?] believe that the divine act itself of mind, which results from a certain viewing or touching of things divine, is not in itself interrupted because of inferior actions, even though it is interrupted, insofar as it pertains to our own awareness, in the lower powers, and though the acts of the rational intellect (or of the intellectual reason) resulting from discursive reasoning are usually interrupted because of inferior operations and vice versa.

Yet why are we not aware of the wondrous spectacle of that di- 6
vine mind which is ours? Perhaps it is either because, given that we are continually used to seeing it, we have lost the habit of admiring and noticing it, or because the intermediary faculties of the soul, the reason, and the phantasy, being for the most part more involved in life's daily affairs, do not clearly view the works of the divine mind. The like happens when the eye sees something in front of it but when the phantasy, being preoccupied with other things, does not recognize what the eye may see. But when the in-

clare persentiunt, sicut quando oculus praesens aliquid aspicit, phantasia tamen in aliis occupata quod oculus videat non agnoscit. Sed quando mediae vires agunt otium, defluunt in eas intellectualis speculationis illius scintillae velut in speculum. Unde et vera ratiocinatio nascitur ex intellegentia vera, et humana intellegentia ex divina. Neque mirum est aliquid in mente illa fieri quod nequaquam persentiamus. Nihil enim advertimus[23] nisi quod in medias transit vires. Ideo licet saepe vis concupiscendi esuriat atque sitiat, non prius hoc animadvertimus quam in phantasiam transeat talis passionis intentio. Nonne nutriendi virtus assidue agit? Assiduam tamen actionem eius haudquaquam perpendimus. Itaque neque perpetuam mentis intellegentiam, neque ex hoc est intellegentia illa debilior quod intellegere nequaquam nos agnoscamus, immo est potius vehementior. Saepe enim dum canimus aut currimus, canere nos et currere nequaquam excogitamus, atque ex hoc attentius operamur. Animadversio enim actionis intentionem distrahit animae ac minuit actionem.

7 Tirones in qualibet arte opera eius artis sine attentione non agunt, veterani autem etiam si non attendant, habitu quodam et quasi natura operantur. Quid prohibet talem esse continuam mentis intellegentiam? Quoniam vero lumen lumini iunctum sine confusione conspirat in unum (nam et ubique sunt ambo et alterum secerni potest ab altero), efficitur ut mentes hominum menti divinae coniunctae unum quodammodo fiant[24] cum mente divina et unum invicem, neque tamen inter se confundantur, non aliter ac multae lineae a circumferentia in centrum reflexae per puncta sua medium circuli tangunt punctum, ibique[25] unum quodammodo fit lineae[26] cuiusque punctum cum puncto circuli medio. Unum quoque quodammodo fiunt puncta invicem singula, et quae non

termediary powers are in repose, the sparks of that intellectual contemplation dart down into them as into a mirror. Thus from true understanding is born true reasoning, and from divine understanding, human understanding. Nor is it surprising that something can come to be in that divine mind that we do not see. For we notice nothing except what passes through the intermediary powers. Although our power of desiring may hunger or thirst, we do not therefore notice it until the "intention" of such a passion crosses over into the phantasy. Isn't our power of nutrition continually at work? And yet we do not pass judgment on its continual action. Hence we do not pass judgment on the mind's perpetual understanding, and yet, far from being any weaker because we do not recognize that it understands, it is stronger. For when we are singing or running, we often do not think about the fact that we are singing and running, and accordingly perform these actions more adroitly. For awareness of an action distracts the soul's intention and detracts from the action.

Novices in some craft cannot perform the works of this craft 7
without paying attention, whereas veterans can do so, even if they are not paying attention, out of a particular habit or nature as it were.[49] What stops the mind's understanding from being similarly continuous? Since one light joined to another light combines without confusion into one light (for they are both present everywhere and neither can be distinguished from the other), consequently men's minds joined to the divine mind are united in a way with the divine mind and united together, and yet they are not mutually confused. Analogously, the many lines, having returned from the circumference to the center, through their points touch the midpoint of the circle; and there the point of each line is made one in a way with the midpoint of the circle. The individual points are also made one in a way with each other, and though neither position nor time distinguishes them, the reason does. In the same way, a very large number of concepts in the mind can be combined

discernit situs aut tempus, ratio tamen ipsa discernit, quemadmodum plurimae notiones in mente tum invicem, tum menti absque ulla confusione coniunctae. Profecto sicut sphaerae minores intra maiorem sphaeram centris suis centrum maioris attingunt, ita mentes quasi minores intellegibilis mundi sphaerae sub bonitate divina comprehensae tamquam sphaera maiori sub ipsaque revolutae proprie per centra sua, id est per unitates suas intellectibus praestantiores, unitati divinae tamquam universi centro se copulant. Ac si forte disiunguntur[27] circuli, disiunguntur et centra, utpote quae unita fuerant potius quam confusa. Disiungi vero numquam vult Plotinus, ne aeternae mentium sphaerae minus unitae permaneant cum sphaera ipsarum summa, quam temporales visibilis mundi sphaerae cum sphaera maiori. Sed hoc ipse viderit. Nos autem ad institutum ordinem revertamur.

8 Ex iis omnibus quae ex Platonis et Plotini fontibus hausimus, concluditur hominis mentem ad mentem divinam in ipsa sua intellegentia ita ferme comparari, quemadmodum materia comparatur ad formam. Sane si mens nostra quotidie formatur divinae mentis ideis perque illas opus proprium agit, quis non videat mentem nostram subire divinam, ceu materia subit formam, nec aliter se habere ad divinas formas quam materiam primam ad naturales? Unde non minus immortalis debeat esse quam illa, praesertim quia quanto mens purior est et simplicior corporibus atque animis et ob hoc magis est una, tanto ex duabus illis mentibus una congredientibus arctior provenit copula, quam provenire soleat aut ex quibuslibet rebus corporalibus una mixtis, aut ex animis invicem concurrentibus, aut ex anima cum corpore coeunte. Auget huius copulae nodum, quod deus ipsa unitas est et ipsa bonitas. Et cum per unitatis vim rerum omnium copula uniatur, per vim quoque bonitatis ubique attractio fiat et propinquatio, nusquam unio ve-

both with each other and with the mind without any confusion. As the lesser spheres within the greater sphere touch with their centers the center of the greater, so minds — which are as it were the lesser spheres of the intelligible world included under the divine goodness as under the greater sphere, and under it having revolved by way of their own centers, that is, their own unities which are superior to their intellects — so minds, I say, link themselves to the divine unity as to the center of the universe. If the circles are perchance disjoined, so are the centers too, for they were united together, not confused. Plotinus claims that they will never disjoin, lest the mind's eternal spheres were to remain less united to their highest sphere than the visible world's temporal spheres to its greater sphere.[50] But this is Plotinus' concern. Let us return to our theme.

From all we have imbibed from the springs of Plato and Plotinus we conclude that the mind of man is prepared in its understanding for the divine mind almost as matter is prepared for form. If our mind is formed daily by the ideas of the divine mind, and does its own work through them, isn't it obvious that our mind is subject to the divine mind as matter is to form, and stands in the same relationship to the divine forms as prime matter to natural forms? Hence it should not be any less immortal than prime matter, especially because, to the degree mind is purer and simpler than bodies or souls and hence more unitary than them, so the bond that comes about from the meeting of these two minds is to that degree tighter than the bond that usually results either from various corporeal things being mixed together, or from two souls meeting, or from a soul accompanying a body. The strength of this bond is the greater because God is unity itself and goodness itself. Since through the power of unity the knot of all things is tied as one, and since too through the power of goodness attraction and union are everywhere effected, nowhere does truer union emerge than where mind is in harmony with divinity. 8

rior provenit quam ubi mens cum divinitate conspirat. Item, si deus menti ab ipso proxime[28] perpetuoque emananti infinita tum puritatis tenuitate intus illabitur, tum virtutis amplitudine eam penitus implet partesque mentis quasi iuncturas ipse tamquam nervus connectit intrinsecus invicem et ad totam, totamque essentiam ipse velut nodus intimus cum esse devincit, ideoque interior menti est quam ipsa sibi, quid mirum deum ipsi in ipsius intellegentia uniri tamquam formam, postquam in essentia et vita iam unitus est plusquam forma?

9 Signum illius unionis maximae[29] hoc est praecipuum, quod per veram intellegentiam intima substantia rei semper inspicitur, utpote quae in rei ideam profundius penetraverit quam aut visus in coloris speciem aut in coloris simulacrum phantasia, cum sensus et phantasia rerum superficies dumtaxat attingant. Ideo Mercurius inquit ex divinitatis et mentis conspiratione unum spiritum coalescere. Et Ioannis theologia docet contemplatores divinae rationis in unum cum ipsa ita consummari, sicut ipsa[30] unita est deo.

10 Nempe si in genere corporalium tanta est unio ut materia, quae ultimus eorum est terminus, unum quiddam efficiatur non solum cum mediis omnibus, verumetiam cum supremo generis corporalis, quis negabit aequalem saltem esse in genere intellectualium unionem, ut mens humana, quamvis ultimus illorum terminus sit, cum omnibus tamen intellectualibus formis ac etiam cum suprema unum aliquid fiat? Non fit autem ex animo ac deo tertia quaedam natura a tertio aliquo componente utrumque invicem et ad tertium actum dirigente utrumque, sicuti fit in naturalium re-

Again, if God flows down into mind which emanates immediately and perpetually from Him, and fills it inwardly with the infinite fineness of His purity and abundantly with the abundance of His power; and if like a tendon[51] for the joints He Himself joins the parts of mind within to each other and to the whole, and ties the whole essence like an inner knot to existence and so is more internal to mind than mind to itself—then is it any surprise that like a form God is united to mind in its understanding, since far more than a form He is already united to mind in its essence and life?

The principal evidence of this greatest of unions is that the innermost substance of a thing is always examined by way of true understanding, because the understanding has penetrated more deeply into the idea of that thing than the sight into the form of color, or the phantasy into the image of color, since sense and phantasy touch only upon the surface of things. Hence Mercury says that from the harmony of divinity and mind coalesces a single spirit.[52] And the theology of John teaches us that the contemplators of the divine reason are [eventually] as consummately united to it as it is united to God.[53] 9

If the union that occurs in the class of corporeal entities is so close that matter, which is their lowest limit, is made one not only with all the mean points but with the highest point of the class of bodies, then who will deny that at least an equivalent union occurs in the class of intellectual entities, such that the human mind, in spite of being their lowest limit, is yet made one with all the intellectual forms and even with the highest form? However no third sort of nature is made from the soul and God by some third agent compounding them together and directing them both towards a third act, as is the case in the compounding of natural objects. For in the contemplating soul, since God is both the prime mover and the ultimate giver of form, so [its] whole act is God, and God Himself is always in this act, and the soul becomes, at least at some point in time, divine. And just as nature transmits the order 10

rum compositione, sed quia in animo contemplante deus et primus motor est et formator ultimus, ideo totus actus est deus, quo quidem actu et ipse semper est deus, et animus fit saltem quandoque divinus. Et sicut natura per naturalem motum tradit materiae formarum ordinem, sic deus per divinam immortalemque vitam tradit menti perspicuam formarum possessionem, ut eidem divina immortalisque competat vita, cui divinarum immortaliumque intellegentia convenit. Atque ut materia, licet sub inferioribus fluat formis, sub formis tamen sublimibus, ut quidam putant, quiescit semper, ita mens hominis, quamvis per sensibiles imaginariasque perfluat formas, potest tamen sub divinis quandoque in aeternum quiescere. Quod etiam modo facit, ut vult Plotinus et Iamblichus et Theodorus, ut quemadmodum materiam perficit semper quantitatis interminata dimensio, sic mentem divinae amplitudinis virtus immensa. Per huius vim, in huius luce, ad huius finem mens continue aeternis formatur ideis. Et quia per congruentiam formatio omnis efficitur, non potest subiectum hoc esse mortale quod formis continue formatur aeternis. Incorruptibilis est materia prima, in quam formae quaedam penetrant sempiternae, quamvis ipsa non penetret in illas: nonne immortalis quoque mens erit, quae non modo penetratur ab illis, sed et penetrat cognoscendo et reflectitur in eas agnoscendo?

11 Praeterea, ubi prima mens est, ibi vita prima, quoniam mens est reflexio vitae[31] in esse unum. Ubi vita prima, ibi et esse primum, quoniam vita est primus et intimus ipsius esse motus. Profecto, deus prout per se existit, et vere id quod existit perpetuo permanet, primum apud multos esse vocatur. Prout non torpet otio, sed operatur assidue secum, vita dicitur. Prout actus talis, qui non effluit extra, refluit[32] in se ipsum, mens appellatur. Nam ea re-

of the forms to matter by means of natural movement, so God transmits the transparent possession of the forms to mind by means of divine and immortal life. The result is that divine and immortal life accords with mind just as the understanding of things divine and immortal accords with it. And just as matter, though it flows under the lower forms, yet always comes to rest (some believe[54]) under the higher forms, so the mind of man, though it flows through the sensible and imaginary forms, yet is able at some point in time to come to rest in eternity under the divine forms. It is only able to do this according to Plotinus, Iamblichus, and Theodore,[55] because just as quantity's unlimited extension always perfects matter, so the immeasurable power of the divine abundance perfects mind. Through the force of this power and in its light and to its end mind is formed unceasingly by the eternal ideas. And because all forming is effected through coming into accord, the subject that is continually formed by the eternal ideas cannot be mortal. The prime matter into which certain eternal forms penetrate is incorruptible, although it does not itself penetrate them. Surely that mind too will be immortal which is not only penetrated by the forms, but which in coming to know them penetrates them, and in knowing them is reflected into them?[56]

Furthermore, the prime mind is there where the prime life is, 11
for the mind is the turning back of that life towards the one being. And where the prime life is the prime being is, for life is the first and innermost movement of being itself. Certainly, according as God exists through Himself (and as that which truly exists endures forever), among many He is called the prime being. According as He never succumbs to idleness, but is unceasingly active within Himself, He is called life. According as such an act never flows out of itself but flows back into itself, He is called mind. For in that turning back He is conscious of Himself. Since what is highest in some genus has no part of a contrary genus either

Xexione se ipsum animadvertit. Quoniam vero quod est in genere aliquo summum, nihil contrarii generis aut immixtum habet aut proximum, fit ut neque prima mens vel in se vel iuxta se ipsam demens aliquid patiatur, neque prima vita mortale quicquam, neque primum esse aliquid in nihilum ruiturum, neque prima unitas aliquid dissolubile, neque prima bonitas aliquid morbo subiectum. Quare mens quae menti iungitur primae, sicut in ea coniunctione nihil reservat dementiae, sic mortale nihil admittit aut perdibile aut dissolubile morbove subiectum, quia per mentem primam primae quoque vitae copulatur et esse primo similique unitati et bonitati. Quid mirum si intellectualis vita propter congressum cum prima vita immortalis permaneat, cum caelestia corpora, ut volunt Platonici, per se quidem dissolubilia sint, quia et mobilia et composita sive ex naturis pluribus sive partibus, ex eo tamen indissoluta perdurent, quod nullo alio corpore interiecto immortali animae copulantur. Quae vero per aliud medium dissolvuntur, qualia sunt corpora ex pluribus elementis composita, quae immortalem animam, ut Magi tradunt, per corpus caeleste suscipiunt.

: V :

Confirmatio superioris rationis prima, per visum.

1 Animas hominum de corporibus in corpora transmigrare et praecedentis vitae artes in sequentibus recordari Plato non suo sensu tractavit, sed ex quorundam Aegyptiorum opinione recensuit, quorum opinionem Augustinus Aurelius reprobavit. Quod autem anima hominis ab ipso suo formatore formis rerum insignita descendat atque his formis non sufficienter rerum substantias com-

mixed in with it or close to it, accordingly the prime mind suffers nothing mindless in or near itself; the prime life, nothing mortal; the prime being, nothing that is about to tumble into non-being; the prime unity, nothing divisible; and the prime goodness, nothing subject to malady. Thus mind is joined to the prime mind, and just as it retains nothing mindless in this union, so by the same token it admits nothing mortal or dissoluble or subject to disease. For it is linked through the prime mind also to the prime life and the prime being, and likewise to the prime unity and goodness. Is it surprising if the intellectual life because of its union with the prime life remains immortal, when heavenly bodies, according to the Platonists, though in themselves liable to dissolution because they are mobile and composed from many natures or parts, yet remain without dissolution precisely because they are linked without any other intervening body to immortal soul. But those linked through another medium suffer dissolution, for example, bodies composed of many elements; and these, as the Magi tell us, receive an immortal soul only by way of a heavenly body.[57]

: V :

The first confirmation of the previous argument: by way of sight.

When Plato treated of the transmigration of men's souls from 1
bodies to bodies and their recalling the skills of an earlier life in later lives, he did not present his own view but that of certain Egyptians, a view that Augustine condemned.[58] However, that man's soul comes down stamped with the forms of things by the Giver of form Himself, that it does not adequately comprehend things' substances by means of these stamped forms, but that

prehendat, sed per eas tamquam praeparationes ideis reformata comprehendere valeat, hoc inquam et Plato ex mente propria saepe affirmasse videtur, et Augustinus summopere comprobasse. Ergo per Augustini vestigia gradientes ad superioris sententiae confirmationem iterum contendamus. Procedamus autem triplici calle: visu, auditu et ratione.

2 Visu primo hunc in modum. Anima qua vivunt corpora omnibus corporibus potior est, quia vitam dat corporibus. Hac profecto quae sensum habet excellentior est. 'At vero in animo humano quiddam praestantius est, non dico quo sentit sensibilia, sed quo de sensibilibus iudicat. Iam vero illud videre facile est, praestantiorem esse rem iudicantem illa de qua iudicatur neque iudicat. Non solum autem rationalis vita de sensibilibus, sed de ipsis quoque sensibus iudicat: Cur[33] in aqua remum fractum oporteat apparere, cum rectus sit,[34] et cur ita per oculos sentiri necesse sit. Nam ipse aspectus oculorum renuntiare id potest, iudicare autem nullo modo. Igitur rationalis vita sensuali praestat'.

3 'Itaque si ratio secundum se ipsam iudicat, iam nulla est natura praestantior. Sed quia clarum est eam esse mutabilem, quando nunc imperita, nunc perita invenitur, tanto autem melius iudicat quanto est peritior, et tanto peritior quanto alicuius artis vel disciplinae vel sapientiae est particeps, ipsius artis natura quaerenda est. Neque nunc artem intellegi volo quae notatur experiendo, sed quae ratiocinando indagatur'.

4 'Sed certe quaerendum est cur nos offendat, si duabus fenestris non supra invicem, sed iuxta invicem locatis, una earum maior minorve sit, cum aequales esse potuerint, si vero super invicem fuerint, ambaeque dimidio quamvis impares, non ita offendat illa

through them as by way of preparation, having been re-formed by the ideas, it can comprehend—all this it seems Plato often stated as his own view, and Augustine fully confirmed it. So treading in Augustine's footsteps, let us seek confirmation once more of our earlier argument. Let us proceed by way of three paths: by way of sight, of hearing, and of reason.

First via the sense of sight. The soul that animates bodies is 2 more powerful than all bodies because it gives life to bodies. More excellent than this is the soul that possesses sense. "But more outstanding still is something in man's rational soul, not, I say, that it senses sensibles, but that it makes judgments about them. For it is easy to see that what does the judging is superior to what is being judged and does not judge. But rational life makes judgments, not only about sensibles, but also about the senses themselves—why an oar has to look bent in the water when it is in fact straight, and why the eyes have to see it thus. For the eyes' vision can report the information, but not judge in any way. Therefore rational life is superior to sensual life."[59]

"Thus, if reason judges on its own, no nature is higher. But be- 3 cause reason is clearly liable to change—sometimes we find it has had experience, sometimes not, and it makes the better judgments the greater its degree of experience, and its degree of experience depends on how far it has participated in some skill or learned discipline or wisdom—and because this is so, we must inquire into the nature of art itself. Now I am not talking here about an art that is picked up by experiencing, but about the one that is tracked down by reasoning."[60]

"But we should certainly ask ourselves in the case of two win- 4 dows set side by side and not one above the other, why it bothers us if one is bigger or smaller when they could be equal, whereas, if the windows are one on top of the other, and one is twice the size of the other, the difference does not bother us. Or again why, with two such, we do not really care how much bigger or smaller one of

inaequalitas, et cur non multum curemus quantum sit una earum aut maior aut minor, quia duae sunt. In tribus autem sensus ipse videtur expetere ut aut impares non sint, aut inter maximam et minimam ita sit media, ut tanto praecedat minorem, quanto a maiore praeceditur. Ita enim primo quasi natura ipsa consulitur quid probet. Ubi potissimum notandum est, quemadmodum quod solum inspectum minus displicuit, in melioris comparatione respuatur, ita reperitur nihil esse aliud artem vulgarem, nisi rerum expertarum placitarumque memoriam, usu quodam corporis atque operationis adiuncto. Quo si careas, iudicare de operibus possis, quod multo est excellentius, quamvis operari artificiosa non possis'.

5 'Sed cum in omnibus artibus convenientia placeat, qua una servata pulchra sunt omnia, ipsa vero convenientia aequalitatem unitatemque appetat vel similitudine parium[35] partium vel gradatione disparium, quis est qui summam aequalitatem vel similitudinem in corporibus inveniat audeatque dicere, cum diligenter consideraverit, quodlibet corpus vere ac simpliciter unum esse, cum omnia vel de specie in speciem vel de loco in locum transeundo mutentur et partibus constent sua loca obtinentibus, per quae in spatia diversa dividuntur? Porro, ipsa vera aequalitas ac similitudo atque ipsa vera et prima unitas nullo sensu sed mente intellecta conspicitur. Unde enim qualiscumque appeteretur in corporibus aequalitas, aut unde convinceretur longe plurimum differre a perfecta, nisi ea quae perfecta est mente videretur?'

6 'Et cum omnia quae sensibiliter pulchra sunt, sive natura edita sive artibus elaborata, locis et temporibus pulchra sint, ut corpus et corporis motus, illa aequalitas et unitas menti tantummodo co-

them is, but with three, our sense itself seems to demand that either they should be equal, or that the one in between should measure halfway between the biggest and the smallest. To begin with, one could say that Nature herself gives advice on what should be approved. We should, however, be careful to note that, as with something which causes no displeasure when we first see it, but which we reject when we compare it with something better, so we discover that art in the vulgar sense is nothing else but the memory of things we have tested and approved in conjunction with some use of the body and its activity. If you lack all this, you can still judge the results; and this is a far superior activity, even though you are unable to make the artifacts."[61]

"Since it is symmetry that gives pleasure in all the arts, and all 5
things are beautiful if this is preserved intact, but since symmetry itself desires equality and unity, either in the likeness of equal parts or in the proportion between unequal parts, then who can find the highest equality or likeness in bodies? And who dares say, having given the matter careful consideration, that any body can be truly and simply one, since all bodies change by moving either from one species to another, or from one location to another, and are constituted of parts occupying their own places and thus spatially distributed? Furthermore, true equality and likeness, and true and prime unity are not themselves perceived by the sense, but by the mind's understanding. For whence would our desire for some kind of equality in bodies derive, and how would we be convinced it differs so very much from perfect equality, if our mind had not seen perfect equality?"[62]

"Since all which are beautiful in terms of the senses (whether 6
produced by nature or elaborated by art) are beautiful in time and space, like body and the movements of body, so the equality and unity known only to mind (according to which we judge the corporeal beauty brought to us by way of the senses) is neither extended in space nor unstable in time. It cannot be correct to say

gnita, secundum quam de corporea pulchritudine sensu internuntio iudicatur, nec loco tumida est, nec instabilis tempore. Non enim recte dici potest secundum eam iudicari rotundum templum, et non secundum eam rotundum vasculum aut rotundum denarium. Similiter in temporibus atque in motibus corporum ridicule dicitur secundum eam iudicari aequales annos et non secundum eam aequales menses. Sed sive per haec spatia sive per horas sive per breviora momenta convenienter moveatur aliquid, eadem una et incommutabili aequalitate iudicatur. Quod si minora et maiora spatia figurarum atque motionum per eandem legem parilitatis vel similitudinis vel congruentiae iudicantur, ipsa lex maior est iis omnibus. Sed potentia, ceterum spatio aut loci aut temporis nec maior, nec minor. Quod si maior esset, non secundum totam iudicaremus minora; si autem minor esset, non secundum eam iudicaremus maiora. Nunc vero, cum per totam quadraturae legem iudicetur et forum quadratum et lapis quadratus; rursus, si per totam aequalitatis legem iudicentur convenire sibi motus pedum currentis formicae et per eam gradientis elephantis, quis eam dubitet locorum intervallis ac temporum nec maiorem esse nec minorem, cum potentia superet omnia? Haec autem lex omnium artium, cum sit omnino incommutabilis, mens vero humana, cui talem legem videre concessum est, mutabilitatem pati possit erroris, satis apparet supra mentem nostram esse legem quae veritas dicitur'.

7 'Nec iam illud ambigendum est incommutabilem naturam, quae supra rationalem animam sit, deum esse, et ibi esse primam vitam et primam essentiam ubi est prima sapientia. Nam haec est illa incommutabilis veritas, quae lex omnium artium recte dicitur et ars omnipotentis artificis. Itaque cum se anima sentiat nec corporum speciem motumque iudicare secundum se ipsam, simul

that we use this equality to judge the roundness of a temple, but not the roundness of a vase or a silver coin. Likewise with times and with the movements of bodies, it would be ridiculous to say that we use equality to judge the equalness of years, but not that of months. Whenever something is consistently moved, however, whether through these larger intervals or through hours or through still briefer moments, it is judged by one and the same unchanging equality. But if the lesser and greater dimensions of figures and motions are judged by the same law of equality or likeness or congruity, then the law itself must be greater than all of them. But it is greater in power, since in extent of time and place it is neither larger nor smaller; for were it larger we could not use the whole of it to judge what is smaller; and were it smaller, we could not use the whole of it to judge what is larger. In point of fact, however, since we use the whole law of "squareness" to judge a forum square and a stone square, and likewise if we use the whole law of equality to judge that the feet of a scurrying ant are coordinated, and use the same law for a lumbering elephant, who will doubt that this law is neither larger nor smaller in terms of the intervals of space or time, even though it is superior to everything in power? But since this law which applies to all the arts is totally immutable, whereas the human mind which is permitted to observe this law can be subject to the mutability of error, it is quite apparent that above our mind exists the law called truth."[63]

"We should no longer doubt that this unchanging nature [i.e. truth] which is above the rational soul is God, and that the prime life and the prime essence dwell where the prime wisdom is. For this is that unchanging truth, which is properly called both the law of all the arts and the art of the omnipotent artificer. Therefore, since the soul realizes that it does not judge the species and motion of bodies according to itself, it ought at the same time to recognize that, while its nature is superior to the nature of the object it is judging, the nature according to which it judges and about 7

oportet agnoscat praestare suam naturam ei naturae de qua iudicat, praestare autem sibi eam naturam, secundum quam iudicat et de qua iudicare nullo modo potest. Possum enim dicere quare similia sibi ex utraque parte respondere membra cuiusque corporis debeant, quia summa aequalitate delector, quam non oculis sed mente contueor. Quapropter tanto meliora esse iudico quae oculis cerno, quanto pro sua natura viciniora sunt iis quae animo[36] intellego. Quare autem illa ita sint nullus potest dicere, nec ita esse debere quisquam sobrie dixerit, quasi possint esse non ita'.

8 'Quare autem nobis placeant et cur ea, quando melius[37] sapimus, vehementissime diligamus, nec id quisquam quidem, si ea rite intellegit, dicere audebit. Ut enim nos et omnes animae rationales secundum veritatem de inferioribus recte iudicamus, sic de nobis, quando eidem cohaeremus, sola ipsa veritas iudicat. De ipsa vero nec iudicat pater. Nec enim minus est quam ipse. Et ideo quae pater iudicat, per ipsam iudicat. Omnia enim quae appetunt unitatem hanc habent regulam vel formam vel exemplum, quoniam eius similitudinem sola, a quo esse accepit, implevit'.

9 'Mens omnia iudicat, quia super omnia est, quando cum deo est. Cum illo est autem quando purissime intellegit, et tota caritate quod intellegit, diligit. Ita etiam quantum potest lex ipsa et ipsa fit per quam iudicat omnia, et de qua iudicare nullus potest. Sicut in istis temporalibus legibus, quamquam de his homines iudicant quando eas instituunt, tamen cum fuerint institutae atque firmatae, non licebit iudici de ipsis iudicare, sed per ipsas. Conditor tamen legum temporalium, si vir bonus est et sapiens, illam ipsam consulit aeternam, de qua nulli animae iudicare datum est, ut per eius incommutabiles regulas, quid sit pro tempore iubendum vetandumque discernat. Aeternam igitur legem mundis animis fas est agnoscere; iudicare non fas est'.

which it can make no judgment is superior to it. For I can say why on either side of any one body the members should correspond to each other: it is because I am delighted by the highest equality, which I see not with my eyes but with my mind. So I judge that the things I see with my eyes are better to the extent that they are closer (as far as their nature permits) to the things I understand in my rational soul. But why these [in turn] are the way they are, no man can say; nor can anyone claim in all seriousness that they have to be like this (as if they could be otherwise)."[64]

"Why they give us pleasure, or why we love them so intensely when we understand them better, this too no one, if he properly understands them, will dare to say. Just as we and all rational souls make correct judgments about inferior things according to the truth, so truth itself alone makes judgments about us when we adhere to it. And not even the Father judges the truth; for it is no less than He; and so what the Father judges, He judges through the truth. For all that desire unity has this as its measure or form or exemplar, since truth alone took on the full likeness of Him whence it had its being."[65] 8

"The mind judges all things because it is above all things when it is with God. And it is with God when it understands most purely and loves what it understands in total charity. Thus, insofar as it can, it too becomes the law itself whereby it judges all things, and about which none can judge. Similarly with temporal laws: although men make judgments about them when they institute them, once they have been instituted and established, the judge is not going to be permitted to make judgments about them but only through them. Yet the establisher of temporal laws, if he is a good and wise man, looks to that eternal law, concerning which no soul is allowed to judge, so that he may learn through its immutable principles what should or should not be permitted in the world of time. So pure souls are permitted to acknowledge the eternal law but not to judge it."[66] 9

10 'Sane secundum ipsam de animo et corpore iudicare possumus, hic minus actus[38] aut minus vehemens est quam debuit, hoc minus candidum est quam debuit. De ipsa vero lege nullo modo quis iudicat. Cum enim quis dixerit aeterna temporalibus esse potiora aut septem et tria esse decem nemo dicit ita esse debuisse, sed tantum 'ita est,' agnoscens non ut examinator corrigit, sed tamquam inveniens delectatur'.

11 'Sed multis finis est humana delectatio, nec volunt tendere ad superiora ut iudicent cur ista sensibilia placeant. Itaque si quaeram ab artifice, uno arcu constructo cur alterum parem contra in alteram partem moliatur, respondebit, credo, ut paria paribus aedificii membra respondeant. Porro si pergam quaerere idipsum cur eligat, dicet hoc decere, hoc esse pulchrum, hoc delectare cernentes. Nihil audebit amplius. Inclinatus enim recumbit oculis et unde pendeat non intellegit. At ego, virum intrinsecus oculatum et invisibiliter videntem, non desinam commonere cur[39] ista placeant, ut iudex esse audeat ipsius delectationis humanae. Ita enim superfertur illi nec ab ea tenetur, dum non secundum ipsam, sed ipsam iudicat. Et prius quaeram utrum ideo pulchra sint quia delectant, an ideo delectant quia pulchra sint. Hic mihi[40] sine dubitatione respondebitur, ideo delectare quia pulchra sint. Quaeram ergo deinceps quare sint pulchra, et si titubabit, subiiciam, utrum ideo quia similes sibi partes sunt et aliqua copulatione ad unam convenientiam rediguntur'.

12 'Quod cum ita esse compererit, interrogabo utrum hanc ipsam unitatem, quam convincuntur appetere, summe impleant aut longe

"We can of course use this law to make judgments about the rational soul or body: [for instance] that the soul is less busy or less vehement than it should be, or the body less clear-complexioned than it should be. But no one makes judgments in any way about the law itself. When someone says that things eternal are more powerful than things temporal, or that seven and three make ten, he is not declaring that they should be so, but only that this is the reality. In this recognition he is not an examiner who corrects, but someone who is delighted by what he finds."[67] 10

"For many people, however, human delight is the goal; they do not want to aim at higher things in order to judge why the sensible objects here give delight. Thus, if I ask a builder who has built one arch why he is laboring to erect another one like it on the opposite side, he will answer, I imagine, that equal parts of the construction should correspond to each other. If I go on to ask him why he chooses to do it in this way, he will say that it looks correct, that it is beautiful, that it gives pleasure to those who see it. He will not venture further. He is content to rely on his eyes and does not understand the source of his dependency. But with a man who has eyes within and sees what is invisible, I shall not cease reminding him why it is that these pleasures please him, in order that he may venture to be the judge of human pleasure itself. For he is set above it and is not possessed by it when he judges it itself and does not simply judge through it. First I shall ask him whether things are beautiful because they give pleasure, or give pleasure because they are beautiful. He will answer me, with no hesitation, that they give pleasure because they are beautiful. Then I shall ask him why they are beautiful, and, if he falters, then ask him whether it is because the parts are alike and joined in some union for one harmony's sake."[68] 11

"When he realizes that this is so, I shall ask him whether they fully achieve this unity we have shown they desire, or whether they fall far short of it, and, so to speak, pretend to possess it. Now if 12

infra iaceant et eam quodammodo mentiantur. Quod si ita est—nam quis non admonitus videat, neque ullam speciem neque ullum omnino esse corpus, quod non habeat unitatis qualecumque vestigium? neque quantumvis pulcherrimum corpus, cum intervallis locorum necessario aliud alibi habeat, posse assequi eam quam sequitur unitatem?—flagitabo ut respondeat ipse ubi videat unitatem hanc, aut unde videat. Quam si non videret, unde cognosceret et quid imitaretur corporum species et quid implere non posset? Nunc vero cum dicitur corporibus: "vos quidem, nisi aliqua unitas contineret, nihil essetis; sed rursus si vos essetis ipsa unitas, corpora non essetis"; recte dicitur. Unde igitur nosti istam unitatem secundum quam iudicas corpora? Quam nisi videres, iudicare non posses quod eam non impleant. Si autem iis corporeis oculis eam videres, non vere diceres, quamquam eius vestigio teneantur, longe tamen ab ea distare. Nam iis oculis non nisi corporalia vides. Mente igitur videmus eam. Sed ubi videmus? Si hoc loco esset ubi corpus nostrum est, non eam videret qui hoc modo in Oriente de corporibus iudicat. Non ergo isto continetur loco. Et cum adest ubique iudicanti, nusquam est per spatia locorum, et per potentiam nusquam non est'.

13 Cum anima multis illusionibus phantasmatum hinc inde perturbantium concitatur, et tamen falsa haec esse agnoscit, ubi est verum quod mente conspicitur? 'Illa lux vera est, qua haec omnia non esse vera cognoscis.[41] Per hanc illud unum vides, quo iudicas unum esse quicquid aliud vides,[42] nec tamen hoc esse quod illud est quicquid vides mutabile'.

14 Praeterea, 'quaere in corporis voluptate quid te delectat: nihil aliud invenies quam convenientiam. Nam si resistentia vel discrepantia pariunt dolorem, convenientia pariunt voluptatem. Agnosce igitur quae sit summa convenientia. Noli foras ire. In teipsum redi. In interiore homine habitat veritas. Et si tuam naturam mu-

this is so — for who cannot see, once alerted, that there is no form and no body at all which does not have some trace of unity, but that no body, however beautiful, because inevitably it is different in different parts of space, can attain the unity it seeks — I shall insist that he tell me where he himself sees the unity and from what source he sees it. Were he unable to see this unity, then how would he know both what the bodies' form is imitating and why it cannot achieve it? Now when you say to the bodies, 'Unless some unity contained you, you would not exist; but if on the other hand you were unity itself, you would not be bodies,' you are telling them what is true. Whence, therefore, do you come to know the unity according to which you judge bodies? If you have not seen it, you cannot judge that bodies fail to achieve it. But if you have seen it with these bodily eyes, you would not be saying truthfully that, though bodies are onto its track, yet they are a long way from it. For with these eyes you only see things corporeal. So we must see this unity with the mind. But where do we see it? If it were in the same place where our body is, somebody in the East making judgments about bodies in this way would be unable to see it. So it cannot be confined to this location here. And since it is present wherever someone is making judgments, it is nowhere in terms of space; but it is not nowhere in terms of power."[69]

Since the soul is aroused by a multitude of illusory images 13
bombarding it on every side yet recognizes they are false, where is the truth the mind perceives? "That is the true light, by which you know all these images are not true. Through it you see the One by which you judge something else you see is one, and yet this One is not that something which you see is changeable."[70]

Furthermore, "ask what gives you pleasure in the body's plea- 14
sure. You will find it is nothing other than harmony. For if conflict and dissension breed pain, harmonies give birth to pleasure. Learn then what is the highest harmony. Do not go outside. Return into yourself. Truth dwells in the inner man. And if you discover your

tabilem inveneris, transcende teipsum. Sed memento, cum te transcenderis, ratiocinantem animam te transcendere. Illuc ergo tende, unde ipsum lumen rationis accenditur. Quo enim pervenit omnis bonus ratiocinator nisi ad veritatem, cum ad se ipsa veritas non utique ratiocinando perveniat, sed quod ratiocinantes appetunt, ipsa sit?'

15 Et cum[43] disputando ambo videmus verum esse quod dicis, et ambo videmus verum esse quod dico, ubi quaeso hoc videmus? Hoc utique nec ego in te, nec tu in me, sed ambo in ipsa quae super mentes nostras est incommutabili veritate videmus. Ibi sane formam ipsam secundum quam haec temporalia facta sunt visu mentis aspicimus, atque inde conceptam rerum veritatem et notitiam tamquam verbum apud nos habemus.

16 'Vide ibi convenientiam qua superior esse non possit, et ipse conveni cum ea. Confitere te non esse quod ipsa est, siquidem se ipsa non quaerit. Tu autem quaerendo ad eam venisti, non locorum spatio, sed mentis affectu, ut interior homo cum suo inhabitatore spiritali voluptate conveniat. Aut si non cernis quae dico et an vera sint[44] dubitas, cerne saltem utrum de his[45] te dubitare non dubites. Et si certum est te esse dubitantem, quaere unde sit certum. A lumine "quod illuminat omnem hominem venientem in hunc mundum," quod iis oculis videri non potest, nec illis quibus phantasmata cogitantur, sed illis quibus ipsis phantasmatibus[46] dicitur: "Non estis vos quod ego quaero, neque illud estis, unde ego vos ordino, et quod mihi inter vos foedum occurrerit improbo, quod pulchrum approbo, cum pulchrius sit illud unde improbo et approbo. Quare hoc ipsum magis approbo, et non solum vobis,

nature is mutable, transcend yourself. But remember as you transcend yourself you are transcending yourself as a reasoning soul. Aim for the place whence the reason's light was kindled. For where does every good reasoner arrive if not at the truth, given that the truth does not arrive at itself by reasoning, but is itself the goal reasoners long for."[71]

15 When we both realize, in the course of an argument, that what you say is true, and we both realize that what I say is true, where, may I ask, do we see this truth? I do not see it in you, nor do you see it in me; but we both see it in that unchangeable truth which is above our minds. There we perceive with the sight of the mind the form itself according to which these temporal things are made. Having conceived this form, we possess the truth and conception of things like a word amongst ourselves.

16 "Look there for the harmony than which none can be greater, and put yourself in harmony with it. Admit that you are not the same as it, because it does not seek itself. But you have come to it through seeking—not through space, but through the mind's desire—that the 'inner man' may be united in pleasure with his spiritual guest. If you do not see what I am saying, or if you doubt whether it is true, at least see whether you are not in doubt about doubting all this. And if it is certain you doubt, ask where this certainty comes from. It comes from the light 'which lighteth every man that cometh into this world,'[72] and which cannot be seen with these eyes, nor with those by which we conceive of images. Rather it is seen with the very eyes with which we say to the images, 'You are not what I am looking for, nor are you what enables me to establish an order for you and to condemn what I find ugly amongst you, and to approve what is beautiful, when that by virtue of which I condemn and praise is more beautiful still. Wherefore I approve it the more, and choose it in preference, not only to you, but to all those bodies from which I have derived you.' When you see these things it is with the light that is without spatial and tem-

sed illis omnibus corporibus unde vos hausi antepono". Ubi videntur haec, ibi est lumen sine spatio locorum et temporum, et sine ullo spatiorum talium phantasmate. Numquid ista ex aliqua parte corrumpi possunt, etiam si omnis ratiocinator intereat? Non enim ratiocinatio talia facit, sed invenit. Ergo antequam inveniantur, in se manent, et cum inveniuntur, nos innovant.[47] Ita renascitur interior homo, et exterior corrumpitur de die in diem'.

17 Inter mentem nostram, qua illum intellegimus patrem et veritatem, id est lucem interiorem per quam illum intellegimus, nulla interposita creatura est. Quare ipsam quoque veritatem nulla ex parte dissimilem in ipso et cum ipso veneremur, quae forma est omnium quae ab uno facto sunt et ad unum nituntur. Unde apparet per hanc formam facta esse omnia, quae sola implet quod appetunt omnia.

: VI :

Secunda confirmatio, per auditum secundum Augustinum.

1 Hactenus per ea quae aspectu percipiuntur, duce Augustino, eo pervenimus ut inveniremus mentem nostram divina mente formari. Deinceps, duce eodem, per ea quae audiuntur ad idem proficiscamur.

2 'In sonis concinnis est aliquis numerus, hinc et in actu sentiendi certus fit numerus, quia numerosus sonus numerose sentitur. Est et numerus aliquis in ipsa sensus natura. Non enim aliter aut mul-

poral dimension and without any image having such dimensions. Surely these things can never be in any way corrupted even if every person who reasons were to perish? For such reasoning does not create but discovers truths. So, before they are discovered, they remain in themselves, and when they are discovered, they make us anew. 'Thus the inner man is born again, and the outer perishes from day to day.'"[73]

No creature is interposed between our mind by which we un- 17
derstand Him as Father and the truth, that is, the inner light through which we understand Him. For we also worship the truth itself, which is in no way different from the Father, in Him and with Him; and this truth is the form of all things which are created by the One and which strive towards the One. Thus it is clear that all things are created through the form that alone satisfies the yearning of all things.

: VI :

The second confirmation: by way of hearing and according to Augustine.

Led by Augustine by way of what our sight perceives, we have 1
reached the point of discovering that our mind is formed by the divine mind. Again following his lead, let us next pursue the same goal by way of what we hear.

"In harmonious sounds some number exists. Hence some num- 2
ber also occurs in the act of perceiving, because a numbered sound is perceived in a numbered way. Some number also exists in the very nature of the sense [of hearing]; for otherwise it would not be delighted by the harmony of sounds or offended by their harshness. So whatever it is when something sounds according to which

ceretur sonorum concinnitate aut absurditate offenderetur. Idipsum ergo, quicquid est quo aut annuimus aut abhorremus, non ratione sed natura, cum aliquid sonet, ipsius sensus numerum voco. Non enim tunc fit in auribus meis, cum sonum audio, haec vis approbandi et[48] improbandi. Aures quippe non aliter bonis sonis quam malis patent. Vide potius ne ista duo sint minime confundenda. Nam si versus quilibet modo correptius,[49] modo productius pronuntietur, spatium temporis non idem teneat necesse est, quamvis eadem pedum ratione servata. Ut ergo ipso suo genere aures mulceat illa vis facit, qua concinna asciscimus et absurda respuimus. Ut autem breviore tempore sentiatur, cum celerius quam cum tardius promitur, non interest aliquid, nisi quamdiu aures tangantur sono. Affectio ergo haec aurium, cum tanguntur sono, nullo modo talis est ac si non tangantur. Ut autem differt audire ab eo quod est non audire, ita differt hanc vocem audire ab eo quod est alteram audire. Haec igitur affectio nec ultra porrigitur nec infra cohibetur, quam est mensura eius soni qui eam facit. Altera est ergo in iambo, altera in tribracho, productior in productiore iambo, correptior in correptiore, nulla in silentio. Quod si in numerosa voce fit, etiam ipsa numerosa sit necesse est, neque esse possit cum abest effector eius sonus. Similis est enim vestigio in aqua impresso, quod neque ante formatur quam corpus impresseris, neque remanet cum detraxeris. Naturalis autem illa vis et iudiciaria quae auribus adest, non desinit esse in silentio, nec nobis eam sonus inserit, sed ab ea potius sonus probandus sive improbandus excipitur'.

3 Quis negaverit in anima esse vim numerorum, cum anima hos numeros agat quos in venarum pulsu invenimus et reciproco spiritu? 'Cum aliquando correptius sive productius, dum serviam

we either give approval or are averse, not rationally but naturally, I call the sense's number. For this power of approving or condemning does not happen in my ears when I hear the sound; for ears are open alike to good and bad sounds. Rather, make sure that these two sounds are not confounded. For if some verse is pronounced in a way that is now too clipped, now too drawled, it necessarily does not last the same length of time even though you have observed the same ratio or principle underlying the prosodic feet. Thus, in this genre [of prosody], for the verse to delight our ears derives from the power by which we approve of concords and reject discords. But the fact that the verse is heard in a shorter time when we pronounce it faster and not more slowly is the outcome of how long our ears hear the sound. So our ears' perception itself when they hear a sound is not the same at all as it would be if they did not hear it. But just as hearing is different from not hearing, so hearing one voice is different from hearing another. So the perception lasts no longer and is no shorter than the measure of the sound producing it. The measure is different in an iamb than it is in a tribrach;[74] and it is more extended in a more extended iamb, briefer in a briefer one, and non-existent in silence. If it is produced in a sound containing number, then it must itself be numbered; and it cannot exist when the sound producing it does not exist. It is like a print impressed in water, which is only formed after you impress some object in the water, and does not remain when you remove it. But the natural and judgment-making power that is present in the ears does not cease to exist when there is silence. Sound does not sow this power in us, but rather the power itself selects a sound for approval or rejection."[75]

Who would deny that the power of numbers is in the soul, since the soul sets into motion the numbers [or rhythms] we find in the pulsing of the veins and in respiration? "When I recite the verse more rapidly at one point or more slowly, so long as I submit to the rule of the meter, by which the feet accord as the single to 3

temporum legi, qua simplo ad duplum pedes conveniunt, versum pronuntio, nulla fraude iudicium tui sensus offendo. Atqui sonus ille qui correptioribus et quasi fugacioribus syllabis editur, non potest plus temporis occupare quam sonat. Iudiciales autem illi numeri si vinclo temporis in tanto spatio tenerentur, quanto isti sonantes digesti sunt, non possent ad eorum sonantium, qui paulo productius eadem iambica lege funduntur, aspirare iudicium. Hos igitur mora temporum qui iudicando praesident, illa non tenet. Sed si nulla tenerentur, quantolibet productius competentibus intervallis et invicem respondentibus iambicos proferrem sonos, nihilominus ad iudicandum adhiberentur. Nunc vero si ederem unam syllabam quanta mora peraguntur (ne multum dicam), tres passus incedentis, et aliam duplo, atque ita deinceps tam longos iambos ordinarem, simpli et dupli lex illa nihilominus servaretur, nec tamen naturale illud iudicium iis dimensionibus approbandis adhibere possemus. Tenentur ergo et ii iudiciales nonnullis finibus temporalium spatiorum, quos iudicando excedere nequeunt, et quicquid excedit haec spatia, non assequuntur ut iudicent'.

4 'Temperant tamen isti singulas actiones. Quod enim nos vel ambulantes ab imparibus passibus, vel percutientes ab imparibus intervallis plagarum, vel edentes ab imparibus molarum motibus, scalpentes denique ab imparibus unguium ductibus, et quod nos in qualibet attentione agendi aliquid per corporis membra ab imparibus motibus refrenat et cohibet et quandam parilitatem tacite imperat, idipsum est iudiciale nescio quid.' Quod facit ut homines sensum ac delectum habeant pulchritudinis et decoris magis quam bestiae, quae ad sua quaelibet incitamenta sedandae passionis corporalis causa praecipitantur, non pulchritudinis gratia aviditateque

the double, I am not offending or deceiving the judgment of your sense. And yet the sound that is produced in more rapid and so to speak more fleeting syllables cannot occupy more time than the sound itself lasts. If the judging numbers[76] were bound in time's fetter to the same duration as the audible numbers, they could not aspire to making a judgment with respect to audible numbers, which, though produced more slowly, are based in the same iambic meter. So temporal duration does not possess the numbers that preside over it in judging. But if they were not limited by duration at all, and I could draw out the iambic sounds as long as I liked in the appropriate and mutually corresponding intervals, they would still be summoned to judgment. But in reality if I were to utter one syllable that takes (not to make it too large) as long as it takes a person to walk three steps, and then another twice that length, and if I kept on thus lengthening out the iambs, yet preserving the rule of the simple and the double, nonetheless we could not bring the natural judgment [of our ears] to approve of these dimensions. So [in reality] these judging numbers are limited to certain boundaries of time and space, which in making judgments they cannot exceed. Anything that exceeds these limits they are not in a position to judge."[77]

"Yet the judging numbers do temper our individual actions. For whatever it is that prevents and checks us from walking with uneven strides, or beating time to uneven intervals, or chewing with uneven bites of our teeth, or scratching ourselves with uneven digs of our nails, and whatever it is in any concern that checks us from unbalanced movements when we do anything using the body's limbs, and silently commands us to observe a certain symmetry, this is in fact some judging thing." This is what gives men much more than the beasts a sense of, and appreciation for, beauty and charm. For beasts respond immediately to certain stimuli keyed to satisfying physical passion: they are not drawn by the grace of, or by the desire for, beauty. Horses do not choose a more beautiful 4

alliciuntur. Unde equi non formosiorem deligunt equam quam ament, sed ad quamlibet aequali furore trahuntur. 'Iudiciale autem illud conditorem animalis insinuat deum, quem certe decet credere auctorem[50] omnis convenientiae atque concordiae'.

5 Praeterea numeri et qui in sono sunt et qui fiunt in sentiendo, 'in quantum eorum intervalla potest memoria custodire, in tantum iis iudicialibus iudicandi offeruntur atque iudicantur. Numerus namque iste qui intervallis temporum constat, nisi adiuvemur in eo memoria, iudicari a nobis nullo modo potest. Cuiuslibet enim brevis syllabae, cum et incipiat et desinat, alio tempore initium est, et alio finis sonat. In audienda itaque vel brevissima syllaba nisi memoria nos adiuvet, ut eo momento quo iam non initium sed finis syllabae sonat, maneat ille motus in animo qui factus est cum initium ipsum sonuit, nihil nos audisse possumus dicere. Hinc est illud, quod plerumque alia cogitatione occupati, loquentes nihil nobis videmur audisse. Quapropter iudiciales illi numeri, qui numeros intervallis temporum sitos iudicare non possunt, nisi quos eis tamquam ministra memoria obtulerit, nonne ipsi existimandi sunt per certum spatium temporis tendi?'

6 Licet enim in iis spatia temporum minime videamus, non tamen adhibentur nisi ad ea iudicanda, quae in spatiis temporum fiunt, nec ipsa quidem omnia, sed quae possunt articulari memoriter. Cum versus ille canitur: 'deus creator omnium,' numeros ipsius versus per numeros sentiendi audimus et per iudiciales numeros delectamur, et nescio quibus aliis existimamus de ista delectatione,

mare to love; they are attracted with equal lust to any mare. "But as the Creator of the animal the judging principle introduces God, God whom it certainly behooves us to believe is the author of all that is fitting and harmonious."[78]

Furthermore, the numbers which are present in sound and 5
those which come into being in our hearing "are brought before the judgment of these judging numbers and are judged only to the extent that their temporal divisions are retained in the memory. For the sort of number that subsists in temporal divisions we cannot judge in any way without the help of the memory. Now with any brief syllable whatsoever, since it both begins and ends, the beginning of the sound is at one moment, the end at another. In hearing therefore even the briefest syllable, unless the memory helps us to retain in the rational soul the movement made at the sound's beginning at the very moment when it is no longer the beginning but the end of the syllable that is sounding, then we cannot say that we have heard anything. Hence it is that, preoccupied with another train of thought, we often appear not to have heard anything from those talking to us. Surely, therefore, we must assume that the judging numbers, which cannot judge numbers situated in temporal intervals unless the memory ministers to them like a servant, are themselves extended over a certain period of time?"[79]

For although we cannot perceive temporal intervals in the judg- 6
ing numbers, nevertheless they cannot be brought to bear except to judge what occurs in temporal intervals; and not all of them, but only those that can be articulated by the memory. When we sing the hymn "Deus creator omnium," we hear the numbers of the verse itself through the numbers in the hearing, yet we take pleasure in them through the judging numbers. And by means of [still] other numbers I do not know about, we reflect on that pleasure; and this we might describe as the judgment on the judging numbers, since above them by way of other numbers we can offer

quae quasi sententia est iudicialium istorum, cum per alios super hos[51] latentiorem sed certe veriorem ferre possimus sententiam. Aliud est enim delectari sensu, aliud existimare ratione. Aliud quippe est annuere vel renuere motibus numerosis, quod fit in delectatione convenientiae[52] et offensione absurditatis talium motionum, et aliud est existimare utrum recte an secus ista delectent, quod fit ratiocinando. Ac si recte nobis visum est, nisi quibusdam numeris esset ipse delectationis sensus imbutus, nullo modo eum potuisse annuere paribus intervallis et perturbata respuere, recte etiam videri[53] potest ratio, quae huic delectationi superimponitur, nullo modo sine quibusdam numeris vivacioribus de numeris, quod infra se habet, posse iudicare. Iam nunc, si placet, illi qui nobis surrexerant ad principatum obtinendum sensuales nominentur, et iudicialium nomen, quoniam est honoratius, ii accipiant, qui excellentiores comperti sunt.

7 'Age nunc accipe vim potentiamque rationis, quantum ex operibus eius aspicere possumus. Ipsa enim, ut id potissimum dicam quod ad huius operis susceptionem attinet, primo quid sit ipsa bona modulatio consideravit, et eam in quodam motu libero et ad suae pulchritudinis finem converso esse perspexit. Deinde vidit in motibus corporum aliud esse quod brevitate et productione temporis variaretur, in quantum magis esset minusve diuturnum, aliud localium spatiorum percussione in quibusdam gradibus celeritatis et tarditatis; qua divisione facta, id quod in temporis mora esset modesto intervallo et humano sensui accommodato articulatum, varios efficere numeros; eorumque genera et ordinem usque ad modulos versuum persecuta est. Postremo attendit quid in his moderandis, operandis, sentiendis, retinendis ageret anima, cuius caput ipsa esset, hosque omnes animales numeros a corporalibus

a judgment that is hidden but certainly truer. For to be delighted by the sense is one thing, to reflect with the reason is another. It is one thing to give assent to, or to reject, numbered motions—a consequence of the delight taken in the motions' harmony or the repulsion felt at their dissonance. But it is another to reflect whether it is proper or not that they should delight us; and this comes in reasoning. If it rightly appears to us that the sense of delight, unless it were itself endowed with certain numbers, could in no way approve of equal intervals and reject disordered ones, then it can also rightly appear that the reason which is set over this delight cannot make judgments about the numbers inferior to itself without having other, more enduring numbers. At this point, if you agree, let us call the numbers that had initially risen up before us claiming primacy the sensual numbers, and keep the term "judging," since it is more honorable, for those numbers we have found to be superior.[80]

"Consider now the strength and power of reason insofar as we 7
can perceive it from its works. For reason first considered—to confine myself to what is relevant to the aim of this work—what good modulation itself is, and saw it consisted in a certain freedom of movement directed towards the goal of its own beauty. Next in the movements of bodies it observed that variation from the abbreviation or lengthening of time was one thing (in that it lasted for a longer or shorter period), but variation in the actual metrical beat, in the particular degrees of quickness or slowness, was another. Then the reason noted that, if time's duration were divided up into a modest interval and one conforming to the human sense, then it produced different numbers; and it pursued the different kinds of numbers and their ordering until it arrived at the meters of verses. Lastly the reason addressed the question of the role of the soul (of which reason is the head) in moderating, producing, perceiving, and remembering these numbers; and it separated all the soul-belonging numbers from the corporeal ones.

separavit, seque ipsam haec omnia neque animadvertere neque distinguere neque certe numerare sine quibusdam suis numeris potuisse cognovit, eosque ceteris inferioris ordinis iudiciaria quadam aestimatione praeposuit'.

8 'Et nunc cum ipsa sua delectatione, qua temporum momenta perpendit et talibus numeris modificandis nutus suos exhibet, sic agit: Quid est quod in sensibili numerositate diligimus? Num aliquid praeter parilitatem quandam et aequaliter dimensa intervalla? An ille pyrrhichius pes sive spondeus sive anapaestus sive dactylus sive proceleumaticus sive dispondeus nos aliter delectaret,[54] nisi partem suam parti alteri aequali divisione conferret? Quid vero iambus, tribrachus, trochaeus pulchritudinis habent, nisi quod minore sua parte maiorem suam in tantas duas aequaliter dividant? Iam porro sex temporum pedes num aliunde blandius sonant atque festivius, nisi quod utraque lege partiuntur, scilicet aut in duas aequales partes terna tempora possidentes, aut in unam simplam ex qualibet parte et alteram duplam, id est ut maior habeat bis minorem, et eo modo ab[55] illa dividatur aequaliter duobus temporibus quatuor tempora in bina dimetiente atque secante?' Et in reliquis omnibus simili ratione. Atque usque adeo delectamur aequalitate, ut eam non modo in vocum intervallis, sed etiam in silentiorum spatiis exigamus.

9 'Quaerit ergo ratio et carnalem animae delectationem, quae iudiciales partes sibi vendicabat, interrogat, cum eam in spatiorum temporalium numeris aequalitas mulceat, utrum duae syllabae breves, quascumque audierit, vere sint aequales an fieri possit ut una earum edatur productius, non usque ad longae syllabae modum, sed infra quantumlibet, quo tamen excedat sociam suam. Num negari potest fieri posse ut haec delectatio ista non sentiat et inaequalibus velut aequalibus gaudeat? Quo errore et inaequalitate

And the reason recognized that it could not itself be aware of, distinguish, or number all of them with certainty without particular numbers of its own. These it preferred, using a certain judging power, before the rest of the numbers in the lower order."[81]

"Now in the case of the pleasure it takes in weighing the tem- 8
poral moments and lending its approval to the modification of particular numbers, the reason asks, 'What is it that we like about numbers we hear? Is it anything else but a certain symmetry, and intervals equally measured? Doesn't the pleasure we get from the pyrrhic foot, or the spondee, the anapaest, the dactyl, the proceleusmatic, or the double spondee[82] come only from the fact that, when equally divided, one of their parts is matched to the other? What is beautiful about the iamb, the tribrach, or the trochee except that in their minor part they are dividing their major part into two halves? Don't feet of six measures sound both more soothing and festive only because they are divided following two metrical rules: either into two equal parts possessing three measures each, or into one single part from any of the parts and one double, such that the larger part is twice the smaller and in this way is divided by the smaller equally into two measures, as it measures and cuts the four measures into two.'"[83] And likewise with the rest. And we so delight in symmetry that we demand it not only in the intervals of sounds but in the pauses of silences as well.

"So the reason questions the soul's carnal delight, which was 9
claiming the judging roles for itself. Since in the numbers of temporal intervals the reason is charmed by equality, it asks whether the two short syllables (whichever of them it hears) are truly equal or whether it is possible that one of them lasts longer, not quite as long as a long syllable but only a little bit less so, yet long enough to exceed its fellow. Surely one cannot deny that it could happen that our sense of delight might not notice this, and thus take pleasure in unequal syllables as though they were equal? What is worse than this error and inequality? We should be warned by

quid turpius? Ex quo admonemur ab his avertere gaudium quae imitantur aequalitatem et utrum impleant comprehendere non possumus; immo quod non impleant fortasse comprehendimus. Et tamen in quantum imitantur, pulchra esse in suo genere et ordine suo negare non possumus'.

10 'Aequalitatem illam quam in sensibilibus numeris non reperiebamus certam et manentem, sed tamen adumbratam et praetereuntem agnoscebamus, nusquam profecto appeteret animus, nisi alicubi nota esset. Haec autem alicubi non ⟨in⟩[56] spatiis locorum et temporum, nam illa tument et illa[57] praetereunt; non in corporis formis, quas aequales numquam dicere possumus; aut in temporum intervallis, in quibus similiter utrum aliquid aliquanto quam oporteat productius vel correptius transeat, quid[58] sensum fugiat, ignoramus. Illam quippe aequalitatem quaero ubi esse arbitreris, quam intuentes cupimus aequalia esse quaedam corpora vel corporum motus, et diligentius[59] considerantes eis fidere non audemus? Ibi puto, ubi regnat quod est corporibus excellentius. Sed utrum in ipsa anima an etiam supra animam quaeramus?'

11 Artem istam rhythmicam[60] vel metricam, qua utuntur qui versus faciunt, putamus habere aliquos numeros, secundum quos fabricant versus. Quicumque isti sunt numeri, non praetereunt cum versibus, sed manent. Consentiendum est ergo ab aliquibus manentibus numeris praetereuntes aliquos fabricari, et hanc artem non aliud putamus quam affectionem quandam animi artificis. Quod si omnia quae ad numeros pertinent ille interrogetur qui numquam didicit, nonne censes hanc artem posse cognoscere? Non transibunt ii numeri ab eo qui docebit in eum qui discet, sed discens intrinsecus apud mentem suam, movebit se ad aliquid unde menti eius imprimantur hi[61] numeri et illam faciant affectio-

this to set aside any delight derived from those syllables that merely imitate equality and where we cannot know for certain whether they achieve it. Rather we know perhaps that they do not. And yet we cannot deny that, to the extent that they do imitate it, they are beautiful in their way and in their own order."[84]

"In sensible numbers we did not find equality either reliable or 10
permanent, but we recognized it only as shadowy and ephemeral. But the rational soul would nowhere desire it unless it were known from somewhere. This somewhere could not be anywhere in the intervals of time or space, for the former expand and the latter perish. It is not in the body's forms, which we can never call equal; and it is not in the intervals of time, wherein similarly we do not know whether something which flees the sense takes a somewhat longer or shorter time than it should. So, I ask, where do you think exists that equality which we desire when we gaze at particular equal bodies or movements of bodies, and yet do not dare put our trust in them on closer scrutiny? We would find it, I believe, only there under the rule of what is superior to bodies. But let us ask whether it is in the soul, or even above the soul."[85]

We believe that the art of rhythm or meter, which is employed 11
by those who make verses, possesses certain numbers, in accordance with which they compose their verses. Whatever those numbers are, they do not pass away with the verses, but remain permanently. We must agree then that certain ephemeral numbers are manufactured by certain permanent numbers. We would suppose this art is nothing else but a certain disposition of the artificer's rational soul. Now if you questioned a man who had never learned this art about everything pertaining to numbers, don't you suppose that he could learn it? The numbers do not pass from teacher to student, but the student learns them internally in his own mind; and he will gravitate towards something that will print these numbers on his mind and produce that disposition which is called [the metrical] art; and he will realize the truth of

nem quae ars dicitur, et ea quae interrogabitur vera esse intelleget atque respondebit. Quoniam vero hi[62] numeri, de quibus ita quaeritur, incommutabiles sunt, ideo sunt aeterni, neque ulla in eis est inaequalitas. Unde vero credendum est animae tribui quod aeternum est et incommutabile, nisi ab uno, aeterno et incommutabili deo? Ergo qui discit alio interrogante, sese intus ad deum movet, ut incommutabile verum intellegat.

: VII :

Tertia confirmatio, per mentem secundum Augustinum.

1 Satis per visus indicia primum, deinde per auditus admonitiones propositum nostrum investigavimus. Nunc indagemus per indicia rationis.

2 'Aliter unusquisque homo loquendo enuntiat mentem suam, quid in se ipso agatur attendens; aliter autem humanam mentem speciali aut generali cognitione definit. Itaque cum nihil de sua propria loquitur, utrum intellegat hoc aut illud an non intellegat, et utrum velit an nolit hoc aut illud, credo. Cum vero de humana specialiter aut generaliter verum dicit, agnosco et approbo. Unde manifestum est aliud unumquemque videre in se, quod sibi alius dicendi credit, non tamen videt, aliud autem in ipsa veritate, quod alius quoque possit intueri, quorum alterum mutatur per tempora, alterum incommutabili subsistit aeternitate. Neque enim oculis corporeis multas mentes videndo per similitudinem colligimus generalem vel specialem mentis humanae notitiam, sed intuemur in-

the matters he is being questioned about, and respond. But since the numbers under discussion are unchangeable, they are eternal and no inequality exists in them. Whence do we suppose the soul receives what is eternal and unchangeable if not from the one, eternal, and unchangeable God? Thus the student who learns from someone else's questioning turns within himself towards God in order that he may understand the unchanging truth.[86]

: VII :

The third confirmation: by way of the mind and according to Augustine.

We have adequately examined our thesis first through the evidence of the sight, and then through suggestions arising from the hearing. Let us explore it now in terms of the evidence of the reason. 1

"In speaking each individual reveals his own mind, paying attention to what is going on within himself; but this is different from his defining the human mind in terms of special or general knowledge. So when he speaks to me about his own mind—whether he does or does not understand or does or does not will this or that particular thing—I just believe him. But when he speaks the truth about the human mind in terms of species or genus, I recognize it and give my assent. Hence it is clear that for an individual to see in himself what another just believes by being told is different from his seeing in the truth what someone else can also see. The one changes over time, the other subsists through unchanging eternity. We do not assemble the notions of the human mind's special or general knowledge by seeing many minds with our corporeal eyes and noticing the similarities. We observe the inviolable truth, and from it we derive a definition, as perfectly 2

violabilem veritatem, ex qua perfecte, quantum possumus, definiamus non qualis sit uniuscuiusque hominis mens, sed qualis esse sempiternis rationibus debeat'.

3 Praeterea, cum 'impii cogitant aeternitatem, et multa recte reprehendunt recteque laudant in hominum moribus, quibus ea tandem regulis iudicant, nisi in quibus vident, quemadmodum quisque vivere debeat, etiam si nec ipsi eodem modo vivant? Ubi eas vident? Neque enim in sua natura, cum proculdubio mente ista videantur eorumque mentes constet esse mutabiles, has vero regulas immutabiles videat, quisquis in eis et hoc videre potuerit, neque in habitu suae mentis, cum illae regulae sint iustitiae, mentes vero eorum esse constet iniustas. Ubinam sunt istae regulae scriptae? Ubi quid sit iustum[63] etiam iniustus agnoscit? Ubi cernit habendum esse quod ipse non habet? Ubi ergo scriptae sunt nisi in libro lucis illius quae veritas dicitur? Unde omnis lex iusta describitur et in cor hominis qui operatur iustitiam, non migrando, sed tamquam imprimendo transfertur, sicut imago ex annulo et in ceram transit et annulum non relinquit. Qui vero non operatur, et tamen videt quid operandum sit, ipse est qui ab illa luce avertitur, a qua tamen tangitur. Qui autem nec videt quemadmodum sit vivendum, excusabilius quidem peccat, quia [non] est transgressor legis incognitae. Sed etiam ipse splendore aliquotiens ubique praesentis veritatis attingitur, quando admonitus confitetur'.

4 Denique superior haec Aureliana discursio quatuor finibus terminatur: quod videlicet mens ad summa non surgit, nisi eius quod est summum trahatur instinctu; quod aeternis rationibus non ute-

as we can, not of the nature of the mind of one particular man, but of what the nature ought to be like in terms of everlasting rational principles."[87]

Moreover, when "the godless think about eternity and rightly blame and rightly praise many aspects of human behavior, by what rules do they finally judge unless by those which enable them to see how each man ought to live, even if they themselves do not live in that same way? Where do they see these rules? Not in their own nature, for such things are undoubtedly seen by the mind, and yet it is generally agreed that the minds of such godless men are mutable. But whosoever sees the rules as immutable is able to see this [immutability] in the rules, not in the habit of his own mind (since the rules pertain to justice, but the minds of the godless, it is agreed, are unjust). But where are these rules inscribed? Where does even the unjust man recognize what is just? Where does he see what he ought to possess but does not himself have? Where else are the rules written down but in the book of that light which is called truth? From it every just law is copied and inscribed in the heart of the man who acts justly; and it comes down, not by literally crossing over, but by being as it were imprinted, as the image from a ring is transferred into the wax and yet does not leave the ring. The man who does not act, yet sees how he ought to act, is turning away from the light, and yet he is touched by it. But the man who does not see how he ought to live has more excuse for sinning, for he is not a transgressor of a law he knows about. Even he is touched at times, however, by the splendor of truth present everywhere, when, being admonished, he confesses [his sins]."[88] 3

The preceding Augustinian discussion leads to four conclusions: 1) that the mind does not ascend to the highest unless it is drawn by the impulse of that which is the highest; 2) that the mind cannot draw upon eternal principles of its own freewill to arrive at judgments unless it is able to attune itself to eternity; 3) 4

retur pro arbitrio iudicando, nisi aeternitati se posset aequare; quod immutabilia ratione immutabili non apprehenderet, nisi regulam ipsam immutabilitatis attingeret; quod animi multi eandem non caperent veritatem, nisi aut unus esset in multis intellectus humanus, quod fieri nequit, aut saltem multi intellectus humani in eundem se fontem veritatis immergerent, quasi tunc optime aliqui ordinem artificii sint cognituri, quando rationem ipsam unam, per quam artifex opus construxerat, penetraverint.

5 Haec autem Augustini sententia duobus modis potissimum confirmatur, primo per communem virtutem argumentandi, deinde per communes notiones veritatis, bonitatis et esse. Omnis intellectus apprehendit necessariam consequentiam in rebus et contingentibus et non existentibus. Haec enim consequentia est necessaria: Si Plato currit, Plato movetur, licet Plato et cursus et motus eius contingentia sint. Quinetiam haec est necessaria: Plato olim, dum disserebat, loquebatur, licet neque Plato neque disputatio sua neque sermo sint in praesentia. Talium itaque consequentiarum necessitas immutabilis in rebus illis temporalibus non fundatur, quae vel non sunt ullo modo, vel sunt contingentes, neque in solis cogitationibus animae, alioquin non esset vera necessitas, sed figmentum, immo neque immutabilis esset, cum cogitatio nostra sit mobilis. Fundatur igitur in aeterna et necessaria rerum serie, quam divina mens, omnium ordinatrix, intra se continet, ubi mutuam rebus habitudinem tribuit. Quapropter omne verae ratiocinationis lumen a prima veritate accenditur et in eandem reflectitur, postquam omnis consequentiae necessitas in summa totius naturae necessitate fundatur.

6 Docent hoc communes quoque veritatis bonitatisque ipsius intellegentiae, quas in superioribus probavimus inesse mentibus om-

that the mind cannot grasp things unchanging with an unchangeable reason unless it can attain the very principle of immutability; and 4) that many minds could not grasp the same truth unless either a single human intellect were to exist in them, which is impossible, or at least many human intellects were to bathe themselves in the same fountain of truth, just as the best way people come to know an artist's design is when they have penetrated to the single rational principle he used to construct his work.

We can find support for Augustine's views principally in two 5
ways: first through the universal force of reasoning, and second, though the universal notions of truth, goodness, and being. Every intellect is aware of a necessary consequence in things which are contingent or non-existent. For instance, it is a necessary consequence that, if Plato runs, he moves, even though Plato, his running, and his moving are themselves contingents. It is necessary too that when Plato argued Plato was talking, although neither Plato nor his argument nor his enunciation of it are occurring in the present. The unchanging necessity of such consequences is not based on the things in time, which are either totally non-existent or contingent; nor does it rest solely on the thoughts of the soul, or it would not be true necessity but a mental fiction, or rather it would not be immutable since our thinking changes. So it rests on the eternal and necessary series of things that the divine mind, which sets everything in order, contains within itself, and where it gives things their status relative to each other. Therefore true reasoning's every light is lit from the prime truth and reflected back towards it, since the necessity of every consequence is based on the supreme necessity of the whole of nature.

We are taught the same by the universal concepts of truth and 6
goodness, which we have shown above to be present in the minds of all insofar as they continually compare things true and good [to these concepts]. Now if God is truth and goodness itself, it follows that it is God who illumines the minds of men whenever

nium, ex eo quod vera et bona assidue comparant. Quod si veritas ipsa et bonitas deus est, sequitur ut deus totiens mentibus hominum illucescat, quotiens per deum tamquam normam vera et bona diiudicamus. Docet idem esse ipsius notio omnibus insita. Nam omnes homines iudicant: illud quidem nullo modo esse, istud vero esse, sed imperfecto modo, hoc esse modo perfectiori. Talis autem in essendo gradatio neque fit neque cognoscitur, nisi per accessum ad esse summum, qui deus est, atque inde recessum. Accessum vero ad ipsum et recessum ab ipso videre non potest, nisi qui ipsum videt. Vident autem ipsum viri peritiores, alio insuper pacto, quando videlicet omnia rerum genera subalterna ad generalissima et illa usque ad ipsum, quod dicitur ens simplex absolutumque, resolvunt. Tale ens aut figmentum falsum est aut est deus. Non potest autem ens ipsum falso esse, si modo aliquid in rebus est vere. Si comparatio illa[64] de rerum gradibus atque haec resolutio non fit nisi per ipsam summi et absoluti esse virtutem, utique fit per deum, quo formatus intellectus et comparat et resolvit.

7 Accedit ad haec quod ipsum esse usque adeo perspicue fulget, ut nequeat cogitari non esse. Sicut enim ipsum quod dicitur nihil, occurrit nobis ut expers omnino essendi, ita esse occurrit ut expers penitus non essendi. Itaque in esse neque potentia ulla prorsus apparet ad non essendum, neque aliquis defectus essendi. Ex prima parte aeternum est, ex secunda est tota essendi perfectione plenissimum, id est deus. Hac ratione, ⟨quando⟩ esse occurrit nobis evidentissime et recte animadvertentibus, occurrit ut deus. Quod duabus praeterea rationibus confirmatur. Prima, quia esse usque

we make judgments, with God as our normative measure, about things true and good. And the notion of being itself, which is implanted in us all, teaches us the same. For all men judge that one thing is completely non-existent, that another exists but imperfectly, and that another exists more perfectly. But such a scale of being cannot occur or be understood unless it is by way of our approaching the highest being, which is God, or of withdrawing from Him. But approaching Him and withdrawing from Him can only be evident to a person who sees God Himself. However, men with greater mental training also see God in another way, namely when they resolve all the secondary classes of things into the primary classes, and these [again] into what is called simple and absolute being. Such a being is either a deceptive fiction or it is God. But absolute being cannot be a deception, if something truly exists in things. If comparison of different levels of being on the one hand and resolving them on the other do not occur except through the power of the highest and absolute being, then obviously it occurs through God; for it is He who has formed the intellect which compares and resolves.

One might add that being itself shines out so transparently that 7
it cannot be thought not to exist. Just as what we call nothingness presents itself to us as totally devoid of being, so being presents itself as totally devoid of non-being. In being, therefore, there is obviously no potentiality at all for non-being, nor any defect in its being. On the first count, it is eternal; on the second, it is completely filled with the total perfection of being which is God. Thus, when we see being most clearly and in the proper way, it presents itself to us as God. Two further arguments confirm this. 1) Being is so manifest that in individual known things it is always known. If someone declares Plato is running, he is saying that as a being he is running. If he says Plato is a man and is white, he is saying that he exists in the species a) of man and b) of what is white. Finally being is itself understood in the different modes

adeo manifestum est ut in singulis quae cognoscuntur, semper cognoscatur et ipsum. Qui Platonem affirmat currere, affirmat eum esse currentem. Qui eum vocat hominem aut album, esse in hominis specie ait et albi. Denique in singulis essendi modis, per quos res constant singulae, ita esse ipsum subintellegitur, quemadmodum in omnibus animalium speciebus subintellegitur animal. Secunda ratio: quia per ipsum esse cetera cognoscuntur, ipsum vero per semetipsum. Siquidem in cognitione quae fit per intuitum, illud quod dicitur non ens, per ens cognoscitur; ens in potentia per ens actu, ens actu per actum noscitur existendi. Talis actus esse ipsum exigit.[65] Si per esse[66] quod cuiuslibet entis actus est, quodlibet ens agnoscitur, sequitur ut per esse quod cunctorum existentium actus origoque est, existentia cuncta noscantur. Ac si ponatur super esse in potentia et esse in actu ens ipsum simpliciter, quod neque sit potentia neque actu, ens ipsum aut figmentum erit aut erit deus aut quaedam significatio dei ut placet Platonicis. Deus autem actus est, omnium auctor existentium, perque actionis excessum prius, vehementius, diutius movet mentem quam reliqua quae offeruntur; immo eius virtute reliqua mentem movent. Ipsum ergo esse absolutum, ipse scilicet purus actus, effector[67] omnium existentium, qui deus est, primum est quod mentibus miro quodam pacto sese offert, quod illabitur, quod effulget, quod cetera omnia patefacit. Cuius formam et notionem, quamvis perpetuam quodammodo in nobis possideamus perque illam et in illa reliqua cognoscamus, non tamen istud animadvertimus, sicut neque oculus considerat se videre solis lumen continue ceteraque per ipsum atque in ipso, neque ratio animadvertit se continue ratiocinari, cum semper ferme ratiocinetur. Nam diutius consueta animadvertere non solemus. Quis enim se spirare considerat?

8 Ubi Platonici deum summum vocant ipsum esse, intellegi volunt non esse quod in essentia est, sed huius esse principium, esse

of being from which individual objects are constituted, just as animal is understood in all the different species of animals. 2) Everything else is known through being itself, whereas being is known through itself. In intuitive cognition what is called a non-entity is understood through an entity, a potential being through a being in act; and a being in act is known through the act of existing. Such an act requires absolute being. If every being is known through the being that is the act of every being, it follows that all existing things are known through the being which is the act and origin of them all. If above being in potentiality and being in act we set the absolute being which is neither in potentiality nor in act, then this being will either be a mental fiction or be God or be a signification of God (as the Platonists put it). But God is the act, the author of all existing things; and through the overflowing of His act He moves the mind prior to, more vehemently, and more lastingly than all other objects presented to it. Or rather, other things move the mind through His power. So absolute being itself, that is the pure act, the effective cause of all existing things, God in other words, is the first thing that in a wonderful way presents itself to minds, and flows into them, and fills them with light, and reveals all other things to them. Though we have within us its everlasting form and have a notion of it, and though we know everything else through it and in it, yet we do not realize this. Similarly the eye is not always aware that it is continually seeing the light of the sun and other things through it and in it; and the reason does not notice that it is continually reasoning even though it is reasoning virtually all the time. For we do not normally notice things to which we have long become accustomed. For who thinks about himself breathing?

When the Platonists call God on high being itself, they mean 8
not the being which is in essence, but the principle of that being, the being above being, whatever is conceived by way of some proper rational principle of being or comprehended in some no-

videlicet super esse, quodcumque propria quadam essendi ratione concipitur et aliqua notione comprehenditur. Summum enim deum proprie unitatis bonitatisque, sequentem vero deum de deo lumenque de luce entis nomine nuncupant, a prima unitate in tria deductum, scilicet in essentiam vitamque et mentem. Et quia in quolibet trium modo suo sunt et reliqua, tria in novem usque producunt, unde fiat ut in angelis novenarius sit numerus observandus, similisque in animabus felicibus gradus. Mentem vero contemplantem formari quidem a deo summo per unitatem, mentis caput, deo[68] vero sequente per intellectum. Sed haec ipsi viderint; nobis autem sufficit animam divinitate formari.

9 Ex omnibus superioribus concluditur, rationem humanam in ordine⟨m⟩ rerum considerando versari semper circa rationem divinam, rerum omnium ordinatricem, non minus quam mundi sphaerae circa medium mundi punctum. Quod si revolutio quae naturaliter et assidue ex se ipsa perpetuum ambit centrum, perpetua est, oportet rationem nostram fore perpetuam. Quae quoniam intellegendo per deum atque in deo sine medio in deum reflectitur, plane testatur se a deo sine medio processisse. Quis autem neget, quod proxime ab aeternitate fit, aeternum fore? Atque etiam videt in deo speciem sempiternam, prout sempiterna est, dum certa illam ratione sempiternam esse concludit. Ita vero videt, ut suscipit inde; sequitur igitur ut per modum suscipiat sempiternum. Et quia suscipit ut est ipsa, siquidem pro natura capit sua, fit ut ipsa perpetua sit, postquam modo perpetuo suscipit. Ratio autem haec nostra nihil est aliud quam vita intellectualis. Semper ergo vivet, immo et intelleget semper, si semper erit.

tion [of it]. For, strictly speaking, they refer to God on high by way of unity and goodness, but reserve the term being for the subsequent "God of God, Light of Light," who has descended from primal unity into a trinity, the trinity of essence, life, and mind.[89] And because any two members in this triad dwell in the other one in its own way, the Platonists multiply the three into nine.[90] Hence one must look to nine as the number dividing the angels, and a similar gradation among the souls of the blessed.[91] They say that the contemplating mind is formed by God on high through the unity that is the mind's head, and by the second god through the intellect. But that is the Platonists' affair. It suffices for us that the soul is formed by the divinity.

From all of the foregoing one may conclude that the human 9
reason, in contemplating the order of things, always revolves around the divine reason, which bestows the order on all things, no less than the spheres of the world revolve around its mid-point. But if a revolution, which naturally, continuously, and of its own accord rotates around a center that is everlasting, is itself everlasting, then our reason ought to be everlasting. Since in understanding it is turned back without an intermediary to God through God and in God, this clearly testifies that it has itself proceeded without an intermediary from God. For who is going to deny that what comes directly into being from eternity will itself be eternal? Moreover, it is in God that our reason sees an eternal species qua eternal, when it concludes, with unswerving logic, that the species is eternal. But it sees the species as it receives it. It follows then that it receives in an eternal way. And since our reason receives as it is in itself (in that it grasps in accordance with its own nature), it follows that it is itself eternal since it receives in an eternal way. But this reason of ours is nothing other than intellectual life itself. So it will live forever; or rather, if it is going to be always, it will understand forever.

10 Sed iuvat hic cum Augustino, ut saepe solemus, paulo latius pervagari. Quando ratiocinamur, animus id agit. 'Non enim id agit, nisi qui intellegit. Nec corpus intellegit, nec animus auxiliante corpore, quia cum intellegere vult, a corpore avertitur. Quod enim intellegitur, eiusdem modi est semper, nihilque corporis eiusdem modi est semper. Non[69] igitur potest adiuvare animum ad intellectum nitentem, cui non impedire satis est'.

11 Si per se ratiocinatur animus, ac ratiocinando veritatem attingit, attingit utique per se veritatem. Quapropter ipsi veritati, per quam vera sunt quaecumque intellegendo attinguntur, propius[70] haeret quam aut rebus sensibilibus aut earum imaginibus, quas non per se attingit, sed per instrumenta et reliqua media. 'Non enim eam posset contemplari animus per se ipsum sine maxima coniunctione cum ipsa'. 'Ea quae sensu capiuntur, extra etiam nos esse sentiuntur et locis continentur, unde nec percipi quidem posse affirmantur. Ea vero quae intelleguntur, non quasi alibi posita intelleguntur quam ipse qui intellegit animus. Simul enim etiam intelleguntur non contineri loco'.

12 'Quare ista coniunctio intuentis animi et eius veri quod intuetur, aut ita est ut subiectum sit animus, verum autem illud in subiecto, aut contra subiectum verum et in subiecto animus, aut est utrumque substantia. Horum autem trium si primum est, tam est immortalis animus quam veritas illa et summa ratio rerum, quae inseparabiliter inhaeret animo et inesse nisi vivo non potest. Eadem necessitas est in secundo, nam si verum illud quod ratio dicitur nihil habet commutabile, sicut apparet, nihil commutari potest, quod in eo tamquam in subiecto est. Remanet igitur omnis

I should like to pursue the matter a little further, travelling, as we so often do, in the company of Augustine. "When we reason, it is the rational soul that reasons. For nothing reasons unless it understands. The body does not understand and neither does the soul with the help of the body; for when the soul wishes to understand, it turns aside from the body. For what is understood is always of the same nature, whereas nothing corporeal is always of the same nature. So the body cannot help the soul in its striving for understanding; the best it can do is not to be in the way."[92] 10

If the soul of itself reasons and in reasoning attains the truth, then obviously it attains the truth through itself. So it cleaves to the truth by virtue of which all the things it attains in understanding are true; and it cleaves more closely than it does to sensible objects or their images, which it does not attain through itself but through [various] instruments and other means. "For of itself the rational soul could not contemplate the truth unless it were intimately united with it. . . . The objects we grasp with our sense we perceive to be outside ourselves and contained in space, so that we cannot even really say we perceive them. But the objects we understand are not thought to be anywhere else but in the rational soul that understands them; for simultaneously we understand that they are not located in space."[93] 11

"So with this joining of the intuiting mind and of the truth it intuits [we have three options]. Either the rational soul is the substrate [or substance] and the truth is in the substrate; or the reverse, the truth is the substrate and the mind is in the substrate; or each of them is a substance. If it is the first of the three, then our rational soul is just as immortal as that truth, that supreme and universal reason, which cleaves inseparably to our rational soul and which cannot exist in it unless it is living. The same necessarily follows with the second option; for if the truth (which is called the reason)[94] contains nothing liable to change, as is clearly the case, then nothing that is in it, as in a substrate, can be liable to change. 12

pugna de tertio. Nam si animus substantia est, et substantia ratio cui coniungitur, non absurde quis putaverit fieri posse, ut manente illa hic esse desinat. Sed manifestum est quod quamdiu animus a ratione non separatur, sed ei cohaeret, necessarium est eum manere atque vivere. Separari autem qua tandem vi potest? Num corporea, cuius et potentia[71] infirmior, et origo inferior, et ordo separatior? Nullo modo. Animali ergo? Sed etiam id quomodo est? An alter potentior animus, quisquis est, contemplari rationem non potest, nisi alterum inde separaverit? At neque ratio cuique contemplanti defuerit, si omnes contemplentur. Et cum nihil sit ipsa ratione potentius, quia nihil est incommutabilius, nullo pacto erit animus qui nondum est rationi coniunctus, eo qui est coniunctus, potentior. Restat ut aut ipsa ratio a se ipsum separet, aut ipse animus ab ea voluntate separetur. Sed nihil est in illa natura invidentiae quo minus fruendam se animis praebeat. Deinde quo magis est eo quicquid sibi coniungitur, magis facit ut sit, cui rei[72] contrarius est interitus. Voluntate autem animum separari a veritate quis dixerit, qui nihil umquam avidius studet quam veritati coniungi? Quid ergo? Iamne, concludendum est animum esse immortalem? An ne etiam, si separari non potest, exstingui potest? At vero si illa vis veritatis ipsa sua coniunctione afficit animum (neque enim non efficere potest), ita profecto afficit ut ei esse tribuat. Est enim maxime ipsa veritas ubi summa etiam incommutabilitas intellegitur. Itaque quemcumque ex se afficit, cogit esse quodammodo. Non ergo extingui animus potest nisi a ratione separatus; separari vero non potest; non potest igitur interire'.

The dispute then swirls around the third option. For if the rational soul is a substance, and the [supreme] reason to which it is attached is also a substance, then it is not absurd to imagine the possibility of the latter remaining while the former ceases to exist. But it is clear that as long as the rational soul is not separated from this reason but cleaves to it, the soul must necessarily abide and live. Well then, what force could separate it? Surely not a corporeal force, whose power is weaker and whose origin is inferior and whose order is far separate from it? Certainly not. Is it a power of the soul then? But how could even that be so? Are we saying that one stronger soul (whosoever it is) cannot contemplate this supreme reason until it has separated another soul from it? And yet this reason is never wanting to anyone contemplating it, if all contemplate it. And since nothing is stronger than this reason, since nothing is more unchanging, it will never be possible for a soul that is not yet united to it to be stronger than one that is. The remaining possibilities are either that this reason separates the rational soul from itself, or that the soul is separated by the will. Yet there is nothing of envy in this reason that would prevent it from offering itself to souls for their enjoyment. Again, the more something exists, the more it makes that to which it is united exist; and the contrary to this is extinction. But who would declare that the rational soul is voluntarily separated from the truth, given that it never desires anything more keenly than to be united with the truth? What then? Should we now conclude that the soul is immortal? Or is it liable to extinction, even though it cannot be separated? Surely if the power of truth affects the rational soul by being united with it (and it is impossible that it should not), it must affect it by giving it being. For the truth is understood to be greatest where immutability too is greatest. So in a way truth of itself compels each soul it affects to exist. So the soul cannot be destroyed unless it is separated from this reason. But it cannot be separated. So it cannot perish."[95]

13 'Quod vero infert dubitationem, illud est: quod animus stultus separari ab ipsa ratione videtur et in quodam defectu esse, et in essentia certiore atque pleniore sapiens. Sed si (quod nemini dubium) tunc est animus sapientissimus cum veritatem, quae semper eodem modo est, intuetur eique immobilis inhaeret divino amore coniunctus, et ex illa essentia omnia sunt, quae quoquomodo sunt, quae summe maximeque est, aut ab illa est animus in quantum est, aut per se ipsum est. Sed si per se ipsum est,[73] quoniam ipse sibi causa existendi est et numquam se deserit, numquam interit. Si vero ex illa, diligenter opus est quaerere quae res ei possit esse contraria, quae animo auferat animum esse, quod illa praebet. Quid est igitur? An forte falsitas, quia illa veritas? Sed manifestum est atque in promptu situm, quantum nocere animo falsitas possit. Non enim amplius potest quam fallere. At nisi qui vivit, fallitur nemo. Non igitur falsitas interimere animum potest. Quod si haec non potest, quae contraria veritati est, auferre animo animum esse, quod ei veritas dedit, ita enim est invictissima veritas, quid aliud invenietur quod auferat animo id quod est animus? Nihil profecto. Nam nihil est contrario valentius ad id auferendum, quod fit ab eius contrario. At si veritati contrarium ita quaeramus, non in quantum veritas est, sed in quantum summe maximeque est (quamquam in tantum est id ipsum, in quantum est veritas, siquidem veritatem eam dicimus, qua vera sunt omnia quantumcumque sunt, in tantum autem sunt, in quantum vera sunt), tamen nullo modo id defugerim, quod mihi evidentius suffragatur. Nam si nulla essentia, in quantum essentia est, habet contrarium aliquid, multo minus habet contrarium prima illa essentia quae dicitur veritas in quantum essentia. Primum autem verum est. Omnis enim essentia non ob aliud essentia est nisi quia est. Esse autem non habet contrarium nisi non esse. Unde nihil essentiae

"What gives us pause here is that a stupid soul appears to be separated from reason and to be in some sense defective, while a wise soul appears to be in its essence more certain and more complete. Nobody can doubt that if the soul is wisest when it contemplates the truth which always exists in the same way, and if it cleaves to the truth immovably (united to it by divine love), and if all things, howsoever they exist, come from the essence which exists to the highest and greatest degree, then either the rational soul comes from that truth as it exists, or it comes from itself. If it exists through itself, then, since it the cause of its own existence and never abandons itself, it never perishes. If it comes from the truth, we must ask ourselves carefully what could be opposite to the truth which might deprive the soul of its being soul, which is the gift of truth. What then? Could it perchance be falsehood, since the other is truth? But the extent to which falsehood can harm the soul is well known and no secret. For it can do nothing further but deceive; but unless someone is alive, he is not deceived. So falsehood cannot kill the soul. But if falsehood, which is truth's contrary, cannot deprive the soul of its being soul—the gift given it by truth, truth being absolutely invincible—what else can one stumble on that can deprive the soul of its being soul? The answer is nothing. For nothing is more capable of destroying what is made by its contrary than its contrary. But if our quest is for the contrary of truth, not insofar as it is truth, but insofar as it exists to the highest and greatest degree (although it totally exists insofar as it is the truth, since we call the truth that by which all things are true insofar as they exist, and they exist insofar as they are true), then I would certainly not avoid an argument which obviously supports my thesis. For if no essence qua essence contains its contrary, then still less does that prime essence, which is called the truth insofar as it is essence. But what is first is true. For all essence is essence for no other reason than that it is. But being has no contrary except non-being. So no entity is the contrary of es- 13

est contrarium. Nullo igitur modo res ulla esse potest contraria illi substantiae quae maxime ac primitus est. Ex qua si[74] habet animus idipsum quod est (non enim aliunde hoc habere potest qui ex se non habet, nisi ab ea re quae illo ipso est animo praestantior; nec habet esse animus ab alio quam a veritate, siquidem ab ea sola sortitur et bene esse), sequitur ut nulla res sit qua id amittat,[75] quia nulla res ei rei contraria est qua id habet, et propterea esse non desinit. Sapientiam vero, quia per conversionem habet ad id ex quo est, aversione potest amittere. Conversioni namque aversio contraria est. Illud vero quod ex eo habet, cui nulla res est contraria, non est unde possit amittere. Non potest igitur interire'.

sence. So there cannot possibly exist a contrary to that substance which exists to the highest and first degree. The rational soul derives its very being from that substance (the fact that the soul is not self-derived results from this substance which is more outstanding than the soul itself, and it does not derive its being from anything other than the truth, since truth alone allots it well-being). And if this is so, it follows that no thing exists whereby soul may lose being, since no thing exists contrary to that thing whereby it has being; and therefore it does not cease to be. But since it acquires wisdom by turning towards its source of being, so by turning away it can lose wisdom. For turning away is the opposite of turning towards. But what it derives from something to which nothing is contrary it does not derive from what it can lose. Therefore the soul cannot perish."[96]

LIBER TERTIUS DECIMUS[1]

: I :

Quantum anima corpori dominatur a multis ostenditur signis, ac primum ab affectibus phantasiae.

1 Hactenus divinitatem animae rationibus demonstravimus, deinceps vero signis idem paene similiter confirmabimus. Phantasiam quatuor sequuntur affectus: appetitus, voluptas, metus ac dolor. Hi omnes quando vehementissimi sunt, subito corpus proprium omnino, nonnumquam etiam alienum afficiunt. Quantos ardores vel cupiditas vindictae ciet in corde vel libido voluptatis in iecore, immo et in pulsu! Ex cuius mutatione cognovit medicus Erasistratus Antiochum esse amore Stratonicae captum. Rursus cupido nocendi frequenti intuitu quam perniciose pueros aliosque quoslibet molliores fascinat! Quam manifeste praegnantis mulieris aviditas tenerum foetum inficit rei cogitatae nota! Quam varios filiis suis gestus figurasque parentes (et quantum sibi dissimiles) imprimunt propter vehementem rerum diversarum imaginationem qua dum coeunt casu aliquo afficiuntur! Quo fit ut dissimiliores sint admodum inter se homines figura gestibusque et moribus, quam quaevis inter se in quavis specie bruta. Quam saepe malefica voluntas exsecrationibus suis et veneficiis vulgo fertur nocuisse hominibus et brutis et plantis! Adde quod glutones nonnulli epulas quasdam avidius cogitantes salivam suam simili quodam sapore inficiunt.

BOOK XIII

: I :

Many signs demonstrate how much the soul dominates the body. The first sign is from the phantasy's emotions.

Thus far we have demonstrated the soul's divinity by resorting to reasons. Next we will confirm the same in virtually the same way by resorting to signs. Four emotions accompany the phantasy: desire, pleasure, fear, and pain. When they are at their most intense, they immediately and totally affect their own body and even sometimes another's. What frenzied ardor the desire for revenge stirs up in the heart or the desire for pleasure in the liver, yea in the pulse too! It was by changes in his pulse that the doctor Erasistratus knew that Antiochus had been seized with love of Stratonica.[1] Moreover, how perniciously does the desire of inflicting harm by constant gazing [i.e. through the evil eye] bewitch boys and others of an impressionable age. How obviously does the greed of a pregnant woman affect the tender fetus with the stamp of what is on her mind! Look at the various gestures and signs parents impress upon their children (howsoever unlike they are to themselves) and that come from the vehemence of their phantasizing about the various things that happen to affect them when they are mating! Consequently human beings are considerably more unlike each other in form, gestures, and manners than particular beasts are among themselves in any [one] species. How often is it commonly said that an ill will by way of its curses and sorceries has harmed men, beasts, and plants! Moreover, certain gluttons, when they are thinking eagerly about particular dishes, convey a like taste to their saliva. Children too and pregnant 1

Pueri quoque et gravidae mulieres propter nimiam vetiti cibi vel potus aviditatem liquescunt, diffluunt, dilabuntur. Haec et similia permulta efficit appetitus.

2 Laetitia quoque vehemens non minora. Haec perimere subito potest corpus et saepe morbo levare. Nonne Sophocles et Dionysius Siciliae tyrannus obiere repente uterque accepto tragicae victoriae nuntio? Mater viso filio e Cannensi pugna redeunte subito exspiravit. Quid contra dolor possit, nullus ignorat. Molestia quinetiam tetri cuiusdam spectaculi gustum inficit et provocat nauseam solo aspectu. Pueri, nonnumquam et grandiores, cum amaram potionem offerri vident alicui, statim sentiunt amaram in ore salivam, quam vehemens movit imaginatio. His nonnumquam tali quadam cogitatione alvus quoque laxatur. Et quod mirabile est, nonnullis stupefiunt dentes et aspectu aliquo et auditu. Quid misericordia, quae dolor quidam est, nonne miserantis corpus ita nonnumquam afficit male, ut corpus alterius videt affectum? Quod declarant ii qui sanguinis humani aspectu statim spiritu deficiente labuntur, et ii quibus dolet cubitus dum vident aut audiunt alterius cubitum vulneratum. Quid metus? An non saepe altis e fenestris in terram despicientes prae formidine caligamus e contremiscimus, quandoque etiam ruimus? Pallent repente timentes, sicut et verecundi rubent. Timore subito trepidat cor, arrectae stant comae, vox faucibus haeret, deficit quoque vita vel morbi diuturni sequuntur. Nonnumquam vero morbos quosdam curat metus, ut singultum et quartanam febrem. Quando autem metus vehementissimus cum vehementissima aviditate concurrit, nonnumquam effectus mirabilis provenit. Hinc, ut est apud Herodotum, cum Croesum regem quidam ex Persis interficere vellet, filius Croesi antea mutus propter ingentem tum mortis paternae timo-

women languish on account of excessive greed for a forbidden food or drink, and waste away and die. These and many similar effects are the result of desire.

Extreme gladness produces no less effects. It can suddenly kill the body and often rid it of disease. Didn't Sophocles and Dionysius, the tyrant of Sicily, both suddenly die when each heard that a tragedy of his had been victorious?[2] A mother died suddenly when she saw her son returning [safely] from the battle at Cannae.[3] On the other hand, nobody is ignorant of what pain can do. Furthermore, the offensiveness of some disgusting sight affects the taste: even just glancing at it provokes nausea. When they see a bitter drink being offered to someone, children and sometimes older people too taste a bitter saliva immediately in their mouths, so vehement is the force of the imagination! And sometimes just such thinking loosens their bowels even. An extraordinary fact is that for some people a mere sight or sound sensitizes their teeth. Doesn't pity, which is a kind of pain, sometimes afflict the body of the pitying person with the affliction it sees in the other person's body? People whose spirit weakens and who faint at the sight of human blood demonstrate this too, as do others who have an elbow that hurts when they see or hear about the injured elbow of another. What about fear? When gazing at the ground from high windows don't we often grow dizzy and tremble with terror and sometimes even plunge down? Those who are fearful at once grow pale, just as those who are shy blush. The heart pounds with fear in an instant, our hair stands on end, our voice sticks in our throat, and life drains away or chronic diseases ensue. But sometimes fear cures certain ailments like the hiccups and quartan fever. When fear at its most intense combines with desire at its most intense, a marvelous effect sometimes occurs. Hence, as we find in Herodotus, when one of the Persians wanted to kill the king Croesus, Croesus's son, who had hitherto been mute, out of overwhelming dread of his father dying and his overwhelming desire to 2

rem tum clamandi cupiditatem subito solvit linguam ac magna voce clamavit: 'o vir, ne interficias Croesum'. Unde[2] vocalis est factus.

3 Quamobrem affectus illi quatuor corpori penitus dominantur, cum illud undique mutent. Sunt autem hi motus ipsius animi. Nam quantum animus bonum quippiam iudicat aut malum, tantum cupit, gaudet, timet et dolet. Unde sequitur naturam corporis animae motibus penitus subiici. Hinc fit ut vultus humanus tum inclinationum animi perspicua signa, tum affectuum singulorum indicia certissima prae se ferat. Illa quidem soli physiognomi, haec etiam vulgares intellegunt. Quis non facile agnoscat cupientem, timentem, iratum, gaudentem animum et maerentem? Hinc accidit rursus, ut solus homo rideat, solus et lachrymetur, ex eo quod animi motus plurimum in corpus habent imperium.

4 Ex hoc autem, quod rationalis animae motibus omnino corpus subiicitur, duo quaedam coniicimus. Unum, quod anima haec forma excellentissima est ac per se subsistens, quia non dominatur corpori forma illa, quae per corpus existit. Alterum, quod corpus humanum animae suae cedit facillime. Non cedit facile, quod propter abundantiam terrae solidum est et durum. Ideo corpus nostrum, si ad cetera animalia comparetur, quam minimum terrae, et illud quidem subtile possidet, sublimiorum elementorum quam plurimum, quocirca caelestis est animae receptaculum. Cui quidem rei documento esse potest, quod viri ingeniosiores saepenumero molles carne sunt, graciles, valetudinarii, corpusque illorum quam minimis ipsorum motibus plurimum variatur, quod de Aris-

cry out, suddenly found his tongue and bellowed in a loud voice, "You there, don't kill Croesus!" From this moment on he had the use of his voice.[4]

So these four emotions entirely dominate the body, since they alter it in every way. But these emotions are motions of the rational soul; for the soul desires, rejoices, fears, or feels pain to the extent it adjudges something good or bad. Consequently the nature of the body is entirely subject to the motions of the soul. Hence the human face shows both the clearest signs of the rational soul's motions and the unmistakable indications of individual emotions. The physiognomists alone understand the signs of the soul's motions, but even the vulgar understand the signs of the emotions. Who does not easily recognize the desiring, fearing, enraged, rejoicing, grieving soul? Hence it is that only man laughs and only he weeps, because his rational soul's motions hold the greatest sway over his body. 3

Because the body is utterly subject to the motions of the rational soul, we can deduce two things. The first is that the soul is the most excellent of forms, the one subsisting of itself, since the form that exists through the body does not dominate the body. The second is that the human body yields to its soul with the utmost ease. What is solid and hard because of an abundance of earth in it, however, does not yield easily. So, when compared to the rest of the animals, our body possesses the least possible earth and even that of a subtle kind, but possesses the most possible of the higher elements, and on this account is the receptacle of a celestial soul.[5] One can adduce as evidence of this the fact that men of great intelligence often have soft flesh and are slender and frequently sick. From the least of their motions their bodies are subject to the greatest change, witness what we have read about Aristotle, Pyrrho, Speusippus, Carneades, Chrysippus,[6] and Plotinus.[7] Plato perceived this in the *Timaeus* when he said that God could have made man's body so strong that it would not be injured by exter- 4

totele, de Pyrrhone, Speusippo, Carneade, Chrysippo, Plotino legimus. Quod in *Timaeo* sensit Plato cum diceret deum potuisse tam solidum hominis corpus facere, ut ab externis minime laederetur, sed voluisse mollius facere, quo esset speculationi paratius, quasi non ad hanc habitationem, sed ad caelestem speculationem simus progeniti. Addit etiam animi potentissimi motiones proprium corpus et resolvere et dissolvere. Quod non in affectu solum, verumetiam in speculationis intentione contingat. Scribit et in *Charmide* Magos illos, animae corporisque medicos, Zalmoxidis Zoroastrisque sectatores,[3] arbitrari omnia corporis tum bona tum mala ab anima fluere in ipsum corpus, quemadmodum oculorum qualitas fluit a cerebro, cerebri qualitas a toto corpore; atque ut impossibile est oculos curari nisi curetur cerebrum, et cerebrum curari nisi corpus totum, ita corpus totum, nisi anima bene valeat, non posse bene valere. Valetudinem vero animae curari Apollineis incantationibus quibusdam, id est philosophicis rationibus. Socrates praeterea narravit vulgatum esse apud Thraces eos medicos tali quadam curatione nonnullos homines servare immortales consuevisse. Tantum est animae in corpus imperium, tanta potestas. Magica haec opinio videtur cum illa Hebraeorum Christianorumque sententia consentire: Adae primi parentis animo prius quidem sano sana fuisse omnia; deinde vero infirmo infirma omnia evasisse.

5 Ceterum de nostris motibus hoc est diligenter animadvertendum, quod aliqui incipientes a corpore non penetrant ad animam, alii penetrant, aliqui incipientes ab anima non redundant in corpus, alii vero redundant. Primi huiusmodi sunt, quando temperatissimus aer corpori circumfusus, licet aliquo modo corpus moveat, tamen neque caloris praebet nobis sensum neque frigoris. Secundi sunt, quando ita movet ut aliquid sentiamus. Tertii sunt,

nal things, but that He wished to make it softer so that it would be better prepared for contemplation.[8] It is as if we were born not for this present habitation but for heavenly contemplation. Plato adds that the motions of an extremely powerful rational soul both resolve and dissolve its body. This happens not only with emotion but with intensity of contemplation. In the *Charmides* too he writes that the Magi, those doctors of the soul and body who were disciples of Zalmoxis and Zoroaster, thought that all the goods and evils alike of the body flow from the soul into the body.[9] Similarly (he says) the quality of the eyes flows from the brain and the quality of the brain from the whole body; and just as it is impossible for the eyes to be healed without the brain being healed, and the brain to be healed without the whole body being healed, so the whole body cannot be well unless the soul is well. He writes that the soul's sickness, however, is cured by certain Apollonian incantations, that is, by philosophical reasons.[10] Moreover Socrates said that it was well known among the Thracians that these very doctors were accustomed to keeping several men immortal with a cure like this. So immense is the soul's sway over the body, so mighty is its power. This opinion held by the Magi seems to be in accord with the teaching of the Hebrews and the Christians; for earlier, when the soul of our first parent Adam was well, all things were well, but later, when it became sick, all things fell sick.

5 With regard to our motions we should take careful note of the fact that, of those beginning from the body, some do not penetrate to the soul while others do penetrate, and of those that begin from the soul, some do not flow over into the body while others do. An example of the first sort is when air tempered to the highest degree, having enveloped the body and though it may move the body in a way, gives us no sense still either of heat or of cold. The second sort is when the air moves us in such a way that we are aware of temperature. The third sort is when the mind quietly contemplates something, or the phantasy considers some airy matter with

quando mens tranquille aliquid speculatur aut phantasia leve aliquid modice intuetur, ex iis namque cogitationibus corpus non agitatur. Quarti denique, quotiens seu mens sive phantasia vehementius sese confert ad aliquid, aut noxium valde aut utile multum iucundumque existimat. Tunc enim corpus aliquid patitur.

6 Profecto, quando per animi affectum motus aliqui in corpus redundant, non per vim corporis, sed per animi imperium in corpus videntur descendere. Corpus enim vim non habet agendi atque accipit subito motus illatos ab animo, nulla intercedente mora. Nam subito pallescit vultus animo metuente et per animi agitationem dumtaxat expallet. Quando vero, calefacto nimium corpore, anima id aegre fert, perturbatio huiusmodi non prius accidit animo, quam et passionem corporis senserit et noxiam iudicaverit. Sentire et iudicare actus est animi. Itaque per suum actum proprie, non per corporis violentiam animus perturbatur, ideoque se ipsum movet, non movetur a corpore. Quod ex hoc plane conspicitur, quia ex vehementiore cogitatione animi et affectu semper agitatur et corpus, neque potest illi corpus obsistere; ex passione vero et cruciatu corporis non necessario animus de suo statu deiicitur. Diogenes Cynicus nudus glaciem nivemque hieme, aestate ardentes calcabat harenas atque interim ridebat et iocabatur; Polemon Academicus rabidissimos canum morsus dum sentiret, ne expalluit quidem. Anaxarchus Abderites philosophus a Nicocreonte Cypri tyranno iussus est in saxum concavum coniici ferreisque malleis caedi. At philosophus poenam corporis negligens inquit: 'Tunde, tunde Anaxarchi vasculum, Anaxarchum ipsum nihil terres'. Iussit tyrannus illi praecidi linguam. Tunc ille praecisam mordicus in ty-

due moderation; for the body is not disturbed by these considerations. Finally the fourth sort is whenever the mind or the phantasy vehemently turns to something and decides it is either very harmful or extremely useful and pleasant; for then the body does experience sensation.

Indeed, when certain motions overflow into the body because 6
of the soul being affected, they seem to descend into the body through the soul's command, not through the body's power. For the body does not possess the power of acting, and it immediately accepts motions imparted to it by the soul without any intervening delay. For when the soul is afraid, the face suddenly turns pale: it turns ashen only because of the soul's tumult. But when the soul is troubled as the body becomes hot and feverish, the perturbation does not assail the soul until it has perceived the body's suffering and judged it harmful. To perceive and to judge are acts of the soul. So properly speaking the soul is perturbed through its own act, not through the body's violence; and thus it moves itself but is not moved by the body. This is evident from the fact that the body too is always agitated by a particularly vehement thought or feeling of the rational soul, and the body cannot resist such. On the other hand the rational soul is not necessarily thrown out of its equilibrium by the passion or suffering of the body. Diogenes the Cynic trod barefoot on the ice and snow in winter and on the burning sands in summer and laughed and joked all the while.[11] Polemon the Platonist did not even blench when he endured the bites of frenzied dogs.[12] The philosopher Anaxarchus of Abdera was ordered by the tyrant Nicocreon of Cyprus to be pitched into the concave bowl of a stone mortar and bludgeoned with iron hammers; but the philosopher, ignoring his body's punishment, exclaimed: "Pound, pound the little dish of Anaxarchus, you will not terrify Anaxarchus himself." The tyrant ordered his tongue cut out. Then Anaxarchus bit off his own tongue and spat it in

ranni faciem conspuit. Aliique innumeri, maxime omnium Christi martyres talia fecisse commemorantur.

7 Ex quibus apparet non per corporalem naturam, sed per animae ipsius iudicium passiones corporis posse in animam penetrare. Iudicium vero non semper naturam sequitur corporis. Variatur quippe iudicium ad coniecturarum varietatem etiam simili corporis complexione manente; saepe etiam manet idem complexione mutata. Constat igitur animum corpori per se obesse, ipsum vero nisi a se ipso laedi non posse. Laesio vero quae a se ipso infertur, controversia quaedam est potius quam pernicies. Nihil enim a se ipso perimitur.

: II :

Signum secundum: ab affectibus rationis.

De philosophis.[4]

1 Animam nostram corporis esse dominam ab affectibus phantasiae satis narravimus. Coepimus quoque idem partim a rationis affectibus indicare. Hanc vero partem diffusius prosequamur. In hac parte ponimus philosophantes, poetas, sacerdotes, praesagos et prophetas.

2 Epimenidem Cretensem annos quinquaginta dormisse aiunt, id est, ut opinor, a sensibus vixisse semotum; similiter[5] decem latuisse Pythagoram, Zoroastrem vero viginti. Socrates, ut scribit Plato, a solis ortu usque ad solem alterum orientem inconnivens, immobilis, iisdem vestigiis et ore atque oculis in eundem locum directis[6] cogitabundus et abstractus a corpore stabat. Plato cum frequenter contemplationis intentione longe secessisset a corpore,

Nicocreon's face.[13] Numberless others, most of all the Christian martyrs, are famous for having performed such deeds.

It appears from this that the body's passions can penetrate to 7
the soul, not through the corporeal nature, but through the judgment of the soul itself. But the judgment does not always follow the body's nature. For the judgment varies according to the variety of opinions even when the body's complexion stays almost the same; and often the judgment stays the same even when the complexion changes. So it is agreed that the soul in itself opposes the body, but that the soul cannot be harmed except by itself. The harm that it suffers from itself, however, is a kind of reverse rather than total ruin. For nothing is destroyed by itself.

: II :

The second sign: from what the reason accomplishes.

On the philosophers.

Using the phantasy's emotions as evidence, we have said enough 1
about our soul being the ruler of the body, and we began to disclose the same in part using what the reason accomplishes. Let us now pursue this category more fully. In it we put philosophers, poets, priests, seers, and prophets.

They say that for fifty years Epimenides of Crete slept, that is, 2
in my opinion, he lived separated from his senses.[14] Similarly Pythagoras, they say, lay hidden away for ten years,[15] and Zoroaster for twenty.[16] Socrates, Plato writes, stood motionless in the same spot from one sunrise to another without closing his eyes and with his face and gaze directed towards the same place, deep in thought and abstracted from his body.[17] Plato, though he had withdrawn far from his body frequently in the intensity of contemplation, eventually left his body's chains behind entirely in this very state of

tandem in ea ipsa abstractione a corporis vinclis decessit omnino. Eius discipulus Xenocrates singulis diebus integram horam abstrahebatur a corpore. Archimedes Syracusanus geometricis figuris intentus, tumultuosum excidium pereuntis patriae et imminentem supra caput hostem non sentiebat. Porphyrius, Plotini discipulus, scribit Plotinum saepe solitum solvi a corpore, mutare vultus, tunc mira quaedam invenire, quae postea scriberet. Quater autem affuisse se asserit iis Plotini miraculis, se ipsum vero, cum ageret octavum et sexagesimum aetatis annum, a numine correptum semel inter contemplandum affirmat. Multis annis ante istos idem fecisse Heraclitum et Democritum legimus. Utrique in solituditinem secesserunt. Alter intentione studii subtristis videbatur aspectu, alter cum mentem a sensibus avocare coepisset et impediretur ab oculis, sese excaecavit. Quid multa? Quicumque magnum aliquid in quavis arte nobiliori adinvenerunt, id fecere praecipue, quando digressi a corpore in arcem animi confugerunt. Hinc Plato scribit in *Phaedro* philosophorum mentes praecipue alas quibus ad divina vola⟨n⟩tur recuperare, quia videlicet semper divinis incumbant. Et alibi quidem divinos, alibi vero dei filios nominat, quia quodammodo renascantur ex deo. Ob id scribit Aristoteles omnes in qualibet arte viros excellentes melancholicos extitisse, sive tales nati fuerint, sive assidua meditatione tales evaserint. Quod ego ob eam causam arbitror evenire, quoniam humoris melancholici natura terrae sequitur qualitatem, quae numquam late sicut cetera elementa diffunditur, sed arctius contrahitur in se ipsam. Ita melancholicus humor animam et invitat et iuvat ut in se ipsam se col-

abstraction.[18] Every day his disciple Xenocrates was abstracted from his body for a whole hour.[19] Archimedes of Syracuse was so intent on examining geometrical figures that he perceived neither the tumultuous slaughter that was destroying his homeland nor the enemy towering over his head.[20] Porphyry, the disciple of Plotinus, writes that Plotinus was often in the habit of being released from his body, of changing his expression and then coming upon certain marvels which he would afterwards write down. He says that he was present four times at these miraculous moments for Plotinus, and he claims that in his sixty-eighth year he was once swept up himself by a divinity in the midst of contemplation.[21] Many years before them we read that Heraclitus and Democritus had done the same. Both withdrew into solitude: one appeared forlorn of aspect from the intensity of his study,[22] and the other, when he began to withdraw his mind from his senses and was still hampered by his eyes, blinded himself.[23] In short, the people who have discovered something important in any of the more noble arts have principally done so when they have abandoned the body and taken refuge in the citadel of the soul. Hence Plato writes in the *Phaedrus* that it is the minds of philosophers that principally recover the wings that bear them aloft to the divine, and this is because they are always devoting themselves to things divine.[24] Elsewhere Plato calls philosophers divine,[25] and in other places, sons of God[26] because in a way they are reborn from God. For this reason Aristotle writes that all men who excelled in any art lived as melancholics whether they were born as such or whether they emerged as such from assiduous contemplation.[27] I believe the reason for this is that the nature of the melancholic humor accompanies the quality of earth, which is never widely diffused like the other elements but contracted tightly into itself. Thus the melancholic humor both invites and helps the soul to gather itself into itself. Again, if the soul frequently thus gathers these very spirits into itself, then because of the continual agitation

ligat. Rursus, anima, si frequenter ita ipsos in se spiritus colligit,[7] propter continuam agitationem partibus humorum subtilibus resolutis complexionem corporis multo magis terream efficit quam acceperit, praesertim cum habitudinem corporis se colligendo reddat compressiorem.[8] Talis autem est terrae natura.

3 Mitto quod talis quoque est natura Mercurii atque Saturni, per quam, dum spiritus in centrum colligunt, animi aciem quodammodo ab alienis ad propria revocant sistuntque in contemplando et ad centra rerum conferunt penetranda. Neque tamen planetae vel humores eiusmodi tamquam efficientes causae id operantur, sed vel praebent occasionem vel impedimenta repellunt. Animus autem ipse et invitatus et expeditus talia perficit.

4 Magnum certe est mentis imperium, quae virtute sua a compedibus corporis solvitur. Ingens opulentia mentis, quae quotiens pretiosos dei et naturae cupit thesauros, non ex terrae visceribus, sed ex proprio eruit sinu. Maxime vero in illis apparet quantum corpori ratio dominatur, qui cum flagitiosam adolescentiam egerint, ante ipsam senectutem subito vel inspirante deo vel homine exhortante ita mores mutant, ut ex intemperatis temperati vel continentes evadant. Quod statim fecisse Polemon traditur eodem die quo audivit Xenocratem de pudicitia disputantem. Idem Diogenes cum audiret Antisthenem disserentem de libertate. Solet natura, quicquid longo tempore inolevit, non aliter quam longo tempore abolere. Habitum igitur diuturna consuetudine roboratum momento labefactare non naturae corporalis est, sed excelsioris atque divinae.

and the liberation of the subtle parts of the [other] humors, it renders the body's complexion much more earthy than when it had first received it; and especially since, by gathering itself in, it [the soul] makes the body's habitual condition more compressed. But such is the nature of earth.

I shall not dwell on the fact that this too is the nature of Mercury and of Saturn, and when through that nature they gather our spirits around a center, they recall the mind's attention in a way from alien matters to its own concerns, and bring it to rest in contemplation, and enable it to penetrate to the centers of things. Yet the planets and such humors do not do this as efficient causes: they only provide the occasion or remove impediments. It is the rational soul itself, an unhindered and invited [guest], that perfects these things. 3

The empire of the mind is certainly immense and by its own power the mind is freed from the bonds of the body. The wealth of the mind is vast and whenever it yearns for the precious treasures of God and nature, it extracts them, not from the entrails of the earth, but from its own bosom. How much the reason dominates the body appears most in those who, having passed a profligate youth and before reaching old age, and whether because of divine inspiration or human exhortation, suddenly change so their behavior that they emerge from their intemperance as temperate and continent men. Polemon is said to have done this instantly on the day he heard Xenocrates discussing modesty.[28] Diogenes [the Cynic] did the same when he heard Antisthenes talking about liberty.[29] Nature usually takes a long time to abolish what it has grown accustomed to for a long time. Therefore to shake off in an instant a habit that daily custom has made strong is not in the power of corporeal nature, but of a nature more excellent and divine. 4

De poetis.

5 Praeterea, poetas considera quos Democritus et Plato divino quodam furore correptos affirmant. Hoc ostendunt prae ceteris duo Platonis dialogi, *Phaedrus* et *Ion*. Cuius quidem rei tria affert signa. Primum, quod artes singulas singuli homines sine deo longo vix tempore assequuntur, legitimi vero poetae, quales fuisse vult Orpheum, Homerum, Hesiodum, Pindarum, omnium artium suis operibus certa quaedam indicia et argumenta inseruerunt. Secundum, quod multa furentes canunt et illa quidem mirabilia, quae paulo post defervescente furore ipsimet non satis intellegunt, quasi non ipsi pronuntiaverint, sed deus per eos ceu tubas clamaverit. Tertium quod non prudentissimi quique et ab ineunte aetate eruditissimi optimi evasere poetae, verum insani potius aliqui, qualem fuisse constat Homerum atque Lucretium, aut rudiores, qualem se fuisse[9] testatur Hesiodus et quales extitisse Ionem et Tynnichum Chalcidaeum scribit Plato, qui praeter artem subito in rebus poeticis mirandi prodierint. Addit ineptissimos quosdam homines a Musis ideo corripi, quia divina providentia declarare vult hominum generi non hominum inventa esse praeclara poemata, sed caelestia munera. Cuius illud affert signum in *Phaedro*, quod nullus umquam, licet diligentissimus et in omnibus artibus eruditus, excelluit in poesi, nisi ad haec accesserit ferventior illa animi concitatio, quam sentimus quando

est deus in nobis, agitante calescimus illo.
impetus ille sacrae semina mentis habet.

Veniamus ad sacerdotes.

On the poets.[30]

Consider moreover the poets whom Democritus[31] and Plato both say are seized by a kind of divine frenzy. Two of Plato's dialogues show us this especially, the *Phaedrus*[32] and the *Ion*.[33] He adduces three pertinent signs. First, without God individual men, even after a long time, can scarcely acquire the individual arts, yet the legitimate poets, such as Plato held Orpheus, Homer, Hesiod and Pindar to be, inserted into their works the particular signs and subject matters of all the arts. Second, poets in a frenzy sing of many things, and marvelous ones at that, which a little later, when their frenzy has abated, they themselves do not sufficiently understand: it is as if they had not pronounced the words but rather God had spoken loudly through them as through trumpets. Third, men of great prudence and those most learned from their youth have not turned out to be the best poets. Rather, some of the poets were mad, as was said of Homer and Lucretius; but others were uneducated as Hesiod himself bore witness, and so too, according to Plato, were Ion and Tynnicus of Chalcis, both of whom suddenly beyond all art stepped forward as wonderfully gifted in poetic matters.[34] He adds that certain wholly unskilled men are enraptured by the Muses precisely because divine providence wishes to declare to mankind that splendid poems are not men's inventions but the gifts of heaven. He gives evidence of this in the *Phaedrus* when he says that no man, however diligent and learned in all the arts, ever excelled in poetry, unless to these accomplishments was added that quickening fervor of the soul[35] which we experience when

> there is a god within us; and when he quickens us we burst
> into flames:
> his is the impulse that bears the seeds of the sacred mind.[36]

But let us come to the priests.

De sacerdotibus.

6 Divum Paulum theologum tres caelestium hierarchiarum caelos in divina abstractione animi conscendisse scripta eius, gesta discipuli monstrant. Galilaei quoque nonnulli olim subito inspirante deo ex piscatoribus summi evasere theologi. Sacerdotes multos ante horum tempora instinctu daemonum solitos debacchari et mirabilia quaedam effari omnis testatur antiquitas. Cornelium sacerdotem castissimum scribit Aulus Gellius Patavi mente motum fuisse, eo tempore quo Caesar et Pompeius in Thessalia confligebant, adeo ut et tempus et ordinem et exitum pugnae videret. Plinius quoque tradit Harmonis[10] Clazomenii animam relicto corpore vagari solitam et multa ac vera e longinquo nuntiare, donec cremato eo inimici eius, qui Cantaridae vocabantur, remeanti animae velut vaginam ademerunt. Idem facere consuevisse scribit Maximus Tyrius platonicus et Herodotus animam Aristei Praeconesii. Aurelius Augustinus refert sacerdotem Calamensem solitum se suo arbitratu a corpore avocare,[11] praesertim cum querula harmonia[12] demulceretur. Iacebat, inquit, simillimus mortuo, sine anhelitu et, cum ureretur et secaretur, non sentiebat; experrectus autem dicebat se nihil praeter ipsam melodiam et voces loquentium in ipsa abstractione sensisse. Quod significat animam illam nihil tunc operari solitam in corpore, cum nullus esset motus aut sensus tangendi aut anhelitus; aliquid tamen in se ipsa agere, cum harmoniam ante auditam excogitaret vocesque perciperet. Atqui[13] et Cornelius ille et Harmon et Aristeus, quos supra narravi, cum se a corpore abstulissent, nihil vidissent remotius quam antea, nisi

On the priests.

His writings[37] (the deeds of a disciple[38]) demonstrate that the divine theologian Paul, in the divine abstraction of his soul, ascended to the third heaven of the celestial hierarchies. One day, with God inspiring them, several Galileans too were suddenly transformed from being fishermen into sublime theologians.[39] All antiquity testifies that in times prior to them many priests, inspired by demons, often danced in frenzy and proclaimed marvels. Aulus Gellius writes that Cornelius, a priest of utmost purity, was so inspired in Padua at the time Caesar and Pompey were fighting in Thessaly that he could envision the time, the course, and the result of the battle.[40] Pliny too writes that the soul of Hermotimus of Clazomenae, having left his body, customarily roamed abroad and brought back news from afar that was abundant and true, until his enemies, who were called the Cantharidae, burned his body and took away its "sheath" from his wandering soul.[41] Maximus of Tyre and Herodotus both write that the soul of Aristeas of Proconnesus customarily did the same.[42] Aurelius Augustine tells of a priest of Calama who was accustomed to withdrawing himself from his body of his own free will, especially when he was soothed by a plaintive harmony. The priest used to lie there, Augustine says, like a corpse without breathing and felt nothing when he was burned or cut, but after he revived, he used to declare he had heard nothing in his abstraction but the melody and the voices of those talking.[43] This means that when no motion, sensation or breathing occurred there, usually the soul was doing nothing in the body; yet in itself it was doing something, since it was pondering the harmony it had heard beforehand and listening to the voices. Yet these people whom we mentioned above, Cornelius, Hermotimus and Aristeas, having taken themselves out of the body, would have seen nothing farther away than they had before, if the soul, when it escapes from its little body, did not live more 6

anima, cum a corpusculo isto eximitur, viveret liberior et latius vagaretur. Nec Calamensis anima se sua sponte abstulisset a corpore et semota egisset aliquid, si corporis sui pedissequa fuisset omnino.

7 Haec his Platonis verbis in *Phaedro* confirmari videntur. Divinis, inquit, meditationibus qui recte utitur perfectisque mysteriis semper imbuitur, perfectus revera solus evadit. Ab humanis autem studiis segregatus divinoque numini semper inhaerens, vulgo carpitur[14] quasi extra se positus, sed ipse deo plenus vulgus latet.

De fatidicis et prophetis.

8 Diximus de philosophis, poetis, sacerdotibus; iam de fatidicis prophetisque loquamur. Longior esse cogar, si augures, haruspices, auspices, mathematicos, magos commemoravero. Horum quidem opera peritissimas indicant mentes. Mentes vero divinas illa prae ceteris praesagia indicant, ut in *Phaedro* vult Plato, quia sine arte et consilio fiunt, qualia sunt quae de Diotima vate et Socrate et Epimenide Plato refert; quae de Sibyllis Varro una cum Platone; quae de Pythiis oraculis historici narrant et philosophi paene omnes confirmant, praesertim Platonici; quae de somniis experiuntur omnes; quae de divinis prophetis tradunt Hebraei. Horum omnium mentes tunc maxime loca plurima circumlustrabant et tria in unum tempora complectebantur, quando se a corpore secernebant. Ergo quando animus hominis omnino erit seiunctus a corpore, omnem, ut est apud Aegyptios, comprehendet locum et omne tempus. Immo vero iam paene est talis animus suapte natura

freely and wander farther afield. Nor would the soul of the priest from Calama have escaped from its body of its own accord and done something apart from it had it been entirely dependent on its body.

All this seems to be confirmed by what Plato says in the 7
Phaedrus. The man who makes correct use of divine meditations and is always steeped in the highest mysteries, alone emerges truly perfect. But divorced as he is from human concerns and cleaving always to the divinity, he is said to be almost mad by the slanderous multitude: though filled with God, he is unrecognized by the rabble.[44]

On seers and prophets.

We have discussed philosophers, poets, and priests; now let us 8
speak of seers and prophets. I would be forced into a long detour if I dealt with augurers, diviners, soothsayers, astrologers, and mages. Their works speak to their minds' great skill and expertise. But it is pre-eminently their predictions that testify to their minds' divinity, as Plato signifies in the *Phaedrus*, because they are made without art or counsel.[45] Witness the predictions which: a) Plato attributes to the priestess Diotima, to Socrates, and to Epimenides;[46] b) Varro, following Plato, attributes to the sibyls;[47] c) historians narrate of the oracles at Delphi[48] and almost all the philosophers, especially Platonists, confirm; d) everyone experiences in dreams; and e) the Hebrews tell of the prophets divine. The minds of all these travelled across very many places and embraced the three "times" in one[49] chiefly when they separated themselves from the body. Thus when man's soul has been completely disjoined from the body, he occupies all place and all time, as the Egyptians maintain.[50] Or rather the rational soul is already by its very nature everywhere and always or virtually so. In order to survey a multitude of places, even the most remote, and to recollect

ubique et semper. Qui ut multa loca et remotissima circumspiciat atque ut totum recolat praeteritum tempus et futurum anticipet, non cogitur extra se progredi, sed relicto corpore in se reversus, id prorsus assequitur, aut quia natura sua ubique est et semper, ut arbitrantur Aegyptii, aut quia cum in naturam suam se recipit, statim numini coniungitur omnes et locorum et temporum terminos comprehendenti. Ceterum qua[15] via praesagium cadat in animum, si placet, altius repetam.

9 Tres rerum ordines ad humanam animam pertinere videntur: providentia, fatum, natura. Providentia est series mentium, fatum series animarum, natura series corporum.

10 Principio sub deo mentes illas omnino solutas a corpore ponimus secundum Platonem, quos vocat Dionysius angelos purissimos, scilicet intellectus. Addimus inferiorem mentium gradum, earum scilicet quae iam corporibus uniuntur et quasi quidam angeli videntur esse, obtinentes quodammodo gradum infimum angelorum, quorum in numero sunt animae omnes rationales, sive mundi, seu mundanarum sphaerarum, siderum, daemonum atque hominum. Tertio loco sunt globi caelorum, elementorum, humorum. Proinde angelorum caput deus est, quia radium suum rerum omnium creandarum rationibus praeditum per angelos omnes demittens, gradatim format omnes, ita ut in singulis universam describat mundi figuram. Neque solum sublimes illos intellectus angelosque purissimos sic exornat, verumetiam per illos tamquam medios in mentes quoque rationalium animarum quasi quosdam infimos angelos radium eundem traducit,[16] iisdem praeditum rationibus. Huiusmodi rerum dispositio lexque divina inscripta mentibus providentia nuncupatur.

11 Sequitur fatum. Animae quippe rationales non modo vim illam habent intellegendi, per quam angelicae sunt et in ordine provi-

all past time and anticipate future time, it does not have to proceed outside itself: it achieves this totally when, having abandoned the body, it has turned within. And this is either because by its very nature it is everywhere and always, as the Egyptians suppose, or because, when it betakes itself to its own nature, it is immediately united with the divinity which comprehends all the boundaries of space and time. But let me, if you are agreeable, trace in greater depth how prophecy befalls the soul.

Three universal orders obviously pertain to the human soul: 9
providence, fate, and nature. Providence is the succession of minds, fate is the succession of souls, nature is the succession of bodies.

Following Plato, we first place under God those minds which 10
are liberated entirely from the body and which Dionysius calls the purest of the angels, namely the intellects. Then we have the lower level of minds, those which are already united with bodies and appear to be particular angels as it were: they occupy in a way the lowest order of angels, and in their number are all rational souls—those of the world, of the world spheres, of the stars, of the demons, and of men. In third place are the spheres themselves of the heavens, of the elements, and of the humors. Accordingly, the head of the angels is God, because, by sending His ray, which is endowed with the rational principles for creating all things, down through the hosts of angels, He forms all things in sequence, such that He inscribes the universal figure of the world in single entities. He not only thus adorns the sublime intellects and the purest of the angels, but through them as intermediaries He also transfers His ray, endowed with these same rational principles, into the minds too of rational souls as if they were the lowest angels. This universal disposition, this law divine inscribed in minds, is called providence.

Next comes fate. Rational souls have not only the power of un- 11
derstanding (via which they are angelic and numbered in the order

dentiae numerantur, verumetiam vim illam vivificam rectricemque corporis, quae alit corpus in corpore, sentit corporalia per corpus, movet corpus per locum regitque in loco, quam vim idolum, id est simulacrum rationalis animae Platonici nuncupant. In hoc idolo insunt semina motionum et qualitatum omnium quae in corpore explicantur ab anima. Omnes animae rationales tum nostrae, tum quae supra nos sunt, vires illas habent intellegendi. Habent et has vivificas rectricesque corporum facultates.

12 Sequitur natura. Nam in quolibet corpore animato est certa quaedam eius affectio sive complexio efficax atque vitalis, quam virtus animae suae vivifica corpori tribuit. Hanc volunt esse Platonici naturam corporum, quasi quoddam vestigium animae in corpore sive umbram, quam Proclus esse vult una cum divisione corporis divisibilem seminibusque plenam vitamque corporis ab animae vita manantem.

13 Resumamus in hunc modum. Omnes mentes, sive sublimes et super animas sint sive inferiores et inditae animabus, ita invicem connexae sunt, ut ab earum capite deo incipientes longa et continua serie procedant, ac superiores quaelibet inferioribus radios suos dispertiant.

14 Videamus quid hinc oriatur. Quando quis caput summum recti ligni humi iacentis digito pulsat, usque ad[17] alterum ligni extremum pulsatio vel levissima resonat. Idem in chorda fit tensa, cuius si apex tangatur tota tremit et sonat. Si tendas aequo intervallo duas in lyra fides, altera pulsata, tremit et altera. Si duas lyras ad eandem intentionem fidium temperes, sonante altera, altera reboat. Quorsum haec? Ut intellegamus hinc ex omnium mentium mutua et invicem temperata connexione idem fieri, ut scintillae primarum in medias, mediarum in infimas usque refulgeant et

of providence), but also the life-giving power. This is the ruler of the body: it nourishes the body in the body, perceives things corporeal through the body, and moves and rules the body through and in space. The Platonists call this power the idolum, that is, the simulacrum of the soul.[51] In it are present the seeds of motions and of all the qualities which are unfolded by the soul in the body. All rational souls, whether ours or those existing above us, possess the powers of understanding. But they also possess these life-giving faculties ruling over bodies.

Next comes nature. In every animate body exists a particular disposition or complexion which is effective and vital and which the life-giving power of its soul gives to its body. The Platonists mean this to be the nature of bodies, to be as it were a vestige or shadow of the soul in the body. Proclus wants it to be divisible along with the division of the body, to be full of seeds, and to be the life of the body emanating from the life of the soul.[52] 12

Let us summarize this in the following way. All minds, whether sublime and above souls, or lower and introduced into souls, are so mutually bound that, beginning from God as their head, they proceed in a long continuous succession; and those that are more eminent distribute their rays to those that are less so. 13

Let us look at the consequences. When someone taps with his finger the end of a straight stick lying on the ground, the pulsation, even the lightest, resonates to the other end of the stick. The same happens with a taut musical string: if its top is plucked the whole vibrates and sounds.[53] If you take two equally tuned strings in a lyre, when the one is plucked, the other vibrates. If you take two lyres and attune the strings to the same pitch, when the one lyre sounds, the other will resound. What is the goal of this argument? That we might understand that from the mutual and mutually tempered connection of all minds issues the same result, namely that the sparks of the first minds are refulgent in the middle minds, and the sparks of the middle in the lowest; and that 14

a postremis per medias in sublimes iterum reflectantur. Harum connexionem hanc mutuam scintillarumque infusionem, a superioribus ad inferiores continue demanantem, providentiam appellamus.

15 Mittamus mentes in praesentia; accipiamus idola, id est simulacra animarum. Caput omnium sit idolum animae[18] mundi, huic connectantur idola duodecim, animarum duodecim sphaeras duodecim agitantium. Quoniam vero in qualibet sphaera plures sunt animae, harum idola ad unum idolum unius communisque animae, quae totam illam regit sphaeram, religentur. Atque ita omnia animarum rationalium idola mutua quadam conspiratione ex uno pendent idolo summo, ita ut nutus quilibet idoli primi in media et mediorum in infima transeant, et semina rerum omnium corporalium a primis idolis, idolis sequentibus inserantur. Conspirationem huiusmodi seminumque traductionem fatum esse arbitrabamur.

16 Eadem ratione per corpora procedamus. Complexiones sive affectiones sive naturae duodecim sphaerarum duodecim uni et summae naturae ipsius mundanae materiae copulentur. Singulae vero naturae singulorum corpusculorum sphaerae cuilibet adhaerentium ad naturam sphaerae suae universalem similiter referantur. Atque haec dependentia series naturalis cognominatur, in qua naturarum superiorum instinctus in naturas inferiores transfunditur. Ita omnes mentes tamquam lumina ad unam mentem tamquam lumen; omnia animarum idola et simulacra ad unum universalis animae idolum; omnes naturae corporum quasi animarum umbrae, proprie ad communem naturam unius corporis, quasi umbram unius animae reducantur. Anima nostra per caput suum, id est mentem, superioribus mentibus nectitur, per vim infimam, id est idolum quo regitur corpus, cum idolis animarum superio-

they are reflected back in turn from the lowest through the middle to the highest. This mutual connection of theirs, this continual emanation and pouring forth of sparks from the highest to the lowest, we call providence.

For the present let us leave aside the minds and take up the 15
idola, that is, the simulacra of the souls. The head of them all is the idolum of the World-Soul; and connected to this are the twelve idola of the twelve souls moving the twelve spheres. But since many souls inhabit any one sphere, their idola must be bound to the one idolum of the one common soul that rules the whole sphere. And thus all the idola of the rational souls depend in a mutual accord on the one highest idolum, such that any commands of this first idolum pass down to the middle idola; and those of the middle idola, to the lowest idola; and the seeds of all corporeal things are sown by the first idola in the subsequent idola. We believe this concord, this transmission of seeds, to be fate.

Let us proceed through bodies following the same principle. 16
The twelve complexions or affective dispositions or natures of the twelve spheres must be joined to the one highest nature of the world's matter. But the individual natures of individual little bodies clinging to any sphere must similarly refer to the universal nature of their sphere. And this dependence is called the natural succession or order: in it the instincts of the higher natures are transmitted to lower natures. Thus like lights all minds are reflected back to the one mind as light; all the idola and simulacra of souls, to the one idolum of the universal soul; and all the natures of bodies, the soul's shadows so to speak, to the common nature appropriately of the one body, to the shadow as it were of the one soul. Through its head, that is, its mind, our soul is bound to higher minds; through its lowest power, the idolum, with which it rules the body, our soul is in accord with the idola of the higher souls; and through its body's nature into which the idolum is wo-

rum conspirat, per naturam corporis sui, cui idolum se insinuat, conciliatur naturis corporum mundanorum, quas natura huius corporis sequitur. Ergo iis quasi tribus rudentibus toti machinae colligamur, mente mentibus, idolo idolis, natura naturis, non aliter ac foetus in alvo toti corpori materno per continuata ligamenta connectitur; unde et animae maternae et corporis et spiritus materni ipse quoque per animam suam, corpus et spiritum percipit passiones.

17 Anima igitur per mentem est supra fatum, in solo providentiae ordine tamquam superna imitans et inferiora una cum illis gubernans. Ipsa enim, tamquam providentiae particeps ad divinae gubernationis exemplar regit se, domum, civitatem, artes et animalia. Per idolum est in ordine fati similiter, non sub fato. Siquidem animae nostrae idolum natura sua cum supernis idolis concurrit ad formandum corpus atque movendum. Per naturam quidem corpus est sub fato; anima in fato naturam movet. Itaque[19] mens super fatum in providentia est; idolum in fato super naturam; natura sub fato supra corpus. Sic anima in providentiae, fati, naturae legibus, non ut patiens modo ponitur, sed ut agens. Ideo Plato in libro *De republica* decimo virtutem animi, inquit, non esse servilem; daemonem vitae ducem ac rursus vitae fortunam eligi a nobis, non nos a daemone vel fortuna; culpam eligentis esse, non dei. Zoroaster quoque ita praecipit:

Μὴ σύ γ' αὔξανε τὴν εἱμαρμένην

id est: 'Ne tu augeas fatum,' quasi in tuo arbitrio sit cedere fato atque non cedere.

18 Cum vero ex tribus illis partibus astringamur partim rerum ordini, partim non astringamur, ex quarta praecipue solvimur nostrique sumus omnino. Haec ratio est, quam inter mentem animae

ven, our soul is united with the natures of the world's bodies (natures which this body's nature follows). Thus we are bound to the whole machine [of the world] by these three ropes as it were: by our mind to minds, by our idolum to idola, by our nature to natures. Similarly the fetus in the womb is bound to the whole maternal body by way of connected cords, whence through its soul, body, and spirit it also perceives the passions of the mother's soul, body, and spirit.

So through its mind the soul is above fate solely in the order of 17
providence, imitating as it were things supernal and with them governing things inferior. For the soul as a participant of providence and according to the model of divine governance rules itself, the home, the state, the arts, and the animals. Likewise through its idolum the soul is in the order of fate but not under fate, since the idolum of our soul through its nature joins with the supernal idola to form and move the body. Through the nature the body is under fate, [whereas] the soul moves the nature in fate. Therefore the mind is above fate in providence; the idolum is in fate above nature; the nature is under fate above the body. Thus the soul is positioned with regard to the laws of providence, fate, and nature, not just as a passive subject, but as an active agent. Thus Plato in the tenth book of the *Republic* says that the power of the rational soul is not a slave: the demon, our life's leader, and our life's fortune in return are chosen by us, and not us by the demon or by fortune, the blame [for a wrong choice] being the chooser's not God's.[54] Zoroaster too proffers this advice, "Do not augment fate,"[55] as if it were your choice to cede or not to cede to fate.

Since in terms of the trio of the mind, the idolum, and the na- 18
ture we are partly bound and partly not bound to the universal order, it is mainly in terms of a fourth part that we are freed and become entirely our own masters. This part is the reason that we locate as a mean between the mind (the soul's head) and the idolum (the soul's foot). For the mind is present to the soul not

caput et idolum animae pedem[20] mediam collocamus. Mens enim animae inest non quantum anima proprie est, sed quantum angelica et a supernis mentibus occupata. Idolum quoque illud animae, id est rectrix potentia corporis, non est animae purae officium, sed animae iam vergentis ad corpus. Verum ratio interponitur, vis quaedam verarum propria animarum, per quam in universali conceptu a principiis rerum ad conclusiones temporali successione discurrunt, effectus resolvunt in causas, causas iterum in effectus deducunt; discurrunt etiam conceptu particulari ad discursionis universalis exemplar. Sed in prima ipsa[21] et universali discursione ratio intellectualis vocanda est; in discursione particulari ratio cogitatrix et opinatrix. Mens autem illa, quae est animae caput et auriga, suapte natura angelos imitata, non successione sed momento quod cupit assequitur, immo habitu quodam et, ut vult Plotinus, actu simul continet omnia. Ac merito post mentem hanc animae stabilem angelos imitantem sequitur ratio mobilis animae propria. Huius pedissequae sunt vires illae sentiendi brutae, quae sunt in idolo, phantasia scilicet confusa, quae instinctum sequitur naturalem, imaginatioque quinque sensuum congregatrix. Idoli pedissequa est natura. Mentem nostram soli cuidam nostro, rationem solis huius lumini, idolum luminis huius radio, naturam radii reflexioni, id est splendori et, ut rectius loquar, umbrae Platonici comparant.

19 Atque ut ad vim revertar rationalem, saepe eam aiunt ita se ad mentem habere, ut sermonem ad animam se habere videmus, et in motu perpetuo liberoque versari. Denique facultas illa rationalis, quae propria est animae verae natura, non est ad aliquid unum determinata, nam libero motu sursum deorsumque vagatur. Primus

properly as soul but as something angelic, as something possessed by the supernal minds. The soul's idolum too, the ruling power of the body, is not performing the office of the pure soul but of the soul already inclining towards the body. But the reason is interposed as a power that is properly that of true souls. Through it souls begin with a universal concept, then in temporal succession proceed discursively from the principles of things to conclusions, and resolve effects into causes, and educe causes into effects. They begin too with a particular concept and reason back to the exemplar or model of universal discursive reasoning. But in this universal, this prime reasoning, the reason should be called intellectual, whereas in particular reasoning it should be called the cogitative or opinion-forming reason. But the mind, which is the soul's head and charioteer and which by its very nature imitates the angels, attains what it desires not in temporal succession but in an instant; or rather, it contains all things in a particular habit and act simultaneously, as Plotinus supposes.[56] And justly, after this unmoving mind of the soul that imitates the angels, comes the moving reason that is properly the soul's own. Attendant on it are those [two] irrational perceiving powers located in the idolum, namely the confused phantasy, which follows natural instinct, and the imagination, the assembler of the five senses. Following the idolum is the nature. The Platonists compare our mind to a private sun, our reason to this sun's light, our idolum to a ray of this light, our nature to the ray's reflection or splendor, or (to put it more accurately) its shadow.

But to return to the rational power. They often say its relationship to the mind is apparently that of speech to the soul, and that it is engaged in perpetual and unencumbered motion. That rational faculty which is the proper nature of the true soul is not confined then to one particular thing; for in its free motion it ranges up and down [the ladder of creation]. For the first motion is that which is located in the nature proper to the soul, since the soul is 19

enim motus est, qui in propria animae natura locatur, cum ipsa sit essentia tertia, cuius virtus est per se mobilis. Primus autem motus non hic motus est aut ille, non huc solum fertur aut illuc, sed communis motus est, et tamquam fons motionis perfluit liber, paribusque in omnem partem momentis prolabitur. Quamobrem licet per mentem, idolum, naturam quodammodo communi rerum ordini subnectamur—per mentem providentiae, per idolum fato, per naturam singularem universae naturae—tamen per rationem nostri iuris sumus omnino, et tamquam soluti modo has partes, modo illas sectamur. Quandoque ratio menti cohaeret, ubi surgit in providentiam, quandoque idolo obsequitur et naturae, ubi fatum suo quodam subit amore, dum sensibus confisa huc et illuc rerum sensibilium occursu distrahitur, quandoque omissis aliis in se ipsam se recipit, ubi aut res alias perquirit argumentando aut indagat semetipsam. Usque adeo vis haec media propriaque animae et libera est et inquieta. Et quando aliquid in nostra incurrit extrema, puta in mentem, idolum vel naturam, fieri quidem potest ut anima statim illud quoquomodo percipiat, non tamen prius animadvertit se illud percipere quam in potentiam transeat mediam.

Cum enim potentia media sit per quam nos homines sumus, immo et quod ipsi sumus, quod pertinet ad eam, evidentissime ad homines pertinet. Movent saepe colores aut voces oculos sive aures, confestim visus et auditus suum explent officium, hic videt, ille audit, nondum tamen animus et videre se et audire animadvertit, nisi media nostri potentia sese ad haec intendat. Quod patet in his qui obvios sibi non comprehendunt, dum aliud quippiam attentius cogitant. Sic mentes superiores movent semper nostram mentem illis[22] annexam; impulsum tamen huiusmodi ideo non

the third essence whose power is to be self-moving. But the first motion is not this or that motion and is not being borne hither or yon, but is the common motion: as the fount of motion it overflows freely and cascades down in equal moments to every part. Therefore, although we are joined to the universal order through our mind, idolum, and nature — through the mind to providence, through the idolum to fate, and through our single nature to universal nature — yet through the reason we are entirely a law unto ourselves, and like free beings we can pursue now these faculties and now those. When the reason cleaves to its mind, it rises into providence; when it follows its idolum and nature, then, subject to a particular love, it submits to fate (and while it relies on the senses, it is dragged hither and thither by its encounter with things sensible); and when, leaving all else aside, it withdraws into itself, then in arguing it delves into other things or it investigates itself. To this extent the reason is the intermediate and proper power of the soul, and it is free and never at rest. And when something strikes our non-intermediate faculties, namely the mind, idolum, or nature, then it becomes possible for the soul to perceive it in a way immediately; and yet the soul does not recognize that it perceives it until it transfers itself to our middle power [i.e. to the reason].

Since a middle power exists by virtue of which we are men, or 20
rather we are ourselves, then what pertains to it clearly pertains to men. Colors often move the eyes, and sounds the ears, and the sight and hearing straightway fulfill their office, the one sees, the other hears; and yet the rational soul does not yet recognize that it sees and hears unless our middle power focuses on these [two] senses. This is obvious in the case of those who do not recognize the people they meet when they are concentrating on something else. Thus the higher minds are always moving our mind which is united to them, yet we do not notice this imparted motion because our middle power, in its wandering through lower things, turns it-

advertimus, quoniam vis media per inferiora circumvaga a superioribus se divertit. Eadem ratione idola animarum superiorum pulsant semper idolum nostrum; hunc nos influxum haud agnoscimus, quando pars illa media aliud quicquam firmius speculatur. Similiter corporum ampliorum naturae continue lacessunt corporis nostri naturam; hunc instinctum saepissime ratione eadem nequaquam advertimus.

21 Huius rei exemplum habemus in corpore. Saepe enim nulla re lacessiti, nobiscum subirascimur. Nullis malis turbati nuntiis aut portentis territi torpescimus, maeremus et trepidamus, nullis bonis permulcti gestimus ipsi nobiscum et canimus. Haec unde? Causam certe novam habent tam novi effectus. Haec utique est varia pro variis temporibus affectio corporis, sive in felle vel iecore crocea bilis exaestuet, seu bilis ferveat atra in splene, seu claro sanguine cor abundet. Huiusmodi corporis affectiones atque naturae, quia proximae sunt vivificae potentiae quae idolo continetur et continet ipsas, eam variis incitant pulsibus, dum occasionem praebent ut illa et aliter et obnixius operetur in complexione corporis vivificanda quam soleat. Huiusmodi operatio reddita concitatior vim sentiendi, quae eodem idolo continetur, tactum praesertim, titillat sensim pungitve latenter eiusmodi idoli phantasiam, ceu per naturae indigentiam pungitur stomachus. Punctio illa et titillatio latens ad mediam animae partem non transit quando illa in aliud inhiat; transit autem quando vacat. Tunc per rationem cogitatricem repente subirascimur quodammodo vel maeremus vel gaudemus. Ratio intellectualis haec advertit, unde assentitur quandoque, quandoque etiam consiliis et remediis haec fugit et fugat.

self away from the higher minds. For the same reason the idola of the higher souls are always influencing our idolum, yet we do not notice their influence since that middle power is gazing more intently at something else. Similarly the natures of the greater [heavenly] bodies continually excite the nature of our body, and yet most often and for the same reason we never notice this excitation at all.

We have an example of this in the body. For unprovoked by 21
anything we are often rather angry with ourselves; without being disturbed by bad news or frightened by portents we grow listless, sad, and fearful; and without being cheered up by good news, we are inwardly elated and burst into song. And why? Such unexpected effects certainly derive from an unexpected cause, and this is the varied affective state of the body at various times, depending on whether the yellow bile is boiling up in the gall-bladder or liver, or the black bile is raging in the spleen, or the heart is full of pure blood. Such affective states or natures of the body, because they are next to the life-giving power which is contained in the idolum and which contains them, excite this power by imparting various motions to it: they give it the occasion to begin imparting life to a different degree and more vigorously than usual to the body's complexion. When this operation has become even more excited, it gradually titillates the power of sensation, which is contained in the same idolum, especially the touch, or secretly goads this idolum's phantasy, just as the stomach is goaded by [the] nature's craving. This goading and hidden titillation do not pass over into the soul's middle part when it is coveting something else, but only when it is empty. Then through the cogitative reason we suddenly become rather angry in a way or sad or joyful. The intellectual reason [in turn] notices these moods: at times it assents to them, but at other times, by way of counsels and cures, it either flees from them or puts them to flight.

22 Summatim his saepe pulsamur affectibus longo ordine a naturis universalibus per propriam in nos descendentibus, et unde nobis ingerantur penitus ignoramus. Si ita est, cur non etiam mentes superiores menti nostrae coniunctae semper eam pulsent? Quem impulsum nos minime advertamus, quando pars media nostri ita est suis actibus occupata ut usque ad eam non transeat mentis influxus. Ea vero vacante, quid prohibet angelicam aliquam rationalibus viribus cogitationem irrepere, licet unde surrepat non videamus? Quod indicant illi qui absque praeceptore ex sola vacuae rationis intentione aut etiam tranquillitate saepe multa et praeclarissima, etiam dum non inquirerent, reppererunt, quasi sua sponte solis lumen in serenum aerem subito se transfundat. Ac licet dispositio mundi, quae tota simul est in mentibus rationibusque supernarum animarum inscripta, perenni quadam continuatione tota simul nostrae menti se offerat, temporalis tamen mundanorum seminum vicissitudo, sicut paulatim in idolis naturisque illarum animarum sibi ipsi succedit, ita simili quadam successionis continuatione per omnium animarum idola omniumque corporum naturas descendit usque ad idolum animae nostrae et corporis nostri naturam, ut ecce ratio pluviae cras futurae hodie regnat in animarum caelestium idolis caelorumque naturis. Eadem per elementalium animarum idola elementorumque naturas demanat, quousque idolum animae nostrae simulque naturam pulset humorum. Pulsatio idoli nostri fit ab idolis, naturae nostrae pulsatio ab illis naturis et idolo nostro.

In short, we are often struck by these emotional affects descending upon us in long and orderly descent from the universal natures via our own nature; and we are entirely ignorant of the source of their being heaped upon us. If this is so, then surely the higher minds, which are united to our mind, also strike our mind? We do not ourselves notice this impulse when our middle part [the reason] is so preoccupied with its own acts that the influence of mind cannot transfer into it. But when it is empty, what is stopping some angelic process of thought from stealing into [our] rational powers, although we cannot see where it is subtly coming from? As evidence, take those who, without a teacher and solely from concentrating their reason (having emptied it of all else), or being even in a state of calm, have often discovered many absolutely outstanding things even when they were not actually looking for them: it is as though the light of the sun were suddenly to diffuse itself of its own accord through the air serene. The world's disposition, which is totally and simultaneously inscribed in the minds and reasons of the supernal souls, offers itself totally and simultaneously to our mind by way of an endless and continuous succession. Though this is so, the temporal alternation of worldly seeds, just as it gradually succeeds itself in the idola and natures of those same supernal souls, so it descends in a like continuous succession through the idola of all souls and the natures of all bodies as far as our soul's idolum and our body's nature. Look, for instance, at the rational principle of the rain which coming tomorrow holds sway today in the idola of the celestial souls and the natures of the heavens. The same principle flows down through the idola of the elemental souls and the natures of the elements until it strikes simultaneously against the idolum of our soul and the nature of the humors. The shock to our idolum comes from the idola, but the shock to our nature comes from the natures and from our own idolum. 22

23 Quando mentium ille influxus rationem nostram sortitur otiosam sive menti vacantem, ipsi aliquid ostendit eorum, quae ad universalem aeternarum rerum cognitionem seu mundi gubernationem pertinent, ut vel dei legem et ordines angelorum vel saeculorum restitutiones et regnorum mutationes praevideat.[23] Quando idolorum naturarumque instinctus rationem omnino et phantasiam offendit vacuam, aliquid sibi portendit eorum quae ad temporum vicissitudines elementorumque turbationes attinent, ut futuram praevideat pluviam, terraemotus atque similia. Qua via istud? Vis illa supernorum idolorum pluvias inductura ad pluvias praefigurat caelorum rotas, hae aerem humefaciunt, aer udus pituitam movet nostram (humorem scilicet aquaeum), pituita spiritum, ex ea praesertim parte qua et ipse est aquaeus. Siquidem spiritus cum sit vapor sanguinis et in sanguine quatuor insint humores, in spiritu sunt quatuor humorum elementorumque virtutes. Igitur virtus illa spiritus aquaea a pituita irritata vivificam animae nostrae instigat potentiam, ex ea parte qua aquaticorum semina vis vivifica possidet. Vis haec suscitat eas imagines quae in vacante phantasia rationeque sunt ad pituitam pertinentes, ut subito cogitemus flumina, imbres, angues, anguillas, pisces atque similia. Eodem pacto vis supernorum, calores et aestus procreatura, congruis mediis choleram, id est bilem, in nobis et cholericum spiritum movet; hic virtutem vivificam; haec igneas imagines in phantasia rationeque latentes, ut incendia imaginemur rubeosque colores et flavos.

When that influence of the higher minds is allotted to our reason at the moment it is no longer busy or is emptying itself for the mind, it reveals to the reason something of all that pertains either to the universal knowledge of things eternal or to the world's governance, in order that the reason might foresee either God's law and the orders of the angels or the [cyclical] recurrence of the ages and the mutations of realms. When the power or instinct of the [supernal] idola and natures strikes the completely empty reason and phantasy, the reason predicts for itself something of what pertains to the vicissitudes of the times and the violent changes of the elements, so that it can foresee a future rainstorm or earthquake or the like. How? The power of the supernal idola which is about to cause the rains prefigures the heavens' turning wheels for the rains; these wheels make the air wet; the wet air provokes our phlegm (our watery humor that is), and the phlegm moves our spirit, using that part especially where it is itself watery. Since our spirit is a blood-constituted vapor and the four humors are present in the blood, the four powers of the humors and of the elements are present in the spirit. The watery power of the spirit therefore, excited by the phlegm, incites the vivific power of our soul, drawing on that part where the vivific power possesses the seeds of watery things. This power arouses the images pertaining to the phlegm which are in the unoccupied phantasy and the reason, so that we suddenly think of rivers, showers, snakes, eels, fish, and the like. In the same way the power of the supernal idola, which is going to produce heat waves and torrid fevers, moves in us the choler (that is, the bile) and the choleric spirit using means that are appropriate. This spirit excites the vivific power, and the power excites the fiery images lying hidden in the phantasy and the reason so that we imagine fires along with red and yellow colors. 23

Septem vacationis genera.

24 Verum quando ita vacamus ut huiusmodi advertamus influxus? Septem sunt vacandi genera: somno, syncopi,[24] humore melancholico, temperata complexione, solitudine, admiratione, castitate vacamus.

25 Quoniam anima operationes suas movendi et sentiendi in hoc corpore crassiore per spiritum sibi proximum explet, ideo quando vel propter defatigationem spiritus in membris exterioribus resolvuntur vel propter vapores humoresque meatus illi cerebri opplentur,[25] per quos huiusmodi spiritus ad sensum motumque idonei solent ad membra transmitti, tunc animus sese quodammodo colligit, neque in sentiendis corporalibus qualitatibus, neque in regendis movendisque membris sui corporis, neque in tractandis externis negotiis occupatur, quod facile fit in somno. Quanto autem magis exterior actus remittitur, tanto intenditur magis interior. Interiores actus sunt phantasiae visa rationisque discursiones. Sed plurimum ita intenditur phantasia, cuius nutu plurimum agimus vitam, ut imagines suas acerrimo intuitu in se ipsa volutet. Revolutae acrius imagines illae usque ad communem illum sensum, quem more platonico vocamus imaginationem, relucent, inde in sensus inferiores et spiritum; imago vero in sensibus iis spirituque relucens solet pro re vera asseverari.[26] Nam vigilantes hominem se videre aiunt, quando ad hominis imaginem in iis[27] micantem sese vertunt. Similiter dormientes affirmant hominem se videre, quando eius imago a phantasia ipsius conservatrice per imaginationem in sensum resplendet et spiritum. Resplendent autem imagines illae prae ceteris ad quas phantasia magis afficitur, sive cogitatio sive perturbatio praeterita sive tumultus praesens dominantium humorum id faciat. Atque haec insomnia vana sunt

The seven kinds of emptiness or release.

When do we empty or free ourselves so that we can notice these influences? There are seven kinds of emptying or release: in sleep, in syncope or swoon, in the melancholic humor, in the tempered complexion, in solitude, in wonder, and in chastity. 24

The soul fulfils its activities of moving and perceiving in this gross body by way of the spirit (which is closest to it). Accordingly, when the spirits are banished to the outer limbs because of fatigue, or when the brain's passages (through which the spirits suitable for sensation and motion are customarily transmitted to the limbs) are choked up because of vapors and humors, then the rational soul in a way gathers itself together and is occupied neither in perceiving corporeal qualities, nor in governing and moving the limbs of its body, nor in negotiating external affairs. This all easily happens in sleep. To the extent external activity is increasingly remitted, however, internal activity is more and more intensified. The internal activities are the visions of the phantasy and the discursive arguments of the reason. But for the most part the phantasy, which most guides the way we live our life, is so intent that with sharpest gaze it ponders its own images within itself. These intensely envisioned images blaze out to the common sense, which we call in the Platonic manner the imagination, and beyond to the lower senses and the spirit. But it is common to claim that this image shining back in the senses and in the spirit is a reality. For people who are awake say that they see a man when they turn to the image of a man flickering in their senses. Similarly people who are asleep say that they see a man when an image of him shines out from the phantasy preserving it and passes through the imagination into the sense and the spirit. But the images that shine out most are those to which the phantasy is more drawn, whether the cause of them is a thought or a past feeling or the present tumult of the dominant humors. These are vain dreams 25

et nihil praeferunt vaticinii, nam aut ex vigiliarum reliquiis aut corporis turbatione nascuntur.

26 Talibus insomniis homines illi solent illudi qui voluptuosae vitae dediti ad ea quae movent sensum vehementer afficiuntur, et phantasiam ad haec vel tamquam bona adsciscenda vel tamquam mala reiicienda affigunt acerrime. Quo fit ut eorum reliquiae[28] phantasiam turbent in somnis. Accedit quod nimio gravati cibo vel potu phantasiam in somno expeditam habent numquam. Nam propter immoderatam humorum vaporumque[29] redundantiam imagines illae in phantasia saepe moventur, quae tetra spectacula praeferant. In iis quoque propter vini calorem, incitata virtute genitalis seminis expultrice, moventur imagines amatae personae quas servat phantasia, unde cogitatur amplexus. Ex iis rationibus Plato in nono libro *De republica* concludit rationem saepe in somno usque adeo occupari ut non libere influxus superiores persentiat. Percepturam autem veritatem inquit quotiens non turbabitur.

27 Sunt et multi voluptuosae vitae contemptores, rerum tamen civilium studiosi vel imperii et gloriae cupidi. In his dormientibus consopitur interdum etiam phantasia, at ratio tunc privata et publica tractat negotia, et iis plurimum occupatur. Sunt nonnulli tam voluptatum quam humanae gloriae contemptores, sed indagationi rerum divinarum et naturalium dediti. Horum in somno cessat aliquando non phantasia solum sed rationis etiam activae anxia consultatio. Resurgit autem consueta illa rationis speculatricis investigatio, ut vel metiri caelum videamur, vel elementa partiri, vel animalium[30] species numerare. Nullis eorum quos numeravimus communiter convenit vaticinium, licet postremi ii philosophantes

and exhibit nothing of prophecy, for they are born either from the vestiges of our waking lives or from the body's agitation.

The people who are deluded by such dreams are usually those who are devoted to the life of pleasure and vehemently attracted to the things that move the sense, and who sharply focus the phantasy on these either as goods to be acquired or as evils to be rejected. Hence it is that the vestiges of such things disturb their phantasy in dreams. Moreover, weighed down in sleep by excessive food or drink, they never have an unencumbered phantasy. Because of an intemperate surplus of humors and vapors, the images set into motion in their phantasy are those that portray hideous spectacles. In these men too, because of the heat of wine and the stimulation of the power to ejaculate generative seed, images of the person they love are set into motion and preserved by the phantasy and they think, accordingly, of sexual intercourse. For these reasons Plato concludes in the ninth book of the *Republic* that in sleep the reason is often so occupied that it is not free to perceive the higher influences. But whenever it is not troubled, he says, it will perceive the truth.[57] 26

There are also many men who despise the life of pleasure but yearn for the life of politics or power or fame. When they sleep, their phantasy too is put to sleep; but then the reason treats of private and public affairs and is preoccupied with them. And there are some men who are contemptuous of pleasure and human fame alike, but dedicated to investigation into matters divine and natural. In the sleep of these men not only does the phantasy sometimes stop but so too does the busy consulting of the active reason. However the customary investigating of the speculative reason reawakens so that we seem to be measuring the sky or dividing the elements or numbering the species of animals. But prophecy commonly is suited to none of the men we have listed, although the last, those who philosophize, do truly reason even when they are sleeping; and indeed, they occasionally find things 27

vere ratiocinentur etiam dormientes, immo et inveniant quandoque quae diu quaesita non invenerant vigilantes, quia ratio est tranquillior. Tale quiddam contigit Galeno, qui scribit, cum circa diaphragma aegrotaret, se somniasse[31] liberatum iri si sanguinem mitteret ex vena quae est inter pollicem[32] et indicem, minuisse sanguinem, convaluisse.

28 Neque desunt aliqui, licet perpauci tales reperiantur, qui domitis voluptatibus civilibusque rebus neglectis ita suam vitam instituant, ut veritatis quidem assequendae flagrent cupiditate, eam tamen humanis vestigiis, quibus ambigua mens naturalium philosophorum plerumque solet confidere, investigari posse diffidant. Itaque deo se[33] dedunt, ipsi moliuntur nihil. Apertis et purgatis oculis, quid maxime divinitus ostendatur expectant, quod et praecepisse dicitur Socrates et fecisse. Hi pii homines et religiosi vocantur. Horum animus in vigilia vacat prae ceteris; vacat in somnis omnino. Quapropter supernus impulsus ab eo facile animadvertitur.

29 Sed horum hominum duo sunt genera. Alii templum hoc dei, mundi scilicet machinam, admirantur frequentius, alii templi huius numen impensius venerantur. Illorum animo per somnum quieto passiones mundi monstrantur, et illae prae ceteris ad quas magis afficitur, ut pluviam videat futuram, bellum, pestem atque similia. Demonstrationis modum et ordinem supra diximus. Ceterum saepe difficilis somnii interpretatio est, saepe etiam facilis. Difficilis, quando postquam pluvia futura expressa est in phantasia, vis phantasiae imaginem pluviae non satis attente commendat

they have sought after for a long time but never found when they were awake because the reason is more tranquil in sleep. Something like this happened to Galen who writes that, when he was suffering chest pains, he dreamed he would free himself of them if he drew blood from the vein between the thumb and the index finger, and he writes that he drew blood and recovered.[58]

There are not wanting some men, though only a very few are to be found, who have tamed the pleasures, who neglect politics, and who so arrange their life that they burn with the desire to attain the truth. Yet they have no faith they can pursue the truth by following the trail of human footsteps to which the changeable mind of the natural philosophers is accustomed for the most part to entrust itself. So they abandon themselves to God but undertake nothing themselves. Having opened and purged their eyes, they wait principally for what might be shown them from on high. And this Socrates is said to have taught and done himself. These men are called pious and devout. In wakefulness their rational soul is more emptied than other men's; in sleep it is entirely emptied. So the movement imparted from on high, the supernal impulse, is easily noticed by this soul. 28

Two kinds of such men exist however. Some more frequently admire this very temple of God, namely this world machine, whereas others more devoutly venerate the divinity of this temple. To the soul of the former, quiet in sleep, are shown the passions of the world, and the things to which it is more attracted compared to the rest, so that it sees future rain, war, pestilence, and the like. The mode and order of this showing we have described above. That aside, the interpretation of a dream is often difficult, but often easy too. It is difficult when, after the coming of rain has been imprinted in the phantasy, the power of the phantasy does not entrust the image of the rain with sufficient care to the memory. As something too quick and nimble, once it has been impelled forward, it slips and slithers through similar and subsequent images, 29

memoriae, sed tamquam velox nimium et versatilis, ut semel impulsa est, currit lubrica per similes et consequentes imagines, ut ex pluvia excitetur ad ventos cogitandos, ex ventis ad altissimos montes, ex montibus ad nives. Ita praetergressa expergiscitur atque experrecta nivis postremo visae magis memor est quam pluviae. Unde futuram praedicit nivem, non pluviam. Quapropter oportet interpretem somniorum esse sagacissimum venatorem, ut sciat ex proximo vestigio recurrere ad remotum, ab illo rursus ad remotius aliud, ac videat quid apprime ex quoque sequatur, quousque ad primum perveniat. Quod solemus in quotidianis sermonibus observare, quando ex uno sermone in alium rursusque in alium transgressi, tandem sermonem primo propositum in promptu non satis habemus. Tunc novissima verba consideramus, e quibus potissimum verbis sequi potuerint, et iterum ex quibus illa, donec prima planissime recolamus. Solertia venatoria velox et versatile requirit ingenium; praesaga facultas, si modo perspicue debeat praevidere, pacatum atque quietum. Haec tamquam repugnantia in eodem non facile concurrunt. Ideo plurimum non iidem praesagi sunt perspicui et interpretes, et saepe qui praesagiunt nesciunt quid presagiant maxime, et qui interpretantur velociter errant magis in praevidendo. Quod in *Timaeo* significavit[34] Plato, cum dixit alios esse vates, alios vatum interpretes.

Sed ut ad rem redeamus, eorum somnia interprete indigent, qui propter cholericos et igneos spiritus curriculo phantasiae currunt velocius. In quibus vero propter complexionem spirituum temperatam vel melancholicam phantasia incedit maturius; praevisae res firmiter inhaerent memoriae neque novis et variis imaginibus con-

so that from the rain it is provoked to thinking about the winds, from the winds, about the highest peaks, and from the peaks, about the snows. Having traversed these, it awakens, and having awoken it has a more vivid memory of the snow it saw at the end than of the rain. So it predicts snow for the future not rain. Wherefore the interpreter of dreams has to be the most skillful of hunters: he must know how to follow the track immediately in front of him to another farther away, and thence to another even more remote, and above all to see what trail he is following until he arrives at the very first track. We are accustomed to witnessing this in our daily conversations, when, having passed from one discourse to another and then on to another, in the end we no longer have the discourse that was first proposed sufficiently in front of us. At that point we turn to consider our most recent words, and from what words they mainly derive, and then the words that preceded them, until we plainly recall our first words. Whereas skill in hunting requires a quick and nimble wit, the prophetic faculty, if it is going to see clearly as it must, requires a calm and peaceful one. These two opposing conditions are not easily reconciled in the same person. So clear-sighted prophets are not for the most part the same people as interpreters: those who prophesy most often do not know what they are prophesying, and those who interpret with rapidity err more in prophesying. Plato signified this in the *Timaeus* when he said that some men are prophets and others are interpreters of prophets.[59]

But let us return to our theme. The dreams of those who run 30
with greater rapidity in the race of the phantasy, because of their choleric and fiery spirits, need an interpreter. But in interpreters themselves the phantasy proceeds at a more timely pace because of the tempered or melancholic complexion of their spirits. Things they have foreseen stick more firmly in their memory and are not confounded by new and different images. Therefore the predictions of such men do not need interpretation, being the predic-

funduntur. Propterea horum praesagia interpretatione non indigent. Atque haec sunt praesagia somniorum, quae religiosis illis conveniunt, qui divinam hanc aedem admirantur et stupent. Qualia sibi obtigisse tradit Hippocrates, qui cum Democritum, qui insanire vulgo ferebatur, curaturus adiret, per quietem accepit a deo, non Democritum insanire, sed vulgus. Eadem ratione Socrates futuram Platonis excellentiam praedixit ex somnio. De his satis.

31 Illis vero religiosis, qui templi huius potius numen adorant, cum per somnum quiescunt, id accidit ut mens eorum divinae cupida maiestatis pulsetur numine vehementer et talis quaedam menti illorum succurat de deo cogitatio, qualem maxime solet vigilans affectare. Puta sedem operationemque dei nosse desiderabat. Quiescenti rationi lux infinita invisibilisque occurrit, quae ubique tota et in se ipsa sit seque ipsam per se sine oculo videat. Hic si phantasia ad motum sit tardior, plana manet et perspicua notio, quam experrectus animus immaculatam, ut acceperat, hominibus aperit. Sin velocior sit, statim ipsa post rationem, ut solet, suum opus aggreditur. Volutat consuetas imagines, atque imitata pro viribus rationem, lucem fingit solis immensam, totam oculis omnium ubique micantem et in se ipsam perpetuo se circuitu revolventem. Hic ergo est opus interprete, qualis Ioseph fuit et Daniel, qui regia somnia interpretabantur. Hac divinatione polluit Mercurius Trismegistus, quod eius liber de dei potentia et sapientia e graeca lingua in latinam a nobis translatus ostendit. Haec vaticinii species religiosis quidem, ut diximus, maxime convenit, aliis quoque nonnumquam, si quando vel providentia aliqua vel casus prosperitate iaceant sobrii curisque vacui. Unde Alexandro regi dormienti draco herbam monstravit, qua Ptolemaeum curaret graviter vulneratum. Praecipue vero prope ortum solis sedata paulum vaporum externarumque curarum turba id accidit. Quamquam, quod vulgo fertur, matutina somnia esse veriora, non ob id solum provenit quod magis sobrii sumus (saepe enim sobrii dormitum accedimus, neque tamen tunc fiunt perspicuae visiones), verume-

tions of dreams proper to those pious men who admire this divine temple [of the world] and marvel at it. Hippocrates is said to have had such when he was about to cure Democritus whom the crowd thought insane; in his sleep he received a message from God that it was the crowd who were insane not Democritus.[60] For the same reason Socrates predicted from a dream the future excellence of Plato.[61] But enough of this category.

Take those [other] pious men, however, who adore rather the divinity of this temple. When they are in the quietness of repose, it happens that their mind, desirous as it is of the divine majesty, is vehemently struck by that divinity: a thought concerning God comes to the aid of their mind (a thought such as a man usually aspires to most when he is awake). Suppose it was eager to know the seat and the activity of God. An infinite and invisible light floods into the quiescent reason; and this light is everywhere whole and integral, and it sees itself through itself without needing an eye. At this point, if the phantasy is very slow to move, the notion remains plain and clear, and the rational soul, having awoken, discloses it to men just as it had received it in its purity. But if the phantasy is quicker, it usually embarks on its work immediately after the reason. It mulls over its accustomed images, and having copied the reason as best it can, it feigns the immense light of the whole sun shining in the eyes of all men everywhere and revolving on itself in its perpetual circuit. Here one needs an interpreter such as Joseph and Daniel who interpreted the dreams of kings. Mercurius Trismegistus was potent in this art of divination, as his book on God's power and wisdom shows (we have translated it from Greek into Latin).[62] This species of prophecy is best suited, as we said, to men of piety, and sometimes to others too, whenever, by some providence or stroke of prosperous fortune, they remain temperate and empty of cares — hence it is that a serpent showed the sleeping king Alexander a herb by which he could cure Ptolemy who had been badly wounded.[63] And it hap- 31

tiam ex eo quod et solis Phoebique vatis accessu vaticinium roboratur, et sanguinei igneique spiritus ea hora dominantes claritate sua ad claram conferunt visionem, et quod videmus, quia statim expergiscimur, turba[35] imaginum consequentium non confundimus. Quae de somno dicta sunt, his Orphei versibus confirmantur:

ἄγγελε μελλόντων, θνητοῖς χρησμῳδὲ μέγιστε·
ἡσυχίᾳ γὰρ ὕπνου γλυκεροῦ σιγηλὸς ἐπελθών,
προσφωνῶν ψυχαῖς θνητῶν νόον αὐτὸς ἐγείρεις,
καὶ γνώμας μακάρων αὐτὸς καθ' ὕπνους ὑποπέμπεις,
σιγῶν σιγώσαις ψυχαῖς μέλλοντα προφωνῶν,
οἷσιν ἐπ' εὐσεβίῃσι θεῶν νόος ἐσθλὸς ὁδεύει,

id est: 'Nuntie futurorum, mortalibus vaticinator maxime. Accedis ad animas somni quiete demulctas, easque compellans suscitas mentem. Sententias numinum beatorum eis per somnum subinseris. Silens silentibus animis ventura praenuntias, his inquam animis, quorum mens divino cultu rectissime utitur'.

32 Satis de ea vacatione animi quae per somnum fit diximus. Sequitur vacatio quae fit per syncopam, id est per casum corporis semivivi, quando cordis defectu spiritus ad membra non mittuntur, et qui in membris sunt, retrahuntur ad cordis debilitati praesidium, quo in statu perinde ut in somno provenit vaticinium. Quo excelluisse Hercules dicitur Arabesque permulti, qui comitiali morbo corripiebantur. Hinc Plutarchus in libro primo *De anima*: 'Enarchus', inquit, 'nuper aegrotans, tamquam iam mortuus a medicis fuit relictus et brevi tempore in se ipsum[36] postea reductus, dicebat se mortuum fuisse et in corpus iterum restitutum, nec eo morbo moriturum; reprehensosque aiebat vehementer a domino suo eos spiritus qui animam eius duxerunt; ad Nicandam enim

pens especially near dawn when the riot of vapors and outer cares for a brief while is calm. Although, as the vulgar maintain, morning dreams are more true, it happens not only because we are more tempered (for often in fact we fall asleep tempered, and yet the visions at that time are not made especially clear), but also because prophecy is strengthened by the coming of the sun and of Apollo, the prophet; and the sanguineous and fiery spirits dominant in that solar hour contribute by their clarity to the clarity of the vision. What we see, because we are immediately aroused, we no longer confuse with the throng of subsequent images. The things that have been said about sleep are confirmed by these verses of Orpheus, "O herald of future things to mortals, o greatest prophet. You come to souls lulled in the quietness of sleep, and, accosting them, you revive the mind. As they sleep you plant in them the judgments of the blessed spirits. Silently to the silent souls you predict things to come, to the souls, I say, whose mind scrupulously practices the worship of the gods."[64]

We have said enough about the emptying of the rational soul 32
that occurs through sleep. We turn now to the emptying that results from syncope or swoon, that is, the fainting of the half-dead body, when, because of the heart's failure, the spirits are not dispatched to the limbs, and those that are in the limbs are withdrawn to the citadel of the weakened heart. In such a state, prophecy arises exactly as it does in sleep. Hercules is said to have excelled in this kind of prophecy and very many Arabs who were seized by epilepsy.[65] Hence Plutarch says in the first book of his *On the Soul*, "Enarchus who had lately fallen sick was left as dead by his doctors, and when he came to himself a short time later he declared that he had been dead and had been restored to his body again, and that he was not going to die of that disease. And he said that those spirits who had led his soul away had been vehemently reprimanded by their master; for they had been dispatched for Nichandas and not for him. But Nichandas was a tanner and

missos, non ad ipsum fuisse. Nicandas autem coriarius erat et in palaestris non ignobilis, qui eo tempore quo Enarchus revixit, in maximas incidit febres ac repente mortuus est. Hic autem vivit superstesque est, felicissime nobiscum manens'.

33 Tertius vacationis modus fit ex melancholici humoris contractione animam ab externis negotiis sevocantis, ut anima tam vacet[37] homine vigilante, quam solet dormiente quandoque vacare. Certe, quemadmodum commodissimum instrumentum carere oportet motu proprio, ne forte, quando faber movere ipsum ad dextram statuit fabricando, ipsum interim feratur motu proprio ad sinistram, sic animum illum, quo divina providentia uti ad vaticinium statuit quasi aliquo instrumento, quietum esse necessarium est, quales sunt melancholici saepe. Sed et hi quando numine[38] rapiuntur, tanto ceteris concitatiores fiunt, quanto corpora densa; si accendantur, ferventius urunt quam corpora rara. Hac ratione Socrates, quem Aristoteles melancholicum iudicavit, daemonis familiaris inspiratione multa praesentiebat, cuius rei testes sunt Plato, Xenophon, Antipater Maximus, Apuleius. Siquidem Timarchus cum ab eo convivio discessisset ubi Socrates discumbebat, Socratis daemone prohibente, inde ea perpetravit, quorum causa est occisus. Charmides in Nemea certavit vetante Socrate ac certasse paenituit. Critoni contra Socraticum consilium rusticanti ramulus aliquis percussit oculum. Idem[39] etiam Socrates dum fugeret una cum aliis nonnullis impetum[40] hostium, ut ventum est in trivium, eadem qua ceteri fugere noluit,[41] quia deterrebatur a daemone. Tum quidem ii qui alia via fugerant in equitatum hostium inciderunt. Aristides et Thucydides aliique permulti quamdiu Socrati

not without a reputation in the wrestling ring. At the very time Enarchus revived Nichandas succumbed to a raging fever and suddenly died. But Enarchus lives and survives and happily dwells amongst us."[66]

The third kind of emptying comes from the contraction of the melancholic humor: it separates the soul from external affairs so that the soul is emptied in the waking man as it is customarily emptied at times in the sleeping. Certainly, just as the most useful instrument must lack its own motion so that, when the artisan decides to move it to the right in making something, it is not meanwhile born by its own motion haply to the left, so a rational soul, which divine providence has decided to use for prophecy as if it were a tool, must be calm as melancholics often are. But when melancholics are seized by the divinity, to the extent their bodies are dense, they become more excited than do the other types, and if they catch fire, they burn more fervently than rare bodies. For this reason Socrates, whom Aristotle adjudged a melancholic,[67] had a presentiment of many things under the inspiration of his familiar demon; Plato,[68] Xenophon,[69] Antipater Maximus,[70] and Apuleius[71] all testify to this. Indeed Timarchus, when he had left that dinner party where Socrates was reclining, though warned not to by Socrates' demon, then committed the crimes that were the cause of his being executed.[72] Charmides trained for the Nemean games when Socrates told him not to, and regretted having done so.[73] When Crito went to work in the country against Socrates' advice, a small branch struck him in the eye.[74] And Socrates himself, when he was fleeing the enemy onslaught along with several others and had arrived at some cross-roads, refused to escape along the same way as the others because his demon was deterring him; those who had fled down the other way then ran straight into the enemy cavalry.[75] Aristides and Thucydides and many others, as long as they stayed close to Socrates (and even if Socrates himself said nothing) made exceptional progress in their 33

propinquabant, etiam Socrate ipso tacente, in philosophiae studiis proficiebant quamplurimum daemonis illius instinctu; quanto longius recedebant a Socrate, tanto reddebantur ad philosophiam ineptiores. Idem cum morti propinquaret, ut scribit Xenophon, praedixit Anyto filium eius, qui tunc modestus videbatur, fore flagitiosissimum, atque ita evenit.

34 Est et quartus a temperata complexione vacandi modus, siquidem talis complexio nullum infert tumultum alicuius superantis humoris, qui ad ullam imaginem commoveat phantasiam. Sunt etiam huiusmodi viri in affectibus suis et actibus moderati, ideo animo[42] adeo tranquillo vivunt, ut etiam vigilantes supernis subiiciantur influxibus, quod Pherecydi Syro, Pythagorae, Plotino dicitur contigisse. Plotinum prae ceteris admiror qui, ut narrat discipulus eius Porphyrius, mores hominum, errata, eventus persentiebat,[43] et cum ipse Porphyrius se ipsum interficere cogitaret, id ille perspexit divinitus atque prohibuit. Ob hanc rationem, ut scribit iunior Plinius, Curtio Rufo dum Africam obtineret et inclinato die spatiaretur in porticu, oblata est mulieris figura humana grandior pulchriorque. Haec praedixit eum venturum Romam honoresque gesturum, atque etiam cum summo imperio in eandem provinciam reversurum ibique moriturum. Facta sunt omnia.

35 Quinta vacatio fieri videtur a solitudine, ubi animus nullis humanorum negotiorum curis distractus paulo vel numinum vel caelorum momento eadem quotidie cogitat, quae caelestia numina cogitant facere. Quod quidem Zoroaster, magorum princeps, solitudine viginti annorum dicitur assecutus, ubi de omni divinandi arte multa conscripsit et fecit. Similia operatum fuisse Orpheum in Thraciae desertis eius scripta Musaeo declarant.

philosophical studies under the impulse of that demon, but the further they got from Socrates the more unsuitable for philosophy they became.[76] When Socrates was close to death, as Xenophon writes, he predicted to Anytus that his son, who seemed at the time to be well behaved, would become utterly degenerate, and so it turned out.[77]

There is a fourth kind of emptying too that results from a tempered complexion, since such a complexion does not admit the tumult that comes with some dominant humor that might move the phantasy towards any one image. Men exist of this kind who are moderate in their feelings and activities, and thus they live with such a tranquil rational soul that even when they are awake they are subject to supernal influences. This is said to have happened with Pherecydes of Syros,[78] Pythagoras,[79] and Plotinus.[80] I admire Plotinus more than all the others, for he, as his disciple Porphyry tells us, clearly saw into the characters of men, their errors, and their fortunes; and when Porphyry himself was thinking of suicide, Plotinus, divinely inspired, perceived it and forbade it.[81] This is the reason, as Pliny the Younger writes, that the figure of a woman of superhuman stature and beauty appeared before Curtius Rufus when he was governor of Africa and strolling as the day declined in the colonnade of his house. She predicted he would go to Rome, hold public office, return to the same province with supreme authority, and die there. All this happened.[82] 34

The fifth emptying seems to result from solitude, when the rational soul, no longer distracted by the troubles of human affairs [and] under the impulse a little of the divinities or of the heavens, thinks daily about the same things that the celestial divinities are thinking of doing. Zoroaster, the prince of the Magi, is said to have achieved this in twenty years of solitude when he wrote about and performed the many things pertaining to every aspect of the art of divination.[83] Orpheus' verses to Musaeus show that he performed similar feats in the wilds of Thrace.[84] 35

36 Sexta fit ab admiratione vacatio. Sibyllae et Pythiae sacerdotes, cum secederent in Iovis aut Apollinis antrum, ibi numen ipsum adesse credebant; tanto admirationis venerationisque stupore de maiestate numinis cogitabant, ut sensus, phantasia, ratioque actus suos illico praetermitterent. Tunc mens soli exposita numini, sive deus ille fuerit sive daemon, supernos persentiebat nutus, eos praesertim qui ad ea negotia pertinebant, de quibus nuper deliberaverant. Similiter affectum fuisse Cornelium sacerdotem Patavii tradit Aulus Gellius. Et tales quosdam inducit Orpheus Corybantes. Hac vaticinii specie[44] praecellebat Albigerius Carthaginiensis: hic paene quicquid egisset quisque aut cogitavisset, afflatu daemonum respondebat. Huius divinationibus saepe se affuisse Aurelius Augustinus affirmat.

37 Septima et omnium praestantissima ea animi alienatio est quae fit castitate mentis deo[45] devotae, quemadmodum Orpheus in hymno deorum omnium Musaeum docet. Talis quippe mens non ad tempus, ut aliae, sed ferme semper pacatum est dei templum, cuius ostium, ut Ioannes inquit theologus, deus pulsat primum, quod statim apertum ingreditur, quod inhabitat sedulo, in quo hominem pascit ambrosia. Per hanc, ut refert Aurelius Augustinus, rusticus quidam suis temporibus secedebat a corpore et vigilare se sciebat, dum tamen videret mira quaedam oculis non corporeis. Per hanc Ioannes, theologus omnium divinissimus, in Pathmo universum vidit ordinem saeculorum; per hanc Ezechiel campum ossibus mortuorum inspexit refertum et ossa postmodum resurgentia; per hanc Isaias deum sedentem a Seraphin circumdatum.

The sixth emptying results from wonder. The Sibyl's and the Pythia's priests,[85] when they would retire into the cave of Jupiter or Apollo, believed the divinity itself was present there: they thought about the divinity's majesty with such overwhelming awe and veneration that their senses, phantasy, and reason instantly intermitted their activities. At that time the mind, exposed as it was to the divinity alone whether god or demon, perceived the divine commands, and especially those which concerned the affairs they had just been considering. Aulus Gellius says that Cornelius, the priest of Padua, was similarly affected.[86] And Orpheus attributes the same to certain of the Corybantes.[87] Albigerius of Carthage excelled in this kind of prophecy: under the inspiration of demons, he used to repeat almost everything that every one had done or thought. Aurelius Augustine affirms that he had often been present himself at his divinations.[88] 36

The seventh and most outstanding of all the soul's alienations is that which results from the chastity of a mind devoted to God, as Orpheus teaches Musaeus in the hymn to all the gods.[89] Not just for a time, as is the case with other minds, but well-nigh for ever such a mind is the irenic temple of God, upon whose door, as St. John declares, God first knocks, and which He will enter directly it is opened; it is the temple where God will eagerly dwell and where He will feast man on ambrosia.[90] Aurelius Augustine reports that it was through this alienation that a certain peasant who was his contemporary used to leave his body, and even as he gazed upon certain marvels with non-corporeal eyes, he knew nonetheless he was awake.[91] It was through this alienation that John, the most divine theologian of all, saw on Patmos the universal order of the ages;[92] that Ezekiel saw the field strewn with dead men's bones and the bones presently rising up again;[93] and that Isaiah saw God enthroned surrounded by the seraphim.[94] But all these men, like those who were dreaming, took whatever they were seeing with the mind and immediately concealed it under the 37

Sed ii omnes, quemadmodum et somniantes, quicquid mente cernebant, phantasiae velaminibus statim operiebant, ita ut visa mentis, phantasiae umbraculis obscurata, interprete indigerent.

38 Concludamus iam per septem vaticinii species tantam esse humanae animae adversus materiam excellentiam, ut et domito et sopito et semivivo corpore multo clarius videat multoque praestantius operetur, quam corpore operante, quasi ad magnifica quaevis efficienda subsidio corporis non indigeat. Ubi apparet quanta sit animae cum caelestibus concordia, quanta cum deo cognatio, quae quotiens in se redit, caelestium arcanorum et divinae fit providentiae particeps.

: III :

Tertium signum: ab artium et gubernationis industria.

1 Cetera animalia vel absque arte vivunt vel singula una quadam arte, ad cuius usum non ipsa se conferunt, sed fatali lege trahuntur. Cuius signum est quod ad operis fabricandi industriam nihil proficiunt tempore. Contra homines artium innumerabilium inventores sunt, quas suo exsequuntur arbitrio. Quod significatur ex eo quod singuli multas exercent artes, mutant, et diuturno usu fiunt solertiores, et quod mirabile est, humanae artes fabricant per se ipsas quaecumque fabricat ipsa natura, quasi non servi simus

veils of the phantasy in such a way that their mind's visions, obscured beneath the shadows of the phantasy, needed an interpreter.

Let us now conclude by way of these seven species of prophecy that the excellence of the human soul so far exceeds matter that, in a body that has been mastered and calmed and that is only half in life, it sees much more clearly and operates much more and much more perfectly than it can in an active body. It's as if it no longer needs the body's help to perform wondrous deeds. In all this it is obvious how perfectly the soul accords with things celestial, how close is its kinship with God: as often as it returns to itself, it becomes a participant in the celestial mysteries and in providence divine. 38

: III :

The third sign: from purposeful activity in the arts and in governance.[95]

The rest of the animals live either without an art or skill or just with a single one to whose deployment they do not [freely] betake themselves but to which they are drawn by the law of fate. An indication of this is that they never improve over time in doing what they do. Men by contrast are the inventors of numberless arts that they pursue at their own choosing. Evidence is the fact that individual men practise many of the arts and they develop and become more skilled as a result of daily practice; and what is marvelous is that human arts make on their own whatever nature itself makes: it is as if we were not her slaves but her rivals. Zeuxis so painted grapes that the birds flew up to them.[96] Apelles so painted a mare and a dog that horses passing by whinnied and other dogs barked.[97] Praxiteles sculpted a marble statue of Venus in a temple 1

naturae, sed aemuli. Uvas ita pinxit Zeuxis, ut aves ad eas advolarent. Apelles equam ita pinxit et canem, ut praetereuntes equi hinnirent, latrarent canes. Praxiteles in quodam Indorum templo Venerem marmore adeo venustam expressit, ut vix a libidinosis transeuntium conspectibus tuta et pudica servaretur. Archytas Tarentinus columbam e ligno mathematica disciplina fecit, libravit, inflavit spiritu adeo ut volaret. Egyptii, ut tradit Mercurius, deorum statuas construebant tales ut loquerentur et irent. Archimedes Syracusanus aeneum caelum fecit, in quo omnes septem planetarum motus verissime conficiebantur ut in caelo, et ipsum volvebatur ut caelum. Mitto Aegyptiorum pyramides, Romanorum Graecorumque aedificia, metallorum officinas et vitri. Denique homo omnia divinae naturae opera imitatur et naturae inferioris opera perficit, corrigit et emendat.

2 Similis ergo ferme vis hominis est naturae divinae, quandoquidem homo per se ipsum, id est per suum consilium atque artem, regit se ipsum a corporalis naturae limitibus minime circumscriptum, et singula naturae altioris opera aemulatur. Et tanto minus quam bruta naturae inferioris eget subsidio, quanto pauciora corporis munimenta sortitus est a natura quam bruta, sed ipsemet illa sua copia construit alimenta, vestes, stramenta, habitacula, suppellectilia, arma. Ideo cum ipse sua facultate se fulciat, fulcit uberius quam bestias ipsa natura. Hinc proficiscitur inenarrabilis varietas voluptatum hos quinque sensus corporis oblectantium, quas ipsimet nobis proprio ingenio machinamur. Bruta brevissimis naturae claustris concluduntur. Non solum ad corporis necessitatem noster animus respicit, sicut bestiae naturae imperio mancipatae, sed ad oblectamenta sensuum varia, quasi quaedam pabula phantasiae. Neque solum per varia blandimenta ipsi phantasiae animus adula-

of the Indians that was so alluring that it could scarcely be kept safe and unspotted from the lustful gazes of passersby.[98] Using his mathematical learning, Archytas of Tarentum made a dove out of wood, adjusted its balance, and inflated it with spirit so that it could fly.[99] Mercurius reports that the Egyptians constructed statues of the gods in such a way that they would speak and walk.[100] Archimedes of Syracuse made an orrery or bronze model of the heavens in which the seven motions of the planets were all reproduced exactly as they are in the heavens, and the whole revolved exactly as the heavens do.[101] I won't go into the pyramids of the Egyptians, the edifices of the Romans and Greeks, the workshops of metals and of glass. In sum, man imitates all the works of divine nature, and perfects all the works of lower nature, correcting and emending them.

Man's power is very like the power of divine nature, since man rules himself through himself, that is, through his own counsel and art: uncircumscribed by the limits of corporeal nature, he emulates the individual works of higher nature. He needs the help of lower nature far less than the animals to the extent that he has been allotted fewer protections for his body than the brutes; and he has used his own resources to grow his own food, and to make his own clothes, coverings, dwellings, furnishings, and arms. Since he therefore supports himself by his own ability, he supports himself more lavishly than nature herself supports the beasts. This is the source of an untold variety of pleasures that delight the body's five senses, pleasures that our own wit and inventiveness devise for ourselves. The brutes are enclosed within the narrow limits of nature. Our rational soul not only looks to our body's need, just as the beasts are bound to nature's sway, but to the various delights of the senses too, the particular dishes as it were of the phantasy. The rational soul not only flatters the phantasy by way of various blandishments, daily it wins it over with various games as if in jest. But in the meantime the cogitative reason also acts 2

tur, dum quasi per iocum diversis ludis delinit quotidie phantasiam, verumetiam agit interdum cogitatrix ratio serius, et suae prolis propagandae cupida emicat foras, et quanto polleat ingenio, evidenter ostentat per variam lanificiorum sericique texturam, picturas, sculpturas et aedificia. In quibus componendis saepe nullum corporis respicit commodum, nullum sensuum blandimentum, cum aliquando sponte ex iis incommodum et molestiam patiatur, sed facundiae suae amplificationem approbationemque virtutis.

3 In iis artificiis animadvertere licet, quemadmodum homo et omnes et undique tractat mundi materias, quasi homini omnes subiiciantur. Tractat, inquam, elementa, lapides, metalla, plantas et animalia, et in multas traducit formas atque figuras, quod numquam bestiae faciunt. Neque uno est elemento contentus aut quibusdam ut bruta, sed utitur omnibus, quasi sit omnium dominus. Terram calcat, sulcat aquam, altissimis turribus conscendit in aerem, ut pennas Daedali vel Icari praetermittam. Accendit ignem et foco familiariter utitur et delectatur praecipue ipse solus. Merito caelesti elemento solum caeleste animal delectatur; caelesti virtute ascendit caelum atque metitur. Supercaelesti mente transcendit caelum. Nec utitur tantum elementis homo, sed ornat; quod nullum facit brutorum. Quam mirabilis per omnem orbem terrae cultura! Quam stupenda aedificiorum structura et urbium! Irrigatio aquarum quam artificiosa! Vicem gerit dei qui omnia elementa habitat colitque omnia, et terrae praesens non abest ab aethere. Atqui non modo elementis, verumetiam elementorum animalibus utitur omnibus, terrenis, aquatilibus, volatilibus ad escam, commoditatem et voluptatem, supernis caelestibusque ad doctrinam magicaeque miracula. Nec utitur brutis solum, sed et imperat.

with greater seriousness, and desirous of propagating its offspring, blazes forth externally. It displays for all to see the powers of its ingenuity and skill by way of the varied textures of wools and of silk, and through pictures, sculptures, and edifices. In making these it often has no regard for the body's comfort or for delighting the senses (since at times it voluntarily endures discomfort and annoyance from them); rather it looks to the full display of its eloquence and to confirmation of its power.[102]

In these artifacts one can observe how man uses all the world's 3
materials and uses them everywhere as though they were all subject to him: he uses the elements, stones, metals, plants, and animals, fashioning them into many forms and figures, which the beasts never do. Nor is he content with just one of the elements or with particular elements like the brutes: he employs them all as though he were the lord of all. He tramples on the earth, furrows the water, ascends into the air in the tallest towers—and I am leaving aside the wings of Daedalus and Icarus.[103] He kindles fire and he alone uses and delights especially in the familial hearth. In justice only a celestial animal delights in the celestial element: with heavenly power he ascends and measures the heavens; and with his superheavenly mind he transcends the heavens. Man not only uses the elements, he adorns them, which no brute does. Throughout the whole globe how marvelous is [man's] culture of the earth! How stupendous is the construction of his buildings and his cities! How skillful is his use of water in irrigation! In inhabiting all the elements and cultivating them all, he performs the office of God: while present on earth he is not absent from the aether. Not only does he use the elements, he uses all the animals living in the elements, the terrestrial, the aquatic, those who fly, for his food, convenience, and pleasure; and he uses the supernal and celestial beings for instruction and for the wonders of magic. And not only does he use the beasts, he rules over them. It can happen at times that particular beasts armed with the weapons given them

Fieri quidem potest, ut armis quibusdam a natura acceptis bruta nonnulla quandoque vel impetum in hominem faciant vel hominis effugiant impetum; homo autem acceptis a se ipso armis et vitat ferarum impetus, et fugat et domat. Quis vidit umquam homines ullos sub bestiarum imperio detineri, quemadmodum ubique videmus tam immanissimarum ferarum quam mitium armenta per omnem vitam parere hominibus? Non imperat bestiis homo crudeliter tantum, sed gubernat etiam illas, fovet et docet. Universalis providentia dei, qui est universalis causa, propria est. Homo igitur qui universaliter cunctis et viventibus et non viventibus providet est quidam deus. Deus est proculdubio animalium qui utitur omnibus, imperat cunctis, instruit plurima. Deum quoque esse constitit elementorum qui habitat colitque omnia. Deum denique omnium materiarum qui tractat omnes, vertit et format. Qui tot tantisque in rebus corpori dominatur et immortalis dei gerit vicem est proculdubio immortalis.

4 Sed artes huiusmodi, licet materiam mundi figurent et animalibus imperent, atque ita deum naturae artificem imitentur, sunt tamen artibus illis inferiores, quae regnum imitatae divinum humanae gubernationis suscipiunt curam. Singula bruta vix ad sui ipsius vel brevem natorum curam sufficiunt; homo autem unus tanta abundat perfectione, ut sibi ipsi imperet primum, quod bestiae nullae faciunt, gubernet deinde familiam, administret rempublicam, regat gentes et toti imperet[46] orbi. Et quasi qui ad regnandum sit natus, est omnino servitutis impatiens. Adde quod boni publici gratia subit mortem, quod bruta non agunt, utpote qui singula haec mortalia despicit bona, communis aeternique boni firmitati confisus.

5 Ceterum ad praesentem vitam artes huiusmodi pertinere alicui forsitan videbuntur, quamvis non sit tanta cura ad vitam praesentem necessaria, sed spectet potius ad divinitatis providentiam imi-

by nature either attack man or flee from his attack, but man armed with the weapons he has given himself both repels the attack of wild beasts and puts them to flight and tames them. Who has ever seen people subject to the sway of any beasts in the same way we see herds of completely wild and domestic animals alike everywhere obeying herdsmen throughout their lives? Man rules the beasts with cruelty but he also governs, fosters, and teaches them. Universal providence is properly God's who is the universal cause. So man who universally provides for all living and non-living things is a kind of god. Doubtless he is god of the animals since he uses and rules them all, and instructs many of them. He is also manifestly god of the elements since he lives in and cultivates each one; and finally he is god of all materials since he handles, changes, and forms them all. He who rules over the body in so many and in such important ways, and who performs the role of immortal God is undoubtedly himself immortal.

Although these arts fashion the matter of the world and rule 4
over the animals and so imitate God as the artificer of nature, yet they are inferior to the arts that, in imitating the kingdom divine, undertake the task of governing men. Individual beasts are hardly able to take even brief care of themselves or their young. But one man abounds in such perfection that first he gives commands to himself, which none of the beasts do, then he governs his family, administers the state, reigns over peoples, and commands the whole world. Born as it were to rule, he is completely impatient of servitude. Moreover, he submits to death for the public good, which beasts never do, inasmuch as he despises these perishable goods and puts his trust in the steadfastness of the common and eternal good.

Perhaps these arts, however, will strike someone as pertaining 5
to this present life, even though such an intense concern with them is unnecessary for this present life but aims rather at imitating the providence of the divinity. Let us consider those arts,

tandam. Consideremus igitur artes illas, quae non modo corporali victui necessariae non sunt, sed plurimum noxiae, quales sunt omnes scientiae liberales, quarum studia corpus enervant et vitae impediunt commoda: subtilis computatio numerorum, figurarum curiosa descriptio, linearum obscurissimi motus, superstitiosa musicae consonantia, astrorum observatio diuturna, naturalium inquisitio causarum, diuturnorum investigatio, oratorum facundia poetarumque furores. In iis omnibus animus hominis corporis despicit ministerium, utpote qui quandoque possit, et iam nunc incipiat, sine corporis auxilio vivere.

6 Unum illud est in primis animadvertendum, quod artificis solertis opus artificiose constructum non potest quilibet, qua ratione quove modo sit constructum discernere, sed solum qui eodem pollet artis ingenio. Nemo enim discerneret qua via Archimedes sphaeras constituit aeneas eisque motus motibus caelestibus similes tradidit, nisi simili esset ingenio praeditus. Et qui propter ingenii similitudinem discernit, is certe posset easdem construere,[47] postquam agnovit, modo non deesset materia. Cum igitur homo caelorum ordinem unde moveantur, quo progrediantur et quibus mensuris, quidve pariant, viderit, quis neget eum esse ingenio, ut ita loquar, paene eodem quo et auctor ille caelorum, ac posse quodammodo caelos facere, si instrumenta nactus fuerit materiamque caelestem, postquam facit eos nunc, licet ex alia materia, tamen persimiles ordine?

therefore, which are not only unnecessary for the body's sustenance but for the most part harmful to it. Of this kind are all the liberal arts whose study weakens the body and prevents us from living a comfortable life: the subtle computing of numbers, the meticulous describing of [geometrical] figures, the obscurest motions of [astronomical] lines, the exacting consonance of music,[104] the daily observation of the stars, the interrogation of natural causes, the investigation into things of long duration, the eloquence of orators, the frenzies of the poets. In all these, man's rational soul scorns the body's assistance like someone who is able to live at some point (and who may begin to live even now) without the body's help.

We must pay especial attention to one fact. Not just anybody 6
can take the work of a clever artisan that has been skillfully constructed and discern by what rational principle or manner it has been constructed: this can only be done by someone who has acquired the same skill in the art. For nobody would be able to discern how Archimedes put the bronze spheres together and gave them motions like the heavenly motions unless he were endowed with a like genius.[105] And the person who did discern this because he had a like genius would certainly be able to construct them once he knew [how], and as long as he had the materials to hand. Since this person sees the order of the heavens, whence they are moved, whither they proceed, with what measures, and to what they give rise, who will deny both that he has almost the same genius, so to speak, as the author of the heavens, and that he is capable in a way of making the heavens, should he ever obtain the instruments and the celestial material, since in fact he is making them now, albeit from a different material, yet in the same order?

Quatuor hominis dotes in artibus.

7 In humanis artibus quatuor animi nostri emicant dotes excellentissimae: facilitas ad percipiendum velocissima, memoria amplissima ac penitus indelebilis,[48] sagacissima praedictio futurorum, verborum usus innumerabilium.

8 Quam divinum putas in Homero viguisse acumen, qui et caecus et inops tot et tanta percepit, tam egregie cecinit, ut cunctas in eum tum humanas tum divinas artes Plato asserat concurrisse. Quam divinum in Didymo Alexandrino, quem scribit Hieronymus a pueritia excaecatum postea tamen dialecticen, physicen, theologiam prae ceteris ebibisse, et quod mirum est, geometram evasisse mirabilem et geometricas figuras describere solitum et docere; egregia quoque theologiae opera condidisse. Divinum certe iis lumen ea nascentibus infudit et quaerentibus revelavit quae impossibile fuisset humanis studiis invenire. Et si Plato Aristotelesque in libris civilium institutionum scribunt regiones alias aliis esse exercendo ingenio aptiores, compertum tamen habemus non in oriente solum atque meridie, sed etiam in occidente septentrioneque et complurimos homines, et frequenter in qualibet arte mirifice claruisse. Si regionum saeculorumque diversitas diversitatem maximam necessario efficit in corporum habitu, in ingeniis vero minimam, et hanc ipsam consilio studioque corrigimus, quis non videat ingenium hominis natura sua locis et temporibus non esse subiectum?

9 Sequitur indelebilis illa memoria, qua excelluerunt quamplurimi. Mithridates duarum ac viginti gentium rex singulis absque interprete ius dicebat. Cyrus et Lucius Scipio omnium suorum ci-

Man's four gifts in the arts.

In the arts of men four excellent gifts of our rational soul are most striking: a lightning fast, perceptive acuity, a memory that is stocked and well-nigh imperishable, a razor-edged ability to predict future events, and an ability to deploy a huge vocabulary. 7

Consider how divine an acuity flourished in Homer: though blind and destitute, he saw so many mighty deeds and sang about them so well that Plato asserted that all the human and divine arts alike met in him.[106] How divine an acuity waxed in Didymus of Alexander whom St. Jerome describes as blind since childhood; and yet later he quaffed down dialectic, natural science, and theology more deeply than all the others, and became, wondrous in itself, a wondrous geometer accustomed to describing and to teaching geometrical figures; he also composed marvelous works of theology.[107] Certainly the divine light poured such learning into these men when they were born, and revealed to their inquiring minds what it was impossible for the studies of man to discover. If in their books on political institutions Plato and Aristotle write that certain regions are more suitable for the exercise of mental acuity than others,[108] nonetheless we have frequently stumbled on many men not only in the east and the south, but in the west and north too who have achieved a remarkable distinction in some art. If the diversity of regions and of epochs necessarily induces the greatest diversity in the habit of bodies, but the least diversity in mental skills (and this diversity we correct by advice and study), isn't it obvious that the mental skill of man is not, in its own nature, subject to place and time? 8

Next follows the imperishable memory in which so many men have excelled. Mithridates, the sovereign of twenty-two peoples, used to issue his edicts without an interpreter to each people individually.[109] Cyrus and Lucius Scipio knew the names of all their fellow citizens.[110] Fabius Maximus and Lucullus knew from mem- 9

vium scieba⟨n⟩t nomina. Fabius Maximus et Lucullus omnes omnium gentium historias memoria tenebant.[49] Seneca inquit se duo milia nominum recitata eodem ordine reddidisse, ducentos quoque versus a discipulis pronuntiatos se ordine retrogrado recitasse. Scribit Augustinus fuisse quendam suis temporibus qui multa legerat neque aliquid umquam eorum quae legerat oblitus fuerat; fuisse Romae alium qui comoediam totam, dum recitaretur, mandavit memoriae. Tot tantarumque rerum capacitas, tanta in iis quae sunt accepta stabilitas angusto cerebri angulo comprehendi et fluxa eius labilique materia servari non potest, sed amplissimo eget stabilissimoque divini animi receptaculo.

10 Est et futurorum praedictio illa qua pollebant Chaldaei et Aegyptii mathematici. Certe illa substantia in futuro non deficit, cuius praesaga virtus ita totum futurum anticipat, sicut memor potentia totum praeteritum recolit. Est autem substantia haec aeterna quae in aeternum momentum[50] colligit labilia temporum intervalla.

11 Postremo loquendi usus atque scribendi homini proprius divinam quandam indicat nobis inesse mentem, qua careant bestiae. Absque sermone ita nos possemus vivere, sicut et bestiae et homines muti. Ideo ad excellentius aliquod opus est nobis sermo tributus, videlicet tamquam mentis interpres, infinitorum inventorum praeco et nuntius infinitus.

12 Neque somniet Epicurus bestias sicut et nos ratione pollere, verum deesse illis sermonis et manuum usum, per quem intus latentem extra significent rationem. Quoniam natura in[51] rebus necessariis non deficit, superfluis non abundat, arboribus non dedit pedes, non brachia; terrenum enim illarum corpus solo fixum ubique terrea alitur alimonia. Brutorum corporibus tamquam mi-

ory all the histories of every people.[111] Seneca says he had taken the recitation of two thousand names and had repeated them in order, and had taken two hundred verses recited by his disciples and repeated them in reverse order.[112] Augustine writes that one of his contemporaries who had read widely never forgot anything of what he had read, and of someone else at Rome who committed a whole comedy to memory while it was being recited.[113] The capacity for so many and such extensive memories, and such a steadfastness in those which we have stored up, cannot be encompassed by some narrow corner of the brain or preserved by its changing and fleeting material; it needs rather the receptacle, in all its amplitude and stability, of the divine soul.

There is also the prediction of future events in which the Chaldaean and Egyptian astrologers excelled. Certainly that [soul-] substance, whose prophetic power anticipates the whole future just as its recollective power remembers the whole past, is not going to fail in the future. Rather, this very substance, which gathers the fleeting intervals of time into an eternal moment, is itself eternal. 10

Finally the fact that it is proper for man to speak and to write indicates that a divine mind, which the beasts lack, is present in us. We are able to survive without speech just as beasts and dumb men do, so speech has been granted us for some more excellent work: to be as it were, the mind's interpreter, the herald and infinite messenger of infinite discoveries. 11

Don't let Epicurus dream that the beasts are potent in reason as we are, but that they lack the use of speech and of hands by which they might externally signify the reason latent within them.[114] Because nature is not lacking in necessities but does not abound in superfluities, it does not bestow feet or arms on trees; for the earthy body of trees is rooted in the earth and everywhere nourished by nutriment from the earth. But food that is completely earthy does not everywhere suffice for the bodies of beasts, since they are less earthy; and so they have been equipped with feet the 12

nus terrenis non omnis terreus cibus est ubique sufficiens, ideo ad quaerendum commodius alimentum pedibus sunt instructa. Phantasia illorum paucos aliquos et confusos conceptus habet et ad usum dumtaxat corporis necessarios, qui mugitu, latratu, hinnitu, garritu,[52] gannitu, fremitu seu nutibus sufficienter exprimi possunt. Verum mens hominis, infinitarum distinctarumque inventrix rerum, usu sermonis innumerabilis suffulta est, quasi quodam digno eius interprete; manibus quoque munita tamquam aptissimis instrumentis ad inventa mentis innumerabilia fabricanda. Quae quidem instrumenta Natura eadem dedisset et bestiis, si illis inesset artifex idem interior talibus instrumentis usurus. Ergo tot concipit mens in se ipsa intellegendo, quot deus intellegendo facit in mundo. Totidem loquendo exprimit et in aere. Totidem calamo scribit in chartis. Totidem fabricando in materia mundi figurat. Quapropter dementem esse illum constat, qui negaverit animam, quae in artibus et gubernationibus est aemula dei, esse divinam.

: IV :

Quartum signum: ab effectu miraculorum.

1 Non solum vero in formanda et figuranda per rationem artis materia, sicut diximus, mens humana ius sibi divinum vendicat, verumetiam in speciebus rerum per imperium transmutandis. Quod quidem opus miraculum appellatur, non quia praeter naturam sit nostrae animae, quando dei fit instrumentum, sed quia, cum magnum quiddam sit et fiat raro, parit admirationem. Hinc admiramur quod animae hominum deo deditae imperent elementis, citent ventos, nubes cogant[53] in pluvias, nebulas pellant, humano-

better to search for food. Their phantasy has a few, confused conceptions that are necessary for the body's use alone and that can be given sufficient expression by lowing, barking, neighing, chattering, yelping, snorting, or by nods. But man's mind, the inventor of infinite, distinct things, has been undergirded by the use of speech in its immeasurable richness as in a way its worthy interpreter. It has also been protected by hands as the most suitable instruments for fashioning the mind's numberless inventions. The same nature would have given these instruments also to the beasts if the same inner artisan [the mind] had been present in them to make use of such instruments. Therefore the mind in understanding conceives as many things in itself as God in understanding creates in the world: in speaking it utters them in the air; it writes them down on sheets with a quill; in fabricating it figures them forth in the material of the world. So anyone who denies the divinity of the soul, which is God's emulator in the arts and in governance, is clearly demented.

: IV :

The fourth sign: the evidence from the effect of miracles.

Not only in forming and shaping matter through the rational principle of art, as we said, does the human mind appropriate for itself the divine right; it does so too through [its] sovereignty in transmuting the species of things. The resulting work is called a miracle, not because it is the supernatural work of our soul when it becomes God's instrument, but because it induces wonder, being a mighty event and one that happens rarely. Hence we are in awe when souls of men dedicated to God command the elements, rouse winds, compel clouds to rain, dispel mists, cure the diseases of human bodies, and so on. The poets of various nations sing 1

rum corporum curent morbos et reliqua. Quae palam facta fuisse quibusdam saeculis apud varias nationes poetae canunt; narrant historici; non negant excellentissimi quique philosophi nostri, praesertim Platonici; testantur theologi veteres, Mercurius in primis et Orpheus; posteriores quoque theologi verbo et opere comprobarunt.

2 Miraberis forsitan si miraculorum rationes exquiram. Sed audi. In primo libro disputatum est essentiam tertiam esse sub angelo et super totam mundi materiam; a numine formari, formare materiam; accipere quidem formas spiritales a numine, dare vero materiae corporales. In tertio quoque libro constitit essentiam tertiam nihil esse aliud quam rationales animas tam nostras quam nostris superiores. Hinc efficitur apud Platonicos sectatoresque Avicennae, ut omnis rationalis anima per essentiam suam atque potentiam super totam sit mundi materiam, totam movere possit atque formare, videlicet quando ad haec dei fit instrumentum.

3 Verumtamen talis est ordo rerum: habent omnes animae rationales, ut diximus, intellectuale caput, rationale medium, infimum vero vivificum. Media haec vis est animae proprietas; vis autem intellectualis est radius quidam superioris intellectus demissus in animam et in superiorem intellectum iterum se reflectens; vis quoque vivifica actus est animae redundans in corpus et inde resultans in animam, sicut lumen solis in nube secundum proprietatem suam splendor est: ut solem respicit, radius; ut nubem implet, est pallor. Intellectus intellegibile suspicit et circa ipsum intellegibile permanet in se ipso. Ratio currit, sed in se ipsam. Vivifica vis infra se currit usque ad aliud, dum implet corpus. Quoniam vero per hanc infimam sui partem sive umbram animae longissime a sua di-

that in particular ages these miracles were openly performed, and the historians tell the same story. Certain of our most excellent philosophers, especially the Platonists, do not deny it; the ancient theologians bear witness to it, especially Mercurius Trismegistus and Orpheus; and later theologians too confirm it orally and in writing.

Perhaps you will be surprised if I inquire into the reasons behind miracles. But listen to me. In the first book it was argued that there is a third essence under the angel but above the whole matter of the world, an essence which is formed by the divinity but itself forms matter, and which receives spiritual forms from the divinity but gives corporeal forms to matter. In the third book it was also established that the third essence is nothing other than [all] rational souls, both our souls and souls higher than ours. It follows that for the Platonists and the followers of Avicenna every rational soul through its essence and power is above the whole matter of the world and can move and form the whole—when, that is, it becomes God's instrument for doing so.[115] 2

Nevertheless the universal order is such that all rational souls, as we said, have an intellectual head, a rational middle, and a life-giving base. The middle power is the property of the soul, while the intellectual power is a ray of the higher intellect sent down into the soul and reflecting back to the higher intellect; and the life-giving power is an act of the soul flowing down into the body and leaping up again into the soul. In the same way the light of the sun in a cloud is splendor in and of itself, but as it refers to the sun it is a ray, and as it fills a cloud it is the cloud's pale color. The intellect receives what is intelligible, but with regard to this intelligible it rests in itself; the reason moves discursively but returns to itself; and the life-giving power flows down under itself to another when it overflows into the body. Since souls depart furthest from their dignity, however, via this lowest part, this shadow of theirs, when they approach bodies, the result is that these powers govern- 3

gnitate discedunt corporibus propinquantes, factum est ut vires huiusmodi rectrices corporum (remissa quodammodo vel intermissa amplitudine illa dominationis, quam anima super universitatem corporum possidet), singulae sint singulis distributae corporibus, quibus astrictae dum sunt, propriam suorum corporum agunt curam, ac ferme negligunt alienam. Quid eas corporibus alligat? Ut Plato vult, amor, id est vitae exuberantis affectus ad proxima sibi vivificanda proclivior. Diversis autem animarum rationalium speciebus proximae sunt diversae corporum species. Hinc fieri vult, ut aliae rationales animae cum aliis corporibus conspiraverint, aliae cum sphaeris, aliae cum sideribus, cum aliis aliae, denique aliae cum corporibus hominum. Atque ex certis quibusdam seminum intimorum dispositionibus a providentia constitutis aliae humanae animae aliis humanis corporibus regendis magis conveniunt. Et, ut summatim dicam, cuiusque animae rationalis vis illa vivifica, quoniam ad tertiam essentiam pertinet, aequam vim habet ad corpora quaelibet, sed per amatorium quendam instinctum corporibus aliis aliae sese[54] movendis accommodant, conferente ad hoc videlicet temperatione divina, et uno quodam instinctu cessante, vis illa vivifica evadit libera, ut novo affecta instinctu corpus aliud quodammodo regat et moveat.

4 Si pars haec infima naturas omnes corporum superat, multo magis media atque summa. Suprema, id est mens, usque adeo supereminet, ut nihil umquam sapiat corporale, divinorum dumtaxat avida, stabilis natura, intellegentia subita. Media, id est ratiocinandi facultas, eminet quidem et ipsa magis quam infima, et nunc quidem, ut diximus alias, ascendit in mentem, quando susceptis a mente principiis demonstrandi, universales rerum naturalium ra-

ing bodies (and which have been remitted or intermitted in a way by the amplitude of the sway the soul exercises over the universal realm of bodies) are individually distributed to individual bodies. And as long as they are bound to such, they take proper care of their own bodies and neglect others almost totally. What binds these powers to bodies? According to Plato, it is love, that is, the overflowing desire of an overflowing life to give life to what is closest to itself.[116] But different species of bodies are closest to different species of rational souls. Hence Plato argues that various rational souls harmonize with various bodies: some with the spheres, some with the fixed stars, some with other bodies, and some finally with the bodies of men. From certain dispositions of the inner seeds established by providence various human souls are more suited to ruling various human bodies. In short, the life-giving power of each rational soul, because it pertains to the third essence, has a power appropriate to all bodies. But through a particular amatory instinct various souls devote themselves to moving various bodies, drawn to do so by a tempering divine. But if that one particular instinct ceases, the life-giving power becomes free to be affected by a new instinct and in a way to rule and move another body.

If this lowest part surpasses all the natures of bodies, then the middle and highest parts do so even more. The highest part, the mind, is supereminent to such a degree that it can never have a sense of anything corporeal, being eager only for things divine, steadfast in its nature, and instantaneous in its understanding. The middle part, the faculty of reasoning, is more eminent too than the lowest power: at one time (as we said elsewhere) it ascends to the mind, when—having received from the mind the principles of demonstration—it inquires by way of reasoning into the universal rational principles of natural things; at another time, however, it declines towards the life-giving power when it believes the phantasy, listens to the senses, and fawns upon the body. But 4

tiones inquirit argumentando, nunc autem ad vivificam declinat potentiam, quando credit phantasiae, auscultat sensibus, blanditur et corpori. Ascendit autem in mentem supernorum capiendorum amore, descendit in potentiam infimam amore inferiorum gubernandorum. Merito cum sit utrorumque media, diligit utraque, et tamquam eminentior quam infima, dum infima corpus unum regit solum, ipsa plura movet atque gubernat. Nam dum rectrix facultas corporis tuum solum alit corpus perque sensum et concupiscentiam servit tui corporis alimoniae, ratio tua et tui corporis agit curam et aliorum, atque in externa materia[55] fabricat artificia. Haec quoque cum aeque valeat quaslibet tractare materia, aliis tamen temporibus[56] alias, quocumque rapit amor, tractandas aggreditur. Cessante amore per quem hunc sculpit lapidem, statuam dimittit subito. Trahente amore ad vasa fictilia, aggreditur figulinam.

5 Quando de tractandis corporibus loquimur, mentem illam corporum penitus contemptricem parumper intermittimus, de ratione magis et rectrice potentia loquimur. Hae utique ambae, licet ad quaelibet mundi corpora propter communem naturam essentiae tertiae parem vim habeant, in illud tamen agunt potissimum, in quod magis afficiuntur, divina illa seminum temperatione non prohibente. Affectus animorum illorum qui supra nos sunt, stabiliores sunt nostris atque eundem semper retexunt ordinem, consueto semper tenore progredientes, quoniam in illis tam suprema vis quam media sursum vergit, contemplationi incumbens aeternae. Sola vis infima opera variat, sed vicissitudines agit, et illas quidem ordinatissimas, ita ut in ipsa etiam mutatione videatur esse stabilitas, dum idem observatur tenor, eademque similiter retexuntur. Sed utcumque sit, formae rerum tribus animorum illorum viribus insitae causae sunt formarum, quae in mundanis corporibus expri-

it ascends into the mind by its love of understanding things supernal; and it descends into the lowest power by its love of ruling things inferior. Since it is the intermediary, it justly loves both extremes; and being more eminent than the lowest, it moves and governs many things, whereas the lowest power rules over one body alone. For while the ruling power of the body nourishes your body only, and preserves your body's sustenance through sensation and concupiscent desire, your reason is concerned both with your body and with other bodies, and it fashions artifacts in external matter. This reason, since it is equally adept in handling all materials, also sets about handling different materials at different times, in whatever way love takes it. When the love that moved it to carve stone ceases, it instantly sets the statue aside. When love attracts it to earthenware pots, it takes up the potter's art.

When we speak of handling bodies, we are briefly neglecting 5
the mind that is utterly contemptuous of bodies, and speaking rather about the reason and the ruling power. These two powers, though they are equally potent with regard to all the world's bodies because of the common nature of the third essence, nevertheless act most on the body to which they are more disposed, as long, that is, as that divine tempering of the seeds [within] is not preventing them. The dispositions of the souls above us are more stable than our own and they have always exhibited the same order, progressing as they always do in their even and customary tenor, because in them the highest power and the middle power each turns upward, devoting itself to eternal contemplation. Only the lowest power varies its works. But it enacts its changes—and even these are most ordered—in such a way that stability appears to prevail even in the mutation; and while it preserves the same tenor, the same motions are likewise retraced. But howsoever this happens, the forms of things innate in the three powers of those supernal souls are the causes of the forms that are expressed in worldly bodies. And what one might call the fatal imaginations,

muntur. Atque, ut ita dicam, fatales imaginationes, quae gradatim idolis animorum illorum suboriuntur, quasi praegnantium mulierum affectus vehementissimi, quicquid sibi fingunt, in sphaeris suis sequentibusque tamquam foetibus exprimunt.

6 Nostra quoque anima erga corpus hoc affecta secundum suorum seminum ordinem corpus hoc ex ipsa vi corporis rectrice figurat. Quid huic corpori praestat certam quatuor humorum complexionem, quid faciei colores et liniamenta, nisi anima? Anima quoque contra naturam corporis ponderosi ipsum[57] agit sursum et quatuor invicem vincit contraria. Neque miraculum hoc miratur quisquam. Quantum vero vis eadem per phantasiam valeat in formando vehementioribus affectibus corpore, in superioribus diximus, siquidem pro affectuum diversitate diversas qualitates producit in membris: ira[58] calorem, rubedinem, amarumque saporem et alvi fluxum; timore frigus atque pallorem; maerore sudoris humorem albedinemque caeruleam; anxietate siccitatem atque nigredinem. Harum profecto qualitatum ipsi animi affectus auctores sunt, quia saepe ad tales aliquas qualitates movent priori nostrae complexioni contrarias. Atque, ut Hippocrates docet et Galenus, inveteratus affectus priorem mutat corporis complexionem et in suam trahit naturam. Hoc agit phantasia.

7 Quid autem ratio in artibus et gubernationibus operetur, alias declaravimus; proinde quid a rectrice corporis potentia in proprio corpore fiat per virtutem vivificam et affectus illi servientes, hic explanavimus. Fit insuper ab ea nonnihil in corporibus alienis quae sibi propinquant, quando per naturalem calorem concoquit cibos calefacitque tangentes. Anima quoque materna in corpus alienum agit, quando nutrit foetus in alvo, quod quidem explet ex conti-

which gradually arise in the idola of those souls, like the vehement desires of pregnant women, take whatever they are imagining to themselves and express it in their spheres and in what attends the spheres as though in embryos.

Our soul also, which is disposed towards this body according to the order of its own seeds, fashions the body by way of the very power which rules over the body. Unless it is the soul, what gives this body a particular complexion of the four humors and our face its tones and lineaments? Also, the soul raises a heavy body upwards, contrary to its nature, and prevails in turn over the four opposing elements; and no one is amazed at this miracle. Earlier we said how powerful is this ruling power in using the phantasy to shape the body with vehement desires, seeing that it produces different qualities in the body's parts according to the diversity of its emotions: from wrath comes heat, redness, a bitter taste, and flux of the bowels; from fear comes cold and pallor; from sadness, sweating and a dark, ashen color; from anxiety, dryness and blackness. The emotions of the rational soul are the sources of these qualities because they often impel us towards some such qualities that are contrary to our prior complexion. And, as Hippocrates and Galen teach us, an emotion of long standing changes the body's first complexion and drags it towards its own nature.[117] This is what the phantasy does. 6

Elsewhere we have declared what reason achieves in the arts and in governance;[118] and here we have explained what is produced by the body's ruling power in its own body through the life-giving power and the emotions subservient to it. Moreover, it produces results in foreign bodies close to it when it digests foods through natural heat and heats things in contact with it. The mother's soul acts on a foreign body when it nourishes the fetus in her womb in that she feeds it from the tubes that continually join the fetus to her maternal body. The soul forms not only a body close to it but one also at times remote. Long after semen has been ejaculated by 7

nuatis vinclis quibus foetus materno corpori alligatur. Neque propinquum dumtaxat corpus format, sed quandoque remotum. Iacto siquidem a viro semine in matricem et diu postea, viro absente, virtus formatrix relicta in semine viget ibi et vicem paternae animae gerit in semine corpusque effingit humanum, ceu cum quis lapidem iacit procul, virtus expultrix lapidi immissa a iaciente, quam diu regnat in lapide, tam diu lapidem pellit, ea scilicet aeris plaga et ad illud signum, qua et ad quod iactor ille direxerat. Si pars animae regendo corpori accommodata per vivificam vim aliquid operatur in corpus alienum atque remotum, cur non etiam per vim sensitivam hac eminentiorem, per affectus scilicet phantasiae? Ergo phantasia instar virtutis vivificae format et ipsa proprium corpus, ut diximus, quotiens acrioribus affectibus agitatur. Format etiam fascinationibus et maleficiis alienum. Neque mirum est animam facere talia affectibus suis, si herbae quaedam faciunt aut lapides suis vaporibus, caelestibus tamen animis aspirantibus. Neque deest animae continuatio mediorum, per quae in alienum corpus transigat actionem.

8 Quippe venefici hominis phantasia, infensa infantis teneriori corpusculo, febrem affectat puero. Imaginatio febris spiritus febriles vibrat, id est cholericos, sicut imaginatio coitus seminales spiritus et genitalia membra. Cholericus et febrifer spiritus ille perculsus vapores foetidos atque febriferos, si qui in venefici hominis corpore sunt, exsuscitat. Hi cum primum incitati sunt, una cum spiritu proruunt illuc tamquam sagittae, quo malefica phantasia quasi ad signum intenderat. Maxime vero ex oculis emicant senioris perque oculos pueri transeunt, tamquam ex vitreis materiis perque materias vitreas radii, spiritusque inficiunt pueri et humo-

a man into a fertile womb and he has departed, the formative power remaining in the seed thrives there: it takes the place of the paternal soul and fashions the human body in the seed. The analogy is with someone who hurls a stone a long way: the expulsive power imparted to the stone by the thrower impels the stone as long as it is dominant in the stone, and impels it through that part of the air and to that mark through which and to which the thrower had aimed it. If the part of the soul suited to ruling the body does something to a foreign and distant body through the life-giving power, then why not through the sensitive power too, which is more eminent—through the emotions, that is, of the phantasy? Thus the phantasy, like the life-giving power, also forms its own body, as we said, whenever it is troubled by the more painful emotions. But it forms a foreign body too by way of charms and wicked spells. That the soul can do such things by its emotions is not surprising if certain herbs can do so, or stones with their vapors (when celestial souls are influencing them). An unbroken chain of means is not wanting to the soul and through these means it imparts action to a foreign body.

The phantasy of a sorcerer, hostile as it is to an infant's tender 8
little body, gives the child a fever. His imagining the fever arouses his febrile, that is, his choleric spirits, just as imagining intercourse arouses our seminal spirits and genitalia. This aroused choleric and feverish spirit in turn arouses whatever fetid and fever-causing vapors dwell in the sorcerer's body. As soon as these vapors are aroused, like arrows they speed with the spirit to the spot the evil phantasy had intended as its mark. They dart out mostly from the older person's eyes and cross through the child's eyes, like rays passing from and through things made of glass, and on to infect the child's spirits and humors. For these sorceries, the most potent men of all are those in whom the malign aspect of Saturn at their birth, the earthy seed of their parents, and a correspondingly earthy sustenance[119] have produced a complexion that is melan-

res. Ad haec autem maleficia illi sunt omnium potentissimi, quibus nascentibus Saturni malignus aspectus semenque parentum terrestre ac victus persimilis complexionem conflarunt foetidis vaporibus abundantem et melancholicam; praeterea, saeva Martis potentia bilis igniculos subdidit. Hi quando in senio sunt, aetate terrestri et melancholica, morosi sunt valde, et cuicumque contigerit acerrime irascuntur, animoque infensissimo exsecrantur. Phantasiam certe propter humorem terraeum stabilius efficaciusque suis votis affigunt. Hic humor accensus et urit vehementissime et exstinguitur sero, tamquam ignis in crassioribus lignis et duriori materia. Vapores quoque non desunt maligni, per quos quasi sagittas venenum in adversarium iaculentur.

9 Miraris corpus unius ab animo alterius inquinari? At non miraris animum laedi ab animo, dum per consuetudinem vitia aliena combibimus. Non miraris corpus tuum a vapore alterius corporis morbosi[59] facile infici, quod phthisis, epidimia, lepra, pruritus, dysenteria, pleurisis, oculorumque rubor indicant. Apud Hesperios Aethiopas fuisse traditur bestias, nomine catoblepas, quae solo aspectu homines interimerent, quod et apud Cyrenem faciunt basilisci, tanta est vis in vaporibus oculorum. Cur minus subiiciatur corpus tuum alterius animo, quam alterius corpori? Cur non magis potius, cum sit potentior animus neque desint media per quae agat? Quod facere consuevisse homines quosdam Illyriis[60] et Triballis legimus, qui cum essent irati, si diutius attentiusque intuebantur hominem, perimebant, qui et geminas habebant pupillas in oculis. Idem quoque fecisse feminas nonnullas in Scythia. Tanta est imaginationis potentia, praesertim quando affectibus animi vapores oculorum subserviunt. Auget[61] enim vim attentio illa mirabilis phantasiae non minus quam struthii oculus defixus ad ovum. Uno siquidem affectu fervescente tepescit alter. Ideo in maleficae

cholic and laden with fetid vapors. Moreover, the cruel power of Mars has added the sparks of bile. When these sorcerers enter upon old age, the earthy and melancholic period of life, they are exceedingly morose, and they rage bitterly against whomsoever they happen upon, cursing in a spirit of rancorous hate. Because of the earthy humor they certainly impress the phantasy in a more enduring and effective way with their curses; and thus inflamed, the earthy humor burns with incandescent ferocity and is only extinguished when it is too late, just like fire in the harder woods and in denser material. These sorcerers are not without malign vapors too and through them as through arrows they hurl their evil magic on their foe.

Are you surprised that the body of one man is contaminated by 9
the rational soul of another? But you are not surprised that one soul is harmed by another when we gulp down alien vices from the company we keep. You are not surprised that your body is easily infected by the vapor of another diseased body as is obviously the case with consumption, epidemy, leprosy, the itch, dysentery, pleurisy, and conjunctivitis. Among the western Ethiopians purportedly lived beasts called the catoblepas[120] that would kill men simply by looking at them (basilisks also do this near Cyrene[121]), so effective is the power in the vapors of [their] eyes. Why should your body be less subject to the soul of another than to the body of another? Why not more subject, since the soul is more potent and does not want means via which to act? We read that certain men among the Illyrians and Triballi were accustomed to killing in the same way: when they were angry, if they gazed intently for a long time at a man, they would strike him dead. These men had twin pupils in each eye. Certain women also did the like in Scythia.[122] Such is the power of the imagination and especially when the vapors of the eyes are subject to the emotions of the soul. For this wondrous attending or intensifying[123] of the phantasy increases its power no less than the sparrow's eye fixed upon

phantasiae intentione remittitur paulisper affectus animae naturalis, per quem suo corpori devincitur. Unde a suo corpore facta liberior materiam novam, in quam nuper afficitur quasi recens aliquod suum corpus, incipit transmutare.

Si tantam habet vim malefica phantasia, quantam putas habituram beneficam rationem? Saltem duplo maiorem, et quia ratio superat phantasiam, et quia bonitas malum. Igitur ratio quando ad beneficium aliquod tota animi erga deum intentione defigitur, nonnumquam corpus illud erga[62] quod est affecta, afficit beneficio tam proprium quam alienum. Hoc munere excellunt illi, ut est apud Platonicos, qui divino quodam beneficio prae ceteris complexione temperata caelestique sunt praediti, necnon puris et modicis nutriti cibis, honestis praeterea divinisque moribus educati. Hi medici saepe sunt generis humani, et corpori cui cupiunt bona, si directi prorsus in deum piis votis ardenter exoptant, illico praestant, praesertim si hominis beneficium accepturi animus sit paratus. Hinc Zoroaster inquit:

> Ἐκτείνας πύριον νοῦν
> Ἔργον ἐπ' εὐσεβίας, ῥευστὸν καὶ σῶμα σαώσεις.

Id est: 'Si mentem ardentem ad opus pietatis intenderis, labile corpus servabis'. Talia quaedam miracula facta ab Apollonio Theaneo philosopho narrat Philostratus. Rursus a Pythagora, Empedocle, et Philolao similia quaedam gesta Pythagorei multi affirmant. Scribit insuper Iamblichus Pythagoricos, quotiens narrarentur miracula, facile solitos credere illa a deo per divinas animas fieri, atque in rebus huiusmodi haec Lini carmina semper habuisse in ore:

> Ἐλπείσθαι χρὴ πάντ' ἐπεὶ οὐκ ἔστιν οὐδὲν ἄελπον
> Ρᾳδια πάντα θεῷ τελέσαι, καὶ ἀδύνατον οὐδέν.

Id est: 'Credenda sunt omnia, nihil enim est incredibile. Facilia deo omnia sunt, nihil est impossibile'.

its egg. For when one emotion becomes inflamed, another cools off. Therefore in the intensifying of the malefic phantasy the natural affection of the soul, which binds it to its body, is briefly remitted, with the result that, freed to a greater degree from its body, it begins to transmute the new material to which it has just been attracted, as if to some new body of its own.

If the malefic phantasy has such immense power, how much more immense do you suppose will be the power of the benefic reason? It will be at least double, because the reason rules the phantasy and good triumphs over evil. So when this reason is fixed upon some good work and the soul is wholly intent on God, it sometimes benefits the body to which it is attracted, its own or a foreign one alike. Excelling in this office, the Platonists maintain, are those who have been endowed more than others with a tempered and celestial complexion, the result of a divine favor; who have been nourished by pure foods taken in moderation; and who have been nurtured furthermore in honorable and pious ways. These men are often the doctors of mankind and they instantly bestow benefits on the body to which they wish well, if, directed entirely towards God, they ardently long for [the benefits] with pious prayers, and especially if the rational soul of the man about to receive a benefit is duly prepared. Hence Zoroaster says, "If you focus your ardent mind on the work of piety, you will preserve your perishable body."[124] Philostratus says that the philosopher Apollonius of Tyana performed miracles such as these.[125] And many Pythagoreans affirm that similar deeds were enacted by Pythagoras, Empedocles, and Philolaus. Iamblichus writes, moreover, that the Pythagoreans, whenever they were told about miracles, had no difficulty as a rule in believing that they were performed by God through the agency of divine souls; and that they always had on such occasions these verses of Linus on their lips: "All things are believable, for nothing is unbelievable. All things are easy for God, nothing is impossible."[126]

11 Sed redeamus ad illos iam animos, per quos deus quasi per instrumenta miracula perficit. Quid confert illis ad hanc excellentiam habitudo corporis temperata, ut ratio illorum sit expeditior, nullo excedentium humorum turbata tumultu? Quid modicus purusque victus, ut non sit anima corporis sui sarcina praegravata? Quid educatio illa honesta atque pia, ut et optet hominibus bona et, tamquam deo quodammodo similis, adiuvetur a deo,[63] immo tamquam instrumentum a deo ducatur? Denique cum ratio sit eminentior phantasia, quando ipsa dedita deo tota ad unum hoc opus beneficii conferendi dirigitur, remittitur admodum naturalis ille prior affectus animi quo proprio corpori copulatur, et ab eo soluta agit in alienum. Potest enim facile ad haec tamquam instrumentum a deo duci, cum natura sit super corpora omnia, quamvis affectus olim aliquis ad unius gubernationem rapuerit, non aliter ac si sapientissimus rex potentissimusque, cuius providentiae et dicioni subsint omnes pariter amplissimi regni partes, reliquas negligat[64] ad tempus, partis alicuius amoenitate pellectus, sed amore aliquando partis illius defervescente, se ad alias conferat gubernandas. Mysteria haec Plato noster omnia tetigisse videtur, tyrannidem quidem illam phantasiae, et hoc rursum piae rationis imperium in *Timaeo*, ubi de vi animae in corpus disseruit. In *Phaedro* autem mirabilius quiddam innuit, cum inquit omnem animam universi corporis curam habere atque animam nostram, quando libera est, totum pererrare caelum mundumque una cum caelestibus animis gubernare, alias in aliis figuris circumeuntem. Quando vero sit talis, aperuit in *Epinomide*, ubi affirmavit necessitatem mentis

Let us now revert, however, to those rational souls whom God uses like instruments to perform miracles. To excel in this way what does the temperate condition of their body contribute in order that their reason may be more free and untroubled by any tumult of excessive humors? What does the pure sustenance taken in moderation contribute in order that their soul may not be weighed down by the burden of their body? What does the aforesaid honorable and pious education contribute in order that their soul may choose what benefits men and, being similar to God in a way, be aided by God, or rather be used by God like an instrument? In short, since the reason is superior to the phantasy, when the reason is dedicated totally to God and directed to the one work of bestowing a benefit, then the earlier natural desire of the soul joining it to its own body is fully remitted: released from its own body, the reason acts upon another. For it can easily be led by God as an instrument to do this, since it is naturally above all bodies, even though an affection at one point seized hold of it to govern just one body. Compare it to the wisest and most potent king, to whose providence and sway all the parts of his great kingdom are equally subject, but who neglects for a while the other parts, having been seduced by the charm of one of them. At some point, when his love for that one part cools, he betakes himself to ruling the other parts. Our Plato seems to have touched upon all these mysteries. In the *Timaeus* he deals with the tyranny of the phantasy and also with the sovereignty of pious reason, when he examines the power of the soul in the body.[127] In the *Phaedrus*, however, he hints at something more mysterious when he says that all soul has care of the body of the universe and that our soul, when it is free, wanders through the whole of heaven and governs the world together with the celestial souls, at various times circling round in various figures.[128] When it might be thus free, he revealed in the *Epinomis*, where he declared that the necessity of mind and of soul joined to mind surpasses all necessity, and that 11

atque animae menti coniunctae necessitatem omnem exsuperare, ac tale omne decretum esse fatale. Quinetiam in decimo *De iusto* intellectualem animam appellavit necessitatem, inter cuius genua sit fusus aliquis, circa quem sphaerae mundi volvantur.

12 Quorsum haec? Ut intellegamus fieri posse quandoque ut hominis anima tota rationis intentione in mentem caputque suum vertatur, sicut quandoque vertitur in phantasiam, ut diximus iam, et rationem. Quisnam animus haec agit? Qui phantasiam iubet silere, ac etiam superni numinis desiderio flagrans, consuetis rationis naturalis discursibus non confidit, sola vivit mente, evadit angelus, et toto capit pectore deum. Haec significat Zoroaster, ubi sic inquit:

> *Ψυχὴ ἡ μερόπων θεὸν ἄγξει πως ἐς ἑαυτὴν*
> *Οὐδὲν θνητὸν ἔχουσα, ὅλη θεόθεν μεμέθυσται*
> *Ἁρμονίαν αὐχεῖ γάρ, ὑφ᾽ ἧ πέλε σῶμα βρότειον.*

Id est: 'Anima hominum deum quodammodo contrahit in se ipsam, quando nihil retinens mortale, tota divinis haustibus ebriatur. Tunc quoque exultat in corporis harmoniam'.[65] Huiusmodi animum divi Ioannis theologia nasci iterum dicit ex deo. Siquidem dei summi influxus per mentes angelicas usque ad animam hominis defluens, instigat quotidie animam corpori mersam, ut exuta carneam textam ponat potentias operationesque animales, et pro anima fiat angelus, quemadmodum radius solis vapores tenuat trahitque sursum et in igneam convertit naturam. Qui huic inspirationi totum se committit, cessat esse anima fitque, deo regenerante, dei filius, angelus. Idcirco Plato theologos appellavit dei filios in *Timaeo*.

13 Si anima natura sua excedit mundi machinam perque vires inferiores mira operatur in corporibus etiam alienis, quid illam putamus acturam, quando in caput surrexerit suum evaseritque angelica? Quod oportet fieri posse quandoque, postquam blandimentis sensuum fit saepe brutalis, et inspiratio dei esse non debet vanior

every such decree is fatal.[129] In the tenth book of the *Republic*, moreover, he personified the intellectual soul as the "necessity" between whose knees lies a spindle around which the world's spheres revolve.[130]

To what is all this leading? That we might understand that it is possible for man's soul to be turned at times towards mind, its head, by the total concentration of its reason, just as it is turned at other times towards the phantasy, as we have already said, and towards the reason. Which soul does this? It is the one which orders the phantasy to be silent and which, burning with desire too for supernal divinity, does not trust itself to the customary discursiveness of the reason natural to it, but lives in the mind alone, issues as an angel, and takes God into its whole heart. Zoroaster signifies this when he says: "In a way the human soul contracts God into itself when, retaining nothing mortal, it becomes utterly inebriated on the draughts divine. Then it exults too in the body's harmony."[131] The theology of the divine John says that such a soul is born again from God.[132] For the influence of God on high, flowing down through the angelic minds to man's soul, daily moves the soul, immersed as it is in the body, to cast off its fleshly clothing, to lay aside its own soul-powers and activities, and instead of a soul to become an angel. Similarly, the sun's ray disperses the mists and draws them upwards and converts them into the fiery nature. He who commits himself entirely to this inspiration ceases to be a soul and becomes, being reborn from God, a son of God, an angel. Thus Plato in the *Timaeus* calls theologians the sons of God.[133] 12

If the soul naturally surpasses the world machine, and if it performs wonders even in foreign bodies through its inferior powers, what do we suppose it will do when it ascends to its head and emerges as angelic? This must be possible at some time given that it is often made beastly by the blandishments of the senses, and God's inspiration must never be more ineffectual than the blan- 13

quam sensuum blandimenta. Tunc igitur non unum quendam amplius aut tenerum fascinabit, aut sanabit hominem aegrotantem, sed sphaeris imperabit elementorum. Quamdiu corpori huic addicta est, parvi huius mundi elementa, id est humores quatuor, agitat eisque calorem, frigus, humorem, siccitatem, colores omnes saporesque[66] inducit, ut supra patuit, tum in actu vitali, tum in affectibus phantasiae. Ideo quando soluta ab hoc, emergit in amplum, deo iam plena, animalis huius grandioris humores, id est quatuor elementa maioris mundi, movet ut sua. Siquidem iam quasi evasit anima mundi, eius videlicet mundi partis erga quam afficitur maxime. Ac sicut eadem hominis anima quae cubitale[67] infantis corpusculum rexerat, regit bicubitum aeque et tricubitum ac deinde quatuor cubitorum et decem rursus (ut dicitur de gigantibus), ita si usque ad centum creverit et ducentos, aeque reget. Quod enim naturae ordine et dignitate omne molem corporis antecedit, non minus totam ipsam molem quam molis partem implere potest atque movere. Si vim ab ipso deo videlicet habet vivifica vis rationalis animae in mundi sphaeras, vim quoque habet in eas rationis ac mentis affectus. Solo igitur affectu citabit ventos deo duce ac caelo nubes inducet sereno easque coget in pluvias. Rursus sedabit ventos et aerem serenabit.

14 Quod quidem posse fieri factumve fuisse Hippocrates Cous, theologi Mauri et Arabes confitentur, Maurorum princeps Avicebron, Arabum Avicenna. Mitto quot elementorum turbationes procellasque tum ex daemonum conflictationibus, tum ex casibus

dishments of the senses. So the soul will no longer be bewitching just one body or a young body, or be healing a sick man; it will then govern the spheres of the elements. As long as it is addicted to this human body, it sets the elements of this body's small world, the four humors that is, into motion; and it induces in them heat, cold, wetness, dryness, and all the colors and tastes, as was evident above, both in the act of life and in the emotions of the phantasy. When liberated, it therefore emerges from this body into the great [world] body, and, filled now with God, moves the humors of this greater animal, the four elements, that is, of the greater world, as if they were its own. For it has now emerged as a kind of World Soul, the soul of that part of the world with respect to which it is most disposed. Just as the same human soul, which had ruled over the little body of the infant when it was just a cubit long, now rules in the same way over a body of two or three cubits, and then over a body of four or in turn of ten cubits (as it is purported of giants), so, were the body to grow to a hundred or to two hundred cubits, the soul would still rule over it in the same way. For in the order and dignity of nature what comes before the whole mass of body is able to fill and move that whole mass no less than a part of the mass. If the life-giving power of the rational soul has the power from God Himself over the world's spheres, then the affective power of the reason and the mind will also have power over them. With that power alone, therefore, it will, under God's command, rouse the winds and drag clouds into the clear sky and compel them to rain; then it will allay the winds and clear the air.

That this can or did happen is acknowledged by Hippocrates of 14
Cos, the Moorish theologians and the Arabs, the prince of the Moors being Avicebron[134] and of the Arabs, Avicenna.[135] I will not delve into how many storms and tempests of the elements arise all the time, the Egyptians and the Platonists suppose, both from the conflicts of the demons and from the downfall of souls into bod-

animarum in corpora saepe contingere Aegyptii Platonicique arbitrentur, qua quidem de re Plutarchus et Porphyrius et Proclus diligentissime disputant. Platonis certe Platonicorumque sententia est, a caelo ad terram usque in sphaeris omnibus alias plagas numinibus aliis ab initio distributas ita fuisse, ut quando in regione terrae certis dicata numinibus dispositio ad ipsa numina vel per supernos influxus vel per animorum affectiones praecipue augetur, miracula saepe talibus numinibus congrua vel per se vel per animas ibidem ab eisdem numinibus occupatas efficiantur. Sed de iis[68] alias. Magicam quandam in praesentia sententiam referamus.

Putant Chaldaei posse insuper aliud quiddam ab anima mirabile fieri, ut scilicet radiis effusis in corpus suum ipsum lumine circumfundat et radiorum levitate tollat in altum. Quod in se ipso fecisse patrem eorum Zoroastrem nonnulli referunt. Ego vero, si qua huius miraculi ratio assignari potest, talem forsitan esse opinor. Prima lux in deo est atque ibi est talis ut supereminet intellectum, ideoque non potest lux intellegibilis appellari. Sed lux illa dei, cum infunditur angelo, fit e vestigio lux intellectualis atque intellegi potest. Quando infunditur animae, fit rationalis ac[69] potest non intellegi solum, sed cogitari. Inde migrat in animae idolum, ubi fit sensitiva, nondum tamen corporea.[70] Inde in aethereum vehiculum idoli, ubi fit corporalis, nondum tamen manifeste sensibilis. Denique in corpus elementale, sive simplex aeriumque sive compositum, quod est aetherei vasculum, in quo evadit manifeste visibilis. Atque ego hanc esse puto catenam illam auream quam vidit Homerus a caelo pendentem et in terras usque demissam, qua apprehensa homines sese possint in caelos attollere.

ies. Plutarch, Porphyry, and Proclus discuss this very carefully.[136] Certainly the opinion of Plato and of the Platonists is that various regions — from the heavens to the earth and extending to all the spheres — have been allotted to various spirits from the beginning.[137] They have been so allotted that when the disposition for certain spirits in an earthly region dedicated to them is especially heightened, either through supernal influences or through the emotional good-will of souls, then often miracles proper to such spirits are performed either by the spirits themselves or by souls in that region possessed by the same spirits. But of these matters elsewhere. For the present let us refer to an opinion held by the Magi.[138]

The Chaldaeans think that yet another marvel can be performed by the soul, namely that it can surround its own body with light from scattered rays and with the levity of the rays lift its body on high. Some of them say that their father, Zoroaster, did this to himself.[139] But if it is possible to assign any reason for this miracle, I think it is perhaps the following. The first light is in God and there it is such that it surpasses the intellect, and thus cannot be called intelligible light. But that same light of God when it is poured forth into the angel suddenly becomes intellectual light and can be understood. When it is poured into the soul it becomes rational light and can be both understood and thought about discursively. Thence it passes down to the soul's idolum where it becomes sensitive but not yet corporeal light; and thence to the aetherial vehicle of the idolum where it becomes corporeal but not yet manifestly visible. Finally it crosses over into the elemental body, whether into the simpler and airy or into the composite (which is the vessel of the aetherial body); and in this elemental body it becomes manifestly visible. I believe that this is the golden chain which Homer saw hanging from heaven and stretching down to the earth, and men who have seized it can raise themselves to the heavens.[140]

16 Profecto tanta luce divinitus abundant caelestes animae, ut ingens inde in corpus earum redundet copia luminis, quod videmus in stellis. Si quando anima hominis ita figat aciem suam in deum[71] divinoque lumine impleatur rapiaturque ut ille[72] tunc aeque coruscat, et in vehiculum suum radios effundit uberrimos, perque vehiculum et corpus aerium, in corpus hoc oculis manifestum. Quod tunc plenissima illa copia radiorum effulget, rarescit, attollitur, aethereo ad hoc conferente vehiculo corporeque aereo, quasi stuppa elevata per flammam. Tali quodam igneo curru Magi atque Platonici Heliam Paulumque raptos in caelum fuisse dicerent, ac demum post mundi iudicium corpus, quod nostri glorificatum nominant, similiter raptum iri. Ideo sic praecipit Zoroaster:

Ὅτι ψυχὴ πῦρ δυνάμει πατρὸς οὖσα φαεινόν
Ἡγείσθω ψυχῆς βάθος ἄμβροτον, ὄμματα δ᾽ ἄρδην
Πάντ᾽ ἐκπέτασον ἄνω,
Μηδὲ τὸ τῆς ὕλης σκύβαλον κρημνῷ καταλείψης

Id est: 'Quoniam anima per potentiam patris fit ignis splendidus, dominetur in te immortalis profunditas animae, et oculos omnes una tolle in altum, tunc neque etiam materiale ipsum corpus praecipitio derelinques'. Ignem appellat lucem ipsam, qua et exuberat deus per se et anima per vim patris conversa in patrem abundat. Et quia deus est ipsa unitas super mentem et centrum essentiarum super essentiam, ideoque non unitur illi per mentem proprie, sed per unitatem animae, quae est mentis caput centrumque totius animae, idcirco dicit Zoroaster: 'ducat te animae profunditas immortalis,' id est unitas ipsa, quam impressit quondam deus animae tamquam unitatis divinae characterem, a qua et ad quam omnes aliae vires animae, quasi a centro et ad centrum omnes circuli lineae, pendent. Sequantur 'oculi tui omnes,' id est omnes vires animae quae in cognoscendo versantur. Huc tendit illud: 'Attollite portas, principes, vestras, et elevamini portae aeternales, etc.' 'Una,' id est in unam collectae mentem sive in unitatem, mentis

Certainly the celestial souls abound with so much light from heaven that the overflowing plenty of that light spills over into their body (we see this in the case of the stars). And whenever a human soul focuses its gaze on God and is filled and possessed by the divine light to the point that the person becomes equally coruscating, then it pours the copious rays out into its [aetherial] vehicle and, via that vehicle and the airy body, into this body visible to our eyes. Filled to the brim with the copiousness of the rays it is then set ablaze, rarefied, lifted up, borne thither in the aetherial and airy body like tow wafted through the flame. In such a fiery chariot, the Magi and the Platonists would say, Elias[141] and Paul[142] were swept up into heaven, and eventually, after the Last Judgment, the body that our [theologians] call the glorified body will be similarly enraptured. Thus Zoroaster teaches us: "Because the soul becomes a resplendent fire through the power of the father, may the immortal profundity of the soul dominate you and raise all eyes as one on high, and then even the material body you will not abandon to the precipice."[143] By *fire* he is referring to the light itself in which God of Himself abounds and in which the soul abounds, having been converted through the power of the Father to the Father. And since God is unity itself above mind and is the center of essences above essence, and the soul therefore is united to Him properly not through its mind but through its unity which is the head of the mind and the center of the whole soul, Zoroaster therefore says *May the immortal profundity of the soul lead you,* that is, the unity itself. God once impressed this unity on the soul as a print of the unity divine, and on it all the other powers of the soul depend and to it they return, just as all the lines of a circle proceed from and revert to its center. *All eyes* comes next, meaning all the powers of the soul which are concerned with knowing: the following verse refers to this: "Lift up your gates, o ye princes; and be ye lifted up, ye everlasting doors, etc."[144] *As one* means collected into one mind or into the unity, the head of the mind; and following 16

caput. Tunc eas sequetur corpus, tum caeleste tum terrenum. Propterea dixit 'corpus materiale', id est terrenum, tunc 'non derelinqui praecipitio', quia tunc ipsum quoque tolletur in altum neque relinquetur in infimo loco mundi, quem locum Magi saepe nominant praecipitium. Miraculi huius vim effectumque describit etiam Mercurius Trismegistus, ubi de regeneratione cum filio suo Tatio disputat.

17 De hoc quidem miraculo, quod in proprio corpore mens ostendit, ex Platonicorum opinione satis sit dictum. De illis vero quae in sphaeris mundi demonstrat, tales quaedam apud Platonicos moventur quaestiones, quales dicam, et solvuntur ut dicam.

: V :

Quaestiones sex de miraculis et solutiones.

1 Mens hominis quando corporeas exuit curas, cur passiones elementorum affectat? Quia publicum bonum non despicit divinus animus, summi communisque boni filius. Ergo tamquam deus aliquis ad animalium[73] hominumque commoditatem providenter elementa movebit. An potest adeo supra suum corpus attolli ut mundi sphaeras attingat? Potest utique, si ubique est, ut quidam putant. Sed nonne etiam lumen crassa laterna inclusum paulo momento laterna reclusa emicat eminus et remotissima quaeque illuminat? Neque tamen a laterna discedit; clausa iterum laterna in angulum absque sui offensione colligitur, quod dum locum[74] prius impleret amplissimum, absque sui dissipatione profundebatur. Mira luminis virtus! In angustissimo quiescit loco, implet amplis-

them is the body, both the celestial and the earthly. Accordingly Zoroaster declared that the *material body*, meaning the earthly one, is not to be abandoned to the *precipice* at that time, because it too will be raised on high and not abandoned in the world's lowest place that the Magi often call the precipice. Mercurius Trismegistus describes the power and effect of this miracle when he discusses regeneration with his son Tat.[145]

Enough has been said of the Platonists' view concerning this 17
miracle manifested by the mind in its own body. I will now address the kind of questions raised among the Platonists about the miracles that are manifested in the spheres of the world, and speak to their resolution.

: V :

Six questions about miracles and their resolution.

When man's mind lays aside bodily cares, why does it [still] aspire 1
to the passions of the elements? It is because the divine soul, the son of the highest and universal good, does not scorn the public good; like a god, therefore, it will move the elements providentially for the advantage of animals and men. But can it be so elevated above its own body that it attains the spheres of the world? It can certainly do this if it is omnipresent as some think. Doesn't even a light trapped inside a heavy lantern blaze out afar in a brief moment when the lantern is opened, and illuminate most distant objects? Yet it does not quit the lantern; and when the lantern is shut again, it is confined in a narrow space without its being harmed. This is because, when initially it was flooding the greatest space, it was being poured forth without its being dissipated. Wonderful is the power of light! It remains quietly in the narrowest place and it

simum. Id quippe facit, quoniam lumen quodammodo est incorporeum. Idem facit animus, quia divinum est lumen.

2 Numquid divinus hic animus in iis[75] conficiendis miraculis per omnes sui partes secedit a corpore? Nihil opus est ut officium omnino dimittat contrariorum conciliandorum. Anima utique in corpore per idolum suum quasi crinitae comam in vapore: primum contraria in unum elementa conciliat; deinde, si dissolvitur quicquam, instaurat nutriendo, auget etiam; regit corpus et transfert et reliqua. Videmus apertissime opus transferendi regendique corporis remitti et intermitti quandoque. Cum anima vehementiori corripitur phantasia, officium augendi nutriendique minuitur propter intentissimam rationis indaginem. Ideo non concoquunt cibos philosophantes et anima adulto corpore acutius speculatur quam adolescente, minus in augendo corpore occupata, et sobrium corpus speculationem impedit minus, dum anima ad speculandum est dumtaxat intenta. Quamobrem cum per mentem tanta animi contingit abstractio, ut et phantasia et ratio naturalis intermittantur, quae solent ipsae nutritionem regimenque membrorum debilitare, quid obstat quo minus cadat corpus et nutriatur in corpore nihil? Restabit forsitan solum conciliationis officium, quo anima nondum sinat dissolvi humores atque diffugere. Sed non fiet tunc talis conciliatio, ut fieri solet, per idolum, quod omnino destituit terrenum corpus quando anima nihil sapit terrenum. Tunc enim idolum ita relinquit terrae naturam, sicut ratio terrenorum corporum relinquit imagines.

3 Opinor igitur viri omnino abstracti corpus eo ipso in tempore brevissimo quo est angelicus animus, per virtutem idoli antea

fills up the amplest; and it does this because light in a way is incorporeal. The soul does the same because it is divine light.

In performing these miracles, however, does this divine soul withdraw from the body through all its parts? There is no need for it to abandon entirely its office of reconciling opposites. The soul is certainly in the body through its idolum like the hair of a comet in the aether. First it reconciles opposite elements together; then, if anything dissolves, it restores the body by nourishing it and increases it even; it rules the body and moves it along and so on. At times, manifestly, the work of transporting and ruling the body is remitted and halted. When the phantasy is caught up by the more vehement soul, the office of increasing and nourishing is diminished on account of the reason's extremely intense investigation. So those who are philosophizing do not digest their food; and the soul in the adult body contemplates with greater acuity than in the adolescent one, being less occupied in making the body grow. The tempered body impedes contemplation less when the soul is intent solely on contemplating. Therefore, when it happens that the soul becomes, because of the mind, so totally abstracted that both the phantasy and the natural reason are intermitted (the very faculties which usually weaken the nourishing and government of the limbs), then what prevents the body from totally succumbing and nothing being nourished in the body? The office of reconciliation, wherein the soul does not yet allow the humors to be dissolved or to disappear, alone perhaps remains. But then this reconciling will not occur through the idolum (as it customarily does), [since] the idolum entirely flees the earthly body when the soul no longer savors anything earthly. For at that point the idolum leaves the nature of earth behind, just as the reason leaves behind the images of earthly bodies. 2

I think therefore that the body of the man utterly abstracted in that very briefest of times in which he is an angelic soul is neither moved nor sustained nor contained through the formerly custom- 3

consuetam neque moveri neque sustineri neque etiam contineri. Quod si moveatur vel sustineatur vel continueatur, id fieri arbitror per illud animae centrum, quam paulo ante unitatem vocavimus animae a deo tributam, per quam deo, omnium centro et purae unitati, concilietur; per quam non modo elementa corporis huius, sed etiam mundi conciliet; per quam solam posse deum attingi. Sic aperuit Zoroaster:

Ἐστί τι νοητόν, ὃ χρὴ σε νοεῖν νόου ἄνθει

Id est: 'Est intellegibile aliquid, quod intellegere te oportet mentis flore'. Florem mentis appellat Zoroaster ipsum animae centrum, quod Plato nominat mentis caput. Sententiam hanc nostram illud Pauli divini theologi confirmare videtur, quod inquit animum deo raptum nec esse evidenter in corpore nec extra corpus, videlicet quia non insit corpori per idolum, sed adsit per centrum. Quandiu mirabilia haec animus operatur? Quandiu ita manet abstractus? Manet vero parumper naturali quodam potentiae inferioris affectu ad curam corporis retrahente, sicut et paulisper manere in aere lapis dicitur sursum iactus inter ascensum atque descensum.

4 Sed numquid ordinem mundi animus confundit humanus miracula operando? Nequaquam. Nam, ut platonice loquar, in universali rerum lege et perpetua quadam serie causarum ad idem conferentium sunt huiusmodi praescripta miracula. Ad hoc ipsum conducit providentia mentium sub deo usque ad mentem nostram continue conspirantium. Ad idem divinum fatum animalium idolorum a prima anima ad nostrae animae idolum confluentium. Ad idem divina quaedam naturarum omnium dispositio a primae naturae affectione concurrentium usque ad naturae nostrae complexionem. Idem saepe nobis caelestia signa praenuntiant, per

ary power of the idolum.[146] But if it is indeed moved or sustained or contained, then I believe this occurs because of the soul's center, which a short while ago we called the unity bestowed on the soul by God. Through this unity the soul is united to God, to the center of all, to the pure unity; through this unity the soul reconciles the elements not only of this [human] body but even of the world's body; and through this unity alone it is able to attain God. Zoroaster revealed it thus, "There is something intelligible which you must understand with the flower of your mind."[147] Zoroaster calls "the flower of the mind" the center itself of the soul which Plato calls "the mind's head."[148] The verse of Paul the divine theologian seems to confirm our interpretation when he says that the soul enraptured by God appears to be neither in the body nor outside the body,[149] because, in other words, it is not present in the body via its idolum but it is present to it via its center. For how long does the rational soul perform these miracles? For as long as it remains thus abstracted? But it remains so for only a brief while, because, by a natural longing of its lower power, it is withdrawn to take care of the body, just as a stone thrown upwards is said to stay in the air for just that brief while between ascent and descent.

By working miracles, however, isn't the rational human soul 4
confounding the world's order? Not at all. For, to speak Platonically, these miracles have been prescribed in the universal law of things and in an everlasting series of causes contributing to the same.[150] Contributing to it is the providential care of the minds under God down to our own mind, minds singing in continual harmony. Contributing too is the divine fate of the idola of souls, idola flowing from the first soul down to the idolum of our soul. And contributing finally is a divine disposition found in all natures, running from the affection of the first nature to our own nature's complexion.[151] Celestial signs often foretell us the same, for through the signs as through glances and nods the thoughts of the divine spirits are signified: "The heavens declare the glory of God;

quae quasi per oculos nutusque numinum cogitationes significantur. 'Caeli enarrant gloriam dei et opera manuum[76] eius annuntiat firmamentum'. Non igitur quando animus ille angelicus optat mirabile aliquod opus conficere, puta citare ventos, statim superiores causae huic favent voto et nova cupiunt, quoniam nova animus affectavit, sed contra, quoniam caelestes idipsum decreverunt, iste cupit. Quonam pacto? Futurorum ventorum stat in supernis numinibus praevidentia. Dispositio huiusmodi, ut alias diximus, per tres illas series statim ad animas nostras usque decurrit, praecipue per providentiam in mentem, quodammodo etiam per fatum in idolum, per naturam quoque in corporis nostri complexionem.

5 Sed perturbati hominum animi hos impulsus non capiunt, pacatus autem animus undique supernos capit impulsus. Unde latenter incipit cogitare eadem quae cogitant superi, eademque velle ac nolle, cum naturali, id est divino et intimo inclinetur instinctu. Huic cogitationes omnes affectusque succedunt ad votum, et quicquid a superis postulat, accipit. Nempe quae illi iam daturi fuerant, postulat, et quia daturi erant, ad postulandum provocaverunt, sicut mater quae pomum manu praefert oculis filii, ut hinc invitatus filius petat pomum. Filius videt, petit, accipit—accipit, inquam, non solum quia petit, sed petit etiam quia sit accepturus. Neque vult dare mater postquam filius velit accipere, sed e converso.

6 Nos quidem plurimum non naturalibus divinisve incedimus desideriis, sed illis quos accendit quotidie casus; prout enim alia atque alia sensibus nostris occurrunt, aliter aliterve afficimur. Atque ita rebus contingentibus occupati, raro ut cupimus assequimur, quia raro et sorte quadam cum supernorum voluntate

and the firmament sheweth His handywork."[152] So when that angelic soul yearns to perform some miracle, for instance, to raise up the winds, the higher causes do not immediately favor the prayer; nor do they desire novelties just because the soul has desired novelties. To the contrary, it is because the celestials have decreed the miracle that the soul desires it. How? Foreseeing the coming of winds pertains to the supernal spirits. Such a [prophetic] disposition, as we said elsewhere,[153] descends uninterruptedly down to our own soul via the three series: through providence mostly to our mind, through fate in a way to our idolum, and through nature to the complexion of our body.

Men's troubled souls, however, do not receive these impulses, 5
whereas the soul at peace receives the supernal impulses from every side. Hence it begins in secret to think about the same things that the higher souls are thinking about, and to wish and to not wish for the same things, since it is inclined towards them by a natural, that is, by a divine instinct within. For this soul at peace, all thoughts and desires answer its prayer, and whatever it seeks from those above, it receives. Indeed, the things they are already about to give it it asks for, and because they are about to give them to it, they prompt it to ask for them. A mother similarly dangles an apple in front of her child's eyes and lured in this way the son begs for the apple: the son sees, asks for, and receives: he receives not only because he asks, but he asks because he is about to receive. The mother does not want to give because her son wants to accept, but the reverse.

For the most part we are not impelled by natural or divine de- 6
sires, but by those daily incited in us by chance; for according as various objects impinge on our senses, so are we variously affected. Preoccupied in this way with contingent things, we rarely attain what we desire because we rarely and only by chance come into accord with the will of those above. But the rational angelic soul is in accord with them, since it lives in peace, and it rules the world

concurrimus. Angelicus autem animus et consentit cum illis, quia tranquillus vivit et imperat mundo, quia sua sponte ab hoc corpusculo, quod est mundi particula, solvitur, in sui naturam regressus amplissimam. Talem vero fore animum praevidit deus, talem, inquam, non superno auxilio tantum, sed etiam propria voluntate, quae quidem tunc praecipue agit libere, quando dimissis actionibus in se ipsam originemque contemplandam amandamque se flectit. Talem quoque elegit deus ad mirabilia perpetranda. Cuius orationes etiam circa publicas mundi mutationes non esse vanas, Avicenna in *Metaphysicis* et Proclus Iamblichusque disputant in *Timaeo*. Probant enim vota viri sanctissimi, praesertim si cum illo populi quoque vota concurrant, animos mirabiliter ita coniungere deo, ut una quodammodo dei animique operatio fiat, sed dei quidem velut artificis, animi autem tamquam instrumenti divini. De illis vero miraculis quae deus per se absque instrumento facit, quae longe maiora sunt, in praesentia non tractamus.

7 Miracula huiusmodi numquid naturalia sunt animo? Sunt naturalia quodammodo, ut opinantur Platonici, atque iterum non naturalia. Naturalia quidem quantum recurrit in mentem fitque summi dei pedissequus atque instrumentum. Non naturalia, quantum unius tantum servit corporis usui, cuius amore captus ad tempus, neque virtutis suae explicat amplitudinem, neque divinae fit particeps. Qui quotiens et[77] explicat et fit particeps, ostendit se nullo ictu corporum dissolutum iri, quandoquidem quodammodo praestat omnibus et torquet omnia pro arbitrio.

8 Singula vero quae de miraculis ex Platonicorum mente disseruimus, ita a nobis affirmata sint ut a Christianis theologis approbantur.

since it is freed of its own will from this little body (which is a particle of the world), having returned to its own nature in all its amplitude. But God has foreseen that such a soul is going to exist and exist as such not only because of supernal aid but also because of its own will, a will which acts freely precisely when, having set actions aside, it turns to contemplating and loving itself and its origin. God also selects such a soul to perform miracles. Even when the prayers of this soul concern the public vicissitudes of the world, they are not in vain it is asserted by Avicenna in his *Metaphysics*[154] and by Proclus and Iamblichus.[155] They prove that the prayers of an extremely holy man, especially if the prayers of the people also accord with his, unite souls with God so marvelously that the activity of God and of the soul become in a way one, with God as the maker and the soul as His instrument divine. For the present let us not deal with those far greater miracles which God performs through Himself and without an instrument.

Are the said miracles natural for the rational soul? In a way 7
they are natural, as the Platonists see it, and again they are nonnatural: natural, insofar as the soul has recourse to the mind and is made the attendant and instrument of God on high; non-natural, insofar as it serves the needs of one body alone (by the love of which it is enraptured for a while) and neither unfolds the full extent of its own power nor becomes a participant in the divine power. But as often as the soul does unfold its own power and become a participant [in the divine power], it demonstrates that no blow from bodies is ever going to shatter it, since in a way it rewards and punishes all bodies according to its own judgment.

But individual points concerning miracles, points we have dis- 8
cussed from a Platonic viewpoint, we affirm only insofar as they are approved by Christian theologians.

LIBER QUARTUS DECIMUS[1]

: I :

Quod anima nitatur deus fieri, ostendimus signis duodecim secundum duodecim dei dotes.

1 In principio disputationis duo iecimus fundamenta signorum ad immortalitatem animae pertinentium. In uno tractatur quantum anima corporibus dominatur, quod per quatuor signa transegimus. In altero agitur quod anima deus fieri nititur, de quo per duodecim signa tractabimus secundum duodecim dei dotes. In quo apparebit mira animi magnitudo, cui non satis fuerit aemulari deum iis miris quos diximus modis, nisi etiam fiat deus. Hinc ita exclamavit Zoroaster:

Ὦ τολμηροτάτης φύσεως ἄνθρωπε τέχνασμα

Id est: 'O homo, naturae audentissimae artificium'. Constat apud omnes theologos deum esse primum ipsum verum ac bonum; esse cuncta; esse auctorem universorum; super omnia; in omnibus; semper; providere cunctis; iuste administrare; fortiter, dum administrat, in habitu suo perseverare; temperate suaviterque tractare; opulentissime vivere atque iucundissime; se ipsum adeo beatum intueri, mirari et colere.

2 Has duodecim deo dotes omnis apud omnes gentes tribuit theologia. Quicquid ubique homines agunt, ad harum possessionem referunt, neque aliud quicquam expetunt et conantur quam

BOOK XIV

: I :

We demonstrate that the soul strives to become God by way of twelve indications or signs corresponding to twelve properties of God.

At the onset of the discussion we laid down two basic categories for the signs pertaining to the soul's immortality. The first category concerns the degree the soul governs bodies, and that we have [just] established by way of four signs. The second category deals with the soul's striving to become God, and this we will establish by way of twelve signs, corresponding to twelve properties of God. Herein will appear the wonderful greatness of the rational soul, for which it is not enough to emulate God, in the marvelous ways we have described, if it cannot also become God. Hence Zoroaster exclaimed: "O man, the artifice of nature in all her greatest daring."[1] Among all theologians it is agreed: (i) that God is the first true and the first good; (ii) that He is all things; (iii) that He is the author of all, (iv) above all, (v) in all, and (vi) for all time; (vii) that He provides for all; (viii) that He governs with justice; (ix) that in governing He remains steadfastly in His habitual condition; (x) that He proceeds with moderation and sweetness; (xi) that He lives in superlative magnificence and delight; and (xii) that He gazes upon, marvels at, and cultivates His own beatitude. 1

In every nation all theology attributes these twelve properties to God. Everywhere whatever men do they refer to the possession of these properties, and they seek and strive for nothing else but to procure them as fully as possible for themselves. He who possesses them in the fullest degree is God alone. So the aim of our soul's 2

dotes huiusmodi sibi plenissime comparare. Plenissimus harum possessor solus est deus. Totus igitur animae nostrae conatus est, ut deus efficiatur. Conatus talis naturalis est hominibus non minus quam conatus avibus[2] ad volandum; inest enim hominibus omnibus[3] semper ubique. Ideo non contingentem alicuius hominis qualitatem, sed naturam ipsam sequitur speciei. Naturalis autem motus ad finem aliquem directus non aliam ob causam ad hunc finem potius quam ad alium determinatur, nisi propter quandam naturae suae affectionem, per quam cum tali fine congruit potius quam cum tali, et propter congruitatem amat, ac propter eandem[4] assequi potest quod amat; quemadmodum aer levitate cum ignis concavo congruit; per eandem annititur[5] moveturque ad illud; per eandem rursus attingere potest ipsum et in eo, postquam attigerit, conquiescere. Potest igitur quandoque nixus humanus in deum intentus expleri. Nam quis hunc inseruit animis nostris nisi idem ipse deus quem petimus, qui cum solus[6] sit auctor specierum, proprium speciebus inserit appetitum?

3 A primo namque rerum principio, tamquam a primo bono appetibilique, omnis naturalis ducitur appetitus. Idem primus est motor; idem et finis est ultimus. Siquidem ad agentium ordinem ordo sequitur et in finibus, quia sicut supremum agens sequentia movet agentia, ita ad finem supremi agentis referri oportet fines agentium reliquorum. Quicquid enim agit primum ipsum agens, propter finem suum agit. Ducit autem agitque primum omnes omnium causarum sequentium actiones, movendo ad suam actionem omnes ideoque ad suos fines. Unde sequitur agentium omnium inferiorum fines ab ipso primo ad finem proprium ordinari. Primum agens deus est. Divinae voluntatis finis est sua bonitas. Quapropter sequentia omnia in deum tamquam finem necessario ordinantur, praesertim quia nihil tendit in aliquid tamquam finem, nisi quatenus ipsum est bonum. Quo fit ut bonum sit finis, qua ratione bonum. Quod ergo summum est bonum, est maxime om-

whole endeavor is to become God. Such an endeavor is no less natural to men than the effort to fly to birds; for it is always and everywhere present in all men. So it accompanies the nature itself of man the species and not just the contingent quality of a particular man. But a natural movement aimed towards some end is not aimed towards this end rather than another for any other reason except some particular affection of its nature. Through this affection it accords with one particular end rather than another, and it loves this end because of the accord; and through that same accord it is able to attain what it loves. Likewise through its levity air is in accord with the concave [rim] of fire: it strives and is moved towards this rim through this same levity, and through it it is able to attain the rim, and, having attained it, to come to rest in it. So human endeavor intent on God can at some point be fulfilled. For who has sown this endeavor in our souls but the very same God whom we seek, and who, being the sole author of the species, sows the appropriate appetite in the species?

For all natural desire is led by the first principle of things as by 3
the first desirable good. This same is the first mover and this same is the ultimate end. For if the order in ends follows on the order of agents it is because, just as the supreme agent moves the subsequent agents, so the ends of the remaining agents must be referred to the end of the supreme agent. For whatever the first agent does, it does because of its end. But the first agent leads and moves all the actions of all the subsequent causes by moving all their actions towards its own action and so to its own ends. The result is that the ends of all inferior agents are ordered by the first agent for its own end. The first agent is God. The end of the divine will is His goodness. So all subsequent agents are necessarily set in order with God as their end, especially since nothing aims at anything as its end except insofar as it is good. Hence the good is the end by reason of its being the good. So that which is the highest good is absolutely the end of all things. Moreover, the first good is the

nium finis. Adde quod primum bonum est causa omnibus ut sint bona; ergo est causa ut appetantur. Si autem ipsum est propter quod omnia sunt appetenda, sequitur ut ipsum sit et maxime omnium et ab omnibus appetendum. Est igitur finis omnium, et[7] eo tamen pacto ut mentium finis sit secundum formam, reliquorum vero secundum umbram. Ergo et hominum secundum formam finis existit, quando nihil aliud satis ipsis facit. Ita igitur homines dei formam appetunt, ut a deo tributus sit huiusmodi appetitus. Neque minus a deo accenditur appetitus quo deum desideramus, quam a re quavis obiecta sensibus appetitio corporalis alliciatur. Immo et tanto magis, quanto bonum summum potentius ad trahendum est quam minima bona.

4 Profecto quemadmodum in libro *De amore* disserui, ipsius summi boni splendor fulget in singulis, et ubi fulget accommodatius, ibi praecipue allicit intuentem, concitat considerantem, rapit et occupat propinquantem, cogitque eum venerari splendorem huiusmodi prae ceteris tamquam numen, nihilque aliud anniti[8] quam ut deposita priori natura ipse splendor efficiatur. Quod hinc patet, quoniam aspectu tactuve amati hominis non est contentus et clamat saepe: 'Homo hic nescio quid habet quod me urit atque ego quid cupiam non intellego'. Ubi constat animum divino uri fulgore, qui in formoso homine micat quasi speculo atque ab eo clam raptum quasi hamo trahi sursum ut deus evadat. Esset autem deus, ut ita loquar, tyrannus iniquus,[9] si ea nobis mandaret aggredienda quae numquam possemus implere. Mandat autem ut se quaeramus, dum suis igniculis desiderium in se inflammat humanum. Esset quoque sagittarius imperitus ac nimium temerarius, si desideria nostra velut sagittas ad se ceu signum dirigeret, neque addidisset spiculis pennulas, quibus quandoque signum attinge-

cause in all things of their being good; hence it is the cause of their being desired. But if the first good is the cause of all things being desirable, it follows that it itself must be desired most of all and by all. So it is the end of all, and yet in such a way that it is the end of minds by way of form but of inferior things by way of [form's] shadow. Hence it is the end of men by way of form since nothing else satisfies men. So men desire God's form insofar as such a desire has been given them by God. The desire with which we yearn for God is ignited by God no less than corporeal desire is excited by some object offered to the senses. Or rather it is inflamed the more to the extent the highest good is more powerful than the least of goods in attracting things to itself.

As I have discussed in the book *On Love*, the splendor of the 4
highest good is refulgent in individual things, and where it blazes the more fittingly, there it especially attracts someone gazing upon it, excites his consideration, seizes and occupies him as he approaches, and compels him both to venerate such splendor as the divinity beyond all others, and to strive for nothing else but to lay aside his former nature and to become that splendor itself. The evidence is that he is not content just with the sight and touch of the beloved and often exclaims, "As to this person, I do not know why he has the power to set me on fire and do not understand why I desire him." The book established that the soul burns with a divine radiance which is reflected in the man of beauty as in a mirror, and that, caught up by that radiance secretly as by a hook, he is drawn upwards in order to become God. But God would be, if I may put it this way, a wicked tyrant, if He ordered us to attempt things that we could never achieve. But He commands us to seek Him as long as from His own sparks He ignites the human desire for Himself. He would be an inept and over-bold archer too if He directed our desires like arrows to Himself as to the target and had not added feathers to the shafts that would flight them some day to that target. Finally God would be unfortunate if His whole

rent. Esset denique infortunatus, si conatus suus quo nos ad se rapit, numquam finem suum consequeretur. Quamobrem potest animus noster aliquando fieri deus, postquam ad id naturaliter contendit sollicitante deo.

Non fit deus nisi quod dei induitur formam, sicut neque fit ignis quicquam nisi formam ignis accipiat. Ergo sicut materia aeris quae prius erat sub aeris humiditate atque calore, per ignis vim humorem exuit, servat calorem et accepta siccitate formam ignis induitur, sic animi humani essentia, quae nunc mentem habet viresque inferiores deo exspoliante inferiores quodammodo exuit vires ac mente, immo vero capite mentis unitate servata, substantiam divinam induitur quasi recentem formam, per quam paene fit deus, per quam omnes deinde operationes agit ut deus aliquis potius quam ut anima. Hoc impleri posse quandoque necessarium est, ne frustra ab humana specie quaerente, immo ne temere a deo trahente tentetur. Anima tenebroso huius corporis habitaculo circumsaepta vires omnes inferiores aut numquam aut vix et momento remittit. Quocirca mirabile opus illud in hoc corpore non impletur et vix umquam gustatur ab uno. Naturalia vero desideria et in multis oportet expleri, et non per momentaneam qualitatem, sed per habitum stabilem qualem appetunt. Quod si mens quanto altius ad contemplanda spiritalia elevatur, tanto longius discedit a corporalibus, supremus autem terminus,[10] quem attingere potest intellegentia, est ipsa dei substantia, sequitur ut tunc demum mens divinam subire substantiam valeat, quando fuerit a mortalibus sensibus penitus aliena. Igitur anima ab huius corporis vinclis exempta puraquae decedens, certa quadam ratione fit deus. Deus

endeavor, whereby He seizes us to Himself, were never to achieve its goal. At some point, therefore, our rational soul is able to become God, because, with God inciting it, it naturally strives towards that goal.

It does not become God unless it is clothed with God's form, 5
just as nothing becomes fire unless it receives the form of fire. Therefore, just as the matter of air which was subject first to the humidity and heat of air, through the force of fire then casts off the humidity but preserves the heat, and, having accepted dryness, is clothed with the form of fire, so the essence of the rational human soul, which at the present possesses a mind along with lower powers, with God disrobing it, casts off in a way the lower powers. Having preserved its mind — or rather the head of its mind, the unity — it is clothed with divine substance as with a new form; and through this form it almost becomes God, and through this form it then performs all its operations as some god rather than as a soul.[2] Some day it must necessarily be able to fulfill all this, lest the human species be induced to seek it in vain, lest God, rather, draw it towards this goal for nothing. Imprisoned in the shadowy cell of this body, the soul never resigns all its inferior powers or does so only for a moment. Therefore that wonderful work is not fulfilled in this body and is barely ever tasted [even] by a single person. But in multitudes of people the natural desires have to be satisfied, and not by way of a momentary quality but through the stable habitual condition they yearn for. If the mind separates itself the more from corporeal things the more it is lifted upwards towards the contemplation of things spiritual, but the highest limit which understanding can attain is the substance itself of God, then it follows that the mind only ascends to the divine substance when it has become totally separated from the mortal senses. So the soul, having been delivered from the chains of this body and departing now as a pure being, in a certain sense becomes God. But God and the eternity of God are the same. For

autem ac dei aeternitas idem. Igitur ratione simili fit aeternitas multoque magis fit aeterna. Quem quidem statum Ioannes theologus appellat deo similem fieri, Paulus autem in dei imaginem transformari.

: II :

Quintum immortalitatis signum ab eo quod anima appetit[11] *primum verum et primum bonum.*

1 Ita demum ratio superior nos de immortalitate certiores efficiet, si duodecim illas dei dotes sigillatim percurrentes ostenderimus animam in his quaerendis naturaliter deo se quodammodo aequare conari.

2 Animus noster communem veritatis bonitatisque concipit rationem, per quam commune verum quaerit et commune appetit bonum. In communi veritate omnia vera, in communi bono bona omnia continentur. Hinc fit ut cuncta vera naturaliter quaerat, cuncta naturaliter appetat bona. Quod ex eo patet quod cognita una quadam alicuius rei veritate non quiescimus, sed aliam inquirimus rursusque aliam, quamdiu putamus veritatem aliquam superesse noscendam. Idem in bonis comparandis inspicitur. Omne autem verum et omne bonum deus ipse est, qui primum verum est primumque bonum. Ergo deum ipsum appetimus. Sed quid in eo potissimum affectamus? Illi similes fieri. Omnia enim pro capacitate naturae in ipsum tendunt tamquam finem, et ipsi suo modo cupiunt similia fieri: corpora vita carentia secundum esse tantum; viventia secundum vitam; sensitiva secundum sensum; secundum intellectum rationalia. Non possumus autem deo per intellectum similes effici, nisi deum intellegendo, quippe cum quibuslibet aliis

the same reason therefore the soul becomes eternity and *a fortiori* eternal. The theologian John refers to this state as becoming like God,[3] but Paul refers to it as being transformed into the image of God.[4]

: II :

The fifth sign[5] of immortality is that the soul desires the first truth and the first good.

The argument above will convince us the more of immortality if, in reviewing one by one the twelve attributes of God, we were to show that the soul in pursuing them naturally strives in a way to equal God. 1

Our rational soul conceives of the common rational principle of truth and goodness and uses it to search for what is universally true and to desire what is universally good. All true things are contained in the universal truth, and all good things in the universal good. Hence it naturally searches for all things true and naturally desires all things good. We see this from the fact that we are not content with having known the one particular truth of something; instead we inquire again for another truth and another, as long as we suppose that some truth remains to be known. We see the same in our pursuit of goods. But every truth and every good is God Himself who is the prime truth and the prime good. So we desire God Himself. But what do we long for most in Him? To become like Him. For all things aim at God as their end according to their natural capacity, and they desire to become like Him in their own way: bodies lacking life by way of being only, living things by way of life, animals possessing sensation by way of sense, rational beings by way of intellect. But we cannot become like God through the intellect except by understanding God, since the 2

rebus intellectus tunc fiat similis, quando eas intellegendo se in earum imagines transfigurat. Finis ergo noster est per intellectum deum videre, per voluntatem viso deo frui, quia summum bonum nostrum est summae potentiae nostrae obiectum summum sive actus perfectissimus circa ipsum. Summae autem potentiae nostrae sunt mens mentisque caput atque voluntas. Summum harum obiectum est commune verum bonumque commune et integrum, id est autem deus.

3 Neque obiiciat nobis Arabum aliquis sufficere nobis angelo aliquo frui. Naturale quippe desiderium nobis inest ad causam semper cuiusque effectus inveniendam, neque cessat inquisitio quousque ad causam primam perveniatur. Quoniam igitur cuiusque effectus cogniti optamus causam videre, atque intellectus noster esse ipsum universale cognoscit, efficitur ut naturaliter affectemus esse ipsius causam noscere, quae quidem ipse est deus, neque dicimur finem ultimum assecuti, nisi quiescat totum desiderium naturale. Quare in sola dei sive cognitione sive possessione ultimus finis consistit humanus, quae naturalem sola terminat appetitum. Quod liquido hinc apparet, quia proprii finis adeptio delectat quemque summopere. Animus autem rei nullius possessione tam vehementer, tam pure, tam firmiter gaudet, quantum vel exigua qualibet speculationis divinae gustatione, pro qua, si quando vere persentiatur, et possessio omnis et mundus totus et vita contemnitur. Quisquis enim pie nonnunquam cum deo vivit, is clamat se tunc solum in vita et a malis vixisse semotum et boni aliquid gustavisse, quasi tunc dumtaxat in suum se portum receperit. Huc tendit illud Platonis in libro *De scientia:* 'Mala omnino devitari non possunt. Necesse est enim semper aliquid bono contrarium esse. Apud superos autem mala esse impossibile est, sed circa mortalem naturam locumque inferiorem necessario revolvuntur, quamobrem

intellect becomes like various other things when it transforms itself in understanding them into their images. So our end is to perceive God through the intellect and to enjoy God as seen through the will, because our highest good is the highest object of our highest power or the most perfect act pertaining to it. But our highest powers are the mind and the head of the mind and the will. Their highest object is the universal truth and the universal good entire, that is, God.

Let none of the Arabs confront us with the argument that for 3
us it is enough just to enjoy some angel. There is a natural desire present in us always to find the cause of each effect and not to halt our enquiry until we have reached the first cause.[6] Since we therefore choose to see the cause of each known effect and our intellect knows the universal being itself, we naturally long as a consequence to know the cause of being itself, which is God Himself; and we are not said to have reached the ultimate goal unless our natural desire is wholly laid to rest. So the ultimate human end consists in either the knowledge or the possession of God; and this alone terminates the natural appetite. Demonstrating this clearly is that for anything the acquisition of its own end absolutely delights it. But the rational soul rejoices so vehemently, so purely, so steadfastly in the possession of nothing so much as in some taste, however faint, of divine contemplation. If ever this is truly perceived, all possessions, the whole world, life itself—all are despised for its sake. For whoever at some point lives with God in righteousness, exclaims that only then has he lived in life and been severed from evil; only then when he has returned as it were to his own port has he enjoyed something of the good. This is the point of what Plato says in his book on knowledge [the *Theaetetus*]: "Evil cannot be entirely avoided. For something always has to be the contrary of good. But evil cannot exist among the gods: necessarily it revolves around our mortal nature and this lower realm. So as soon as possible we must flee from here to there. But to flee from

hinc illuc quam primum est fugiendum. Fugere vero hinc illuc nihil est aliud quam deo, quatenus fieri potest, se similem reddere. Similem vero faciunt iustitia et sanctitas cum prudentia'. Haec ille. Merito ita praecipit. Ubi enim bonorum omnium viget bonum, ibi solum invenitur omnium medicina malorum.

4 Neque credendum est Panaetio dicenti optare quidem nos divina, sed numquam ad summum consecuturos, quia plena divinorum possessio et vita quieta non ad animos hominum pertineat, sed ad angelos. Natura ipsa rerum contra nos docet. Nempe elementa, quae naturali cupiditate sua petunt loca, tanto feruntur rapacius, quanto magis locis suis finibusque propinquant. Ideo Aristoteles in libro *De caelo* ostendit motum naturalem rectum non posse ad infinitum vagari, alioquin in suo progressu non esset modo tardior, modo vero velocior. Quapropter quod tale est, ut vehementius postea quam prius tendat in aliquid, non oberrat in infinitum, sed ad certum aliquid sese confert. Hoc autem in ipso sciendi desiderio experimur; quo enim quis magis intellegit, eo ardentius flagrat ad reliquum.

5 Igitur naturale desiderium cognoscendi ad finem aliquem determinatum dirigitur. Quis hic finis? Causa causarum omnium, quae comperta naturalem omnem inquisitionem terminat causarum. Dedit natura corporibus crassis appetitionem inclinationemque qua loca cuperent inferiora; adhibuit illis praeterea gravitatem frigusque, quasi medium per quod ad locum optatum descenderent. Dedit subtilioribus appetitum altioris loci, adiunxit et levitatem caliditatemque, per quae[12] media optatum finem consequerentur. Dedit brutis cibi et coitus appetitum, addidit membra ad esum et

here to there is nothing other than to make oneself as like God as it is possible to be. But justice and sanctity along with prudence make man like Him."[7] So Plato. And his precepts are just; for where the good of all good flourishes, there alone is found the medicine for all ills.

4 We should not believe Panaetius when he says that we do indeed choose things divine but that we will never possess them fully because full possession of them and the life of tranquillity pertain not to men's souls but to the angels.[8] Universal nature herself teaches us the contrary. For the elements, which have a natural desire to seek out their own places, the closer they approach these places and ends of theirs, the more fiercely are they borne along. Thus Aristotle shows in his book *On the Heavens* that a motion that is naturally straight cannot continue to infinity, otherwise it would not be sometimes slower in its progress and sometimes faster.[9] So whatever is such that later it strives for something more vehemently than it strove earlier is not proceeding to infinity but aiming at a definite end. But we find this in the desire to know; for the more someone understands, the more ardently he burns for what still remains to be known.

5 Therefore the natural desire to know is directed towards a determined end. What is this end? It is the cause of all causes that, once discovered, ends all natural delving into causes. Nature gave heavier bodies the desire and inclination to yearn for lower places, and it endowed them with heaviness and coldness furthermore as a means by which they might descend to their chosen place. It gave to more subtle bodies the desire for a loftier place and added lightness and heat as means by which they might attain their chosen end. It gave beasts the appetite for food and sex and gave them body parts designed for eating and coition. But the leader of nature gave the rational soul the longing for the universal true and good in their entirety, a longing which, to the extent it is more continuous, is more natural to it than the appetite for food or co-

coitum praeparata. Dedit naturae dux animo universalis et totius veri bonique votum, quod quidem eo naturalius est quam cibi et coitus appetitus quo illud est magis continuum. Comedere quidem raro corpus exigit, rarius vero coire. Verum autem bonumque singulis optamus momentis. Semper enim novarum rerum imaginationumque et rationum cupidi sumus. Semper oculos patefacimus ad quaelibet occurrentia et longissimo amplissimoque prospectu nimium delectamur, immo solo contenti sumus immenso. Semper arrigimus aures ad quaelibet audienda, quod infantes faciunt et adulti, gnari pariter et ignari, atque omnes in arte qualibet artifices, duce natura. Adde quod domari potest coitus libido, edendi voracitas minui, veri autem bonique voluntas minime. Immo vero decrescunt illa aetate, haec augetur. Adde insuper, quod illa corporalia propter aliud appetuntur, haec autem gratia sui. Quanto igitur naturalior est veri bonique quam cibi coitusque cupiditas, tanto magis a naturae duce provisum est ut finem suum prorsus adipiscatur. Immo vero ob eam maxime causam naturalior est, quia est ad finem acquirendum paratior.

6 Profecto si speciei cuiusque proprietas necessaria est prudenterque ab auctore disposita, sequitur ut rationalis speciei conatus, qui ad totius boni possessionem dirigitur quasi finem, assequi valeat quod contendit. Nempe si impossibilis sit finis ultimi consecutio, universa tum species tum actio speciei contingens est, fortuita et inanis. Quiescit quandoque oculus speciei gratiosae conspectu, quiescit auris melodia, et quisque sensus quandoque suis satiatur et impletur obiectis. Tanta felicitate sensus natura donavit. Ratio vero istorum regina, quae licet angelis inferior sit, brutis tamen est superior, tam infelix erit, tam ab artifice naturae neglecta, ut oberret semper, quiescat numquam? Certe in hac vita numquam.

itus. A body rarely needs to eat and even more rarely to have sex. But every single moment we wish for the true and the good. For we are always desirous of new things and of novel imaginations and reasons. Our eyes are always wide open to gaze upon all that comes into their field of vision and we delight excessively in gazing at the most distant or the widest prospect; or rather, we are content with immensity alone. Our ears are always alert to hear everything. This is the case with children and adults, the wise and the foolish alike, and with every artisan in any art guided by nature. Moreover, [while] the desire for sex can be mastered and the greed for eating lessened, the will for the true and the good is never mastered or diminished; or rather, while the former wane with age, the latter increases. Furthermore, while those corporeal things are desired because of another, the true and the good are desired for their own sake. So to the extent the desire for the true and the good is more natural than that for food or sex, the guidance of nature has made even greater provision for its fully attaining its end; or rather this desire is more natural precisely because it is readier to attain its end.

If the property of each species is necessary and has been wisely 6
ordained by its author, it follows surely that the endeavor of each rational species—which, as its end, is directed to the possession of the good in its entirety—is able to achieve what it is striving for. If attaining the ultimate end were impossible, then both the universal species and the action of that species would be contingent, fortuitous, and in vain. But on occasions the eye does come to rest in the sight of a beautiful shape, the ear in a melody; and each sense is at times satisfied and filled by its object. Nature has given such felicity to the senses. But reason, the queen of the senses, though it is lower than the angels, is yet higher than the beasts. And will this reason be so unhappy, so neglected by the artificer of nature that it will wander forever and never rest? Certainly it will never rest in this life.

7 Neque audiendus hic est Arabum aliquis fingens intellectum humanum, quod hac in vita nequit in singulis, saltem in cunctis hominibus assequi. Primo quidem non est intellectus unus in omnibus inter se penitus repugnantibus, quod alias ostendemus; deinde neque in cunctis quidem simul hominibus umquam animus habitum exoptatum consequitur. Ac dum in singulis hominibus ad divina caecus est, ad eadem ferme similiter in cunctis est caecus. Denique non licet fingere nos ipsas divinarum formarum substantias ex substantiis naturalibus ad votum comprehendere posse. Hae namque substantiae ad materiam declinant; illae vero nequaquam. Intellectus autem humanus quatenus hoc habitat corpus, eatenus cognoscendo quodammodo ad corporalia vergit. Praeterea, naturales effectus divinarum causarum vires substantiasque aequare et demonstrare non possunt. Adde quod divinae formae a naturalibus multo magis distant quam a naturalibus naturales. Ergo si per voces non cognoscuntur colores, quod apparet in caecis, multo minus per naturalia umquam divina comprehenduntur, ut Plato ad Dionysium scribit Syracusanum. Mitto quod substantia virtusque divina tamquam infinita non potest a nobis prius ad votum percipi, quam per ipsammet absolute formemur, quod quidem in anima huic coniuncta corpori sic affecto perfici nequit.

8 Verum ut ad propositam huius capituli argumentationem regrediamur, rationis capacitas appetitioque[13] non quaedam vera aut bona quaedam, sed omnia integraquae requirit. Quae hic ideo numquam assequi videtur, ut Plato inquit in *Epinomide*, quia semper est ambiguus intellectus, semper voluntas est anxia. Haec igitur animus exutus corpore consequetur. Si bonum universum adi-

Here we must not give ear to one of the Arabs who supposes that the human intellect can attain in all men what it cannot attain in this life in individual men.[10] In the first place the intellect is not one in all men who are utterly at odds with themselves (as we will show elsewhere[11]). Next, the rational soul never achieves its elected habitual condition in all men even if viewed collectively. And as long as it is blind to things divine in individual men, it is similarly blind to them in all men, or virtually so. Finally, it is unlawful for us to suppose that we can comprehend at will from natural substances the substances themselves of the divine forms; for the natural substances decline towards matter, but the divine never. In knowing, however, and to the extent it dwells in the body, the human intellect turns in a way towards corporeals. Moreover, natural effects are unable to equal or to demonstrate the powers and substances of divine causes; and add to this the fact that divine forms are more distant from natural forms than natural forms from each other. So if colors are not known via sounds as we see in the case of blind people, much less are divine matters ever comprehended by way of natural ones, as Plato writes to Dionysius of Syracuse.[12] I leave aside the fact that divine as well as infinite substance and power cannot be perceived by us at will prior to our being formed absolutely by that substance; and this cannot be achieved in a soul joined to this body in its present condition. 7

Let us return, however, to the stated theme of this chapter. The reason's capacity and desire seeks not just particular true or good things but all good things and all together. It seems these can never be attained here, as Plato says in the *Epinomis*, because the intellect is always uncertain and the will always troubled.[13] Once divested of the body, however, the soul will attain them. If it attains the universal good, it will in no way lack immortality, which is as great a good as death (which deprives us of all good things) is an evil. And the mind, which will see all things true, will never 8

piscetur, immortalitate nullo modo carebit, quae tantum bonum est, quantum mors est malum, quae cunctis privat bonis. Ac mens quae vera videbit omnia, nullis gaudebit bonis, si se suspicabitur morituram. Ut ergo secura sit finis adeptio et tranquilla, necesse est mentem de aeterna finis possessione certam esse. Quod quidem ita confirmat Aurelius Augustinus in libro *De trinitate* tertio decimo. 'Omnes beati esse volunt atque ideo nolunt perire et consumi, quod beati sunt. Nec nisi viventes beati esse possunt. Nolunt igitur perire quod vivunt. Immortales itaque esse volunt quicumque vere beati vel sunt vel esse cupiunt. Non autem vivit beate, cui non adest quod vult. Nullo modo igitur esse poterit vita vere beata, nisi fuerit sempiterna'. Haec ille. Sed ne Panaetiani diffidant ulterius vitam vere beatam homini convenire, ita concludemus. Cum naturae intellectualis proprium sit cognitione gustare omne bonum, certe eiusdem proprium est affectu etiam vesci omni bono, id est integro. Beatitudo igitur naturae intellectualis est propria. Qualem vero quisque intellectum habet, talem potest beatitudinem consequi. Si verum formalemque intellectum, veram quoque formalemque felicitatem. Sin umbratilem intellectum, umbratilem quoque felicitatem.

9 Hominis anima, licet imago quaedam sit intellectus divinioris, veram tamen in se mentis formam habet, quod tribus probatur signis. Primum est, quod multa vera secundum veram eorum rationem intellegit. Secundum, quod veram veritatis ipsius intellegit rationem. Tertium, quod si anima nostra solam intellectus umbram haberet, non intellegeret definiretve umquam formam et substantiam intellectus, sed accidentia tantum confuse prospiceret. Quoniam igitur anima vim intellegendi possidet non umbratilem tantum, sicut bestiae quaedam sagaciores, sed vere etiam expressam

rejoice in things good if it suspects it is going to die. So for the acquisition of its end to be assured and tranquil, the mind must necessarily be certain about its eternal possession of that end. Aurelius Augustinus confirms this in the thirteenth book of his work *On the Trinity*: "All men want to be blessed and so they do not want their blessedness to perish or to be consumed. They cannot be blessed unless they are alive. So they do not want the fact that they are alive to perish. So all those who are truly blessed or who desire to be so want to be immortal. But the person who lacks what he wants is not living blessedly. So life could not be truly blessed in any way unless it were everlasting."[14] These are Augustine's words. But lest the followers of Panaetius doubt any longer that the truly blessed life is appropriate to man,[15] we will conclude as follows. Since in knowing it is the property of the intellectual nature to taste of every good, in desiring it is certainly the property of the same to be nourished too by every good, every integral good that is. So blessedness is appropriate to the intellectual nature. But each person is able to attain the blessedness that is appropriate to his intellect. If he has an intellect that is true and possessed of the forms, he will attain a happiness that is true and authentic;[16] but if he has an intellect wrapped in shadows, he will attain a happiness that is shadowy too.

Man's soul, though it is an image of an intellect that is more divine, yet it has the true form of mind within itself; and this is proved by three signs. The first is that it understands many truths according to their true rational principle; the second is that it understands the true rational principle of the truth itself; and the third is that, if our soul were to have the shadow alone of the intellect, it would never understand or define the intellect's form and substance but confusedly gaze instead on accidents alone. Therefore, because the soul possesses not only a shadowy power of understanding, like certain of the cleverer beasts, but also a power that is truly distinct and formal, it can at some point therefore 9

atque formalem, idcirco potest quandoque vitam consequi vere beatam. Neque mirum alicui videri debet me intellectum alium umbratilem alium formalem ponere, siquidem Platonici, ut Proculus disputat, omnia rerum genera ita distinguunt, atque in primis unitatem et mentem,[14] animam et naturam.

10 Sed missa haec in praesentia faciamus, videamusque qua ratione Origenes in libris *De principiis* superiora confirmat. Cum consideraret Origenes deum rerum artificem in singulis non necessitati solum utilitatique tum propriae tum communi consulere, sed etiam (neque id quidem minus) pulchritudini rerum admirationique spectantium ubique studere, conclusit, quemadmodum humanus artifex artificia construit quam pulcherrima, ut intuentes alliciantur ad ingenium quo ille construxit considerandum atque admirandum, ita deum artificiosissimum mundi opificium construxisse. Unde effici vult, ut rationum quibus omnia constant inquisitio ab ipsamet ratione dei artificis omnium mentibus sit inserta, et inde quotidie moveatur, ita ut non minus eas nostra mens desideret per naturam, quam oculus colores et gustus escas. Addit ea nos conditione a deo eiusmodi desiderium accepisse, qua aliquando posset expleri, ne frustra a deo sit insitum. Praeterea, quisquis amori huic studio voluntatis indulserit, etiam si parum veritatis consequatur in vita, tamen ex hoc affectu praeparari ad veritatis plenitudinem in futuro comprehendendam. Et quoniam praeparatio talis fit per deum, per deum fore quandoque formationem, siquidem agentes causae non ob aliam rationem disponunt materiam, nisi ut eam forment quandoque dispositam.

11 Hanc Origenis sententiam ita breviter confirmamus, quod videlicet quatenus consideramus quales effectu universi formae sint,

achieve the life that is truly blessed. No one should be surprised that I am postulating a shadowy intellect and a formal intellect, since the Platonists, as Proclus argues, thus distinguish the classes of all things and especially the unity and the mind, the soul and the nature.[17]

Let us leave this aside for the moment, however, and see how 10
Origen confirms the argument above in his book *On Principles*.[18] Since Origen considered that God, the artificer of the world, not only has regard for both particular and general necessity and utility in the case of individual things, but everywhere also has regard (and indeed no less regard) for their beauty and for the admiration of those gazing upon it, he concluded that, just as the human artificer makes his artifacts as beautiful as possible so that people might be drawn to ponder and admire the cunning with which he has constructed them, so too has God constructed the world as the greatest work of art. Hence he wants to conclude that the inquiry into the rational principles constituting all things has been implanted in the minds of all by the reason itself of God the artificer; and that it is daily motivated by Him in such a way that our mind naturally desires these principles no less than the eye desires colors or the taste, delicate foods. He adds that we have received this desire from God on the condition that some day it can be satisfied, lest it has been implanted in us by God to no purpose; and, moreover, that whosoever has tended this love carefully and voluntarily, and even if in this life he attains too little of the truth, has been prepared by this desire nonetheless to understand in the future the fullness of the truth. Because this preparation comes through God, our being perfectly formed will also some day come through God, since active causes predispose matter for no other reason than that some day, once matter has been disposed, they might form it.

Let us briefly confirm Origen's view as follows. To the extent we 11
consider the forms of the universe in terms of their effect, and

atque utrum prosint nobis aut obsint, eatenus a natura creata duci videmur, et vitae corporis obsequi, ac velle formas externas in formam nostram, prout usus postulat, transformare. At quando perscrutamur quibus rationibus singula ita creata ordinataque sint, quod sane inquirimus naturaliter, tunc ab ipsa rerum artifice ratione ad ipsammet allicimur vitaeque studemus aeternae et in formam artificis omniformem animum reformare conamur. Hinc Paulus Apostolus inquit interiorem hominem quotidie renovari, invisibilia nobis aeternaque contemplantibus. Item: 'Nos autem, inquit, revelata facie gloriam Domini speculantes, in eandem imaginem transformamur a claritate in claritatem tamquam a Domini spiritu'.

: III :

Sextum signum: quia animus conatur omnia fieri.

1 Ostensum est animum nostrum in omnibus suis actibus primam illam dei dotem pro viribus comparare, id est totius veri totiusque boni possessionem. Secundam vero illam quaeritne? An conatur omnia fieri sicut deus est omnia? Conatur mirum in modum.

2 Vitam siquidem agit plantae, quatenus saginando indulget corpori. Vitam bruti, quatenus sensibus adulatur. Vitam hominis, prout de humanis negotiis ratione consultat. Vitam heroum, quantum naturalia investigat. Vitam daemonum, prout mathematica speculatur. Vitam angelorum, prout divina inquirit mysteria.

whether they work for or against us, to that extent we seem to be led by created nature and to follow the life of the body, and, as use demands, to be wishing to transform external forms into our form. But when we seek to know (and it is natural for us to inquire) by what rational principles individual things are thus created and arranged, then we are drawn by reason itself, the artificer of things, towards itself. We strive after eternal life and try to reform our rational soul into the omniform form of the artificer. Hence the apostle Paul declares that "the inward man is renewed day by day" in those of us contemplating things invisible and eternal.[19] Again he says, "In gazing upon the glory of the Lord with face unveiled, we are transformed into the same image from brightness to brightness as by the spirit of the Lord."[20]

: III :

Sixth sign: that the rational soul strives to become all things.

In all its acts our soul has been shown to draw on all its strength to procure that first gift of God, the possession of the whole truth and the whole good. But does it seek the second gift or not? Does it strive to become all things as God is all things? It does indeed strive in a marvelous way. 1

It lives the life of a plant insofar as it indulges the body by fattening it up; the life of the beast insofar as it flatters the senses; the life of man insofar as it calls upon reason to handle human affairs; the life of the heroes insofar as it investigates things in nature; the life of the demons insofar as it contemplates mathematics; the life of the angels insofar as it inquires into the mysteries divine; and the life of God insofar as it does all things for God's sake. Every man's soul in a way makes trial of all these in itself, although different souls do so in different ways, and thus human- 2

Vitam dei, quantum dei gratia omnia operatur. Omnis hominis anima haec in se cuncta quodammodo experitur, licet aliter aliae, atque ita genus humanum contendit omnia fieri, cum omnium agat vitas. Quod admiratus Mercurius Trismegistus inquit: 'Magnum miraculum esse hominem, animal venerandum et adorandum, qui genus daemonum noverit quasi natura cognatum, quive in deum transeat, quasi ipse sit deus'. Praeterea, quaecumque sunt, quantum sunt, sunt vera. Quantum vero vim aliquam ordinemque et usum sortita sunt, sunt et bona. Animum supra monstravimus omnia vera et bona omnia quaerere. Res igitur omnes quaerit. Quid autem quaerit aliud, nisi ut per intellectum sciat omnes, per voluntatem omnibus perfruatur? Utroque autem modo fieri cuncta conatur. Sicut sensus, puta visus, colores non cernit, nisi colorum induat formas, fiatque unum ex videndi potentia et formae visibilis actu, ceu ex aere lumineque fit unum, ita neque intellectus res ipsas cognoscit, nisi vestiatur formis rerum cognoscendarum, fiatque ex intellegendi potentia et formae intellegibilis actu unum. Quorum unionem una actio comitatur; una enim intellegendi operatio est utriusque.

3 Quis item neget ex materia corporali et forma illi tributa rem unam fieri, cum ex illo composito unus proveniat actus unusque motus? Multo autem magis, ut placet Platonicis et Averroi, unum quiddam fieri oportet ex potentia intellectus formaque rei intellegendae, tum quia saepe stabilior ex iis provenit compositio (saepe enim diutius manent una quam materia corporalis eiusque forma), tum etiam quia intellectus ipse forma quaedam est. Forma, inquam, inhians materiae instar ad formam ulteriorem. Ideo magis convenit cum forma suscipienda, quam conveniat cum forma propria materia corporalis. Omnes enim formae in mundi materias a superna mente descendunt, quocirca cum mente nostra multo magis conveniunt quam cum materia. Denique mens quanto est

kind strives to become all things, since as a genus it lives the lives of all. Mercurius Trismegistus was struck with wonder by this and declares, "Man is a great miracle, an animal meet to be worshipped and adored; he knows the race of the demons, being naturally their kin, and he turns into God as though he himself were God."[21] Furthermore, all that exist insofar as they exist are true; but they are also good insofar as they have been allotted a power, an order, and a usefulness. We showed above that the rational soul seeks all true and all good things. So it seeks all things. But what else does it seek except to know all through the intellect and to enjoy all through the will? But it strives to become all in both ways. Just as a sense, for instance the sight, does not see colors unless it assumes the forms of colors, and in it the power of seeing and the act of the visible form are united as air and light are united, so the intellect does not come to know things themselves unless it is clothed in the forms of the things to be known, and unless its power of understanding and the act of the intelligible form are united. Following their union is one activity; for pertaining to both is the one activity of understanding.

Again, who will deny a single thing results from corporeal mat- 3
ter and the form bestowed upon it, since this composite gives rise to one act and to one motion? *A fortiori*, according to the Platonists and to Averroes,[22] a single something must result from the union between the intellect's power and the form of the object to be understood, both because a more stable composite emerges from their union (for they often stay united longer than corporeal matter and its form), and because the intellect itself is a kind of form, a form yearning like matter for a higher form. So it is more in harmony with the form to be received than corporeal matter can be in harmony with its own form. For all forms descend into the world's materials from the supernal mind, and this is why they are more in harmony with our mind than with matter. Finally, the mind, insofar as it is more excellent than matter to that extent it

praestantior quam materia, tanto efficacius formam quam exoptat[15] sibi adsciscit et unit.

4 Neque credendum est animum sibi minus unire quae capit quam corpus. Corpus enim cibos vel diversissimos in suam vertit substantiam anima concoquente. Ita et animus quae accipit, immo concipit, in se vertit, et multo magis, siquidem dimensiones corporum mutuam in corporibus impediunt unionem; spiritalia vero sunt unioni admodum aptiora. Itaque rationes rerum intellectarum magis in substantiam transeunt intellectus, ut vult Plotinus, quam in substantiam corporis alimenta. Per haec patet ex mente nostra et forma rei intellegendae unum aliquid fieri. Quod autem ita subit alicuius formam, ut ex ea et se ipso reddat unum, illud ipsum ferme evadit, cuius subivit formam. Quis nesciat materiam aeris quando ignis formam suscipit, effici ignem aut igneam? Ideo intellectus paene res illa fit quam intellegit—fit, inquam, actu res illa. Nam et potentia et quodammodo habitu res eadem erat etiam priusquam intellegeret, ut Plotinus existimat. Tunc sane intellectus intellegit circulum quando ipse actu quasi fit ratio circuli. Immo hoc ipsum actu fieri ipsum intellegere est. Erat autem intellectus eadem ipsa circuli ratio etiam prius, tum secundum potentiam, quoad substantialem pertinet circuli ipsius ideam, tum secundum habitum quoad ideae formulam nobis familiarem. Veritas autem singularum rerum in ipsa firma illarum ratione consistit. Atque ita mens res quaelibet vera fit, quando res ipsas intellegit, se in earum rationes perpetuas convertendo. Sed de hoc alias. Sufficit

acquires and unites the more effectively with the form it desires for itself.

We must not suppose that the rational soul unites itself less to what it receives than does the body. For the body takes in a great variety of foods, and with the [vegetative] soul digesting them, turns them into its own substance. So too the rational soul takes what it receives, or rather conceives, and turns them into itself; and the more so, since the dimensions of bodies impede mutual union in bodies, yet spiritual beings are much better suited to union. So the rational principles of things understood pass into the substance of the intellect, as Plotinus supposes,[23] to a greater degree than nutriments pass into the body's substance. From this it is obvious that a single something results from our mind being united with the form of an object to be understood. But what submits to the form of another (such that a union results from the form and itself) ends up as nearly the same object to whose form it has submitted. Who does not know that the matter of air when it receives the form of fire is made into fire or made fiery? Thus the intellect almost becomes the object it understands—becomes the object itself, I repeat, in act; for it was this same object potentially and in a way habitually even before it understood it, as Plotinus holds.[24] For surely the intellect understands the circle at the moment when it becomes in act as it were the rational principle of the circle; or rather, this actualizing is itself to understand. But the intellect was this same rational principle of the circle even beforehand: potentially insofar as it pertains to the substantial idea of the circle itself, and habitually insofar as it pertains to the idea's formula familiar to us. But the truth of individual things consists in their unchanging rational principle itself. And thus the mind becomes an individual true thing when it understands things themselves by converting itself into their unchanging rational principles. But of this elsewhere.[25] For the present it is enough for us that, since the intellect seeks to understand all things and in un- 4

autem nobis in praesentia, quod cum intellectus quaerat res omnes intellegere et intellegendo formis earum penitus vestiatur, consequens est ut quaerat res omnes effici. Unde nititur deus fieri, in quo sunt omnia, dum nititur omnia fieri. De intellectu satis.

5 Cupit idem et nostra voluntas, quia semper affectat bonis omnibus perfrui. Fruendo autem rebus, se ipsam rebus quibus fruitur unit. Sed interest intellectum inter[16] et voluntatem. Utraque fiunt omnia — intellectus omnia vera, voluntas omnia bona — sed intellectus res in se ipsum transferendo illis unitur, voluntas contra in res transferendo se ipsam. Quonam pacto? Sane noster intellectus modo suo potius res intellegit quam pro natura rerum. Formas utique corporum, quae sunt particulares, materiae immersae, divisae, confusae, infectae ac mobiles intellegit modo quodam universali, absoluto, simplici distincto, puro et stabili. Deum vero et angelos, qui stabiles sunt et simplices mobili ut plurimum et multiplici comprehendat[17] discursione. Ita intellectus noster tam illa quae infra se, quam quae supra existunt, modo quodam percipit suo. Quam ob causam dicitur omnia in suam transferre naturam. Ex quo etiam Platonis illud confirmari videtur, quod mens per innatas formas intellegat, postquam per naturae suae modum intellegit.

6 Voluntas autem primo quidem non sicut intellectus in se permanet, sed animam et corpus movet ad operandum, ut ad res desideratas accedant, deinde non eo proprie modo quo res in anima insunt affectat, sed quo potius in se ipsis. Intellectui aurum cognituro species auri illa universalis et incorporea sufficit, voluntati vero non sufficit. Nam quantum ad humanam vitam spectat, aurum vult particulare istud et corporale, quale est in se ipso.

7 Concludamus animam nostram per intellectum et voluntatem tamquam geminas illas platonicas alas idcirco volare ad deum,

derstanding is entirely clothed in their forms, it seeks consequently to become all things. Hence as long as it strives to become all things, it is striving to become God in whom all things exist. But enough concerning the intellect.

Our will longs for the same thing too, because it always longs to enjoy all that is good. But in enjoying things it unites itself with the things it enjoys. But there is a difference between the intellect and the will. Both become all things — the intellect all things true, the will all things good — but the intellect is united to them by transferring things into itself, whereas the will by contrast is united by transferring itself into things. How? Our intellect understands things in its own way rather than according to their nature. The forms of bodies at any rate that are particular, immersed in matter, divided, confused, tarnished,[26] and changing, the intellect understands in a way which is universal, free of matter, undivided, distinct, pure, and unchanging. But it comprehends God and the angels, who are unchanging and simple, by way of a discursiveness that is for the most part changing and multiple. Thus our intellect in a manner peculiar to itself perceives those things that exist below itself and those that exist above. On this account it is said to transfer all things into its own nature. This also seems to confirm Plato's view that the mind understands through innate forms since it understands by way of its own nature. 5

But the will first of all does not remain in itself as the intellect does, but moves both the soul and the body to act so that they approach the things desired; and next it longs for things, not strictly in the way they exist in the soul, but rather as they are in themselves. The universal and incorporeal species of gold is enough for an intellect that is about to understand gold; but it is not enough for the will. From the perspective of human life, the will wants the gold that is particular and corporeal, gold as it is in itself. 6

Let us conclude that our soul thus flies towards God by way of the intellect and the will as the twin Platonic wings,[27] because it 7

quoniam per eas volat ad omnia. Per primam omnia sibi applicat, per secundam se applicat omnibus. Itaque anima cupit, conatur, incipit deus fieri, proficitque[18] quotidie. Motus autem omnis qui ad terminum aliquem directus incipit quidem primo, pergit deinde, intenditur paulatim et proficit, profecto quandoque perficitur. Eadem namque facultate intenditur qua coepit. Eadem postea proficit qua et intendebatur. Eadem tandem perficitur, qua[19] profecit. Quamobrem animus noster quandoque fieri poterit quodammodo omnia ac deus quidam evadere.

: IV :

Septimum signum et octavum: quoniam animus conatur facere omnia atque item omnia superare.

1 Sequuntur aliae dei dotes: tertia, quod auctor universorum est, quarta, quod super omnia. Has quoque animus noster aucupatur.

2 Diximus alias quemadmodum per varias artes omnia dei opera aemulatur atque ita instar dei efficit omnia. Diximus etiam hominem[20] semper contendere ut et sibi ipsi[21] et ceteris cunctis tum hominibus tum bestiis dominetur. Esse servitutis omnis impatientem. Qui etiam si servire cogatur, odit dominum, utpote qui serviat contra naturam. Superare autem obnixe qualibet in re contendit, pudetque vel in rebus minimis ludisque levissimis superari, tamquam id sit contra naturalem hominis dignitatem. Et omnino

flies towards all things with them. With the first wing it draws all things to itself, with the second it draws itself into all things. So the soul desires, strives, and begins to become God, advancing day by day.[28] But all motion that is directed towards some goal first begins, then proceeds, is gradually intensified, and advances, and at some point is certainly completed. For it is intensified by the same faculty whereby it began; later it advances by the same faculty whereby it was intensified; and eventually it is perfected by the same faculty whereby it advanced. Hence our rational soul at some point will be able to become in a way all things and to emerge as a kind of god.

: IV :

The seventh and eighth signs: that the rational soul strives to make all things and also to master them.

God's other gifts follow next: the third that He is the author of all, the fourth that He is above all.[29] Our rational soul also chases after these. 1

We have declared elsewhere that, just as this soul emulates all God's works through its various arts, so too, like God, it accomplishes all things. We have also declared that man is forever striving to rule over himself and over all others, men and beasts; that he is impatient of all servitude; that even if he is compelled to serve, he hates his master in that to serve is contrary to [his] nature.[30] But he strives resolutely in every thing to achieve mastery and is ashamed to be overcome in even the smallest matters and the most frivolous games as being counter to man's natural dignity. And in general the feeling of shame and diffidence which is proper to humanity signifies that something august, I know not what, lies hidden in us which it is sacrilegious to desecrate, or which de- 2

pudoris verecundiaeque affectus humano generi proprius nescio quid augustum latere in nobis significat, quod nefas sit temerari, quodve sit veneratione dignissimum. De hoc alibi. Sed quantum pertinet ad victoriae cupiditatem, immensam animi nostri magnificentiam ex hoc manifeste licet perspicere, quod non satis illi futurum sit mundi huius imperium, si hoc subacto alium resciverit superesse mundum, quem nondum subegerit. Hinc Alexander cum audiret Anaxarchum Democritium mundos esse innumerabiles disputantem, 'heu me miserum', exclamavit, 'qui ne uno quidem adhuc potitus sum'. Ita nec superiorem vult homo neque parem, neque patitur superesse aliquid ab imperio eius exclusum. Solius dei hic status est. Statum igitur quaerit divinum. Quod inde plane possumus coniectari, quod multi tum philosophi tum principes divinos sibi quaesiverunt honores. Neque satis illis fuit quod boni homines haberentur, nisi haberentur divini; immo tamquam dii voluerunt coli. Quod cum innumerabiles viri tentaverint, inter philosophos Empedocles praecipue, inter principes Alexander Macedo dicitur concupisse. Denique omnes idem affectant, et si successurum sperarent, aggrederentur quasi iure suo vindicent sibi[22] divinitatem.

: V :

Nonum signum et decimum: quod homo affectat ubique esse atque item esse semper.

1 Deus praeterea ubique est et semper. Cupit autem homo ubique esse. Quatuor enim elementis utitur, sicut diximus. Terram metitur et caelum ac profundas Tartari latebras perscrutatur. Non illi caelum videtur altissimum, ut Mercurii verbis utar, non centrum

serves our utmost veneration. But of this elsewhere.[31] But insofar as it pertains to the desire for victory, we can perceive the boundless magnificence of our rational soul from the manifest fact that the empire of this world is not going to be sufficient for it, if, having conquered this one, it learns that another world exists which it has not yet conquered. Hence Alexander, when he heard Anaxarchus, the Democritean, arguing that there were numberless worlds, cried out, "Miserable me, alas, who have not yet taken possession of even one world."[32] Thus man wants neither a superior nor an equal, nor does he suffer anything to thrive outside his dominion. [But] this condition is God's alone. Thus man seeks the divine condition. We can plainly infer this from the fact that many philosophers and princes alike have sought out divine honors for themselves. That they were considered good men was not enough for them unless they were also deemed divine; or rather, they wanted to be worshipped as gods. Though innumerable men have attempted this, among philosophers chiefly Empedocles is said to have coveted it,[33] and among princes, Alexander of Macedon. Finally, all men want the same thing, and if they hope to attain it in the future they will proceed as though they are going to lay claim to divinity as their right.

: V :

The ninth and tenth signs: that man longs to be everywhere and to be forever.

1 Furthermore, God is everywhere and is always. But man longs to be everywhere. For he uses the four elements, as we said. He measures the earth and the sky and he examines the hidden depths of Tartarus. To him the sky does not appear superlatively high—to use Mercurius' words[34]—nor deep the center of the earth. The

terrae profundum. Non temporum locorumve[23] intervalla impediunt quin per omnia currat[24] quaecumque sunt in quibuscumque temporibus aut locis. Nullus paries eius aut obtundit aut retundit intuitum. Nulli fines sibi sunt satis. Ubique studet imperare, ubique laudari. Atque ita conatur esse, ut deus, ubique.

2 Conatur quoque esse et semper, ut deus. Duobus autem id quaerit modis. Primo quod per omne futurum tempus in ore hominum restare contendit, doletque neque potuisse etiam in omnibus praeteritis saeculis celebrari, neque posse in futuris ab omnibus tum hominum nationibus tum brutorum generibus honorari. Id omnes tam adolescentes quam adulti, tam rudes quam eruditi omni ope studioque nituntur, et tanto affectant ardentius quanto magis excellunt ingenio. Quod autem omnes appetunt homines, maxime vero praestantiores, hoc ab illis naturali lege tamquam bonum desideratur. Non igitur frustra quaeritur, siquidem in lege naturae non est temeritas. Temere autem quaereretur et frustra tamquam bonum, si nihil esset quaerentibus profuturum. Non prodest laus quae non sentitur. Quapropter species humana vaticinatur se in saeculis futuris sensu non carituram, cum saepe etiam praesentem contemnat vitam ut a posteris celebretur. Posterorum quoque suorum cum in omni vita, tum in vitae calce summam habet curam, existimans ad se futura saecula pertinere. Haec fieri a bestiis non videmus, quasi earum natura vaticinetur nihil in se esse quod aut veneratione sit dignum aut sensu praeditum sempiterno. Vaticinium vero naturale excellentissimorum praesertim ingeniorum aberrare non potest, quemadmodum Plato in epistola scribit ad Dionysium. Ex quo effici vult, ut animis hominum sensus humanarum rerum supersit.[25] Quod etiam in *Legibus* ex ordine divinae providentiae confirmavit.

3 Alter modus quo noster animus optat esse semper, immo et vivere (siquidem animae idem est esse quod vivere) talis apparet.

intervals of time and place do not prevent him from coursing through all that exists in whatever time or place. No wall blocks or checks his gaze; no boundaries suffice for him. He studies to rule everywhere, everywhere to be praised. And thus he strives to be, like God, everywhere.

Man strives too to be, like God, always. However he wants to 2
be so in two ways. First he strives to remain on the lips of men for all future time, and he grieves too that he could not be celebrated in all the past centuries and cannot be honored in all the centuries to come by mankind's every nation and by every kind of beast. All young as well as adult men, ignorant as well as learned, strive for this [praise] with all their strength and ardor; and the more ardently they long for it, the more they excel in natural ingenuity. But what all men desire, and the more outstanding men desire the most, they desire by a natural law as a good. So it is not sought in vain, since no waywardness exists in the law of nature. Yet it would be sought as a good waywardly and in vain if it were not going to profit those seeking it. Unheard praise, however, is useless. So the human species foresees that it will not lack the ability to hear [praise] in centuries to come, since it even scorns the present life often in order to be celebrated by posterity; and it is supremely solicitous of its own descendents both throughout life and at the end of life's race, believing that future ages are its concern. We do not witness this happening in the case of the beasts, whose nature foresees as it were that nothing exists in it which is worthy of veneration or endowed with everlasting perception. But natural prediction, especially by those with the finest natural abilities, cannot err, as Plato writes in a letter to Dionysius; and so he holds that the perception of human affairs survives in men's souls.[35] He confirmed this view also in the *Laws* arguing from the order of divine providence.[36]

Another way in which our rational soul strives to be always, or 3
rather to live always (since for the soul to be and to live are the

Humanus animus, et is quidem omnis, vitam aliquam cogitat sempiternam, quam statim cogitatam affectat, semperque cupit esse. Omnino appetitus essendi naturalis est, quoniam rebus statim natis inest cunctis atque continuus. Neque consilio advenit, quia inest e vestigio natis, neque casu contingit, quia cunctis et quia continuus. Profecto elementa per virtutem naturalium qualitatum resistunt rebus corruptionem tentantibus, ne esse illis auferatur. Rursus, loca sibi convenientia petunt avidissime repelluntque obstantia motui, ut esse conservent. Hic appetitus essendi ideo dicitur naturalis, quia naturales eorum sequitur qualitates. Plantae quoque vitalis complexionis instinctu humorem sugunt salubriorem, radices ad hunc longissime dilatantes, quo esse conservent. Item, umbras retractis declinant ramusculis atque viminibus quibusdam aduncis implicant sustentacula, ne esse amittant. Quem appetitum dicimus naturalem, quia naturalem sequitur vitae complexionem. Bruta per concupiscentiam naturalem ea adsciscunt, quae esse conservant repelluntque[26] per naturalem iracundiam interimentia. Itaque in iis similiter essendi appetitus est naturalis, quia non consilium aut casum, sed vires sequitur naturales et insitas. Quoniam vero horum naturae vim non habent ullam, per quam esse sempiternum subiecto suo proprie corporique exhibeant, ideo horum nulla semper esse in sua proprie substantia cupiunt, frustra namque contenderent; cupiunt tamen secundum naturam esse sempiternum in specie, ad quod sufficienter naturales eorum vires subserviunt. Hinc similia sibi in specie generant, per quam propagationes species talis rerum perpetua manet in mundo. Quae quidem appetitio non solum in elementis et plantis, sed brutis etiam

same), appears as follows. Our human soul—and this means all of it—thinks about an everlasting life, which, directly it has thought about it, it longs for, desiring to be always. The desire for being is wholly natural, since it is continuously present in all things directly they are born. It does not proceed from deliberation, because it is immediately present in those born, and it does not proceed from chance, because it is in all and in them continuously. Through the power of their natural qualities, the elements certainly resist things introducing corruption lest they be deprived of being. Again, in order to preserve being, they seek out places appropriate for themselves with utmost avidity and repel things obstructing [their] motion. Their desire for being is thus said to be natural because it results from their natural qualities. Plants too by the instinct of their vital complexion suck up the humor that is better for their health, spreading out their roots for this as far as possible in order to preserve being. Likewise they avoid shadows by withdrawing their twigs, and with particular tendrils and their hooks they weave their way into supports lest they lose their being. We call this appetite of theirs a natural one because it is the result of the natural complexion of their life. Through natural concupiscence beasts appropriate those things that preserve being, and through natural irascibility repel things that destroy it. Therefore the desire for being is likewise natural in them, because it results not from deliberation or chance but from their naturally innate powers. Since their natures do not have any power, however, to bring everlasting being properly to their own subject and body, so these beasts never desire properly to be forever in their own substance; for they strive in vain. Yet they naturally do desire an everlasting being in their species, and their natural powers are sufficient to serve that end. Hence they generate things like themselves in their species, and through such generation a particular species of things remains forever in the world. This desire not only in the elements and plants but also in the beasts lacks knowledge;

caret cognitione. Nempe vis generandi, quae ad id servit, nullam prorsus habet cognitionem. Si qua vero sunt corpora, quorum principia sufficiant ad esse in propria substantia sempiternum, illa secundum naturam esse appetunt sempiternum non in specie solum, verumetiam in substantia propria, qualia forte sunt siderum corpora. Redeamus ad nostra.

4 Appetit noster animus esse. Sed numquid naturalis est huiusmodi appetitus? Est absque dubio non minus naturalis animo nostro quam ceteris rebus appetitus essendi. At enim appetit esse semper. Num haec semper essendi cupiditas ita naturalis est, sicut essendi? Est plane. Neque nobis Epicureus quisquam obiiciat quod licet animus esse quidem ipsum appetat naturaliter, quia etiam si non nosset, appeteret, tamen esse sempiternum praeter naturam exoptat, ob id fortasse, quod aeternitatem illam cognovit quidem prius, postea concupivit. Non obstat cognitio illa quominus aeternitatis aviditas sit naturalis. Nam et nostri sensus cibos cognoscunt, quos tamen secundum naturam appetunt. Lupus agnum, canis leporem, postquam viderunt, cupiunt, tamen cupiunt naturaliter, quoniam ex naturali complexione statim ita compelluntur ad appetendum, ut non cupere nequeant. Atque ut oculis naturale est talia sibi obiecta perspicere, ita naturale est concupiscendi potentiae talia inspecta protinus affectare. Eadem ratione intellectui naturale est perspicua obiecta cognoscere, voluntati quae bona iudicata sunt velle.

5 Quicquid perspicue offertur, naturaliter intellectus agnoscit. Quicquid sub boni ratione offertur, voluntas appetit naturaliter. Quare naturale est intellectui esse sempiternum cognoscere, cognitum vero tamquam bonum voluntati naturale expetere. Et sicut appetitus irrationalis sequitur sensum, sic voluntas, quae est ratio-

and indeed the power of generating which serves this desire has no knowledge whatsoever. But if certain bodies do exist whose rational principles suffice for [them to have] everlasting being in their own substance, then they yearn naturally for everlasting being not only in their species but also in their own substance; and of this kind perchance are the bodies of the stars. But let us return to our own bodies.

Our rational soul desires to be. But is such a desire natural? 4
Undoubtedly it is no less natural to our soul than the desire to be in other things. Yes, but it desires to be forever. Then is this longing to be forever as natural as the longing just to be? Plainly it is. Nor can some Epicurean object that although our soul naturally desires being itself (because it would desire it even if it did not know about it), yet it chooses everlasting being preternaturally, on the grounds perhaps that it came to know that eternity first and desired it later. But its knowing does not stop its yearning for eternity from being natural. For though our senses recognize foods, they nonetheless desire them naturally. The wolf desires the lamb, the dog the hare, after they have seen them, and yet they desire them naturally because they are immediately impelled by their natural temperament to desire them to the point that they cannot not desire them. And just as it is natural for their eyes to focus on such things presented to them, so it is natural for their concupiscent power to yearn for them directly they have been seen. For the same reason it is natural for the intellect to know perspicuous objects, and for the will to wish for objects judged to be good.

Whatever is clearly presented the intellect naturally knows. 5
What is presented rationally as good the will naturally desires. So it is natural for the intellect to know eternal being, and natural for the will to seek this known being as the good. Just as the irrational appetite follows the sense, so the will, which is a rational desire, follows the intellect. Therefore, just as the appetite for food is natural because it is instantaneous and not born of deliberation, so

nalis aviditas, sequitur intellectum. Ergo sicut[27] appetitio cibi est naturalis, quia subita est, non nata consilio, sic voluntas immortalitatis est naturalis, quia est actus subitus sequens meram intellectus voluntatisque naturam. Nam cum primum menti esse sempiternum offertur, iudicatur appetendum absque discursione, et appetitur nullo consilio praecedente. Quod si vel casu vel consilio affectaretur, neque omnes, neque semper iidem, neque aeque semper expeterent, sed variaretur istud secundum casus consultantiumque varietatem. Nunc autem omnes et necessario et subito id adsciscunt, impellente natura, quemadmodum et bonum ipsum necessario volumus, hoc autem aut illud non necessario neque natura. Ita esse tale aut tale, hic vel ibi non naturaliter affectamus, esse autem ipsum absolutum, cui nulla privatio miscetur essendi, trahente natura, desideramus. Atque sicut sempiternam vitae privationem impellente natura semper horremus, ita sempiternam vitam natura trahente diligimus. Temperavit autem naturae artifex cum essentia cognitionem, cum cognitione appetitum, cum appetitu finis adeptionem. Ergo sicut brutum esse tantum temporale cognoscit pro naturae suae capacitate ac secundum naturam esse appetit temporale, ita noster animus naturae suae magnificentia sempiternum esse cognoscit et naturaliter appetit. Nam et esse ipsum est secundum naturam appetibile, et eo quidem modo secundum naturam appetibile, quo et cognoscibile naturaliter. Itaque sicut a natura bruti esse cognoscitur tantum ut temporale ac praesens, ita ab illa desideratur similiter secundum naturam. Ab humana vero natura sicut cognoscitur esse ipsum tamquam perpetuum, ita tamquam perpetuum ab ea[28] naturaliter affectatur, ut quod secundum propriam intellectualem naturam dumtaxat notum est, secundum eandem naturaliter appetatur. Quinimmo secundum eandem quod cupimus, consequemur. Rationabile enim

the will's desire for immortality is natural because it is an instantaneous act consequent upon the pure nature of the intellect and the will. For as soon as everlasting being is presented to the mind, without any deliberation it is judged to be desirable; and it is desired without any preceding deliberation. But if such being were desired by chance or as a result of deliberation, then neither would all men seek it, nor would the same men always seek it, nor would they always seek it equally; but it would vary according to chance and the variety of those deliberating about it. But in fact all men opt for everlasting being necessarily and instantaneously, with nature impelling them, just as we necessarily also want the good itself; but we do not necessarily or naturally wish for this or that individual good. Thus we do not naturally desire this or that being, being here or being there, but, with nature attracting us, we desire absolute being itself (wherein is mingled no privation of being whatsoever). And just as, with nature impelling us, we always dread an everlasting privation of life, so, with nature attracting us, do we prize an everlasting life. But the artificer of nature has tempered knowledge with essence, desire with knowledge, the attainment of the end with desire. Accordingly, just as a beast knows only temporal being according to the capacity of its nature and naturally desires temporal being, so our soul by the magnificence of its nature knows everlasting being and naturally desires it. For being itself is naturally desirable, and it is naturally desirable in the way it is also naturally knowable. Therefore, just as being is known only as temporal and in the present by the beast's nature, so is it naturally desired by that nature as likewise temporal and in the present. But just as being itself is known by man's nature as perpetual being, so is it naturally desired by that nature as perpetual being, seeing that what is only known according to the intellectual nature proper is naturally desired according to the same. Or rather, what we desire according to this same intellectual nature, we will attain. For it is logical that in attaining we use the same

est, ut per eandem facultatem attingamus in consequendo, per quam in cognoscendo attingimus et volendo, ut eidem naturalis sit terminus motionis, cui naturalis est motio. Ergo qui per cognitionem et voluntatem sempiternam vitam attingit, non video cur per vitam non attingat, cuius quidem vitae virtute temporalia superante tam intellegentia quam voluntas, quae inde dependent, ultra temporanea sese conferunt ad aeterna.

6 Praeterea, cum non sit frustra desiderium naturale, consequens est ut hominis animus esse perpetuum consequatur naturaliter exoptatum—esse, inquam, perpetuum non in specie tantum, sed in substantia propria—id enim cupit. Merito corporalia, quia propagatione nascuntur, esse perpetuum secundum propagationem affectant. Mens autem esse perpetuum substantiae propriae, quia mens quaeque in se ipsa subsistit fitque a deo: non iacet in aliquo generationis subiecto, neque successione producitur. Quis autem secundum naturam cupit impossibilia? Nam quis aut volare, aut siccis pedibus flumina pertransire? Potest quidem quandoque puer aliquis vanus, casu quodam per sensum[29] commotus, talium sibi miraculorum optare facultatem, sed neque pueri ipsi saepe talia, neque viri umquam cogitant aut cupiunt. Vitam vero sempiternam omnes cupimus atque semper, etiam dum non advertimus cupere. Itaque non est huius assecutio impossibilis.

7 Hoc autem arbitror summopere advertendum, quod vita est naturalior quam scientia, quoniam vita est prior interiorque et magis continua substantialisque quam scientia. Verae igitur vitae appetitus magis naturalis est quam scientiae verae. Vera scientia est, quae est oppositi sui, id est ignorantiae, usque adeo expers ut neque iam habeat illam actu admixtam per fallaciam, ⟨neque⟩ in illam per oblivionem umquam cadere possit. Vera quoque vita est, quae neque secundum actum mixta est mortiferae qualitati, neque secundum ullam proclivitatem obnoxia morti. Cum igitur verae, id

faculty that we use in knowing and in willing, so that a natural terminus of motion might exist for what has a natural motion. Therefore I see no reason why he who attains perpetual life through knowledge and the will should not attain it through life. For it is through the power of this life, which conquers things temporal, that the understanding and the will alike, which depend upon it, transcend the temporal and turn towards the eternal.

Moreover, since natural desire is not in vain, man's rational soul 6
therefore attains the perpetual being it has naturally chosen — perpetual being both in the species and also in its own substance — for this is what it desires. Corporeal objects, because they are born through propagation, aim at perpetual being through propagation and justly so. But the mind aims at the perpetual being of its own substance, because each mind subsists in itself and is made by God: it does not lie in something subject to generation, nor is it produced in [temporal] succession. But who naturally desires impossibilities? Who desires to fly, or to cross dry-shod over rivers? An empty-headed boy can sometimes do so, his sense agitated by a chance wish for the ability to perform such miracles; but for the most part boys do not consider or desire such, and grown men never do. But all of us yearn always for everlasting life even when we do not realize that we are yearning. Therefore its attainment is not impossible.

I believe we should take special notice of the fact that life is 7
more natural than knowledge, because life is prior, more internal, more continual, and more substantial than knowledge. Therefore the desire for true life is more natural than the desire for true knowledge. True knowledge lacks what is opposite to itself, that is, ignorance, to such a degree that in actuality it is not mingled already with ignorance through deceit; nor can it ever fall into ignorance through forgetfulness. True life too is that which in actuality is not intermingled with a lethal quality and which is not exposed to death through any proclivity. Therefore, since the de-

est sempiternae vitae cupiditas multo naturalior sit quam scientiae verae, sequitur ut longe magis naturalis possibilisque sit sempiternae vitae quam verae scientiae consecutio. Immo vero cum vita multo magis quam intellegentia et voluntas cum sempiterna vita conveniat, si intellegendo atque volendo, certe longe magis vivendo vitam consequimur sempiternam. Quae quidem si posterioribus actibus animae, id est intellegentiae voluntatique, se communicat, nimirum vitae iam ipsi, quae prior actus est, se ipsam prius communicavit. Alioquin naturae auctor non tam vehementer nos ad huius rei aviditatem quotidie raperet, sicut neque ad alia quaevis rapit impossibilia. Divine enim Zoroaster:

οὐ γὰρ ἀπὸ πατρικῆς ἀρχῆς ἀτελές τι τροχάζει.

Id est: 'Nihil a paterno principio progreditur aut volvitur imperfectum'.

: VI :

Signum XI, XII, XIII, *et*[30] XIV: *quod cupimus quatuor dei virtutes assequi.*

1 Sunt quatuor quaedam aliae dei dotes ad virtutes quatuor pertinentes. Vocavimus namque illum providum iustum, fortem et temperatum. Quis negaverit deum singula circumspicere? Debitis naturalibusque ordinibus gubernare? In suo statu permanere immobilem dum haec agit, neque defatigari?[31] Tranquillum esse suaviterque singula et moderate tractare?

2 Hominis animam inspice divinae prudentiae aemulam. Quam curiose recolit praeterita, non privata solum vel sua, sed publica omnia et mundana! Quam impense praesentia sciscitatur, aliena

sire for true, that is, everlasting, life is much more natural than the desire for true knowledge, it follows that the attainment of everlasting life is that much more natural and possible than the attainment of true knowledge. Or rather, since life accords with everlasting life to a far greater degree than does the understanding or the will, then, if we attain everlasting life in understanding and willing, *a fortiori* we must do so in living. If this everlasting life communicates itself to the subsequent acts of the soul, namely to its understanding and willing, then certainly it has communicated itself beforehand to its very life, which is the prior act. Otherwise the Author of nature would not enrapture us daily and so vehemently with the desire for this thing [life], just as He does not enrapture us with the desire for other impossibilities. Zoroaster puts it divinely, "Nothing imperfect proceeds or unrolls from the paternal principle."[37]

: VI :

The eleventh, twelfth, thirteenth, and fourteenth signs: that we long to attain four powers of God.

There are four other gifts of God pertaining to the four [cardinal] virtues. For we have called Him provident, just, steadfast, and temperate. Who denies that God has regard for individuals; that He governs by just and natural arrangements; that He remains motionless in His state of rest when He does these things and never wearies; that He is at rest and treats individual things with gentleness and moderation? 1

Look at man's soul emulating the divine prudence. How exactly does it recollect things past, not only its own private affairs but those too of the state and the world! How earnestly does it inquire into things present, even those alien and external to it! How care- 2

etiam et externa! Quam annixe futuris inhiat! Quam diligenter futura anticipat saecula! Quod gravius audire potest homo convitium, quam si inscius et improvidus appelletur? Unde fit ut nemo velit ultro rei aut artis ullius ignorantiam confiteri, utpote qui monstrante natura iudicent nullius rei ignorantiam ad hominem pertinere, sed esse illi rerum omnium ferme perinde ac deo peritiam naturalem.

3 Iustitiam quoque divinam mens nostra venatur. Quot legibus suum subiicit corpus,[32] familiam gubernat, temperat civitatem, moderatur et regna! Quot poenis saevit in peccatores! Quot bonos afficit praemiis! Quam graviter scelestissimis indignamur! Quam ardenter vel a malis viri probatissimi diliguntur! Quanto denique ordine ac paene caelesti societas humana disponitur et in omni gubernatione ad unum seniorem prudentioremque tamquam totus mundus ad deum unum dirigitur! Quinetiam latrones iuste inter se praedam dispertiunt. Et iniqui homines si quam inferunt iniuriam, iuste illam inferre putant, vel acceptas iniurias vindicantes, vel tollentes e medio homines nocituros, vel furantes ea quibus indigent ipsi, abundant alii, ac videri volunt iustissime singula perpetrare. In quibus omnibus apparet humanum genus non minorem sibi velle iustitiam vendicare, quam deus ipse possideat.

4 Damus quoque operam ut dei fortitudinem adipiscamur. Dei profecto fortitudo est status immobilis. Prudentissimi viri hunc sibi statum ex eo pro viribus comparant, quod statuunt animi bonis contenti vivere, neque ullius facere corporis et fortunae commoda vel incommoda, quasi ad se, qui animi ipsi sunt, nihil pertineant. Qui haec mobilia negligunt, immobiles animo perseverant. Imprudentiores autem eundem optant vitae statum, sed alia aggre-

fully does it look to future things! How diligently does it anticipate the ages to come! What graver reproof can a man hear than being called ignorant and without foresight? Hence no person wants voluntarily to confess ignorance of any object or art, inasmuch as, on the evidence of nature, people judge that being ignorant of anything does not pertain to man, and that the practical knowledge of virtually all things is as natural to him as to God.

Our mind pursues divine justice too. To how many laws does it 3
submit its body! It governs the family, it regulates the city, and it moderates kingdoms! It inflicts how many punishments on the guilty! It bestows on the good how many rewards! How fiercely do we rage against the wicked! How ardently are the upright cherished even by the bad! Finally with what order, order almost divine, is human society organized and in every polity looks to one, older, particularly prudent man[38] just as the whole world looks to one God! Even thieves divide up their booty justly among themselves; and whenever evil men commit some injustice they believe they are committing it justly, whether they are revenging injuries received, or eliminating those about to harm them, or stealing things which they themselves need and others have in abundance; and such men want to appear to be committing their individual crimes with perfect justice. In all this, mankind wants in no small measure to lay claim to the justice that God Himself possesses.

We also labor to acquire God's fortitude. God's fortitude is of 4
course a motionless condition of rest. To their utmost ability men of the highest prudence seek this condition for themselves when they decide to live content with the goods of the soul, and to make nothing of the [mere] advantages or disadvantages of a body or of fortune. It is as though none of these pertained to themselves who were rational souls. Men who neglect such changing things remain unchanging in their soul. More imprudent men, however, elect this same state of life, but approach it by another route, thinking that they can thereby acquire it the more easily for themselves.

diuntur via, putantes ea sibi rem facilius successuram. Quid ergo? Expugnant et subiugant pro viribus omnes qui eos posse quandoque ex sua sede et dignitate depellere videantur.

5 Divinam praeterea temperantiam quis non cupiat? Prudentes ita moderari motus animi student ut nulla ex parte dissideant. Imprudentes et corpus et res suas ita componere, ut animum non perturbent. Utrique integram expetunt animi sui concordiam; prudenti quidem res succedit quandoque, imprudenti nequaquam.

6 Denique sicut ceterarum rerum omnium, ita quatuor harum virtutum summae in deo sunt rationes, adeo ut summa prudentia deus sit, summa iustitia, et reliqua summa. Viri autem harum virtutum studiosi summam earum expetunt rationem, dum nihil quod ad ipsarum consummationem pertineat, sibi volunt deesse. Id omnes optant homines, licet alii alia proficiscantur via. Omnes igitur deum quaerunt. Quaerunt autem illi deum rectissimo calle, qui primo per civiles virtutes affectus animi secundos amputant, deinde per virtutes purgatorias eos extirpant, tertio loco per virtutes animi iam purgati affectus primos insuper moderantur. Quibus temperatis denique virtutibus exemplaribus quae sunt in deo formentur. Formari vero quandoque virtutibus exemplaribus proculdubio possumus. Nam praeparatio sive affectio formam habitumque respicit, atque certa quaedam affectio certum habitum. Quapropter causa, quae subiectum aliquod[33] gradatim magis magisque praeparat, ob id praeparat, ut formam inducat substantialem atque praecipuam, et subiectum illud secundum communem naturae ordinem, quemadmodum praeparationis illius fit particeps, ita et principalis formae capax effici potest. Deus, qui virtus

How then? To the utmost of their powers they attack and defeat all those who appear to be capable of depriving them some day of their position and dignity.

Moreover who does not yearn for divine temperance? Prudent 5
men study so to moderate the motions of their soul that they are never in any disaccord. Imprudent men study to so compose their external body and affairs that they do not perturb the soul. Both seek a perfect harmony for their soul: the prudent succeed at some point, the imprudent never.

Finally, just as the highest rational principles of all other things 6
are in God, so are those of the aforementioned four virtues, inasmuch as the highest prudence is God, the highest justice, and so on. Men studious of these virtues seek their highest rational principle when they do not want to lack anything that pertains to their perfection. All men wish for this, although various men set out on various routes. All therefore seek God. But the straightest path to God is taken by those who use the civic virtues first to lop off the rational soul's secondary desires, then the purgatorial virtues to root them out entirely, and third the virtues of the already-purged soul to moderate the primary desires as well. When these desires have been tempered, they may be formed at last by the exemplary virtues that are in God. Undoubtedly, we are capable of being formed some day by the exemplary virtues. For being prepared or affectively disposed concerns form and habit, and a particular disposition concerns a particular habit. So the cause, which gradually but increasingly prepares some subject, does so in order that it might introduce both the substantial and the principal [the exemplary] form to it. And the subject, following the common order of nature, even as it is made a participant in that preparation, so too can it be made capable of receiving the principal form. God, who is the exemplary virtue itself, endows the species of the human soul from the beginning with certain seeds and stirrings of the virtues, through which the rational souls, having been purged by the

ipsa exemplaris est, animae humanae speciem afficit ab initio seminibus quibusdam incitamentisque virtutum, per quae humanis virtutibus (id est civilibus, purgatoriis, purgati animi) ad exemplares divinasque virtutes commode praeparamur. Quod tres eiusmodi virtutes humanae praeparationes sint ad divinas, ex eo coniicimus quod ex divinis inseruntur nobis et excitantur; quod illarum imagines sunt ita perspicuae, ut per ipsas agnoscantur illae; quod ad illas gradatim magis magisque accedunt; quod ita nos afficiunt, ut in his non quiescamus, sed afficiamur ad illas. Ergo et deus immortali divinae virtutis habitu animae speciem formare quandoque debet et animae species formari potest.

: VII :

Decimum quintum[34] signum: quod animus summam expetit opulentiam et voluptatem.

1 Accedit quod vitam dei opulentissimam et iucundissimam posuimus. Nam solus ille summa est opulentia summaque voluptas, qui fons est bonorum omnium, nullius egenus. Si ergo summam opulentiam et voluptatem summam omnes expetunt homines, dii expetunt fieri.

2 Non certa quaedam rerum aliquarum possessio aut species aliqua voluptatis sufficit homini, quemadmodum ceteris animantibus, sed paulum quid in iis[35] adeptum se putat, donec restat aliquid vel minimum acquirendum. Quamobrem prudentes viri, existimantes opulentiam dei gaudiumque in solis intellegentiae honestatisque thesauris revera consistere, sola haec cupiunt, sed ad summum. Imprudentes autem homines, opinantes maiestatem divinam bonis insuper corporalibus perfrui,[36] appetunt insuper cor-

human, that is, the civic and purgatorial virtues, are duly prepared for the exemplary and divine virtues. That these three [kinds of] human virtues[39] are preparations for the divine ones we deduce: a) from their being sown and quickened in us by the divine, b) from their images being so transparent that the divine are recognized through them, c) from their gradually but increasingly approaching the divine, and d) from their so affecting us that we do not rest in them but are moved towards the divine. It follows both that God must some day take the species of the soul and form it with the immortal habit of divine virtue and that the species of the soul can be formed.

: VII :

The fifteenth sign: that the rational soul seeks riches and pleasure in the highest degree.

We have posited additionally that God's life is the most bountiful and the most delightful. For He alone who is the fount of all good things and yet needs none of them is absolute wealth and absolute pleasure. If all men therefore seek the highest wealth and the highest pleasure, they are seeking to become gods. 1

The assured possession of particular things or of a particular species of pleasure does not suffice for man as it does for the other animals. What he has acquired of these he deems paltry as long as something else remains, even the least bit, to be acquired. Wherefore prudent men, in thinking that the wealth and joy of God truly consists in the treasures of understanding and virtue alone, desire these alone, but to the full. Imprudent men, however, in supposing that the divine majesty enjoys corporeal goods besides, also desire things corporeal, and to the full. But everyone knows 2

poralia et ad summum. Constat autem eos neque necessitatis neque commoditatis corporalis gratia dumtaxat talia quaerere. Nempe etiam si arbitrentur habere se quantum sufficiat ad vivendum, et quantum ad vivendum iucunde et copiose, nondum tamen cessant accumulare thesauros et oblectamenta exquisitissima diligenter inquirere, quod Midas, Sardanapallus, Xerxes[37] demonstraverunt. Ille thesauros in immensum accumulabat, hi summa praemia proponebant illis qui nova quotidie invenirent oblectamenta. Non corpori serviunt isti, sed obsunt, neque damni corporalis ignari non corpori obsequuntur, sed divinae felicitatis invidi immensam sibi illius copiam tam rerum quam voluptatum usurpare contendunt, atque ut hanc assequantur corpus suum perdunt, affligtant animum vitamque perturbant. Tandem neque prudentes, licet accedant propius, neque imprudentes hac in vita ingentes illos quos cupiunt thesauros consequuntur; ideo hic quiescunt numquam.

3 Res autem quaelibet in loco suo ac naturali habitu conquiescit. Quam obnixe loca sua repetunt elementa! Quam firmiter illis inhaerent! Plantae conveniens sibi solum situmque congruum quam avide asciscunt! Quam stabiliter in eo pro viribus permanent bruta similiter! Talpae enim sinus[38] terrae, armenta gregesque terrae faciem, pisces aquam et avidissime petunt et in his locis trahunt moras quam libentissime. Tandem haec omnia, ut brevi complectar, quando locum habitumque naturalem nacta sunt, quiescunt. Quod indicat et corpus nostrum quando bene valet, pastum est belle, molliterque recumbit ad votum, tunc neque complexio eius neque sensus eius comes, qui in nobis ipsa est bestia, poscit aliquid ultra. At interim vel ratio intellectualis rerum inquirit causas studiose et anxie de rebus consultat agendis, vel ratio cogitatrix

that such men do not seek such things only for the sake of corporeal necessity or comfort. Even if they think they have enough for living and for living comfortably and abundantly, yet they do not cease nonetheless to amass treasures, and diligently to search out the most exquisite pleasures. Midas, Sardanapallus, and Xerxes are obvious examples. Midas piled up immense treasures; the other two offered huge rewards to those who could daily invent new pleasures. Such men do not minister to but harm the body; nor are they ignorant of the harm to the body. They have no regard for the body, but, being envious of divine felicity, they strive to appropriate for themselves its immense store both of objects and of pleasures; and to acquire this store they destroy their body, afflict their soul, and plunge their life into disorder. Eventually neither the prudent, although they approach much closer, nor the imprudent attain the immense treasures they desire in this life, and so here they never rest content.

Each thing comes to rest, however, in its own place and in its 3
own natural and habitual condition. How strenuously the elements search for their spheres again! How steadfastly they cleave to them! How eagerly do the plants take to the soil that is suitable for them and to a spot that is congenial! How pertinaciously do they remain there as long as they can, and the beasts likewise! For moles seek out the folds of the earth, herds and flocks its surface, and fishes the water, all with utmost eagerness; and they are glad to stay in these places as long as possible. To sum up: all these things come to rest when they have attained their natural place and habitual condition. Our body demonstrates this too when it is in good health or has feasted handsomely or reclines at will on soft down: then neither its complexion nor its accompanying sense (which are the beasts in us) demand anything further. Meanwhile either our intellectual reason studiously seeks out the causes of things and anxiously ponders what to do, or our cogitative reason devises and lays claim to new pleasures.[40] It is goaded by penitence

novas fingit et postulat voluptates. Stimulatur paenitentia, suspicione sollicitatur. Anxietas huiusmodi hominis ipsius est propria, siquidem a viribus animi homini propriis oritur, non elementorum corporalium, non bestiae viribus, quae in nobis sat habent, ut diximus. Quamobrem homo solus in praesenti hoc vivendi habitu quiescit numquam, solus hoc loco non est contentus. Solus igitur homo in regionibus his peregrinatur, et in ipso itinere non potest quiescere, dum ad patriam adspirat caelestem, quam petimus omnes, quamvis propter varietatem opinionis atque consilii diverso calle proficiscamur. Si ergo quae nobis inferiora sunt quandoque naturalem habitum patriamque sedem adepta quiescunt, nos quoque necesse est, ut diximus alias, haec assequi posse quandoque atque quiescere.

4 In vita praesenti non datur merito. Appetimus[39] enim tamquam naturalem habitum finemque nostrum bonum illud quod tres praecipue conditiones habeat, videlicet purum sit, integrum, stabile. In hac autem vita boni possessio neque pura est, quoniam naturalis quidam affectus animae erga corpus, primique ipsi sensuum motus mentes virorum vel excellentissimorum distrahunt et perturbant. Neque integra: oportet siquidem omne illud, cui naturaliter inest ad actus aliquos potentia nixusque, ad eos ipsos pervenire omnino, si quando sit quieturum. Cum ergo insit intellectui humano capacitas naturalis atque conatus ad formas rerum omnium percipiendas et possidendas, tunc demum finem suum naturalem consecutus erit, cum adeptus fuerit omnes. At quia[40] in hac vita talem numquam habitum adipiscitur, bonum hic integrum numquam possidet. Neque stabilis, quippe bonum nostrum actione quadam consistit expedita, secura, continua. Omnis autem hominum in terra viventium actio impedimentum aliquod periculum interpellationemque patitur. Quid quod quaecumque longiore ad incrementum indigent tempore, solent diutius cum sunt adulta

and roused by suspicion. Such anxiety is proper to man, since it arises from the powers of the soul that are proper to man, and not from the powers of the corporeal elements or of the beasts which, as we said, do find satisfaction in us. Wherefore man alone never rests in his present habit of living: he alone is not content with this present place. So man alone is a pilgrim in these regions and cannot rest on the journey as long as he aspires to his celestial homeland, which all of us seek, although we proceed on sundry paths on account of the diversity of opinion and of judgment. So if the things that are inferior to us come to rest at some point, having attained their natural habit and ancestral home, then, as we have declared elsewhere,[41] at some point necessarily we too will be capable of attaining them and of coming to rest.

This is not granted us in this present life, however, and justly 4
so. For we desire as our natural habit and end that good which satisfies three main conditions: that it be pure, entire, and unchanging. But in this life the possession of good is not pure, since a particular natural affection of the soul for the body along with the first motions of the senses distract and trouble the minds of men, even the most excellent. Nor is possession entire, since every thing in which the power and inclination for certain acts is naturally present must wholly arrive at these acts if it is ever going to rest. Since, therefore, the natural capacity and striving to perceive and possess the forms of all things is present in the human intellect, it will eventually attain its natural end when it has acquired them all. But because such a habitual condition is never attained in this life, our intellect never possesses here the good entire. Nor is our possession of the good unchanging. Indeed, our good consists in a particular action that is unimpeded, untroubled, and continuous. But every action of men dwelling on earth suffers from some impediment, danger, and interruption. Why is it that all things needing a longer time to mature usually live much longer when they are adults? But up to extreme old age man anxiously

perseverare? Homo vero usque ad extremam senectutem contendit obnixe ad felicitatis habitum acquirendum, quem tandem ex parte quadam percipit, eumque in hac vita ad tempus quam brevissimum possidet. Quapropter ut habitus, qui ex parte est acquisitus, impleatur quandoque, et qui diutissime crevit permaneat diutissime, necesse est animam corpori superesse. Quae quoniam hic 'Italiam sequitur fugientem' neque patrium portum attingit, sollicitatur maeretque assidue.

5 Porro, quod mirabile est, quotiens otiosi sumus, totiens tamquam exules incidimus in maerorem, quamvis maeroris nostri causam aut nesciamus aut certe non cogitemus. Ex quo factum est, ut homo nequeat solus vivere. Nam ceterorum hominum societate ac insuper multiplici oblectamentorum varietate latentem perpetuamque maestitiam expellere posse putamus. Sed fallimur, heu, nimium! Sane in mediis voluptatum ludis suspiramus nonnumquam, ac ludis peractis discedimus tristiores. Idem accidit nobis quod illis, qui esuriente stomacho dormientes insomnia comedunt nec implentur, quia non imaginem cibi, sed ipsum cibum stomachus appetebat.

6 Nos quoque menti nectar (id est visionis paternae gaudium) sitienti[41] offerimus lethales Lethaei fluminis aquas, dum umbratiles adhibemus ludos corporalium voluptatum quae falsae voluptates sunt, non solum quia brevissimae ac plenae solicitudinis, sed quia mixtae dolori, siquidem appetitio indiga dolor quidam est. Voluptates autem corporis tamdiu percipiuntur, quamdiu egestas et appetitio permanet. Merito igitur oblectamenta terrena non implent animum, sed titillant. Ille siquidem res veras affectat et gaudia vera, res autem corporales umbrae sunt rerum earumque illecebrae umbrae sunt gaudii. Quamobrem si neque alicuius rei temporalis

strives to acquire the habit of felicity that he perceives in the end only in part, and possesses in this life only for the briefest while. Accordingly, in order that the habit that has been acquired only in part might some day be made whole, and that having developed for the longest time might remain for the longest time, the soul must necessarily survive the body. The soul, because "it follows fleeting Italy,"[42] never arrives here at the port of its fathers and remains troubled and stricken with grief.

Next, and this is remarkable, as often as we are idle, we lapse 5
into sadness like exiles, even if we do not know the cause of this sadness or do not think about it certainly. Hence it is that man cannot live alone. For we suppose we can expel our secret and perpetual gloom with the society of other men and with the variety too of many pleasures. But we are, alas, too much deceived! For in the midst of pastimes and pleasures we often sigh, and when the pastimes are over we lapse into even greater sadness. What happens to us is what happens to those who fall to sleep on an empty stomach and who feast in their dreams but are not filled, because their stomach is hungry, not for the image of food, but for real food.

To the mind thirsty for nectar, for the joy, that is, of the pater- 6
nal vision, we offer the lethal waters of the river Lethe as long as we summon up the shadowy pastimes of corporeal pleasures, which are false pleasures, both because they last the briefest time and overflow with trouble and because they are mingled with sorrow (since the appetite in need is a kind of sorrow). But the body's pleasures are perceived just as long as the need and the appetite remain. Deservedly, therefore, earthly pleasures do not satisfy the rational soul: they only titillate it, since the soul yearns for things true and for authentic joys, but corporeal realities are the shadows of things and their delights are the shadows of joys. Wherefore if drinking neither a particular temporal liquor nor all temporal liquors quenches the thirst of the mind, it is thirsting not for a tem-

neque cunctarum temporalium rerum potus sitim mentis extinguit, non temporalem sitit liquorem, sed aeternum. Ac si[42] sitim superno sole accensam impleri oportet quandoque, atque numquam Lethaeo flumine satiatur, aliquando aeterno nectaris haustu satiabitur. Sed iuvat[43] rursus quae dicta sunt, his quae referam priscorum theologorum mysteriis confirmare. Affirmant enim animas in corporibus dormitare, et quaecumque hic agere pative[44] videmur, nihil aliud esse quam somnia, cogitationesque animarum separatarum a cogitationibus coniunctarum multo magis differre quam vigilantium ab insomniis dormientium, similiterque a voluptatibus voluptates. Quod quidem ita probatur.

7 Experimur in nobis non solum quotidie, verumetiam ferme qualibet hora, quotiens pauculus quidam vapor aliquanto crassior et humidior ab inferioribus corporis partibus exhalans caput ipsum petit cerebrique meatus opplet, statim nos somno gravari, mox etiam insomniis imaginibusque deludi. Experimur quoque nonnumquam si vapor aliquis bilis atrae, quam melancholiam Graeci vocant, arcem corporis obsederit expugnaveritque statim reginam inde nostram, ipsam videlicet rationem, ut ita dicam, praecipitari, ac manifesta homines insania corripi. Si fumus quidam exiguus tantam in nobis vim habet, si tam levis motus nos tantum mutat, quanto magis censendum est caelestem immortalemque animum, quando ab initio ab ea puritate qua creatur momento delabitur, id est quando obscuro terreni moribundique corporis carcere clauditur, tunc, ut est apud Platonicos, e suo illo statu mutari! Quippe qui tunc non uno et consueto tantum humoris alicuius fumo, sed omnibus pariter novisque[45] humorum omnium vaporibus atque ipsa insuper humorum membrorumque insueta mole gravatur. Praeterea, informi illa materia, quae a formosissima mentis forma diversissima est, tamquam flumine Le-

poral drink but for an eternal. And if this thirst, set on fire by the supernal Sun, has to be satisfied some day, and if it can never be satisfied by the Lethean river, then some day it will be satisfied by an eternal draught of nectar. But it is helpful to confirm what has been said above by again referring to the mysteries of the ancient theologians. For they declare that souls become drowsy in bodies; that all that we seem to do or to suffer here is nothing other than dreams; that the thoughts of separated souls differ more from the thoughts of souls joined to bodies than the thoughts of men awake from the dreams of those asleep; and that their pleasures differ similarly. This is proved as follows.

Not just daily but almost every hour, whenever a wisp of vapor 7
that is somewhat denser and more humid wafts up from the lower parts of the body, seeks out the head, and chokes up the passages of the brain, we experience in ourselves the sensation of being instantly weighed down by sleep and as instantly deceived by dreams and images. Often too, if some vapor of black bile, which the Greeks call melancholy, besieges and then storms the body's citadel, we immediately experience the sensation of our queen, the reason, being dethroned as it were, and of [her] subjects being gripped by manifest insanity. If a wispy vapor has such power over us, if such a delicate motion moves us so violently, then how much more, one must suppose, does our celestial and immortal rational soul depart from its state of rest, as the Platonists believe, at the moment when it falls away from the original purity of its creation—that is, when it is imprisoned in the lightless dungeon of the earthly and mortal body. For it is weighed down then not only by the familiar single vapor of some humor, but by the new vapors of all the humors equally, and it is weighed down too by the unaccustomed burden of both the humors and the limbs. Moreover, it is drowned in the river of Lethe as it were, in that unformed matter which is at the other extreme from the form of the mind in all its formal beauty. Wherefore the whole time that the sublime ra-

thaeo submergitur. Quamobrem totum id tempus quod sublimis animus in infimo agit corpore,[46] mentem nostram velut aegram perpetua quadam inquietudine hac et illac sursum deorsumve iactari, necnon dormitare semper et delirare Pythagorici et Platonici arbitrantur, singulasque mortalium motiones, actiones, passiones nihil esse aliud quam vertigines aegrotantium, dormientium somnia, insanorum deliramenta, ut non iniuria Euripides hanc vitam umbrae somnium appellaverit. Proinde cum fallantur omnes, ii tamen minus falli solent, qui interea quandoque, ita ut interdum fit in somno, suspicantur secumque ipsi dicunt: forsitan non sunt vera, quae nunc nobis[47] apparent, forsitan in praesentia somniamus. Quicumque inter somniantes sic est affectus, talis certe est ad alios qualis apud inferos ab Homero dicitur esse Tiresias. 'Solus', inquit, 'iste sapit; ceteri vero omnes velut umbrae volitant, immo umbrae volitant'.

: VIII :

Decimum sextum[48] signum: quod colimus nos ipsos ac deum.

1 Superest ut de duodecima illa dei dote loquamur, per quam se ipsum amat et colit, quam homines duobus sibi modis vendicant.

2 Primo, quod omnes non modo, ut cetera faciunt cuncta, se diligunt et tuentur, verumetiam colunt se ipsos magnopere et quasi quaedam numina[49] venerantur. Id agunt prudentes, quatenus externa et corporalia animo tamquam principi subigunt. Toti ex

tional soul acts in the lower body, the Pythagoreans and Platonists think that our mind, as in sickness, is tossed to and fro and up and down in a kind of perpetual restlessness, and dozes besides, and is ever delirious; and that the individual motions, actions, and passions of mortal men are nothing other than the dizzy spells of the sick, the dreams of those asleep, the ravings of the insane, so that not unjustly has Euripides called this life a shadow's dream.[43] Therefore, though all are deceived, yet less deceived usually are those who suspect something at some point (as occasionally happens in sleep) and say to themselves, "Perhaps these things as they now appear to us are not true; perhaps at this moment we are dreaming." Whoever feels like this in the midst of dreamers resembles Tiresias among the dead as Homer describes him: "Alone," he says, "Tiresias knew: all the rest flitted about like shadows, or rather flitted about as shadows."[44]

: VIII :

The sixteenth sign: that we worship ourselves as we worship God.

It remains for us to speak of God's twelfth gift, the gift by which He loves and worships Himself and which men claim for themselves in two ways. 1

The first way is that not only do all men love and protect themselves as all other things do, they greatly worship and venerate themselves as though they were particular divinities. The prudent do so insofar as they subject external corporeal things to the rational soul as to their principle. They are entirely dependent on the mind as on God. They also deem it sacrilegious to desecrate the august majesty of their mind, a divine statue as it were, with vile 2

mente pendent tamquam ex deo. Augustam quoque suae mentis maiestatem velut divinam statuam vilibus cogitationibus terrenisque sordibus temerare nefas existimant. Quae quidem notio naturalis humano generi pudorem verecundiamque ingenuit, ut non modo aliorum hominum conspectum quasi divinorum, verumetiam propriae mentis conscientiam, quod praecepit Pythagoras, tamquam dei faciem vereamur. Quae nos assidue malefactorum paenitentia stimulat, etiam si poenam non metuamus, bene autem factorum oblectat memoria, quasi caelestis animus a terrenis vitiorum maculis semper abhorreat. Idem imprudentes quodammodo faciunt, sed a prudentioribus in consummando hoc opere superantur. Idem rursus, sed aliter agunt homines dementissimi, prout nimium placent ipsi sibi, pertinacissime in sua persistunt opinione, sententiam suam tamquam divinum decretum mordicus tenent. Cuncti denique homines excellentissimos animos atque optime de humano genere meritos in hac[50] vita ut divinos honorant, solutos a corporibus adorant, ut deos quosdam deo summo carissimos, quos prisci heroas nominaverunt. Tanta vero ad se et ad suos reverentia non apparet in bestiis, nedum vilioribus, sed neque etiam in maioribus. Atque hic primus est modus quo homines divinum imitantur cultum, videlicet quia se ipsos ut deos colunt.

3 Est et alter quia scilicet soli nos animantium omnium colimus deum, soli nos deum affectu, gestibus, verbis, delubris, sacrificiis honoramus. Quod[51] Plato[52] in *Protagora* maximum esse vult nostrae divinitatis indicium, quod soli nos,[53] tamquam sortis divinae participes, ob cognationem quandam deum agnoscimus[54] et cupimus tamquam auctorem, invocamus et amamus ut patrem, ut regem veneramur, timemus ut dominum. Sicut enim sol sine sole

thoughts and sordid earthly matters; and this natural notion has implanted in mankind a sense of shame and modesty. Consequently, we revere the sight of other men as of divinities but also revere the conscience of our own mind as, in Pythagoras' precept, the face of God.[45] This both provokes us to the earnest repentance of our evil deeds, even if we are not afraid of being punished, and it delights us with the memory of our good deeds; it is as though the celestial soul always abhorred the stains of earthly vices. The imprudent do the same in a way, but in accomplishing this work they are surpassed by the more prudent. Again, the most foolish men of all do the same but in a different way (in that they are overly pleased with themselves): they persist in their opinion with unyielding pertinacity and dig their teeth into their own view as if it were a divine decree. In sum, all men take the souls of highest excellence, those who have deserved their place among the best of mankind, and honor them in this life as if they were divine; and they adore those released from bodies as if they were in a way gods dearest to the highest God (the ancients called them the heroes). But such devout reverence towards themselves and towards their own alike does not appear in the beasts, not even in the greatest of them, to say nothing of the viler sort. This is the first way in which men imitate divine worship, namely they worship themselves as gods.

The second way is that, of all animate beings, we alone worship 3
God: with love, with [ritual] gestures, with words, with shrines, with sacrifices we alone honor Him. In[46] the *Protagoras*[47] Plato maintains that the greatest proof of our divinity is that we alone —as participants in a divine destiny and because of a certain kinship [with the divine]—know and long for God as our author, love and beseech Him as our father, venerate Him as our king, and fear Him as our lord. For just as the sun is never seen without the sun, and air is never heard without air, but the eye sees light when filled with light and the ear hears the echoing air when filled

non cernitur, sicut aer sine aere non auditur, ac plenus lumine oculus videt lumen, plena aere auris audit aerem resonantem, ita neque deus sine deo cognoscitur. Sed animus deo plenus tantum in deum dirigitur,[55] quantum et divino lumine illustratus agnoscit deum et divino calore accensus sitit eundem.[56] Hinc animus dei templum efficitur, ut Xystus Pythagoricus arbitratur. Dei vero aeterni templum numquam existimat ruiturum. Deum agitat mens humana quotidie. Deo ardet cor. Deum suspirat pectus. Eundem cantat lingua. Eundem caput manusque adorant et genua. Eundem referunt hominum artificia. Si non audit haec deus, forte videtur[57] ignorans. Si non exaudit, forsitan apparebit[58] ingratus. Crudelis quodammodo,[59] si vociferari nos cogit[60] quotidie, quos non[61] exaudiat.

4 Neque audeat[62] quisquam dicere deum humana despicere tamquam minima. Sane commoda[63] habitatio tamquam finis fabrum movet quasi agentem causam, ut certam quandam domus formam excogitet,[64] ob quam formam rursus certam quaerat materiam. Ubi finis movet agentem, agens formam, forma materiam. Idem accidit in civilibus bellicisque consiliis. Quo fit, ut finis sit causa causarum, ideoque omnes causas antecedat. Sunt autem naturalia quaeque[65] certi alicuius finis gratia instituta, cum singula ad singulos potissimum usus conducere videantur. Puta vimen[66] palmitis, quem capreolum vocant: ad hoc natum est ut vitem proximae arbusculae vinciat. Hic[67] vinciendi actus causa est ut ortum sit vimen.[68] Quia vero quod nullo modo est, id neque esse potest essendi causa effectui cuiquam neque causas omnes movere, necessarium est actum huiusmodi et ante vimen[69] et ante reliquas omnes vitis causas exstitisse. Non autem exstitit in corporibus nisi novissime. Ergo in natura quadam incorporea,[70] rectrice corporum, ex-

with air, so God is not understood without God. When filled with God, however, the rational soul is directed towards God alone to the extent that, having been illumined by the divine light, it knows Him, and, having been inflamed by the divine heat, it thirsts for Him. So this soul is made into the temple of God as the Pythagorean Xystus supposes.[48] But he thinks that the temple of eternal God will never perish. Daily the human mind ponders God, the heart yearns for God, the breast sighs for God, the tongue sings of Him, the head, hands, and knees adore Him, and the arts of men tell of Him. Were God not to hear all this, perchance He would appear ignorant; were He not to listen to all this, ungrateful; and were He to compel us to cry out daily but did not listen to us, He would appear in a way cruel.

Nor[49] should anyone venture to say that God despises human matters as trivial. Indeed,[50] a commodious dwelling as the end cause moves the builder who is as it were the agent cause, so that he designs a particular and defined form of the house, and because of this form in turn searches out a particular material. In this instance the end is moving the agent, the agent, the form, and the form, the material. The same occurs in the counsels of civil government and war. Consequently, the end is the cause of causes and thus precedes all [other] causes. But particular natural things have been instituted for the sake of some particular end, since individual things in most instances appear to serve individual uses. Take the shoot or bine of the pruned vine that they call the lead tendril: it has been born to fasten the vine to the nearest shrub. This act of binding is the cause that the bine appears. But since what never exists in any way cannot be the cause of being for any effect and cannot move all the causes [of it], such a binding act must necessarily exist prior to the bine itself and prior to all the other causes of the vine. But this binding act does not exist in bodies except as the very last act. So it exists in an incorporeal nature ruling over bodies long before it exists in the vine. In fact through its own 4

stitit longe prius quam in palmite. Quae quidem natura, vitis artifex, gratia talis actus per formam suam viminis[71] formam in tali quadam materia figuravit.

Sed utrum actus huiusmodi in natura illa praefuit secundum naturae modum, an secundum propositum voluntatis? Certe secundum utrumque. At ex illo idem erat quod agentis forma quaedam et effectus[72] ipsius exemplar; ex hoc erat finis. Ubi autem artificiosae voluntatis propositum est, ibi mens. Quapropter praeest omnibus corporibus[73] divina mens, quae corporalium omnium formas intellectuali modo complectitur et tamquam sagittarius[74] singula ad suos dirigit fines, ad unum denique cuncta. Divinus hic agricola colit pampinos, capreolos et radices. Unde enim aut pampini vertuntur ad solem umbra vitata, aut capreoli tamquam manus ad eam partem praecipue protenduntur, ubi est propinquius sustentaculum, aut radices fugientes ariditatem ad humorem maxime propagantur? Electio quae non errat artificiosi consilii, immo verissimi intellectus est opus. Non tamen inest vera mens vitibus. Ergo adest. Adest insuper abiectissimis quibusque bestiolis, quae in suis artificiis semper eligunt potiora. Colit deus arbores ducitque et pascit beluas, quod et prisci theologi voluerunt. Numquid solos despicit homines, qui soli in terris divinam non despiciunt maiestatem? Absit. Immo vero si deus nullas omnino vel minimas mundi negligit[75] partes, profecto non despicit genus humanum, quod est mundi pars adeo pretiosa ut media sit temporalium rerum et aeternarum, quantum[76] aeterna capit, ordinat temporalia; adeo deo proxima ut sese divinae mentis arcanis insinuans opus hoc dei, ordinem scilicet mundi cognoscat. Mundani ordinis intellegentia eo ipso ordine est excellentior, siquidem ordo huius-

form, that nature, that craftsman of the vine, formed the bine's form in this particular matter and for the sake of this particular binding act.

In that nature, however, did this act take command according to the manner of that nature or to what the will purposed? Certainly according to both. The first ensured that the particular form of the agent and the exemplary model of the effect were the same; the second ensured the end. But where the artistic purpose of a will exists, mind exists. So ruling over all bodies is the divine mind, which embraces in an intellectual way the forms of all corporeals: like an archer, it aims individual things at their targets, and all things eventually to one end. This divine farmer cultivates the vine shoots, the tendrils, and the roots. For how otherwise do the shoots turn towards the sun eschewing the shade, or the tendrils like hands reach out in the particular direction where support is closest, or the roots seek out moisture, always avoiding where it is dry? A choice that is not in error is the work of careful deliberation, or rather of the truest of intellects. Yet true mind is not present inside vines. So God tends them from outside and tends all the little animals too, however humble, which in their artful activities always choose whatever is preferable. God cultivates the trees and directs and nourishes the beasts as the ancient theologians also believed. Surely He does not disregard men alone, who alone among earthly things do not disregard the divine majesty? God forbid! Or rather, if God never neglects even the smallest parts of the world, certainly He does not disregard mankind, which is the part of the world so precious that it is the mean between temporal and eternal things, inasmuch as it comprehends the eternal and rules over the temporal. Mankind is so close to God that it penetrates the secrets of the divine mind and comes to know God's work, the order, that is, of the world. This understanding of the world's order is more excellent than the order itself, given that this same order has been established by and is ruled through under-

modi per intellegentiam est factus et regitur. Si per cognitionem animus noster est mundo praestantior, per vitam quoque praestantior erit. Cuius virtute a corpore separabili idipsum habet, ut per operationem possit a corpore separari, ipsumque mundum vitae, ut ita dixerim, supermundanae virtute transcendere.

6 Quantum vero mundi ordinem intellegentia superet, hinc apparet quod ordo talis dispergitur tempore; intellegentia totum simul ac stabilem possidet. Ordo rursus causam suam sequitur, non assequitur; intellegentia causam assequitur ordinis quando deum eius artificem invenit, ubi tam ampla[77] capit de deo ut mundum deinde velut umbram posthabeat. Rem vero tantam non spernit, nisi qui concipit ampliora. Si tam amplus[78] est animus hominis, cur negligatur a deo rerum vel minimarum procuratore? Si deum sentit animus, cur non et deus sentiat animum, praesertim cum deus hanc ipsam vim actionemque sentiendi animo dederit et servet et ducat? Hinc David interrogat: 'An qui plantavit aurem, non audit? Et qui finxit oculos, non considerat?'

7 Praeterea, si animus ad deum ascendit, cur non descendat quodammodo deus ad animum? Si quae iusta sunt, a deo mens postulat, dum paternam poscit haereditatem, cur non exaudiat deus? Quid postulat a parente indulgentissimo hic natus officiosissimus? Aeternitatem. Impetrabitne? Impetrabit[79] certe. Potest enim deus aeternus eam tribuere, potest capere vita mentis aeternitatem,[80] quam capit eius cognitio et voluntas. Non enim vult nisi cognoscat, neque cognoscit etiam nisi vivat. Quinetiam dari debet aeternitas menti, quae et transcendit tempus, ac pro deo aeterno despicit temporalia. Quod non modo religiosiores, verumetiam impii

standing. If through knowledge our rational soul is more outstanding than the world, it will be more outstanding also through life. By the power of life separable from the body, the soul can be separated through its activity from the body; and by the power of life that is as it were otherworldly it can transcend the world itself.

The degree to which understanding excels the world's order is 6
obvious from the fact that this order is dispersed in time [but] understanding possesses it wholly, simultaneously, and unchangingly. Again, the order follows on its cause, but does not attain it, [but] understanding does attain the order's cause when it discovers God, its artificer; and then it perceives such splendors concerning God that it puts the world aside like a shadow. Yet one does not reject so a vast a thing [as the world] without conceiving of things vaster still. If man's rational soul is so vast, why would it be neglected by God, who cares for even the smallest things? If the soul perceives God, why would God not perceive the soul, especially since God gave this very power and action of perceiving to the soul, and preserves it and guides it? Hence David asks, "He that planted the ear, does he not hear? He that formed the eyes, does he not see?"[51]

Moreover, if the rational soul ascends to God, why would God 7
not descend in a way into the soul? If the mind claims from God all that is just when it asks for its paternal inheritance, then why would God not listen to it? What does this most dutiful son ask for from his most indulgent parent? Eternity. Will he obtain it? Certainly he will. For eternal God can bestow it, and the life of the mind can lay hold of that eternity which its understanding and will understands; for it does not will except to understand and does not understand even except to live. Eternity must be granted, moreover, to the mind that transcends time and scorns things temporal for the sake of God eternal. Not only do the more religious do this, the impious do so in a way too. For those whom the love of God does not attract, at least the fear of God terrifies; and those whom fear does not terrify are troubled at least by a presen-

quodammodo faciunt. Nam quos non allicit amor dei, saltem terret timor. Quos non terret metus, supplicium[81] saltem sollicitat. Itaque homines multi omnia, omnes certe quam plurima vitae commoda temporalis abiiciunt, dei amore vel suspicione[82] vel metu. Deus igitur debet pro temporalibus aeterna tribuere. Nullum vero animalium reliquorum praesentibus abstinet bonis propter futurorum aviditatem. Quo fit ut homo stultissimus sit animalium omnium atque miserrimus, si neque praesenti fruitur vita neque futura. Atque haec eius stultitia misera ac stulta miseria ex eo proveniet, quia se deo sapientissimo felicissimoque crediderit. At enim sicut non potest quicquam ignis propinquatione fieri frigidissimum, ita non potest homo, quia solus haeret deo sapientissimo beatissimoque, stultissimus ex hoc miserrimusque evadere; immo vero ob hoc ipsum fit beatissimus, quod beatissimo se coniungit. Iungit se illi temporalia contemnendo, aeterna desiderando. Si contemnendis temporalibus fit beatus, non aliter talis efficitur nisi aeternarum rerum adeptione.

8 Praeterea, si deus prima et summa est vita, animal quod ipsi propius[83] haeret, vivit diutius. Non autem vivimus diutius corpore. Si deus summa sapientia est, homo tanto est sapientior ceteris animalibus, quanto deo haeret propinquius. In hac autem appropinquatione se iudicat immortalem. Quia vero iudicium huiusmodi verum est quod fit ab animo tunc quando est aliis animalibus et hominibus sapientior, verum est esse animum sempiternum. Si prima veritas non potest fallere, non falletur spes immortalitatis, a prima immortalitate usque adeo nobis inserta ut invitis reclamantibusque omnibus inter quae versamur spem eiusmodi semper retineamus. Si prima bonitas non est malefica, aviditas primi boni nobis ab illa infusa non privat nos temporalibus bonis, nisi ut tri-

timent of Him. So out of the love of God or out of suspicion or fear many men renounce all the comforts of temporal life, and certainly all men renounce a great many comforts. So God must give men eternal things in exchange for things temporal. Not one of the other animals abstains from things present because it yearns for things future. Consequently, man is the most foolish of all the animals and the most miserable if he finds joy neither in the present life nor in the future. And this miserable stupidity and stupid misery of his would derive from his putting his trust in God, in His supreme wisdom and felicity. For just as someone cannot become icily cold next to a fire, so man, inasmuch as he alone clings to God in His supreme wisdom and felicity, cannot become thereby supremely stupid or miserable. He becomes most blessed, rather, in that he unites himself to the Most Blessed, and he does so by despising things temporal and desiring things eternal. If man becomes blessed by despising things temporal, he does it in no other way than by adopting things eternal.

If God is the first and highest life, furthermore, then the living 8
being that clings most to Him lives the longest. But in the body we do not live very long. If God is the highest wisdom, then the more a man clings fast to God the more he excels the other animals in wisdom. In achieving this closeness [to God], he judges himself immortal. But because such a judgment (which is made by the soul at the moment when it is wiser than all other animals and men alike) is true, then true it is that the soul is everlasting. If the first truth cannot deceive, then that hope of immortality (which has been so implanted in us by the first immortality that we always retain it in the midst of all the unpleasant and intractable things we deal with) is not deceived. If the first goodness is not wicked, then the longing for the prime good it has infused in us does not rob us of temporal goods, except to bestow eternal ones upon us. If every opinion is truer to the extent it is better, and better to the extent it renders those who hold it better, then the

buat sempiterna. Si opinio quaeque eo verior est quo melior atque eo melior quo meliores efficit opinantes, opinio immortalitatis omnium verissima est, quia prae ceteris optimos, excellentissimos homines ideoque felicissimos efficit. Quis ignorat id in natura hominis verissimum esse quod maxime ad perfectionem conducit humanam? Si intellectus natura amat deum tamquam ipsum verum bonumque, ac deus et amat intellectum, praesertim pium, tamquam ipsi cognatissimum, et redamat tamquam amantem, fit ut naturalis quaedam inter eos sit amicitia. Amicitiae finis est vitae communio. Potest ergo dei vita intellectui communicari, ea videlicet ratione qua amatur ab illo, siquidem talis est amicitiae finis, qualis est amicitia atque contra. Amatur vero desideraturque perpetua. Quod inde confirmari videtur, quia cum boni proprium sit allicere ad se cuncta seque cunctis communicare, necesse est infinitum bonum, qui deus est, trahere communicareque infinite. Ideo communicat cuique se ad votum, quia idem ipse deus communicat, qui et traxit. Intellectus autem non minus secundum naturam exoptat perpetuam dei vitam, quam certam illius intellegentiam. Denique si deus beneficus, immo ipsa beneficentia est, officio gratitudinis carere non potest. Non potest autem gratus esse erga eum qui divini cultus amore vitam amittit praesentem, nisi post hanc vitam.

: IX :

Religionem esse humano generi maxime omnium propriam et veridicam.

1 Hominem esse brutis praestantiorem opera eius evidentissima[84] testimonio sunt, quod ostendit duodecimo libro *Animalium* Aristo-

belief in immortality is the truest opinion of all, because, before all others, it makes men the best, the most excellent, and therefore the most happy. Everyone knows that the truest thing in human nature is what most leads to human perfection. If the intellect naturally loves God as the true and the good, and God too loves the intellect, especially the devout intellect, as most akin to Himself, and loves what is reciprocally loving Him, then a natural friendship exists between them. The goal of friendship is sharing life. So the life of God can be communicated to the intellect for the very reason that it is loved by the intellect, since the goal of friendship is sharing life just as the goal of sharing life is friendship. But what is loved and desired is perpetual life. Obviously confirming this is the fact that, since it is the property of the good both to attract all things to itself and to communicate itself to all things, then necessarily the infinite good which is God both attracts and communicates infinitely. So He communicates Himself to each at will, since the God who communicates is the same God as the God who attracts. But the intellect chooses the perpetual life of God no less naturally than it chooses a sure and certain understanding of Him. Finally, if God is beneficent, or rather is beneficence itself, He cannot be wanting in duly exercising gratitude. But God cannot extend that gratitude to the person who, out of love of divine worship, loses this present life, except when this life is over.

: IX :

For mankind religion is the most appropriate and truth-telling of all things.

In the twelfth book of his work *On the Animals,* Aristotle shows 1
that the testimony to man's superiority over the beasts is his manifest works.[52] So let us inquire into the gift that chiefly makes him

teles. Quaeramus igitur qua praecipue dote sit praestantissimus. Videtur sane praestare artium et gubernationis ingenio, praesertim quia, ut alias declaravimus, homines variant artificia, utpote qui ipsi artifices sint, non alterius artificis instrumenta. Bestiae vero non variant, quia artificiosae naturae instrumenta sint potius quam artem ipsae possideant. Verum licet artis et gubernationis ingenio ceteris animalibus praecellamus, communis tamen haec nobis est cum brutis industria. Oportet autem humanam speciem, postquam a brutis distincta est, distinctam aliquam propriamque habere perfectionem, cuius non sint bestiae ullae ullo modo participes. Num sermo hic erit? At nutu, clamore et cantu sermonem bestiae imitantur. Num ratio? Ratio certe. Non omnis tamen operatio rationis, nam ratio quidem activa habet et in bestiis vestigia quaedam per artium et gubernationis indicia. Ratio quoque rerum naturalium speculatrix habere videtur nonnihil in bestiis imaginarium. Nam et ipsae morbis suis ciborum remediorumque quorundam electione medentur, et quasi futurarum tempestatum providae argumenta praeferunt futurorum mutantque loca, ut ventura temporum vitent discrimina, quamvis ad hoc ducantur potius natura quam ducant. Quid ergo reliquum est, quod omnino solius sit hominis? Contemplatio divinorum. Nullum enim bruta prae se ferunt religionis indicium, ut propria nobis sit mentis in deum caeli regem erectio sicut corporis in caelum erectio propria. Cultusque divinus ita ferme hominibus naturalis, sicut equis hinnitus canibusve latratus. At si quis curiosus affirmet bestias insuper nonnullas caelestia venerari (quod ego minime credo), respondebunt Platonici huiusmodi bestias vel aliud quodvis tunc facere, cum caelestia honorare videntur; vel si forte honorant, tamen nescire quid agant; vel si sciunt, eas[85] quoque intellegentiae immorta-

preeminent. It seems that he excels in the genius he has for the arts and for government, especially because, as we have argued elsewhere,[53] men produce different artifacts inasmuch as they themselves are the artificers and not the instruments of another artificer. But the beasts, because they are the instruments of an artful nature rather than themselves being the possessors of art, do not produce different artifacts. Although we excel over all the other animals in our genius for art and government, however, we share this industriousness with the beasts nonetheless. But it behooves the human species, inasmuch as it is distinct from the beasts, to have its own distinct perfection which none of them in any way shares. Will this perfection be speech? But beasts imitate speech by way of gesture, sound, and song. Will it be reason? Reason certainly, but not every activity of the reason; for in the beasts too we find certain traces of the active reason, the adumbrations of art and government. Even the speculative reason, the contemplator of natural things, seems to have a shadowy counterpart among the beasts; for they heal their ailments by opting for particular foods and remedies. Moreover, prescient of future storms as it were, they present us with signs of what is about to happen and change their locations in order to avoid the impending dangers of the advancing seasons, although in this they are being led by nature rather than themselves taking the lead. So what is there left which is entirely and solely man's? The contemplation of the divine. For the beasts display no sign of religion. The lifting of our mind to God, the king of heaven, is as properly ours as the raising upright of our body towards heaven. Worshipping the divine is as natural to men almost as neighing to horses or barking to dogs. But if some caviller affirms that some beasts do venerate things celestial (which I do not personally believe), then the Platonists will respond that such beasts are either doing something else when they appear to be honoring things celestial, or if they are honoring them, they do not know what they are doing; or, if they do know, they are also

litatisque participes esse. Sed revera, ut ad propositum revertamur, perfectissimum animal ea proprietate maxime tum perfectione pollet, tum ab inferioribus discrepat, qua perfectissimis, id est, divinis coniungitur. Rursus si homo animalium mortalium perfectissimus est,[86] qua ratione est homo, ex ea praecipue dote est omnium perfectissimus, quam inter haec habet ipse propriam, animalibus non communem. Ea religio est. Per religionem igitur est perfectissimus. Si religio esset inanis, per eam rursus omnium foret imperfectissimus,[87] quoniam per eam, ut paulo ante exponebamus, dementissimus foret atque miserrimus. Non potest autem per eandem sui partem ita contraria perpeti, ut per eam tum summe perfectus sit, tum summopere imperfectus. Est igitur religio vera.

2 An ignoramus vaticinium illud, quod a tota aliqua animalium specie fit verum esse? Reptilia multa oriente sole e terrae sinu surrepunt: aeris caligo portenditur. Cornicum plurima turba vespere a certa aeri plaga pervolant: venti praenuntiantur.[88] Communi quoque hominum vaticinio religio vera est. Omnes namque semper ubique colunt deum vitae futurae gratia. Verum est igitur vitam aliam fore, si modo perfectissima species animalium verissimum habet iudicium illud, quod sibi est maxime omnium naturale. Talem autem esse religionis assertionem apparet non solum ex eo quod solius hominis est, verumetiam ex eo quod omnes hominum opiniones, affectus, mores, excepta religione, mutantur. Cum religionem dico, instinctum ipsum omnibus gentibus communem naturalemque intellego, quo ubique et semper providentia quaedam, regina mundi, cogitatur et colitur. Ad quam certe pietatem causis praecipue tribus inducimur. Primo quidem naturali quadam, ut ita loquar, sagacitate ab ipsamet providentia nobis infusa; deinde philosophicis rationibus ex ipso aedificii ordine archi-

participants in understanding and in immortality. But to return to our thesis. In reality the most perfect animal is joined to the most perfect beings, that is, to the divine beings, by the very property which gives this animal its perfection and which differentiates it from lower things. Again, if man is the most perfect of all mortal animals because of what makes him man, then he is the most perfect chiefly because of the gift among all the gifts which he has for himself and does not share with the animals. This gift is religion. So through religion he is the most perfect. Were religion baseless, he would be the most imperfect of all because of it, since he would be, as we explained a little earlier, the most demented and the most miserable because of it. But he cannot be so subject to contraries that he is both fully perfect and fully imperfect through the same part of himself. Therefore religion is true.

Do we not know that the prophesying that comes from an entire animal species is true? Many reptiles slithering out of the earth's bosom when the sun rises portend fog. Numerous flocks of rooks in the evening flying from a certain region of the sky foretell winds. The prophecy common to men also proves religion true. For all men always and everywhere worship God for the sake of the future life. So it is true that there is going to be another life if the most perfect of the animal species holds that the truest judgment for it is the judgment that is the most natural of all. But we can see religion being affirmed by the fact not only that it is man's alone but also that all the opinions, feelings, and customs of men change while religion does not. When I say religion, I mean that instinct which is common and natural to all peoples and which we everywhere and always use to think about providence and to worship it as the queen of the world.[54] Assuredly we are led to this piety by three main causes. Firstly by a certain as it were natural sagacity infused in us by providence itself; then by philosophical reasons establishing the providence of the architect from the 2

tecti providentiam comprobantibus; postremo propheticis verbis atque miraculis.

3 Quod vero modo de propheta dixi, operaepretium est deinceps argumentis quae et Plato in *Protagora* et Avicenna adducit in *Metaphysicis* confirmare. Homo, ut aiunt, est animal naturaliter sociabile, eget enim necessario multis, quae singuli comparare non possunt, cuncti vero in unum congregati mutua sibi vicissim opera subministrant. Praeterea quod sociabile sit, indicat sermo quasi quidam alterius ad alterum humanae mentis interpres, quem natura homini non dedisset, nisi fuisset in coetu victurus. Quamobrem naturalis est homini congregatio. Verum si absque lege concurrant, paulo post mutuis disgregabuntur iniuriis, disgregati vero tum multorum defectu peribunt, tum velut inermes laniabuntur a feris. Ut ergo vivant, et bene vivant, congregari eos necesse est. Sed rursus ut in coetu permaneant, omnino opus est lege—ea inquam lege, cuius tanta sit auctoritas, ut nemo vel violentia vel dolo praevaricari se posse aut debere confidat. Talis autem esse non potest, nisi legislator sit existimeturque divinus. Denique ut talis sit habeaturque, oportet eum manifestis quibusdam miraculis ad homines divina providentia mitti. Quem sane prophetam humani generis divinum ducem Plato et Avicenna cognominant. Huc tendit Platonicum illud in libro *De regno*: 'Quemadmodum bestiae nequeunt a bestia feliciter sine homine duci, ita neque homines ab homine sine deo'. Rursus in *Protagora* inquit non potuisse homines simul vivere absque lege, neque legem ad hoc sufficientem accipere a Prometheo, id est creata quadam providentia potuisse, sed Iovem ipsum omnium creatorem ad homines una cum lege misisse Mercurium, id est prophetam aliquem et[89] divinae voluntatis interpretem et legis tam divinae quam humanae latorem.

very order of his edifice; and lastly by words of prophecy and by miracles.

It is important to confirm what I have just said about the prophet by referring now to the arguments that Plato adduces in the *Protagoras*[55] and Avicenna in his *Metaphysics*.[56] Man they say is a naturally sociable animal, for he necessarily lacks many things which individuals cannot acquire but which all men gathered into a community can supply for each individual in turn by working together. Speech too shows that man is sociable in that it is the interpreter so to speak of the human mind of one person to another; and nature would not have given it to man unless he were going to live in a community. So assembling together is natural for man. But if men assembled in the absence of law, they would soon be torn asunder by mutual injustices; as such they would perish from the lack of many things, and in their helplessness be devoured by wild beasts. So in order to live and to prosper, they must come together. But in order to stay together in turn, they absolutely must have law, a law whose authority is such that no man is confident that he has the power or the right to violate it by violence or deceit. But the law cannot be such unless the lawgiver is, and is thought to be, divine. But to be and to be deemed divine, he must be sent to men by divine providence accompanied by certain manifest miracles. Plato and Avicenna call such a prophet the divine leader of mankind. The following quotation from Plato's book on the state points in this direction: "Just as beasts cannot be led successfully by a beast without a man, so neither can men be led by a man without God."[57] In the *Protagoras* in turn he says that men cannot live together without law; that they had been unable to receive enough law to do this from Prometheus, from the providence, in other words, that is particular and created; and that Jove himself, the creator of all, had sent Mercury down to men with the law—had dispatched, that is, a prophet, an interpreter of the divine will and a giver of both divine and human law.[58] 3

4 Quod autem deus prophetas[90] certis saeculis ad officium eiusmodi mittat, sic una cum Avicenna ostendere possumus. Si deus humano corpori non solum in rebus omnino necessariis, sed etiam commodis accuratissime providet, velut in superciliis, palpebrisque et plantarum concavitate, multo magis animo totique hominum generi in rebus praecipuis maximeque ad bonum nostrum necessariis providet, praesertim cum bona minora maiorum gratia sint. Ideoque si minora bona ab initio statim nobis adsunt, absque dubio adsunt etiam maiora, quae et adesse possunt et causae sunt ut minora non desint. Quamobrem deus circa legem divinam prophetamque, conditorem eius, ita prospicit, ut de cuius bonitate singula membra corporis iure conqueri nequeunt, multo minus animus ipse, horum dominus, universumve genus humanum ulla umquam ratione conqueri possit. Probat insuper Avicenna animam quidem prophetica lege virtuteque imbutam a divina solum providentia mitti; corpus autem ad animam prophetae suscipiendam idoneum disponi a deo — non tamen proxime, sed per animas caelorum motrices tamquam per ministros ac etiam per caelos ipsos quasi per instrumenta dei. Ita ut divina lex, utpote incorporea, quamvis per caelestia corpora effici nequeat, tamen quodammodo possit indiciis quibusdam a caelo acceptis significari. Quod etiam ex multis Plotini disputationibus comprobatur, in quibus ille demonstrat, quae ad mentem nostram pertinent, a caeli corpore fieri numquam posse, sed tamen significari, siquidem mentes caelorum motrices nostra haec praevident cogitationesque suas saepe caelestibus quasi oculis nutibusque suis indicare videntur.

That God sends prophets in certain ages to perform this office we can demonstrate with an argument from Avicenna.[59] If God painstakingly provides the human body not only with things it absolutely needs but also with advantages such as eyebrows, eyelids, and the arches of feet, then *a fortiori* He provides the rational soul and the whole of mankind with the most important things, with those that are absolutely necessary for our good, especially since lesser goods exist for the sake of the greater. Thus, if lesser goods are with us from the very beginning, then the greater goods are also undoubtedly there: they are able to be present and they are the causes that the lesser goods are not absent. Accordingly, with regard to the divine law and the prophet who establishes it for us, God so provides that the individual limbs of the body cannot justly complain about the law's goodness, and much less can the rational soul itself (the lord of the limbs) or mankind universally ever have any cause to complain. Avicenna proves moreover that the soul that is inspired by prophetic law and virtue is sent by divine providence alone; but that the body suitable for sustaining the soul of a prophet is disposed for it by God—not directly but by way both of the [celestial] souls as ministers and movers of the heavens and of the heavens themselves as instruments of God.[60] Consequently, the divine law, though it cannot be put into effect by the heavenly bodies, being itself bodiless, can yet be signified in a way by certain signs received from heaven. This is also proved by many arguments of Plotinus, in which he shows that whatever pertains to our mind can never be created by heaven's body but can nonetheless be signified by it, since the minds that are the heavens' movers foresee our concerns, and often seem to indicate their thoughts to us by way as it were of their celestial eyes and nods.[61] 4

: X :

Tres obiectiones Lucretianorum et solutiones.

Prima.

1 Non est credendum Lucretianis dicentibus religionem non a iudicio naturali, sed a complexionis corruptione, consilii legibus, caeli impetu provenire.

2 Profecto a complexionis corruptione idcirco eam proficisci non arbitror, quia non est in hominibus complexio deterior quam in bestiis, praesertim ad veritatis iudicium bonique delectum; homines autem soli ac sedulo religionibus occupantur. Sed neque etiam inter homines qui depravatam habent complexionem hi sunt proprie qui colant deum; omnes enim corruptam non habent; omnes tamen quodammodo deum colunt et coluere semper. Neque tamen semper fuit hominum depravata natura, neque rudes tantum homines adorant, sed etiam ingeniosi et sapientes, quod ostenderunt Persarum magi, Aegyptii sacerdotes, prophetae Hebraei, Orphici, Pythagorici, Platonicique philosophi, ac prisci theologi Christianorum. Hi omnes sine controversia mirabili sapientia pollebant et incomparabili sanctitate. Porphyrius de voto disputans inquit praestantissimos quosque apud omnes gentes sapientiae studio votis incubuisse, quales apud Indos Brachmanae, apud Persas magi, similesque apud Graecos Chaldaeosque fuerint. Haec ille. Neque eos simulasse putandum, qui tum perpetuis ope-

: X :

Three objections by the followers of Lucretius and their resolution.

First objection.

First we must not give credit to the followers of Lucretius when they say that religion does not derive from natural deliberation but from the corruption of our complexion, from the laws of a council, and from the impulse of the sky.[62] 1

The reason I do not think religion proceeds from the corruption of the complexion is that in men the complexion is no worse than in the beasts and especially with regard to determining the truth and choosing the good. Men alone, however, are interested in religions and earnestly so. Yet those who worship God are not, properly speaking, among those who have a depraved complexion; for not all men have a corrupt complexion, yet all in a way worship and have always worshipped God. Nor has men's nature always been depraved. Nor do rude men only adore Him, but so do men who are clever and wise. The Magi of the Persians, the Egyptian priests, the Hebrew prophets, the Orphic, Pythagorean, and Platonic philosophers, and the ancient theologians of the Christians have demonstrated this. It is beyond dispute that all these excel in marvelous wisdom and incomparable sanctity. In discussing prayer, Porphyry says that in all nations the men who excel most in the study of wisdom devote themselves to prayers: among the Indians such were the Brahmans, among the Persians the Magi, and the like among the Greeks and Chaldaeans. This is what Porphyry says.[63] And one must not suppose that these men, who confirmed their life's sanctity both with everlasting works and at their own mortal peril, were just pretending. There have been very many other most learned philosophers, barbarian, Greek, and 2

ribus, tum vitae periculo vitae[91] sanctimoniam confirmarunt. Fuerunt et alii complurimi doctissimi philosophi barbari, Graeci atque Latini, qui etsi non tanta excellerent castimonia vitae, quanta illi quos ante commemoravi, honestis tamen moribus duxerunt vitam religionibusque favere non dubitaverunt. Fieri quidem potest, ut aliqua ex parte horum aliqui simulaverint, non tamen omnes credo simulavisse, neque eos qui simulaverunt, omnis fuisse religionis expertes. Difficile enim est naturam prorsus exuere. Impios quidem prae ceteris fuisse traditur Diagoram, Dicaearchum, Epicurum, Lucretium, qui etiam natura cogebantur interdum nonnihil religionibus assentiri, quod eorum libri testantur. Ac sicut isti nonnulla impune contra religiones in medium protulerunt, ita et alii multi philosophi palam impietatis virus evomuissent, si plurimi fuissent impii. Aliud autem est hunc aut illum religionis cultum non admittere,[92] quod faciunt multi, aliud omnem religionem funditus tollere, quod tentaverunt quam paucissimi, et illi quidem suspicantes potius quam prorsus asseverantes.

3 Porro si qui ingeniosi viri ac docti in religione reperiantur[93] ambigui, non est mirandum. Duas enim aetates[94] Plato scribit esse valde religiosas, pueritiam et senectutem. Nam pueri cum lacte religionem sugunt et in iis permanent quae imbiberunt quousque in adolescentia ratio excitetur, quae sua natura singularum rerum causas rationesque requirit. Si in hac aetate aut ea studia capessant aut in eos sermones incidant, quibus diligenter rerum causae perquirantur, incipiunt quasi nihil velle asseverare, nisi cuius ipsi rationem perspexerint. Tunc primum religionem magna ex parte post tergum abiiciunt, nisi forte legibus seniorumque consilio se committant, quia divinorum occultissimae rationes longo vix tan-

Latin, who, though they have not attained the same purity of life as those I recalled earlier, have led nonetheless honorable and upright lives and never hesitated to favor religious observances. It is possible that some of them pretended to some degree, yet I do not believe that all pretended or that all were wanting in religion among those who did pretend. For it is difficult to cast our nature entirely aside. It is reported that Diagoras, Dicaearchus, Epicurus, and Lucretius were impious beyond others, but that occasionally they too were compelled by nature to assent to sundry religious observances, as their books testify. But just as they raised various objections against religion without being punished, so, if the impious were in the majority, many other philosophers too would have openly spewed out the poison of their godlessness. But not to admit, as many do, one or other religious cult is not the same as rejecting all religion entirely. Very few have attempted the latter and they have done so indeed by voicing doubts rather than rooted convictions.

Indeed, it is not surprising that one finds clever and learned 3
men who are doubtful in matters religious. Plato[64] writes that two stages of life are especially religious, childhood and old age.[65] For children suck religion in with their milk and stay with the things they have imbibed, until their reason, which by its very nature searches out the causes and rational principles of individual matters, is first aroused in their youth. At this age, if they engage in studies or participate in conversations that diligently inquire into things' causes, then they begin to want to assert nothing almost unless they themselves perceive its rational principle. Now for the first time and in large part they put religion behind them, unless perchance they can entrust themselves to the laws and to the advice of their seniors. This is because the rational principles of things divine, totally hidden as they are, are perceived only after a long time and scarcely then, and as a result of the utmost diligence and after the mind has been purged. Adolescents are not yet able

dem tempore, exquisitissima diligentia, purgata mente prospiciuntur.[95] Adolescentes illi rationes huiusmodi nondum attingunt, et quia nihil ferme asserunt cuius non videant rationem, si proprio confidant iudicio, religionem quodammodo negligunt. Nonnulli in hac opinione constituti[96] Aristippicis voluptatibus sese dedunt, tandem nihil amplius de religione nisi tamquam de anilibus fabulis cogitantes. Alii vero[97] Pythagoreo ritu purgant mentem a sensibus per morales, physicas, mathematicas, metaphysicas disciplinas, ne tamquam superiores illi lippos adhuc oculos in divinum solem subito dirigentes caligare cogantur, sed gradatim progredientes lumen divinum in moralibus primo tamquam[98] in terra prospiciant, secundo in physicis tamquam aqua, tertio in[99] mathematicis tamquam in luna, quarto in metaphysicis tamquam in sole[100] perspicue salubriterque perspiciant. Hos appellat Orpheus Musarum legitimos sacerdotes, qui tandem in aetate maturiori de religione sentiunt[101] multo melius, quemadmodum legimus apud Platonem in epistola ad regem Dionysium, in *Phaedro*, in primo *De republica*, in decimo *Legum*. Monet autem iuvenes Plato ne temere de divinis sententiam ferant, sed credant legibus, donec aetas ipsa doceat, vel per eos disciplinarum gradus quos narravimus, vel per experientiam, vel per quandam animae[102] a corpore separationem, quam moderata senectus adducit, ut anima in ea aetate res a corporibus separatas quasi e proximo videns clarius discernat quam consueverit.

4 Quapropter cum Plato Dionysio adhuc iuveni divina quaedam mysteria sub quodam velamine tradidisset, adiunxit primum, ut ea diligenter examinaret, nullum enim hoc studium beatius esse posse. Deinde caveret ne in hominum imperitorum aures haec exciderent, quia nulla sint apud vulgus quidem magis ridicula, apud

to attain these first principles; and because they assent to virtually nothing for which they do not see the first principle, trusting as they do in their own judgment, in a way they neglect religion.[66] Some of them who are confirmed in this opinion surrender themselves to Aristippean pleasures, ultimately thinking nothing more of religion than of oldwives' tales. Others follow the Pythagorean rite and purge their mind of the senses by way of the moral, scientific, mathematical, and metaphysical disciplines. They do so: a) lest they are forced, like the Aristippeans, to blind their eyes, dim as they still are, by turning their gaze suddenly towards the divine sun; but b) so that, proceeding step by step, they may descry the divine light, first in moral matters as on earth, second in scientific matters as in water, and third in mathematical matters as in the moon; and fourth see it clearly and beneficially in metaphysical matters as in the sun. Orpheus calls those who at a more mature age form more discriminating judgments about religion the rightful priests.[67] We read the like in Plato: in the letter to King Dionysius, in the *Phaedrus*, in the first book of the *Republic*, and in the tenth book of the *Laws*.[68] Plato warns young men, however, not to proffer rashly an opinion about matters divine but to believe in the laws, until maturity itself instructs them either by way of the ascending scale of the disciplines we have described, or by experience, or by a certain separation of the soul from the body brought on by the moderation of old age (at that age the soul, as in sharper focus, sees things separated from bodies and distinguishes them with greater clarity than it did in the past).

Wherefore, since Plato had conveyed to the still youthful Dio- 4
nysius certain divine mysteries under a veil, he enjoined him first to examine them diligently; for no study can be more blessed than this study. Next he warned him to take care lest they fell upon the ears of ignorant men, since to the vulgar no mysteries are more ridiculous, while to men endowed with an excellent wit none are more marvelous and divine. And he added furthermore that the

autem viros bono ingenio praeditos magis mirabilia et divina. Addit insuper divina mysteria, postquam frequentius, immo semper examinata sunt, vix tandem multo labore tamquam aurum purgari atque lucere, ut etiam multi, et illi quidem acutissimi eruditissimique, cum talia in iuventute atque etiam in trigesimo aetatis anno audientes tamquam incredibilia reprobaverint, postea tamen sive maturioris aetatis sive diligentioris examinis beneficio sive potius divina, ut alibi dicit, revelatione, talia tamquam omnium probabilissima manifestissimaque concesserint, contraria vero tamquam falsa damnaverint. Haec Plato.

5 Accedit ad haec, quod multi in quavis arte excellentes viri vel melancholici sunt, quales Heraclitus, Aristoteles, Chrysippus fuerunt, vel fiunt, quales Democritus, Zeno Citieus,[103] Avempaces Arabs, Averrois evaserunt. Hic humor frigidus est, siccus et ater, quae quidem tres qualitates tribus illis contrariae sunt in quibus vitae consistit vigor, calori videlicet et humori spirituique perlucido. Talis itaque humor tamquam vitae contrarius aufert spem vitalem et animo suspicionem iniicit contra vitam. Quo fit ut de immortalitate animi nonnumquam ambigant et diffidant. Quod sibi contigisse scribit Avempaces. Non ideo diffidunt, quia sunt excellentes ingenio vel doctrina, sed quia ob humorem terreum suspiciosi et timidi. Nam rudes hebetesque homunculi nonnumquam ipsi quoque diffidunt, si eodem illo premantur humore. Et viri egregii saepenumero sperant quam optime, si humore eiusmodi non vexentur, quamquam qui vexantur[104] ab ineunte aetate, si tamen non perverse omnino fuerint educati, inanes[105] suspiciones abiicunt facile et naturalem sequuntur religionis instinctum. Tanta est ipsius naturae vis, tanta stabilitas. Quod Pythagoras, Socrates, Plato, Varro, Apolloniusque Theaneus sunt prae ceteris assecuti. Quapropter suspiciones illae nihil habent momenti ad animorum

divine mysteries, after more frequent, nay unending examination, are eventually and after great difficulty and labor rendered pure and dazzling like gold. Consequently, many men, and indeed the most clever and learned, when hearing about them in their youth and even in the thirtieth year of their age, have rejected them as unbelievable; yet later, whether benefiting from being older or from more diligent examination, or whether rather by divine revelation, as Plato says elsewhere, they have admitted that such mysteries are the most probable and manifest of all, and they have condemned their opposites as false. Thus Plato.[69]

Add to this that many men who excel in some art are either 5
natural melancholics, as Heraclitus, Aristotle, and Chrysippus were, or they become such, as Democritus, Zeno of Citium, Avempace the Arab, and Averroes turned out to be.[70] This melancholic humor is cold, dry, and black, three qualities that are opposite to the three wherein life's vigor consists—opposite that is to heat, to wetness, and to the transparent spirit. Such a humor, being the contrary of life, banishes life's hope and injects doubt, the enemy of life, into the rational soul. Consequently melancholics sometimes doubt and despair of the soul's immortality. Avempace writes that this happened to him.[71] They doubt, not because they excel in intellectual ability and doctrine, but because the earthly humor makes them doubtful and cowardly. For uneducated and obtuse little men also despair sometimes if they are vexed by that same humor; and illustrious men often experience the greatest hope if they are not troubled by the same, although those who are troubled from the earliest age, as long as they have not been nurtured with utter perversity, easily put empty doubts aside and follow their natural instinct for religion. So mighty is the power of nature itself, so enduring its stability! Pythagoras, Socrates, Plato, Varro, and Apollonius of Tyana grasped this better than the others. These doubts therefore play no role in signifying the death of rational souls, since they proceed not from intelligence or wisdom

mortem significandam, cum neque ab ingenio neque a sapientia, sed a morbo proficiscantur. Quinetiam illi saepe sunt acutiores, in quorum ortu Saturnus et Mercurius possunt quam plurimum. Nam hae stellae invitant ad contemplandum, quoniam ad interiora spiritus contrahunt. Hi planetae, si directi sunt optimeque dispositi, ingenium augent, religionem non minuunt. Sin retrogradi neque optime dispositi, undique hominem reddunt formidolosum admodum atque suspiciosum ob terream ipsorum qualitatem non sufficienter aspectu aliorum siderum temperatam. Quo fit, ut non in religione solum, sed in rebus etiam aliis ambigat et diffidat.

6 Ceterum meminisse oportet eam opinionem sive affectionem non satis habere fidei, quae sequitur aut ingenium melancholicum, aegrum et quodammodo vitae contrarium,[106] aut indecentem et noxiam positionem siderum, quae etiam complexionem pervertit humanam ac defectum affert secum, non modo quantum spectat ad vitae fiduciam, sed etiam quantum ad humanarum rerum gubernationem. Unde impii homines plurimum vel ignavissimi sunt, qualis fuisse dicitur Epicurus, vel flagitiosi, qualis Aristippus, vel insani, qualis sectator eorum Lucretius. Qui dum insania propter atram bilem concitaretur, animam suam primo conatus est verbis perdere in libro *De natura rerum* tertio, deinde corpus suum gladio perdidit. Ergo sicut de vini sapore non est aegrotanti credendum, sed bene valenti, ita de fine humanae vitae credendum est humano sanoque ingenio potius quam insano. Sanam vero et naturalem hominis complexionem appello sanguineam ac maxime temperatam. Sanguinea aerea est in calore et humore vitali consistens; temperata caelo est similis, neque veritatis[107] iudicium interturbat. Tales sunt plurimum humanae complexiones ad sanum ingenium prudentiamque accommodatae, quae religionem nobis non afferunt quidem (est enim haec menti infusa divinitus, cum divino-

but from a disease. Moreover, those in whose birth Saturn and Mercury most dominate are often more acute. For these planets invite us to contemplation because they concentrate the spirits on interior things. If they are moving regularly forwards and are best disposed, they enhance the intelligence and do not diminish religion. But if they are retrograde and not best disposed, they render a man extremely fearful and despairing at every turn, their earthy quality being insufficiently tempered by the aspect of the other planets; accordingly he is doubtful and mistrusting not only in religion but in other matters as well.

For the rest, we must remember not to put full trust in that 6
opinion or affection which results either from a melancholic bent, one sick and contrary in a way to life, or from an inappropriate and harmful position of the stars that both perverts the human temperament and brings with it a weakness with regard not only to our confidence in life but also to the governance of human affairs. Hence impious men are for the most part either extremely idle as Epicurus was said to be,[72] or profligate like Aristippus,[73] or mad as was their follower Lucretius. When his madness was roused on account of his black bile, Lucretius first tried to slaughter his soul verbally in the third book of his *On the Nature of Things;* then slaughtered his body with a sword.[74] Therefore, just as in judging a wine we should trust the palate of a healthy person not of a sick one, so in determining life's goal we should trust the intelligence of a sane rather than of an insane person. But in man the complexion I call healthy and natural is the perfectly tempered sanguine one. The sanguine is airy and consists of heat and vital wetness; and, being tempered, it is like the heavens and does not cloud our ability to judge the truth. Such for the most part are the human complexions best suited to prudence and having a balanced personality. It is true they do not give us religion (for religion is poured divinely into our mind, since it orders us to neglect all else for the sake of things divine); but they do not impede religion in

rum gratia negligi cetera iubeat), sed eam nequaquam impediunt neque vanas animo suspiciones iniiciunt. Quod autem in pluribus perfectioribusque est, naturale censetur. Quod in paucissimis et aegrotantibus, monstruosum. At vero naturale quidem veridicum, monstruosum[108] vero fallax esse solet.

7 Iudicium autem religioni favens reperitur in pluribus gravioribusque hominibus, in paucissimis vero levissimisque contrarium, quorum exemplo alii quoque nonnumquam inficiuntur. Atque in illis paucissimis non est hoc iudicium rationis, sed morbus[109] animi formidolosaque suspicio a depravata complexione corporis proficiscens. Quod ex eo patet, quod saepe homines huiusmodi rationes quidem habent animi aeternitati faventes, suspicantur tamen tamquam ii quorum ratio aut iudicat vinum non esse bibendum, pulmones nihilominus sitiunt, aut iudicat nihil esse in via quod noceat, horret tamen sensus in tenebris. Neque solum contracta vel a parentibus vel a sideribus iniqua complexio, sed usu inducta qualitas, ut significavimus ab initio, a religione humanum genus abducit. Solent enim homines in quavis disciplina nimium curiosi propter nimiam cerebri agitationem siccato cerebro quodammodo insanire, quod in *Theaeteto* scribit Plato contra illos qui nihil in rebus stare umquam dicebant, quos, inquit, vertigine affectos ob frequentem revolutionem, putasse omnia verti, cum verterentur ipsi. Itaque non mirum est, si curiosi artium viri nonnumquam et in religione et in rebus aliis manifeste delirant, quorum insaniam declarant tum mores levissimi, tum ridiculae nimium in rebus multis opiniones opinionumque ipsarum contrarietates.

8 Non igitur a corruptione complexionis religio, sed impietas nascitur. Neque solum a depravata complexione, sed a depravatis mo-

any way, and they do not inject groundless doubts into the rational soul. But what exists in the vast majority of men and in the more perfect is adjudged to be natural; what exists in a small minority and the sick, monstrous. But generally the natural is true, the monstrous, false.

In the vast majority of men and in the graver sort, we find a 7
judgment favorable to religion, in a small minority and the most frivolous, an unfavorable one; and it is by the example of the latter that the others are sometimes infected too. But festering in this tiny minority is not the judgment of the reason but a disease of the soul and a cowardly doubting that stems from their body's depraved complexion. Evidence of this is that such men often indeed have reasons favoring the eternity of the soul but are still doubtful: they resemble those whose reason decides a wine should not be drunk but whose lungs are nonetheless thirsty;[75] or whose reason judges nothing dangerous lies on the road ahead but whose fears infest the shadows. For it is not only the unbalanced complexion contracted from one's parents or the stars, but a quality resulting from constant use (as we signified from the onset) that draws mankind away from religion. For men who are overly curious in any discipline because of their brain's excessive agitation usually become in a way insane, their brain having dried out. Plato says this in the *Theaetetus* in countering those who used to declare that nothing in nature ever stands still: having been made dizzy by the constant turning around, he says, they thought everything else was turning when they were being turned themselves.[76] No wonder therefore if men who are overly curious about the arts are sometimes clearly mad with regard to religious and other matters: their insanity is made manifest both by their extremely flippant behavior and by the wholly ridiculous and self-contradictory opinions they hold about many matters.

So from the corruption of the complexion is born not reli- 8
gion, but [Lucretian] impiety. Plato asserts in his letters to the

ribus impietatem nasci Plato in epistolis ad Syracusanos asserit, dicens credendum semper esse priscis sacrisque oraculis asserentibus animam hominis esse immortalem iudicesque habere ac poenas pati maximas cum a corpore fuerit separata; quapropter minus malum existimandum perpeti gravissimas iniurias quam inferre; quae quidem avarus homo mentisque inops aut non audiat aut deridere soleat, voluptatibusque deditus, quasi caecus non cernat quam maximum semper malum viventem se impie necessario sequatur, et post mortem quam misera demigratio ipsum maneat. Haec ibi omnia. Similia quoque in *Gorgia* et in decimo *De republica* et in *Legibus*, ubi addit hanc de anima sententiam necessariis adamantinisque rationibus esse probatam. Quod usque adeo Cleombroto persuasum fuit,[110] ut se hac vita alterius amore privaverit. Demosthenes quoque ait malle honeste mori quam turpiter vivere, postquam Platonem Xenocratemque de animorum immortalitate disserentes audisset. Neque silentio praetereundum puto maximam impietatis causam a Platonicis in genus infimorum daemonum referri solere, qui tacita quadam persuasione vel propter ambitionem in falsam vel propter invidiam in nullam religionem pro viribus nos impellunt.

Secunda obiectio et solutio.

9 Confutavimus obiectionem primam Lucretianorum, qua dicebatur dei cultum humanae naturae depravatione contingere. Ubi apparuit Lucretianos esse potius depravatos, qui naturam hominum ex eo pessimam iudicant, quod deo optimo iungitur. Sed numquid,

Syracusans, however, that impiety is born not just from a depraved complexion but from depraved habits and customs. He declares a) that we must believe the ancient and sacred oracles when they affirm that man's soul is immortal, that it has judges, and that it endures the severest punishments when it has been separated from the body; b) that we must therefore consider it less bad to suffer than to inflict terrible injuries; and c) that a greedy man wanting intelligence either does not listen to these doctrines or is accustomed to deriding them—addicted to pleasures, like a blind man he cannot see what massive evil always and necessarily succeeds his living so impiously, and what a miserable journey awaits him after death. All this is in the letter.[77] He says similar things in the *Gorgias*, in the tenth book of the *Republic*, and in the *Laws*, where he adds that this view of the soul has been proved by necessary reasons, reasons strong as steel.[78] And it so persuaded Cleombrotus that out of love of the other life he deprived himself of this life.[79] Demosthenes too, after he had heard Plato and Xenocrates discoursing on the immortality of souls, said that he preferred to die honorably rather than to live shamefully.[80] Nor should we pass over in silence, I think, the fact that the Platonists customarily refer the chief cause of impiety to the race of the lowest demons who use all their power and mute persuasion to impel us either by way of ambition towards a false religion or by way of envy towards no religion at all.

The second objection and its resolution.

We have refuted the first objection of the followers of Lucretius 9
that maintains that our worship of God is the result of the depravity of our human nature. It has emerged rather that these followers, who judge men's nature at its worst precisely because it is united with God in His goodness, are themselves depraved. However, is the veneration of things divine, as they claim as their sec-

quod secundo afferunt loco, divinorum veneratio a consiliis hominum nascitur et civilibus institutis? Nequaquam.

Dici non potest quam cito hominum inventa mutentur etiam vera, nedum falsa et simulata. Omnia hominum instituta brevi tempore in contraria instituta mutantur. Contrariae quoque eodem in tempore leges diversis sunt gentibus, et quae aliis turpia, aliis honesta censentur. Quid autem religione antiquius? Quidve amplius? Neque hanc invenerunt conditores legum ad populos coercendos, nam ante civitates et domos viguit in orbe[111] religio, et homines sparsi atque silvestres deum colunt, et idem[112] ipsi latores legum numina[113] timuerunt. Quod quidem in *Protagora* Plato confirmat, dicens homines etiam antequam congregarentur vel loquerentur vel artes aliquas exercerent, statim ab initio ob naturalem cognationem deum adoravisse arasque et sacra fecisse. Proinde tam durum religionis iugum tot bonis vitae contrarium quandoque homines alicubi reiecissent, si ficta esset neque veritatis stabilitate constaret. At inquiet forte Protagoras non esse naturalem religionem, sed videri, quoniam a teneris unguiculis eam combibimus. Nos ita Protagorae respondebimus, eum ab infantia loqui et bibere didicisse, nihilominus tamen naturalem esse sermonem atque potum. Ubique et semper loquuntur homines atque bibunt, quoniam est naturale, sed aliis temporibus atque locis alio ordine loquuntur et bibunt, quoniam operationis ordo opinione constat potius quam natura. Similiter apud omnes gentes omnibus saeculis adoratur deus, quia naturale est, quamvis non iisdem sacris ac modis. Sermo quia naturalis est, suum attingit finem, id est voluntatem alterius alteri declarare. Potus quoque suum, id est corporis

ond argument, born from the councils of men and from civic institutions? Certainly not!

How quickly men's inventions alter even if they are true, let alone if they are false and counterfeit, cannot be described. All men's institutions change in a brief while into their opposites; and at any one time contrary laws govern different peoples, and these laws are deemed shameful by some and honorable by others. But what is more ancient than religion? And what is more widespread? The lawgivers did not invent religion to coerce the people, for it flourished throughout the world before cities and households did: men far separated and in the wilds have worshipped God, and these same lawgivers have themselves feared the gods. Plato confirms this in the *Protagoras* when he declares that men, even before they congregated or spoke together or exercised any of the arts and skills, immediately adored God from the onset because of their natural kinship to Him, and erected altars and instituted rites.[81] This yoke of religion, which is so burdensome, so contrary to the good things of life, men would therefore have rejected at some juncture and at some place if it were counterfeit or was not built securely on the foundation of truth. But perhaps Protagoras will argue that religion is not natural and only appears to be natural because we imbibe it in early infancy. To Protagoras we will respond, however, that he had learned to speak and drink in infancy, but that speech and drink are nonetheless natural. In every place and time men speak and drink because it is natural, but they speak and drink at different times and places, and in a different order, since the order for doing so is established by opinion rather than by nature. Similarly, God is adored among all peoples in every century, although not with the same rites and in the same ways, because it is natural [for men to adore Him]. Since speech is natural it achieves its end, that is, to declare one person's wish to another. Drink too achieves its end, which is to refresh the body's

humorem[114] instaurare. Religio cur suum non nanciscatur, non video. Suus finis est frui deo, suum votum perpetuo frui.

Tertia obiectio et solutio.

11 An feruntur homines ad religionem sideribus, quod tertio obiiciunt impii? Minime. Nempe humoribus corporum sidera suffragantur; religio est inimica corporibus. Neque altius desiderium infundere caelum potest quam sphaerarum caelestium, quas etiam spernit homo religiosus. Adde quod religio fatum damnat et asserit libertatem. Quonam igitur pacto idipsum, ut fato repugnet, habebit a fatis? Praeterea[115] coniunctio quaedam planetarum fertilitatem praestat, opposita vero penuriam. Haec pestem, illa salubritatem, bellum similiter atque pacem. Videmus dona caelorum quam cito in contraria permutentur! Itaque si deum colere cogit certa quaedam positio siderum, brevi positio contraria e memoria hominum divinos delebit[116] honores. Nusquam tamen et numquam religionis facta est intermissio, licet alias et alibi aliter deus sit honoratus. Quae etiam varietas humanarum mentium est secuta consilia, quae astris nequaquam subiiciuntur. Humana quippe mens natura sua tamquam divina ad deum sentiendum colendumque ducitur et timendum, sicut natura sua ad amandum bonum malumque vitandum. Verumtamen per liberam suae consultationis electionem dei colendi variat ritus, sicut etiam ad bonum variis graditur callibus pro arbitrio.

12 Superiori disputatione colligitur communem ipsam omnium gentium ad deum unum religionem esse humanae speciei admodum naturalem, virtutemque hominis propriam ideoque excellentissimam. Duo quidem excellentissimi sunt actus hominum, illi

wetness. I cannot see why religion should not attain its end. Its end is to enjoy God and its prayer is to enjoy Him perpetually.

The third objection and its resolution.

But are men led to religion by the stars, which is the impious Lucretians' third objection? No! The stars favor the humors of bodies, but religion is hostile to bodies. The starry heavens cannot inspire us with desire for anything higher than the celestial spheres that a religious man also spurns. Moreover, religion condemns fate and affirms freedom. So how will it receive the very desire to resist fate from the fates? A particular conjunction of the planets furthermore bestows fertility, an opposite conjunction,[82] penury. The latter brings sickness, the former, health, likewise war and peace. How quickly do we see the heavens' gifts change into their opposites! So if a certain position of the planets forces us to worship God, in a brief while the contrary position will erase the honors divine from men's memory. Yet in no place or time has there been an interruption of religion, although God has been worshipped in various times and places in various ways. This variety of human minds results from deliberations that are not subject to the stars. The human mind by its very nature indeed as divine is led towards recognizing, worshipping, and fearing God, just as it is naturally led to loving the good and avoiding the bad. Yet by way of the free choice of its deliberation it varies the rites for worshipping God, just as it proceeds towards the good by choosing different paths. 11

From the foregoing argument we can gather that the religion centered on one God, the religion all peoples share, is entirely natural to the human species; it is a power proper to man and therefore of supreme excellence. Two human acts are of supreme excellence, namely those which dwell in the soul's most excellent part and concern themselves with the object of highest excellence. These acts in our mind are the knowledge and love of God. Hu- 12

scilicet qui in excellentissima parte animae sunt et circa obiectum versantur excellentissimum. Tales sunt in mente nostra dei cognitio atque amor. In hac vita humanus amor in deum humanae praestat cognitioni, quia deum nemo vere cognoscit. Vere autem amant illi deum quoquomodo cognitum, qui spernunt omnia propter ipsum. Rursus, sicut deterius est odisse deum quam ignorare, sic melius amare quam nosse. Adde quod perscrutando deum longissimo tempore minimum quid proficimus; amando brevissimo plurimum. Ob id enim citius propinquiusque et firmius amor quam cognitio mentem cum divinitate coniungit, quia vis cognitionis in discretione consistit magis, amoris autem magis in unione. Quinetiam gratius ipsi deo est amari quam prospici. Nihil enim deo tribuimus intuendo, amando vero tribuimus quicquid et sumus et possidemus. Amantibus ergo deus se ipsum retribuit potius quam scrutantibus. Deinde cognitione dei male possumus uti, scilicet ad superbiam, amore dei male uti non possumus. Et amando deum longe maiorem quam perscrutando percipimus voluptatem, et meliores amando efficimur quam inquirendo. Immo sicut non qui videt bonum, sed qui vult, fit bonus, ita animus non ex eo quod deum considerat, sed ex eo quod amat, fit divinus, quemadmodum materia, non quia lucem ab igne capiat, sed quia calorem, ignis evadit. Hinc illud Porphyrii: 'Animus deum inquirendo purus efficitur, deum imitando fit deus'. Quod quidem ab ipso Platone acceptum est, dicente divinum lumen non inquisitione paulatim a nobis acquiri, sed perfecta vitae coniunctione subito tandem divinitus in nobis accendi.

13 Praeterea cognoscendo deum eius amplitudinem contrahimus ad mentis nostrae conceptum, amando vero mentem amplificamus

man love of God is greater in this life than human knowledge of Him, because nobody truly knows God. But those who truly love God, in whatever way He is known,[83] are those who spurn all things because of Him. Again, just as it is worse to hate God than to be ignorant of Him, so it is better to love Him than to know Him. Moreover, in seeking to know God we least progress and in the longest time, but in loving Him we most progress and in the briefest instant. For love unites the mind with divinity much more rapidly, more closely, and more steadfastly than knowledge does, precisely because the power of knowledge consists more in distinction, the power of love, in union. Besides, for God Himself it is more pleasing to be loved than to be watched for. For in gazing up at God we bring nothing to Him, but in loving Him we bring Him whatever we are and possess. So God gives Himself in return to those who love Him rather than to those who seek to know Him. We can use the knowledge of God badly, to serve our pride that is, but we cannot use our love of God badly. And in loving God we experience a much more intense pleasure than in seeking to know Him, and we are made better by loving than by seeking to know. Or rather, just as it is not he who sees the good who becomes good but he who wills it, so the rational soul becomes divine not because it thinks about God but because it loves Him, just as matter catches fire not because it receives light from a fire but because it receives heat. Hence the saying of Porphyry: "In seeking to know God the rational soul becomes pure, but in imitating God it becomes God."[84] This saying was taken indeed from Plato himself, who said that the divine light is not gradually acquired by our inquiring into it, but that eventually it is suddenly set ablaze in us from on high, in a perfect conjoining to our life.[85]

In knowing God, moreover, we take His vastness and contract it to match the concept of our own mind, but in loving Him we take our mind and expand it to match the immeasurable vastness of the divine goodness. In the former we pull God down to us, in 13

ad latitudinem divinae bonitatis immensam. Illic in nos deum deiicimus, hic attollimus nos in deum. Noscimus enim quantum ipsi capimus, amamus autem et quantum intuemur, et quantum ultra nostrum intuitum vaticinamur bonitatis divinae reliquum superesse. Neque est amor humana cognitione contentus, ea siquidem creata est atque finita. Voluntas in solo primo et immenso quiescit bono. Quoniam vero in hoc ipso amore tota consistit religio, nihil habent homines, ut Plato in *Epinomide* testatur, religione divinius. Quae tanto est a falso alienior quam cetera hominum studia, quanto propinquius deo summae veritati nos copulat. Quare presagium eius verius est quam facultatum aliarum sententiae. Eius vero praesagium bonis digna praemia pollicetur, malis minatur supplicia.

14 Hominis sanctissimi probitati praemium dignum debetur. Probitas per summum habitum confirmata indelebile bonum est, ac si mille annorum millia vixerit, semper similiter aget. Praemium igitur ea dignum nullum est nisi indelebile et aeternum, praesertim cum illud sit convenientissimum praemium sanctitatis, cuius gratia sanctitas agit singula, quodve eius appetitum potest implere. Tale est illud in quo est tota ratio boni. Est igitur eius praemium immensi boni sempiterna possessio. Vivet igitur semper religiosus animus, ut dignum suscipiat praemium. Vivet semper et impius, ut luat supplicia impietatis, qui infinite peccat, quotiens pro finitis commodis dei obliviscitur infiniti, et malignum habitum contrahit indelebilem, per quem mille annorum millia sit peccaturus, si vixerit, postquam statuit semel tam diu peccare, quam diu vivet. Qui tam diu iam deliquit[117] divinae iustitiae, cui futura saecula praesentia sunt, quam diu est, si vixerit peccaturus; infinitum huic debetur supplicium iam infinite peccanti.

the latter we lift ourselves up to God. For we know insofar as we can grasp, but we love insofar as we can see and insofar as we can foresee that something yet remains of the divine goodness beyond our gaze. For love is not satisfied with human knowing, being a created and finite knowing. The will comes to rest in the first, the measureless good alone. But since all religion consists in this love itself, men possess nothing more divine than religion, as Plato proves in the *Epinomis*.[86] Religion is more estranged from falsehood than men's other studies inasmuch as, being closer to God, it binds us to the highest truth. What it foretells therefore is truer than the judgments and opinions of the other faculties. To good men indeed it foretells and promises noble rewards, while to evil men it threatens punishments.

The probity of a truly pious man is deserving of its due reward. 14
The probity that has been strengthened by unvarying habit is an indestructible good, and should it live for thousands of years, it will always act in the same way. So no reward is truly fitting unless it is indestructible and eternal, especially because this is sanctity's most appropriate reward, and for its sake sanctity performs individual deeds or what can satisfy its desire. Such a reward is that wherein the whole rational principle of the good consists. So sanctity's reward is the everlasting possession of the measureless good. So the religious soul in order to receive its due reward will live forever. The irreligious soul will also live forever in order to pay the penalties of its impiety: it sins infinitely whenever it forgets the infinite God to grasp at finite goods, and it contracts an ill-natured and inveterate habit. Because of this habit it will sin for thousands of years if it lives [that long], once it has decided to sin as long as it lives. And as long as it exists, if it has lived to sin, it has already offended divine justice, to whom are present the ages to come. To this already infinitely sinning soul is due an infinite punishment.

15 Adde quod, si verae virtutis praemium est aeternum (deum enim a quo tamquam principio pendet, respicit tamquam finem), sequitur ut vitii, quod deficit ab aeterno tam virtutis praemio quam vitae principio, supplicium sit sempiternum. Nullum tale est in hoc tempore vitae brevissimo, erit igitur in futuro. Hoc pacto adversa, quae in hac vita bonis, et prospera, quae malis contingunt, compensanda videntur, ne et pietas bonis damno sit, et ut in *Phaedone* legitur, impietas malis sit lucro. Bonum quidem prodesse oportet, obesse malum. Obest in hac vita pietas, quae non solum praesentia bona contemnere, verumetiam dei honestique gratia labores et mortem subire compellit. Contra prodest impietas quamplurimum. Igitur ne desit iustitiae locus, alibi est ferenda sententia. Neque putandum est hanc iustitiae partem, quae humana respicit, ad deum non pertinere, ad quem pertinet mundi totius administratio. In quo si singula intellegendo amandoque facit, ut Plato vult, sequitur ut faciendo intellegat ametque singula, atque in toto curando partes—quibus non curatis non curatur totum—non negligat. Haec in *Legibus* Plato.

16 Mundi vero pars non mediocris est hominum species, administratrix et ipsa iustitiae. Si ergo divina iustitia, ut Orphici canunt hymni, elementa suis quaeque distribuit locis, si rebus quibusque vel minimis pro sua cuiusque natura dispertit munuscula, cur non hominibus etiam pro meritis loca, praemia suppliciaque dispertiat? Deus frequenter vel bonos immunes, vel malos relinquit impunes, ut his[118] indiciis nobis ostendat vitam alteram superesse, in qua iustitia, quae falli non potest, pro meritis impleatur. Nonnunquam

Moreover, if the reward of true virtue is eternal (for it is God upon whom virtue depends as its principle and to whom it looks as its end), then it follows that the punishment of vice, which is eternally lacking the reward of virtue and the principle of life, is everlasting. No punishment is everlasting in the diminutive span of this life, so it will be everlasting in the future. This is why the adversities which happen to good men in this life and the prosperous things that happen to bad must, it seems, be balanced, lest piety be an evil to good men (as one reads in the *Phaedo* too[87]) and impiety profitable to bad men. The good must indeed profit men, the bad must harm. [But] in this life piety brings harm: it forces men not only to scorn present goods but also to undergo travails and death for the sake of God and what is honorable. Contrariwise, impiety brings enormous benefits. Lest justice lose its authority therefore, the sentence must be delivered elsewhere. We must not suppose that the part of justice concerning human matters does not pertain to God to whom the administration of the whole world pertains. If He makes individual things in this world by understanding and by loving, as Plato thinks, then in making them He necessarily understands and loves them; and in caring for the whole He does not neglect the parts (if they are uncared for, the whole is uncared for). Plato says this in the *Laws*.[88] 15

The human species is no small part of the world, however, being itself the minister of justice. So if divine justice, as the Orphic hymns sing,[89] arranges all the elements in their places, and if it distributes little gifts to every thing, however small, according to the nature of each, then why would it not distribute to men too, according to their merits, their appropriate places, rewards, and punishments? Frequently God leaves good men without rewards and bad men without punishments, so that by these signs He might reveal to us that another life exists, a life where justice (which cannot be deceived) is administered fully and according to our merits. But sometimes He punishes particularly heinous 16

vero scelera praecipue gravissima in hac etiam vita punit, ut ob hoc eius providentiam cognoscamus. Mitto in praesentia multa providentiae divinae exempla. Philon Iudaeus platonicus in libro *De providentia* scribit legem apud veteres exstitisse sacrilegos vel cremari vel praecipitari vel suffocari. Cumque Philomelus et Onomarchus et Phaylus templum spoliavissent, paucis post diebus absque iudicum opera divina quadam sorte eos in tria haec supplicia incidisse. Praecipit autem in *Legibus* Plato, ne ob id umquam de divina providentia dubitemus, quod iniusti saepe homines hinc impunes[119] videantur abire, quippe cum nesciamus, qua ratione et ubi, prout ordini universi conducit, singula singulis rependantur. Rursus in ultimo *De republica* probat animum per virtutem deo similem ideoque amicum evadere, atque idcirco ita a deo curari, ut quaecumque contingunt, in bonum denique perducantur, et sive in paupertate sive in morbis sive in alia quadam calamitate sit constitutus, singula vel in hac vita vel in futura aliquando conducant ad bonum.

17 Neque ob hoc dicenda est bonitas divina malefica, quod committi peccata permittit punitque commissa. Profecto in regno dei gradum suum obtinet natura rationalis. Huic motus convenit liber. Motui tali datum est, ut progredi possit in melius et naturae bono bonum insuper voluntatis, actionis adeptionisque adiungere, ita ut natura huiusmodi non modo ab alio facta sit bona tamquam patiens, verumetiam se ipsam efficiat bonam tamquam agens. Datum insuper est tali motui, ut possit transgredi in deterius, non quod naturam propriam exuat, sed quod induat alienam et illam

crimes even in this life so that we might thereby recognize His providence. For the present I leave aside the many examples of divine providence. The Platonist Philo Judaeus writes in his book on providence that among the ancients a law existed that the sacrilegious were to be burned or thrown down a cliff or suffocated; and that since Philomelus, Onomarchus, and Phaylus had despoiled a temple, a few days later they suffered these three punishments in what was a divine sentencing and not the sentence of human judges.[90] In the *Laws* Plato admonishes us never to doubt of divine providence merely because unjust men often seem to escape with impunity here, since we do not know why and where—according as it is in harmony with the order of the universe—individuals are repaid for their individual deeds.[91] Again, in the last book of the *Republic* Plato proves that through virtue the rational soul becomes like God and accordingly God's friend, and thus that it is so taken care of by God that whatever happens eventually leads to the good; and whether the soul has to endure poverty or disease or any other calamity, that single events work together at some point for the good, be it in this life or in the future.

Nor should we maintain that divine goodness is maleficent 17
merely because it permits sins to be committed and then punishes them when they have been committed.[92] In the kingdom of God certainly the rational nature finds its proper seat. To this nature belongs free motion. To such a motion has been granted the capacity to advance towards what is better and to join to the good of the [rational] nature the good besides of the will, of action, and of attainment; and to do so in such a way that the nature has not only (qua patient) been made good by another, but also (qua agent) made itself good. To such a motion has also been granted the capacity to pass over into what is worse, not because it casts aside its own nature but because it dons an alien nature and an inferior one at that. Punishment, whether harmful or purgatorial, succeeds this infection; and it does so by a necessary and divine

quidem inferiorem. Hanc infectionem supplicium sequitur vel noxium vel purgatorium — sequitur, inquam, necessaria quadam divinaque lege peccantem intrinsecus ad similia perducente. Et ut in decimo *Legum* inquit Plato, motionis principium in anima est, quo se pro arbitrio talem efficit aut talem. Postquam vero talis evaserit, mox non tam arbitrio quam fatali quadam dei lege in talem conditionem locumque transfertur. Addit quasi divino Davidis ore: Sive ad mundi centrum penetraveris, sive ad superficiem pervolaveris, divinam legem evitare non poteris. Huc illud in decimo *De republica* tendit: Cum neque latere neque effugere divinos oculos manusque possis, cave omnino ne pecces, id est, ne deo dissimilior umquam evadas. Odit enim animas ab ipsius similitudine longe degenerantes. Quinimmo si et Gygis anulum et galeam nactus fueris infernalem, iniustitiam procul effugito.

18 Sed redeamus ad *Leges*. Inquit ibidem mundum partim bonorum, partim malorum esse plenum, deumque nobis deos daemonesque quosdam quasi pastores custodiendis ovibus praefecisse, quorum providentia et devitemus mala, consequamur et bona. Addit eos qui cum multa iniuste rapuerint, muneribus se deos placare confidunt, perinde errare ac si qui dilaniantes oves putent se membris quibusdam ovis pastori redditis pastorem sibi conciliare. Tandem ubique Plato repetit[120] et arbitrio nos peccare et post peccatum necessario pati.

19 Sed iam ad institutum ordinem redeamus. Quid ergo? Si deus et permittit et punit, in permittendo mirabilis humani generis excellentia lucet, in puniendo dei potestas bonitasque immensa. Si peccare permittitur animus, quis non videat hominem sui iuris esse ac dominum suoque arbitrio alias aliter agere? Si delicta punit deus, in ipso delictorum malo iustitiae peragit bonum, quae hunc

law that guides the sinner inwardly towards what resembles him. As Plato says in the tenth book of the *Laws,* in the soul dwells the principle of motion whereby it makes itself one thing or another according to its choice.[93] After the soul has become its choice, however, it is straightway transferred to its proper condition and location not by its choice but by a law of fate, God's law. Plato adds, with the divine lips as it were of a David, "Whether you penetrate to the world's center or fly up to its outermost part, you cannot evade the divine law."[94] This same notion appears in the tenth book of the *Republic:* "Since you cannot hide or flee from the divine eyes and hands, take especial care that you do not sin, that is, that you never become unlike God. For God hates degenerate souls far removed from His likeness. Even if you have acquired the ring of Gyges and the helmet of the underworld, flee far from injustice."[95]

But let us return to the *Laws*. He says in the tenth book that 18
the world is full partly of good things, partly of bad, and that God has put certain gods and demons to rule over us, like shepherds watching over their flocks, by whose providence we can avoid the bad and acquire the good. He adds that those who are confident they can placate God with gifts, having stolen many things unjustly, err in the same way as those who massacre sheep and think to reconcile themselves with the shepherd by returning various parts of a sheep to him.[96] Finally Plato everywhere repeats that we sin of free choice, and, having sinned, are necessarily punished.

Let us return now to the order of our argument. What are the 19
consequences? If God both permits and punishes, then in His permitting blazes forth the marvelous excellence of mankind, in His punishing, His own power and measureless goodness. If the rational soul is allowed to sin, isn't it obvious that man is independent, is a master who does various things variously as he chooses? If God punishes wrongs, then on the very evil of wrongs He inflicts the good of justice, a justice that would have no place here

non haberet locum, nisi delinqueretur. Ac deesse videretur quodammodo pars aliqua virtutis, ut ita dixerim, et iustitiae regno dei, cuius hic perfulget potestas et bonitas infinita, dum contra mali naturam facit ex malis bona, ut tota natura sit mirabiliter ordinata. In qua tanta est amplitudo boni, ut in bonis splendeat atque malis, et quantum valeat in ambobus experiatur. Tanta quoque ordinis observantia, ut animus, qui peccando digredi videtur ab ordine, et in ipso liberi motus ordine gradiatur, etiam dum digreditur, et in ipsum iustitiae ordinem statim patiendo regrediatur, dum propter delinquendi habitum talia patitur, qualia habitui congruunt.

Haec habui quae de immortalitate quantum ad signorum testimonia pertinet dicerem; oportet autem dubitationes deinceps, quae cogunt immortalitati diffidere, diligentissime solvere.

unless wrong had been committed. And it would seem in a way that some part of virtue (if I may put it that way) and of justice would be wanting in the kingdom of God, the power and infinite goodness of which shines resplendently here as it fashions good from ill (contrary to the nature of the ill), so that the whole of nature is marvelously ordered. In this whole the vastness of the good is such that its splendor is revealed in good and ill alike and its power found in both. So strict too is the observance of the order that the rational soul, which in sinning seems to be deviating from the order, is in fact, in the very order of its free motion, advancing even as it deviates; and in suffering punishment it straightway returns to the very order of justice even as, because of its habit of sinning, it endures the punishments proper to that habit.

This is what I have to say about immortality insofar as it bears on the testimonies of the signs. Next, however, we must resolve, and resolve extremely carefully, the doubts that force us to lose our faith in immortality.

Notes to the Text

ABBREVIATIONS

A	The *editio princeps*, Florence, 1482, with printed corrigenda as noted below.
L	Florence, Biblioteca Mediceo-Laurenziana, MS Plut. LXXXIII, 10, the dedication copy written for Lorenzo de'Medici.
M	Florence, Biblioteca Nazionale Centrale, MS Magl. XX, 58, the *codex unicus* of Ficino's *Disputatio contra iudicium astrologorum* (1477).
CPT	The reading of Ficino's *Compendium Platonicae Theologiae*, included in the second book of his letters (1476/77); text from *Opera*, p. 696.
DCR	The reading of Ficino's *De christiana religione* (1474), in his *Opera*, pp. 1–77.
Marcel	The reading of Raymond Marcel's edition, *Marsile Ficin: Théologie platonicienne de l'immortalité des âmes* (3 vols., Paris: Les Belles Lettres, 1964–70).
Opera	The reading of the text in *Marsilii Ficini . . . Opera* (Basel: Henricpetri, 1576; repr. Turin: Bottega d'Erasmo, 1959, 1983; Paris: Phénix Éditions, 1999).

CAPITULA

1. id est *om. in internal chapter headings.*
2. et vaticinatio *om. in internal chapter headings*
3. quartum signum *transposed in the internal chapter headings*

BOOK XII

1. Marsilii Ficini Theologiae De immortalitate animorum liber duodecimus incipit *L*
2. mentes nostras *L:* nostram mentem *Marcel*
3. *omitted by Marcel*
4. e converso *Marcel, Opera*
5. status *repeated in A*
6. aerae *Marcel*
7. lumen *Marcel*
8. latius *Marcel*
9. longius . . . nominant (nominat *Opera*)] recti trianguli longius *before correction in A*
10. simpliciter *Marcel, Opera*
11. per humano *Marcel*
12. e *before correction in A*
13. formandas *L*
14. -que *omitted in L*
15. appetent *Marcel, Opera*
16. quoties *L*
17. mirum est *Marcel, Opera*
18. mens *L*
19. secundam *before correction in A*
20. mentem *before correction in A*
21. fonti suo *L*
22. Putat *Marcel*
23. animadvertimus *Marcel, Opera*
24. fiat *before correction in A*
25. Ubique *L*
26. linae *Marcel*
27. disiungantur *before correction in A*
28. proximae *Marcel, Opera*
29. maximae *AL: Marcel reports this word as the reading of A but deletes it: omitted in Opera*
30. *omitted by Marcel*
31. vita *L*
32. sed refluit *Marcel, Opera*
33. iudicat: cur *Augustine:* iudicat, ut cur *Opera:* iudicat, ⟨ut⟩ cur *Marcel*
34. fit *before correction in A*
35. *omitted in L*
36. anima *before correction in A*
37. medius *Marcel*
38. aptus *Augustine, Marcel*
39. cur *A, Augustine:* cui *L, before correction in A*
40. nihil *Marcel*
41. agnoscis *before correction in A*
42. quo iudicas . . . vides *omitted in L*
43. *omitted in L*
44. sint *A, Augustine:* sit *L*
45. his *L, Augustine:* iis *A, Marcel*
46. phantasmatis (= *phantasmatibus, an Augustinian form) L, Augustine (but with the variant* phantasmatibus *noted in Green's apparatus):* phantasmatibus *A, Marcel, Opera*

47. innovat *Marcel*
48. et *A, Opera, Augustine:* aut *L*
49. correctius *L*
50. authorem *L*
51. his *Marcel, Opera*
52. conveniente *before correction in A*
53. viderit *Marcel*
54. delectare *before correction in A:* delectaret *Augustine*
55. *thus AL, Augustine, but omitted by Marcel*
56. in *Augustine: omitted in AL, added in Opera, Marcel*
57. ista *Augustine*
58. quod *before correction in A, Marcel, Opera, Augustine*
59. diligenter *L*
60. *thus Augustine:* rythimam *AL (sic)*
61. hi *A, Augustine:* ii *L*
62. ii *L*
63. iustum *A, Augustine:* iustus *L*
64. ipsa *L*
65. existit *A, Marcel, Opera*
66. ens *L*
67. affector *before correction in A*
68. a deo *Opera:* ⟨a⟩ deo *Marcel*
69. Homo *before correction in A*
70. prius *L*
71. petentia *before correction in A*
72. cui rei *A, Augustine:* cuius *L*
73. *omitted in L*
74. se *before correction in A*
75. amittat *before correction in L, Augustine, Marcel, Opera:* admittat *A, after correction in L, but the sense demands* amittat

BOOK XIII

1. Marsilii Ficini Florentini liber de immortalitate xiii *A:* Marsilii Ficini Florentini Theologiae de immortalitate animorum liber tredecimus incipit *L*
2. Inde *A, Marcel*
3. Zoroastrique spectatores *Marcel*
4. De philosophis *is part of the chapter heading in L, but not in A; A adds the heading in the corrigenda*
5. similiterque *Marcel*
6. direptis *A*
7. ipsos in se spiritus] se *before correction in A*
8. complessiorem *L*
9. *omitted in L*
10. *sc. Hermotimus*
11. advocare *Marcel*
12. harmoniam *before correction in A*
13. Atque *Marcel, Opera*
14. capitur *Marcel, Opera*
15. quo *Marcel*

16. traducti *Marcel*
17. *omitted by Marcel*
18. anima *L*
19. movet. Itaque] suam corpus *Marcel*
20. pendem *before correction in A*
21. illa *before correction in A*
22. illius *Marcel*
23. praevideant *L*
24. syncope *Marcel, Opera*
25. oppilentur *before correction in A*
26. asservari *before correction in A*
27. his *L*
28. reliquae *Marcel*
29. *L repeats* vaporumque
30. animarum *L*
31. somniavisse *L*
32. pulmonem *before correction in A*
33. ita se *before correction in A (not corrected in Marcel)*
34. significat *Marcel, Opera*
35. turbam *Marcel, Opera*
36. se ipso *L*
37. cavet *Marcel*
38. minime *before correction in A*
39. Inde *L*
40. *omitted by Marcel*
41. voluit *before correction in A*
42. anima *Marcel*
43. praesentiebat *Marcel, Opera*
44. spem *before correction in A*
45. dei *Marcel*
46. imperat *Marcel, Opera*
47. constituere *A*
48. indebilis *before correction in A*
49. tenebat *L, before correction in A*
50. monumentum *Marcel, Opera*
51. *omitted by Marcel*
52. *omitted in L*
53. cogent *Marcel*
54. se *Marcel*
55. materias *Opera*
56. temporalibus *L*
57. ipsam *Marcel*
58. Ita *L*
59. morbo *Marcel, Opera*
60. in Illyriis *Marcel, Opera*
61. Augent *Marcel*
62. ad *L*
63. adeo *A*
64. negligit *before correction in A*
65. harmonia *before correction in A*
66. vaporesque *L*
67. cubitalis *L*
68. his *Marcel*
69. atque *L*
70. corpora *before correction in A*
71. deo *before correction in L*
72. *Marcel emends to* illa
73. anomalium *Marcel*
74. locus *L*
75. his *L*
76. manum *Marcel*
77. *omitted in L*

BOOK XIV

1. XIIII Liber *A*: Marsilii Ficini Florentini Theologiae de immortalitate animorum liber quartusdecimus *L*
2. avium *L*
3. *omitted by Marcel*
4. eadem *before correction in A*
5. amittitur *before correction in A*
6. solum *L*: solius *Marcel*
7. *omitted in A and by Marcel, Opera*
8. amitti *before correction in A*
9. *omitted in L*
10. Supremis . . . terminis *before correction in A*
11. appetit *AL and capitula librorum in A*; petit *Marcel, Opera*
12. perque *A*
13. -que *om. L*
14. et mentem *om. L*
15. expotat *Marcel*
16. inter intellectum *Marcel, Opera*
17. et simplices . . . comprehendat] mobiles intelligit modo quodam universali, absoluto, simplici *repeated erroneously by Marcel through an eyeskip*
18. perficitque *L (note the distinction between* proficit quotidie *and* perficit quandoque.*)*
19. quo *Marcel*
20. *omitted by Marcel*
21. *omitted by Marcel*
22. *omitted by Marcel*
23. -que *L*
24. percurrat *A*
25. supersit aeternus *before correction in A*
26. -que *omitted in A*
27. si *before correction in A*
28. illa *L*
29. sensus *L*
30. *omitted in A and the capitula librorum in A; also by Marcel, Opera*
31. fatigari *L*
32. *omitted in L*
33. *omitted in L*
34. XV *AL and capitula librorum in A*
35. his *L*
36. perflui *A*
37. et Xerxes *Marcel, Opera*
38. sinum *Marcel*
39. non datur. Merito appetimus *A*: non datur? Merito. Appetimus *Marcel*: non datur? Merito appetimus *Opera*
40. Atque quia *L*
41. sentienti *L*

42. *omitted in L*
43. Si iuvat *before correction in A*
44. -que *L*
45. *omitted by Marcel*
46. *omitted in L*
47. nobis nunc *transposed by Marcel*
48. XVI *AL and capitula librorum in A*
49. minima *before correction in A*
50. omni hac *before correction in A*
51. Plato in *Protagora* . . . quos non exaudiat (*to the end of* 14.8.3): *also found in the DCR*
52. Plato noster *DCR*
53. in terris *after* nos *DCR*
54. recognoscimus *DCR*
55. erigitur *DCR*
56. *After* eundem *DCR adds:* Non enim ad id quod supra est et infinitum, nisi virtute superioris, infinitique attolitur.
57. forte videtur] est *DCR*
58. forsitan apparebit *om. DCR*
59. omnino *DCR*
60. compellit *DCR*
61. nos *Marcel*
62. Neque audiat — deus ad animam (14.8.7): *also found in M*
63. Sane commoda — denique cuncta (14.8.5): *also found in CPT*
64. cogitet *Marcel, Opera*
65. omnia *CPT*: omnia *corrected from* quaeque *M*
66. claviculus *CPT*: claviculus *corrected from* vimen *M*
67. Hinc *Marcel*
68. ortus sit capreolus *CPT*: ortus sit capreolus *corrected from* ortum sit vimen *M*
69. capreolum *M*: et ante vimen *om. CPT*
70. incorporali *CPT, M*
71. capreoli *CPT*: capreoli *corrected from* viminis *M*
72. affectus *CPT, Opera*
73. corporalibus *CPT, M*
74. et tamquam sagittarius *om. CPT, M*
75. negligit mundi *transposed in L*
76. in quantum *M*
77. amplissima *M*
78. amplissimus *M*
79. *omitted by Marcel*
80. aeternitatis *L*
81. suspicio *A, Marcel, Opera*: supplicio *before correction in L*
82. suppositione *before correction in A*
83. proprius *before correction in L*
84. -issimo *Marcel*
85. ea *Marcel*
86. *added in the corrigenda of A*
87. Si religio . . . imperfectissimus *omitted in L (an eyeskip)*
88. pro- *before correction in A*

89. *omitted in L*
90. propheta *Marcel*
91. linguae *A*
92. amittere *A*
93. inveniuntur *L*
94. Duas enim aetates—quam consueverit: *(to the end of the paragraph) is also found in DCR (the first two lines paraphrased)*
95. perspiciuntur *DCR*
96. propter superbiam incontinentiamque *after* constituti *DCR*
97. propter mansuetudinem et modestiam *after* vero *DCR*
98. solis lumen *after* tamquam *DCR*
99. *om. DCR*
100. in sole] in ipso sole tam supercaelesti quam caelesti *DCR*
101. sentiunt de religione *transposed in L*
102. animi *DCR*
103. Citticus *Marcel*
104. vexentur *Marcel*
105. manes *AL:* inanes *corr. Opera, Marcel*
106. contrariam *before correction in A*
107. varietatis *L*
108. monstruorum *Marcel*
109. moribus *before correction in A*
110. *omitted in L*
111. more *before correction in A*
112. iidem *L*
113. minima *before correction in A*
114. *omitted by Marcel*
115. Propterea *Marcel*
116. *Marcel's conjecture:* debebit *A:* habebit *L*
117. deliquit *repeated in L*
118. iis *L*
119. impune *L*
120. reperit *Marcel, Opera*

Notes to the Translation

ABBREVIATIONS

Bidez-Cumont	Joseph Bidez and Franz Cumont, *Les mages héllenisés: Zoroastre, Ostanès et Hytaspe après la tradition grecque* (Paris: Les Belles Lettres, 1938).
Baeumker	Clemens Baeumker, ed., *Avencebrolis Fons vitae ex arabico in latinum translatus ab Iohanne Hispano et Dominico Gundissalino*, 2 vols. , continuously paginated (Namur: Aschendorff, 1892–95).
Copenhaver	*Hermetica: The Greek Corpus Hermeticum and the Latin Asclepius*, tr. Brian C. Copenhaver (Cambridge: Cambridge University Press, 1992).
Crouzel-Simonetti	Henri Crouzel and Manlio Simonetti, eds., *Origène: Traité des principes*, 4 vols. (Paris: Cerf, 1978–84).
Des Places	Édouard Des Places, ed., *Oracles Chaldaïques, avec un choix de commentaires anciens* (Paris: Les Belles Lettres, 1971).
Diehl	Ernest Diehl, ed., *Procli Diadochi in Platonis Timaeum commentaria*, 3 vols. (Amsterdam: A. M. Hakkert, 1965).
Diels-Kranz	Hermann Diels and Walther Kranz, eds., *Die Fragmente der Vorsokratiker*, 3 vols. (Berlin: Weidmann, 1906–1910).
Dodds	E. R. Dodds, ed., *Proclus: The Elements of Theology*, 2nd ed. (Oxford: Clarendon Press, 1963).
Ficino, *De amore*	*Commentaire sur le Banquet de Platon, De l'amour (Commentarium in convivium Platonis de amore)*, Pierre Laurens, ed. and tr. (Paris: Les Belles Lettres, 2002).

Ficino, *Opera*	Marsilio Ficino, *Opera omnia* (Basel: Heinrich Petri, 1576; repr. Turin: Bottega d'Erasmo, 1959; Paris: Phénix Éditions, 1999).
Fotheringham	J. K. Fotheringham, ed., *Eusebii Pamphili Chronici canones latine vertit, adauxit, ad sua tempora produxit S. Eusebius Hieronymus* (London: Milford, 1923).
Green, *DLA*	William M. Green, ed., *s. Aurelius Augustinus: De libero arbitrio libri tres,* Corpus scriptorum ecclesiasticorum Latinorum, vol. 74 (Vienna: Hölder-Pichler-Tempsky, 1961).
Green, *DVR*	William M. Green, ed., *s. Aurelius Augustinus: De vera religione liber unus,* Corpus scriptorum ecclesiasticorum Latinorum, vol. 77 (Vienna: Hölder-Pichler-Tempsky, 1961).
Hörmann	Wolfgang Hörmann, ed., *s. Aurelius Augustinus: Soliloquiorum libri duo; De inmortalitate animae; De quantitate animae,* Corpus scriptorum ecclesiasticorum Latinorum, vol. 89 (Vienna: Hölder-Pichler-Tempsky, 1986).
In Phaedrum	Michael J. B. Allen, *Marsilio Ficino and the Phaedran Charioteer* (Berkeley and Los Angeles: University of California Press, 1981).
In Philebum	Michael J. B. Allen, ed., *Marsilio Ficino: The Philebus Commentary* (Berkeley and Los Angeles: University of California Press, 1975; repr. Tempe, 2000).
Kern	Otto Kern, *Orphicorum fragmenta* (Berlin: Weidmann, 1922).
Kühn	Karl Gottlob Kühn, ed., *Medicorum graecorum opera quae extant,* 26 vols. (Leipzig: Knobloch, 1821–33).
Lizzini-Porro	Olga Lizzini and Pasquale Porro, eds., *Avicenna: Metafisica. Testo arabo a fronte, testo latino in note* (Milan: Bompiani, 2002).

PG	Jacques-Paul Migne, ed., *Patrologiae cursus completus. Series Graeca*, 161 vols. (Paris: Migne, 1857–1866).
PL	Jacques-Paul Migne, ed., *Patrologiae cursus completus. Series Latina*, 221 vols. (Paris: Migne, 1844–1891).
Quandt	Wilhelm Quandt, ed. *Orphei Hymni*, 4th ed. (Dublin: Weidmann, 1973).
Riginos	Alice S. Riginos, *Platonica: The Anecdotes concerning the Life and Writings of Plato* (Leiden: E. J. Brill, 1976).
Schiavone	Michele Schiavone, ed., *Marsilio Ficino: Teologia platonica*, 2 vols. (Bologna: Zanichelli, 1965).
Segonds	A.-Ph. Segonds, ed., *Proclus: Sur le prémier Alcibiade de Platon*, 2 vols. (Paris: Les Belles Lettres, 1985).
SF	*Supplementum Ficinianum*, ed. Paul Oskar Kristeller, 2 vols. (Pisa: Olschki, 1937).
SVF	*Stoicorum veterum fragmenta*, ed. Hans Friedrich August von Arnim, 4 vols. (Leipzig: Teubner, 1921–24).
Tambrun-Krasker	Brigitte Tambrun-Krasker, *Oracles chaldaïques, recension de Georges Gémiste Pléthon* (Athens: Academy of Athens, 1995).
Thom	Johan C. Thom, *The Pythagorean Golden Verses with Introduction and Commentary* (Leiden: E. J. Brill, 1995).
Van Riet	Simone van Riet, ed., *Avicenna: Liber de anima, seu sextus de naturalibus* (Louvain: Éditions orientalistes — Leiden: E. J. Brill, 1968).
Westerink	L. G. Westerink, ed., *The Greek Commentaries on Plato's Phaedo*, 2 vols. (Amsterdam — New York: North Holland Publishing Company, 1976–77).

BOOK XII

1. *Seventh Letter* 342A ff. (Note that for "description" Plato has *logos* and for "formula" *epistēmē*). This passage in the letter governs the course of

the following argument. Cf. *Laws* 10.895D; and, for the definition of a circle, *Timaeus* 33B and *Parmenides* 137E.

2. Ibid. 342E.

3. Psalm 4:6's 'Signatum est super nos lumen vultus tui, Domine,' joined to Psalm 36:9's 'et in lumine tuo videbimus lumen'. Cf. n. 43 below.

4. Avicenna, *De anima* 5.2, 5.6 (ed. Van Riet, IV-V, pp. 81–101, 149–153). Algazel or al-Ghazali (1058–1111) was an Arabic philosopher and theologian, most famous in the West for his *Incoherence of the Philosophers*, a work attacked by Averroes; both the *Incoherence* and Averroes' reply were translated into Latin in the thirteenth century and were well known to Western philosophers.

5. Plato, *Seventh Letter* 342E.

6. John 1:1–14, 14:6, 1 John *passim*, esp. 1:1–2,5, 5:7,12. This Johannine identification of the Divine Logos, Reason or Word both with the Light and Life of the world and with Truth is going to be a leitmotif of this first chapter and of chapters 2 and 7 below, where Ficino will turn, once again, to Augustine's *De immortalitate animae*.

7. I Corinthians 6:17.

8. *Seventh Letter* 341CD. Cf. Augustine, *De magistro* 12.40 (*PL* 32.1217).

9. *Second Letter* 312E-313A [?]. Ficino calls Dionysius a "king," not a "tyrant."

10. *Phaedo* 67C-E, 82D.

11. *Republic* 7.517BC.

12. Cf. Eusebius, *Preaparatio evangelica* 11.3.511 (*PG* 21. col. 848).

13. Plato, *Theages* 130E, and in general the whole section from 128D to the end on Socrates' "divine prohibitory" or "spirit-voice." (Note that Ficino regarded this spurious dialogue as genuine). Cf. Ficino's *Platonic Theology* 11.5.8 (this edition, vol. III).

14. *Republic* 6.507D-509B.

15. *De amore* 2.2. (ed. Laurens, pp. 24–25), which also refers to *Republic* 6.507D-509B (as in note 14, above).

16. Note the argument immediately following speaks of God's gift of *essentia* both to minds and to intelligible objects. Alternatively *generatio* could refer to light itself as the eyes' "offspring," given the sentence's conclusion that "without light we see nothing in act," or possibly to the organic or generative life of eyes. More improbably it could refer (in the Scholastic manner) to a "form or species" that if *substantialis* changes the substance which it informs, and if *accidentalis* or *accidentaria* (sic) does not. See Aquinas, *Summa contra Gentiles* 1.53.3c.

17. See note 16 above.

18. John 14:6.

19. John 14:17; 1 John 2:14, 3:24.

20. 1 John 3:2, 4:7, 5:20

21. John 1:9.

22. Plato, *I Alcibiades* 122A.

23. *Pimander* 1.31–32, 5.2, 13.16–22; *Asclepius* 9, 41. In fact Hermes emphasizes the importance of ending, not commencing, with prayer, and says nothing about "sacrifices" (unless Ficino is thinking of the "speech offerings" invoked at 13.21 as the only sacrifice that is acceptable to the father of all). By contrast, Iamblichus, *De vita Pythagorica* 1.1, stresses the importance of beginning with prayer: "All right-minded people, embarking on the study of philosophy, invoke a god." See also ibid., 15.65.

24. Iamblichus, *De vita pythagorica* 1.1, 15.65.

25. Plato, *Timaeus* 25CD, 48DE; cf. *Philebus* 25B, *Critias* 106AB, *Laws* 4.712B, 10.893B, *Epinomis* 980C.

26. *quem rectangulum nominat, tantum posse* is found only in the *Opera* and not in *A* or *L*. The sense demands it however: see Schiavone, 2:166n. ad loc.

27. Porphyry, *Life of Pythagoras* 36; Diogenes Laertius, *Lives* 8.12.

28. Vergil, *Eclogues* 3.60.

29. *Symposium* 212A, and in general Diotima's final revelation from 210A to 212A.

30. 1 John 1:6: "If we say that we have fellowship with him, and walk in darkness, we lie, and do not the truth."

31. John 1:16: "And of his [Christ's] fullness have we all received."

32. Revelation 3:18.

33. II Corinthians 4:16: "the inward man is renewed day by day"; cf. note 73 below.

34. Ibid.: 3:18: "But we all, with open face beholding as in a glass the glory of the Lord, are changed into the same image from glory to glory, even as by the Spirit of the Lord."

35. *Pimander* 1.2–6 and passim, 2.14, 12.14. The same reference occurs at note 52, below.

36. In chapter 4, at note 47 below, Iamblichus is cited as the source of this tactile metaphor.

37. *Phaedrus* 249B-E, *Epinomis* 986CD.

38. *Republic* 7.532A-534E (on dialectic).

39. *Enneads* 5.3.10–16, 5.5.5.

40. *Elements of Theology*. 12, 13, 40, 46; *In Parmenidem* 7.1239–1242.

41. *De divinis nominibus* 5.1–5; *Theologia mystica* 5 [PG 3. 816B-820C, 1048A]. For the many implications of the assumption that Plotinus and Proclus were indebted to the Areopagite, see Allen, *Synoptic Art*, chapter 2 (cited in the Bibliography).

42. [ps.] Olympiodorus [i.e. Damascius; see *Platonic Theology* 8.2.11, note 10, in vol. II of this edition], *Commentarius in Phaedonem* 2.91 (ed. Westerink, 2: 337).

43. Psalm 4:6: "Signatum est super nos lumen vultus tui, Domine"; Psalm 36:9: "et in lumine tuo videbimus lumen." Cf. note 3 above.

44. Galatians 4:9.

45. This seems to be a reference to the well-known Plotinian notion—see for example *Enneads* 3.4.3–4, 3.4.6, 4.8.8, 5.1.10—that part of the soul remains above in the intelligible realm and thus that we are potentially divine. Proclus, *In Timaeum* 3.333.28–334.3, says that Theodore of Asine espoused this view while Iamblichus, his teacher, did not. This is

the obvious reference for modern scholars trying to reconstruct Theodore's position (see for instance Dodds' note in his edition of Proclus' *Elements of Theology*, p. 309). But it was unknown to Ficino who had access only to the first half of Proclus' commentary in (Florence, Biblioteca Riccardiana, MS Ricc. 24), which ends at 191E with the word *sōmasi* (in Diehl's three volume edition at 2:169.4). Thus his source for the Theodore reference is yet to be discovered. Moreover, he seems to have read Iamblichus, *De Mysteriis* 1.5.15.12–16.5 (ed. Des Places, p. 46), as endorsing the Plotinian position. See the epitome in his *Opera*, p. 1876.

46. Source unknown. Marcel refers us to the *De Mysteriis* 2.11 and Ficino, *Opera*, pp. 1880–81, 1907.

47. *De Mysteriis* 1.3.8.3–13 (ed. Des Places, p. 42); see Ficino's epitome in his *Opera*, p. 1874.1.

48. Ibid.

49. Cf. Cicero, *Tusculan Disputations* 2.16.38.

50. *Enneads* 3.4.2; 6.8.9.

51. The Latin *nervus* means either "tendon" or "muscle" and this confusion continued into the medieval period, even though the anatomical distinction had been recognized as early as the first half of the third century BC by Herophilus and his school in Alexandria, and was accepted by Galen (AD 129–199). See Schiavone's note ad loc. (2: 180).

52. See note 35 above.

53. John 17:20–26; 1 John 1:5–8, 2:5, 3:2, 3:24, 4:7–16, 5:7. Cf. note 6, above.

54. Probably Aristotelian students of the heavenly quintessence.

55. See note 45 above.

56. With a nice distinction between *cognoscendo* and *agnoscendo*.

57. A reference to the spiritual "vehicle" of the *Chaldaean Oracles* nos. 14 and 15 (= Des Places, frgs. 104 and 158) as glossed by Pletho (ed. Tambrun-Krasker, pp. 2, 10–12, with commentary and further references on pp. 89–107).

58. Augustine, *De civitate Dei* 10.30, 12.12,14, 13.19; *De trinitate* 12.15.24 (*PL* 42.1011–12).

59. *At vero in animo . . . sensuali praestat:* Augustine, *De vera religione* 29.53.145–146 (ed. Green, *DVR*, p. 38.9–23), abbreviated.

60. *Itaque si ratio . . . indagatur:* ibid. 30.54.147 (ed. Green, *DVR*, pp. 38.24-.39.1).

61. *Sed certe quaerendum . . . non possis:* ibid. 30.54.149–150 (ed. Green, *DVR*, p. 39.6–22).

62. *Sed cum in omnibus . . . videretur:* ibid. 30.55.151–152 (ed. Green, *DVR*, pp. 39.23–40.5).

63. *Et cum omnia quae . . . veritas dicitur:* ibid. 30.56.153–157 (ed. Green, *DVR*, pp. 40.6–41.7).

64. *Nec iam illud . . . esse non ita:* ibid. 31.57.158–159 (ed. Green, *DVR*, p. 41.8–24).

65. *Quare autem nobis . . . implevit:* ibid. 31.58.160–161 (ed. Green, *DVR*, pp. 41.24–42.3).

66. *Mens omnia iudicat . . . non fas est:* ibid. 31.58.162–163 (ed. Green, *DVR*, p. 42.11–24).

67. *De ipsa vero lege . . . delectatur:* Augustine, *De libero arbitrio* 2.34.134 (ed. Green, *DLA*, pp. 70.32–71.3), slightly abbreviated and adapted.

68. *Sed multis finis est . . . rediguntur:* Augustine, *De vera religione* 32.59.165–167 (ed. Green, *DVR*, p. 43.1–18).

69. *Quod cum ita esse . . . nusquam non est:* ibid. 32.60.168–170 (ed. Green, *DVR*, pp. 43.19–44.10).

70. *Illa lux vera . . . mutabile:* ibid. 34.64.181 (ed. Green, *DVR*, p. 46.25–28).

71. *Quaere in corporis . . . ipsa sit:* ibid. 39.72.202–203 (ed. Green, *DVR*, p. 52.4–15).

72. John 1.9.

73. *Vide ibi convenientiam . . . die in diem:* Augustine, *De vera religione* 39.72.203–74.208 (ed. Green, *DVR*, pp. 52.15–53.19), ending with the quotation from II Corinthians 4.16 (cf. note 33 above).

74. A foot of three short syllables.

75. Augustine, *De musica* 6.2.3 (*PL* 32.1164). Ficino quotes this text while suppressing the dialogue form.

76. These judging or judicial numbers are the principles of harmony within that enable us to judge harmonies in the external sensible world.

77. Ibid. 6.7.17–18 (*PL* 32.1172).

78. Ibid. 6.8.20 (*PL* 32.1173–74).

79. Ibid. 6.8.21 (*PL* 32.1174).

80. Ibid. 6.9.23–24 (*PL* 32.1176–77), abridged.

81. Ibid. 6.10.25 (*PL* 32.1177).

82. The pyrrhic foot consists of two short syllables, the spondee of two long, the anapaest of two short and one long, the dactyl of one long and two short, the proceleusmatic of four short, and the double spondee (dispondee) of four long.

83. Ibid. 6.10.26 (*PL* 32.1177–78). Augustine seems to be addressing the rules for caesura.

84. Ibid. 6.10.28 (*PL* 32.1179).

85. Ibid. 6.12.34 (*PL* 32.1181–82).

86. Ibid. 6.12.35–36 (*PL* 32.1182–83), abridged.

87. Augustine, *De trinitate* 9.6.9 (*PL* 42.965–66).

88. Ibid. 14.15.21 (*PL* 42.1052).

89. "God of God, Light of Light" is the phrasing of the Nicene Creed, though the notion of a *sequens deus* raises Arian possibilities. For the divine triad (Platonic in origin) of essence, life, and mind, see Augustine's *De trinitate*.

90. Proclus' has three fundamental metaphysical triads in his *Theologia Platonica* 3.14 and *In Parmenidem* 6.60, and Ficino then read (following the later Neoplatonic tradition) this Proclian ennead back into pre-Proclian Platonic texts, and notably into Plato's *Sophist* 248E-249D. The fascination with three and its multiples is deeply rooted in the mythological and

methodological formulas of antiquity and is central to Platonic metaphysics as well as Christian theology.

91. See Dionysius the [Pseudo-] Areopagite's treatise *On the Celestial Hierarchy* 6.2–9.4 (200D-261D) and passim that establishes three as the number of the angelic hierarchies, each hierarchy having three choirs; and Dante's *Paradiso* 28 (with a reference to the Areopagite at 28.130). Cf. Ficino's own *De raptu Pauli* 6.

92. *Quando ratiocinamur . . . satis est:* Augustine, *De immortalitate animae* 1.1 (ed. Hörmann, p. 102.1–7).

93. *Non enim eam posset . . . contineri loco:* ibid. 6.10 (ed. Hörmann, pp. 110.17–18, 110.20–111.2).

94. See note 6 above. Augustine is identifying the divine Reason or Word (*ratio*) with the Truth (*illud verum*).

95. *Quare ista coniunctio . . . igitur interire:* ibid. 6.11 (ed. Hörmann, pp. 111.3–112.22).

96. *Quod vero infert dubitationem . . . igitur interire:* ibid. 11.18–12.19 (ed. Hörmann, pp. 120.3–122.2).

BOOK XIII

1. Plutarch, *Life of Demetrius* 38.3–4. Ficino probably knew the story through Leonardo Bruni's *Novella di Antioco, re di Siria* (also known under the title *Stratonica*), a popular novel of the fifteenth century. The text is in G. Locella, *Novelle italiane di quaranta autori* (Leipzig, 1879), pp. 238–242.

2. Pliny, *Natural History* 7.53.180.

3. Aulus Gellius, *Attic Nights* 3.15.

4. Herodotus, *Histories* 1.85.

5. Cf. Cicero, *Tusculan Disputations* 1.22.52: "Nam corpus quidem quasi vas est aut aliquod animi receptaculum."

6. Diogenes Laertius, *Lives,* describes Aristotle as being afflicted with a lisp, slender calves and small eyes (5.1.1); Pyrrho as being afraid of a dog (9.11.66); Speusippus as being paralysed and sick (4.1.3); Carneades as

being negligent of his hair and nails and afraid of dying (4.9.62,64); and Chrysippus as being physically insignificant (7.7.182).

7. Porphyry, *Life of Plotinus* 2 describes Plotinus as "often distressed by an intestinal complaint."

8. *Timaeus* 42A, 43E ff., and in general 41B-47E.

9. *Charmides* 156B-157B, and specifically 156E ff. (Socrates recounts what he heard, while serving in the army, from one of the "physicians" of Zalmoxis, the Thracian king); there is no mention of the "Magi." The sole reference to Zoroaster in Plato is in the *First Alcibiades* (if it is genuine as Ficino supposed) at 121E-122A.

10. *Charmides* 157A "by the use of certain charms, and these charms are fair words."

11. Diogenes Laertius, *Lives* 6.2.23, 34.

12. Ibid., 4.3.17. Polemon was the third scholarch of the Academy after Speusippus and Xenocrates.

13. Ibid., 9.10.58–59.; cf. Pliny, *Natural History* 7.23.87. Anaxarchus, a Democritean and master of Pyrrho, the founder of skepticism, had been a companion of Alexander the Great. But after the latter's death, by his outspokenness he incurred the wrath of Nicocreon or Timocreon, king of Salamis in Cyprus, and was pounded to death.

14. Diogenes Laertius, *Lives*, 1.10.109 (which declares that Epimenides's midday snooze in a cave, while looking for a lost sheep of his father's, lasted 57 years).

15. Reference unknown. The story is not found in the ancient biographical literature on Pythagoras.

16. Pliny, *Natural History* 11.97.242. Pliny says that Zoroaster lived off hard cheese for these twenty years! Cf. note 83 below.

17. *Symposium* 220CD. Cf. Aulus Gellius, *Attic Nights* 2.1.2.

18. The story is not found in the ancient biographical tradition on Plato; see Riginos (q.v.). Nor is it found in Guarino Veronese's popular *Life of Plato*, frequently printed with Plutarch's *Lives*.

19. Diogenes Laertius, *Lives* 4.2.11.

20. Cicero, *De finibus* 5.19.50.

21. *Life of Plotinus* 23.

22. Diogenes Laertius, *Lives* 9.1.3–4.

23. Ibid., 9.7.38; Cicero, *Tusculan Disputations* 5.39.114.

24. *Phaedrus* 249A.

25. E.g. *Seventh Letter* 340C, *Laws* 5.726–727A, 10.899D.

26. E.g. *Timaeus* 40DE.

27. *Problemata* 30.1.953a-955a. Cf. Book XIV at note 70, below.

28. Diogenes Laertius, *Lives* 4.3.16.

29. Ibid., 6.2.20–21.

30. The following paragraph occurs (with a few variations) in Ficino's letter to Antonio Pelotti and Baccio Ugolino of 4 March 1474 (*Opera*, p. 634.2).

31. Cf. Cicero, De *divinatione* 1.37.80; Horace, *Ars poetica* 295–297.

32. *Phaedrus* 245A; see Ficino's own *In Phaedrum* 4 (ed. Allen, pp. 82–87).

33. *Ion* 533D-534E (cf. *Meno* 99CD); see Ficino's own *In Platonis Ionem* (*Opera*, pp. 1281–1284); also "The Soul as Rhasode: Marsilio Ficino's Interpretation of Plato's *Ion*," in Allen, *Plato's Third Eye*, No. XV.

34. *Ion* 534D.

35. *Phaedrus* 245A.

36. Ovid, *Fasti* 6.5–6.

37. Notably II Corinthians 12:2–4.

38. "The deeds (*gesta*) of a disciple" may simply be a gloss on "his writings" and refer to Paul himself as a disciple. But it might refer to the deeds narrated in any one of the short treatises now considered parts of the apocryphal *Acts of St. Paul*; or more probably, to the ascent to the third heaven described in the apocryphal *Apocalypse of St. Paul* (which was known to Augustine and enjoyed a great vogue during the Middle Ages, being quoted by Dante in the *Inferno* 2.28). If we add a prefatory *et*, however, then the phrase "and the deeds of a [his?] disciple" could refer to

Dionysius the [Pseudo-]Areopagite whom Ficino and his contemporaries identified, on the evidence of his *De divinis nominibus* 3.2, with St. Paul's first convert in Athens (Acts 17:34). If so, the reference here is probably to the *De divinis nominibus* 4.13 or to Dionysius' *Epistle* 5 (*PG* 3.712AB, 1073A). Incidentally, Marcel translates "et les Actes de son disciple" and refers us to Acts 9:1–16, the story of Saul's blinding and the vision of "a certain disciple at Damascus named Ananias" (but his reference to Luke is incorrect; see note 39 below).

39. Matthew 4:18–22; Mark 1:16–20; Luke 5:1–11.

40. *Attic Nights* 15.18. Cf. note 86 below.

41. *Natural History* 7.52.174.

42. Maximus of Tyre 28; Herodotus, *Histories* 4.14–15 (on Aristeas of Proconnesus). Maximus (c. AD 125–85) was both an eloquent sophist and a follower of Plato who lectured in Athens and Rome (41 of his lectures are extant).

43. *De civitate Dei* 14.24.

44. *Phaedrus* 249CD.

45. Ibid. 244A-E.

46. *Symposium* 201D, 202E-203A; *Phaedo* 85AB; *Laws* 1.642DE.

47. *Apud* Augustine, *De civitate Dei* 18.23; cf. Plato, *Phaedrus* 244B.

48. Plutarch, *De Pythiae oraculis* 397A-D, 399A ff., 404E, 407E; *De defectu oraculorum* 432C-433E, 437D-438D.

49. The past, present and future as Ficino goes on to clarify; cf. Plato, *Timaeus* 37D-38B, which refers to the "created species" or "forms" of time.

50. Ficino must be thinking of the two notable passages in Hermes Trismegistus, *Pimander* 11.20 and *Asclepius* 6.

51. Plotinus, *Enneads* 1.1.12, 4.3.37, 6.4.16 (though Marcel suggests 2.4.5, 4.3.10). Cf. the well-known Chaldaean Oracle 15 (ed. Tambrun-Krasker [= Des Places, frg. 158]): "the idol also has its part in the region bathed in light." See Ficino's own *Platonic Theology* 12.4.11, and Kristeller, *Philosophy*, pp. 369–375, 385 (cited in the Bibliography).

52. *In Timaeum* 2.160; *Elements* 190, 194, 195.

53. The analogy is from Plotinus, *Enneads* 4.4.41.

54. *Republic* 10.617DE; cf. 620DE.

55. *Chaldaean Oracles* no. 4 (ed. Tambrun-Krasker, p. 1 [= Des Places, frg. 103]; cf. p. 6 with Pletho's note, and p. 69 with editorial commentary).

56. *Enneads* 2.9.1–2, 3.9.1.

57. *Republic* 9.571C-572B.

58. Galen, *Commentarium in Hippocratis de humoribus* 2.2 (ed. Kühn, 16: 222).

59. *Timaeus* 71E-72B.

60. ps. Hippocrates, *Epistolae* (ed. Kühn, 23: 775–783).

61. Diogenes Laertius, *Lives* 3.5.

62. In April 1463 Ficino entitled his Latin translation of the fourteen treatises of the *Corpus Hermeticum* known to him as the *Liber Mercurii Trismegisti de potestate et sapientia Dei*. After its publication in 1471, it became known by its alternative title as the *Pimander* (the title of the first treatise).

63. Cicero, *De divinatione* 2.66.135. Ptolemaeus, an intimate friend of Alexander, had been struck in battle by a poisoned arrow. Alexander attended his sickbed and in a dream saw a pet serpent of his mother Olympias appear with a medicinal root in its mouth and naming the place where it grew nearby.

64. Orpheus, *Hymns* 86.2–7 (ed. Quandt, pp. 56–57)—the "Hymn to Dream."

65. For Hercules' epilepsy, cf. Aristotle, *Problemata* 30.953a10–19.

66. Eusebius, *Praeparatio evangelica* 11.36.563–564 (PG 21: 937, 940) with the substitution of Enarchus for Antyllus. The chapter is subtitled *Ex Plutarcho*.

67. *Problemata* 30.953a.26–33.

68. *Euthydemus* 272E; *Phaedrus* 242B; *Apology* 31CD, 40AC, 41D; *Republic* 6.496C; *Theages* 128D-129D (cf. note 72 below)—the "familiar demon" is Ficino's interpretation of Socrates' "divine sign."

69. Xenophon, *Apology* 4.12–13, *Memorabilia* 1.1.2–5.

70. This is Antipater of Tyre, a first century BC Stoic as cited by Cicero, *De divinatione* 1.54.123 (a text Ficino obviously had in mind given the references at notes 74 and 75 below). See *SVF* 3.3.38 (p. 249).

71. *De deo Socratis,* passim.

72. Plato, *Theages* 129A-C.

73. Ibid., 128DE.

74. Cicero, *De divinatione* 1.54.123.

75. Ibid.

76. Plato, *Theages* 130A-E (the Thucydides in question was the son of Melesias). Cf. Xenophon's *Memorabilia* 1.2.15–16, 24–25, which says much the same of Alcibiades and Critias.

77. Xenophon, *Apology* 29.

78. See Diels-Kranz, no. 71 (2: 503–510). Diogenes Laertius (1.116–117) describes his powers of prophecy.

79. Porphyry, *Life of Pythagoras* 30–31; Iamblichus, *De vita Pythagorica* 2.10.

80. Porphyry, *Life of Plotinus* 23.

81. Porphyry, *Life of Plotinus* 11.

82. *Letters* 7.27.2 (though Pliny the Younger says that at the time Curtius was an unknown aide to the governor of Africa and that the woman was the spirit of Africa). See also Tacitus, *Annales* 11.21. This Curtius Rufus (not Quintus Curtius Rufus, the historian of Alexander) was of obscure and humble origin; he became a senator and eventually proconsul of Africa, thus fulfilling a prediction made at the onset of his career.

83. Pliny, *Natural History* 11.97.242. Cf. note 16 above.

84. Orpheus, *Hymns,* the prologue (ed. Quandt, pp. 1–2) [?]. Cf. note 89 below.

85. That is, of the sibyl at the shrine of Zeus at Dodona and of the female medium who uttered the responses of the oracle of Apollo at

Delphi. Plato's *Phaedrus* 244AB refers to "the prophetess at Delphi and the priestesses at Dodona."

86. *Attic Nights* 15.18.1–3. Cf. note 40 above.

87. *Hymns* 39 (ed. Quandt, p. 31), the "Hymn to a Corybant." The Corybantes were the ecstatic priests of Cybele.

88. *Contra academicos* 1.6.17–8.23 (though Augustine speaks of Albicerius not Albigerius).

89. *Hymns*, the prologue, lines 1–2 (ed. Quandt, pp. 1–2). Cf. note 84 above; or the Palinode Ficino found in Eusebius, *Praeparatio evangelica* 13.12.5 (Kern frg. 247); see the free rendering in his 1492 letter to Martin Prenniger (*Opera*, p. 934).

90. *Revelation* 3:20 (adapted).

91. Augustine, *De cura pro mortuis gerenda* 12.15 (*PL* 40.602–03).

92. *Revelation* 1:9–19 and passim.

93. Ezekiel 37:1–14.

94. Isaiah 6:1–3.

95. See Allen, *Icastes*, pp. 147–157 (cited in the Bibliography), for an analysis of this chapter.

96. Pliny, *Natural History* 35.36.65–66.

97. Ibid., 35.36.95 (said of a horse but not a dog). Apelles, the painter, fl. c. 330 BC.

98. Ibid., 36.4.21 (said of the Cnidian Venus). Praxiteles, the sculptor, fl. c. 370 BC.

99. Aulus Gellius, *Attic Nights* 10.12.9–10: "aura spiritus indusa atque occulta."

100. *Asclepius* 24.

101. Cf. Cicero, *Tusculan Disputations* 1.25.63; *De natura deorum* 2.35.88; *De republica* 1.14.21.

102. Or possibly "approval of its virtue."

103. Cf. Ovid, *Metamorphoses* 8.183–235 — the Icarus story.

104. The grammar is wayward here. Ficino obviously means that tracing out the motions of lines, presumably in astronomy, involves delving into greatest obscurities, and similarly that understanding musical consonances means engaging the most exacting distinctions (*superstitiosa*).

105. See note 101 above.

106. *Republic* 10.598DE; *Ion* 537Aff.

107. St. Jerome, *De viris illustribus* 109 (*PL* 23: 705). Didymus the Blind (c. AD 313–398) was head of the catechetical school of Alexandria (former heads had been Clement and Origen in the early third century). Among his pupils were Jerome and Gregory Nazianzenus.

108. Plato, *Laws* 5.747DE; Aristotle, *Politics* 7.7.1327b.

109. Pliny, *Natural History* 7.24.88; Valerius Maximus, *Factorum et dictorum memorabilium libri* 7.16.

110. Pliny, *Natural History* 7.24.88.

111. Cf. Cicero, *Academica* 2.1.2 (on Lucullus).

112. Seneca the Elder (c. 55 BC — c. AD 37), the rhetorician, was famous for his memory (see his *Controversiae* 1, preface 2–3, ed. Kiessling, p. 58); but in the Quattrocento he had not yet been distinguished, since he had exactly the same name, from his famous son (c. AD 1–65), the Stoic philosopher, moralist, and tragedian (though some argued that the tragedian was not the Stoic moralist). Hence the father's works were often adduced as evidence for the son's life, as here. See, for example, Giannozzo Manetti's widely read *Life of Seneca* 12 (ed. S. U. Baldassarri and R. Bagemihl as no. 9 in this I Tatti series), which is probably Ficino's immediate source for the claim and for the undifferentiated attribution. Incidentally, Manetti had, in the Plutarchan manner, deliberately paralleled this biography with a *Life of Socrates*; this too must have attracted Ficino.

113. St. Augustine, *De anima et eius origine* 4.7.9 (*PL* 44.529), but with no reference to anyone memorizing a comedy.

114. Cf. Lucretius, *De rerum natura* 5.1056–1090.

115. Cf. Ficino, *De christiana religione* 10 (*Opera*, p. 15).

116. *Symposium* 186A-188D (the speech of the doctor Eryximachus).

117. Ps.-Hippocrates, *De humoribus* (ed. Kühn, 21:120); Galen, *Ars medicinalis* 23 (ed. Kühn, 1: 367f.).

118. See the preceding chapter.

119. Or "way of life."

120. Possibly a species of antelope or buffalo or the gnu; see Pliny, *Natural History* 8.32.77. It is described as having an awkwardly heavy head as well as lethal eyes. In Greek *katablepō* means to stare, glare or despise.

121. Ibid., 8.33.78.

122. On the Triballi and the evil eye, see Pliny the Elder, *Natural History* 3.149, 4.3, 4.33.

123. The *attentio* of the good phantasy here is parallel to and almost the same as the *intentio* of the bad phantasy two lines later.

124. *Chaldaean Oracles* no. 17 (ed. Tambrun-Krasker, p. 2 [Des Places, frg. 128]; cf. p. 13 with Pletho's note, and pp. 108–116 with editorial commentary).

125. Philostratus, *Life of Apollonius of Tyana* 3.39, 4.45, 7.38.

126. Iamblichus, *De vita Pythagorica* 139 (undoubtedly Ficino's source).

127. *Timaeus* 43A-46E.

128. *Phaedrus* 246B ff. Cf. Ficino's *In Phaedrum* 8 (ed. Allen, pp. 100–107).

129. *Epinomis* 982BC.

130. *Republic* 10.616C-617D.

131. *Chaldaean Oracles* no. 11 (ed. Tambrun-Krasker, p. 2 [= Des Places, frg. 97]; cf. p. 9 with Pletho's note, and pp. 81–83 with editorial commentary).

132. John 1:13, 3:3–7.

133. *Timaeus* 40DE.

134. Avicebron, *Fons vitae* 3.44 (ed. Baumker, p. 178).

135. Avicenna, *Metaphysics* 10.3 (ed. Lizzini-Porro, pp. 1020–1027).

136. Plutarch, *De defectu oraculorum* 419E-F; Porphyry, *De abstinentia* 2.3–5 (Ficino, *Opera*, pp. 1935–6); Proclus, *Elements of Theology* 145 (ed. Dodds, p. 128).

137. Plato, *Statesman* 271D ff., *Timaeus* 41A ff., *Laws* 4.713CD, 5.738D, 740A, 747DE, 8.848DE, 10.906A-C.

138. Ficino means more than just "a magical view."

139. Reference unknown.

140. *Iliad* 8.15–28; cf. Plato, *Theaetetus* 153CD; Macrobius, *In Somnium Scipionis* 1.14.15; Ficino, *In Philebum* 1.27 (ed. Allen, p. 257). The chain is six-linked, six being the first perfect number (as the sum of its factors, including one) and also the first of the nuptial numbers (as the product of 2x3, the first two adjacent numbers, excluding one); see Allen, *Nuptial Arithmetic*, pp. 50–52, 67–68, 129–133 (with further references); cited in the Bibliography.

141. II Kings 2:11–12.

142. II Corinthians 12:2–4. Cf. note 149 below.

143. A compote of citations from three *Chaldaean Oracles* nos.12 (line 1), 21, and 15b (ed. Tambrun-Krasker, pp. 2, 3 [= Des Places, frgs. 96, 112, 158]; cf. pp. 29, 31, 32 with Pletho's notes, and pp. 84–88, 106–107, 123–124 with editorial commentary). Lemmata that Ficino glosses are in italics.

144. Psalm 24:7, 9. Ficino is citing of course from the Roman psalter. The AV reads "Lift up your heads, O ye gates."

145. *Pimander* 10.13,16–18,21 (cf. 13.14).

146. Notice the subtle descent from *moveri* to *sustineri* to *contineri*—repeating the argument at the end of the previous paragraph. The idolum no longer moves the body or nourishes it or even holds it together (i.e. prevents its four humors from dissolving).

147. *Chaldaean Oracles* no. 28b (ed. Tambrun-Krasker, p. 3 [= Des Places, frg. 1]; cf. pp. 16–17 with Pletho's gloss, and pp. 133–135 with editorial commentary).

148. *Phaedrus* 248A3; cf. Ficino's own *In Phaedrum* 7 (ed. Allen, pp. 99–100), *De amore* 7.14 (ed. Laurens, p. 243), and *In Philebum* 1.34 (ed. Allen, p. 353).

149. II Corinthians 12:2. Cf. note 142, above.

150. A reference to "the ordinance of necessity" of *Phaedrus* 248C—cf. Ficino's *In Phaedrum*, summa 24 (ed. Allen, p. 163)—or possibly, following Marcel, to *Laws* 10.903B-904C.

151. Notice the niceties of the descent from *continue conspirantium* to *confluentium* to *concurrentium*—breathing together (air), flowing together (water), and running together (earth).

152. Psalm 19:1.

153. *Platonic Theology* 13.2.8–23, above.

154. *Metaphysics* 10.1 (ed. Lizzini-Porro, pp. 998–1009).

155. Proclus, *In Timaeum* 1.206.26–222.6 (ed. Diehl), glossing *Timaeus* 27C; Iamblichus, *De Mysteriis* 5.26 (ed. Des Places, pp. 181.237.8–182.240.10; tr. Ficino, *Opera*, pp. 1899–1900).

BOOK XIV

1. *Chaldaean Oracles* no. 22 (ed. Tambrun-Krasker, p. 3 [ed. Des Places, frg. 106]; cf. p. 15 with Pletho's note, and p. 125 with an editorial commentary).

2. Note Ficino's circumspect blurring of the line between "God" and "a god"; cf. the end of Chapter 3 below.

3. John 1:12, I John 3:2.

4. Romans 8:29, I Corinthians 15:49, II Corinthians 3:18.

5. The first four signs have been discussed (as category one) in Book XIII. We recall there are sixteen signs in all.

6. Marcel refers us to Thomas, *Summa contra Gentiles* 3.25; cf. note 9 below.

7. *Theaetetus* 176AB.

8. Source unknown, though Marcel refers us to Cicero, *De officiis* 1.14.46, 97. Cf. note 15, below. No similar testimonium can be found in the edition of Panaetius' fragments by M. van Straaten (Leiden: E. J. Brill, 1952), and the doctrine does not seem appropriate to a Stoic.

9. *De caelo* 1.8.277a15–31; cf. Thomas, *Summa contra gentiles* 3.25.13.

10. This philosopher is Averroes who believed that human beings participated in one supreme agent intellect.

11. Book XV passim.

12. *Second Letter* 314A-C. Cf. Plato's *Seventh Letter* 341C-E, 343E-344B.

13. *Epinomis* 973C-974C (though Schiavone cites 976A, 988B, 992C).

14. *De trinitate* 13.8.11 (the conclusion) (*PL* 42.1022).

15. See the earlier reference at note 8, above.

16. Ficino is playing here with the Platonic associations of *formalis*.

17. Proclus, *In Timaeum* 2.135; *In Alcibiadem* 109D 1–6 (ed. Segonds, 2: 276 f.); *Elements* 20 (ed. Dodds, p. 22).

18. The following epitome does not appear as such in Origen's *De principiis*, but see 2.1.1–3, 2.9.6 and 4.1.35–36 (=4.4.8–9) (Crouzel-Simonetti, 1: 234–240, 364–366, 3: 419–427).

19. II Corinthians 4:16–18.

20. Ibid. 3:18; cf. note 4 above.

21. *Asclepius* 6.1–5.

22. Averroes, *De anima* 3.5.

23. *Enneads* 5.3.5.

24. Ibid., 5.3.6–7.

25. *Platonic Theology* 12.1.1–6 (paragraphs also focused on the image of the circle).

26. *Infectus* can be read either as "tarnished" (from *inficio*) or as "unfinished" (from *infacio*). Either sense would pertain here though "tarnished" is countered by "pure" later in the sentence.

27. This simile derives from the *Phaedrus* 246B ff. Cf. Ficino's *In Phaedrum* 2 (ed. Allen, p. 77; cf. pp. 149, 219, 223–225, 229).

28. Or if we accept L's reading, *perficitque,* "perfecting or fashioning itself day by day."

29. See the enumeration in *Platonic Theology* 14.1.1, above.

30. *Platonic Theology* 13.3.1–4.

31. See Chapter 8, paragraph 2, below.

32. Cf. Plutarch, *De tranquillitate animi* 4 (*Moralia* 466D); and Diels-Kranz, 2:238 A11. But the story is frequently cited by Renaissance humanists.

33. Cf. Diogenes Laertius, *Lives,* 8.2.66 ("I go among you an immortal god"), 69–70.

34. Hermes Trismegistus, *Corpus Hermeticum* 10.25: "the human rises up to heaven and takes its measure and knows what is in its heights and its depths" (tr. Copenhaver, p. 36).

35. *Second Letter* 311CD.

36. *Laws* 11.927AB.

37. *Chaldaean Oracles* no. 5 (ed. Tambrun-Krasker, p. 1 [ed. Des Places, frg. 13]; cf. p. 6 with Pletho's note, and pp. 69–70 with editorial commentary).

38. Though *prudens* can mean "wise" and *imprudens* "ignorant," the argument here and following concerns the four cardinal virtues including the virtue of prudence; hence our decision to retain the terms "prudent" and "imprudent."

39. That is, the civic and the purgatorial virtues and the virtues of the already-purged soul as outlined earlier in this paragraph.

40. Ficino is drawing on the scholastic distinction between the *ratio intellectualis* and the *ratio cogitatrix;* see Aquinas, *Summa theologica* 1.q.78.a.4; *Quaestiones disputatae de anima* a.13; *Commentarium II De Anima* 13.

41. *Platonic Theology* 10.8 passim.

42. Virgil, *Aeneid* 5.629.

43. Euripides, *Medea* 1224 (life as a shadow). Schiavone, ad loc. is surely correct in claiming that Ficino is citing from memory and attributing to Euripides a famous phrase in Pindar's *Eighth Pythian Ode* 95 "skias onar

anthrôpos" ("man is the dream of a shadow"). The general description of the soul's entry into the body recalls Plato's *Timaeus* 43A ff.

44. Homer, *Odyssey* 10.494–495, 11.90 ff.

45. Pythagoras, *Golden Verses* 63 (ed. Thom, p. 98); cf. Hierocles 25.6–8.

46. *Plato in Protagora . . . quos nos exaudiat:* this passage also appears in Ficino's *De christiana religione* 2 (*Opera*, pp. 2–3). Cf. note 64, below.

47. *Protagoras* 322A.

48. Ficino is referring to a gnome in a collection of some 451 gnomes, probably non-Christian in origin but with Christian additions, mentioned by Origen. It was wrongly attributed to the Pope Xystus (i.e. Sixtus II who was martyred in AD 258) by, among others, Rufinus (the sometime friend of Jerome), who translated it into Latin under the title *Anulus*. In a letter to Ctesiphon, however, Jerome himself called the collection's author or originator Sextus Pythagoreus and argued against its being the work of Xystus. The gnome is cited in Augustine's *De natura et gratia* 64.77 (*PL* 44. col. 285) as *Templum sanctum est Deo mens pura* and this was probably Ficino's source, even though MSS of Rufinus' Latin version were available to him; in Henry Chadwick's 1959 edition, *The Sentences of Sixtus*, it is numbered 46a. In a quite different text, also known to Ficino and which he eventually translated, Porphyry's *De abstinentia animalium*, book 2 declares, in the course of discussing total abstinence, that "the uncontaminated soul is as it were the temple of God" (tr. Ficino, *Opera*, pp. 1936.3–1937). Cf. the reference in note 84 below.

49. *Neque audeat . . . deus ad animam:* this passage also appears in Ficino's *Disputatio contra iudicium astrologorum* in *M* (= *SF*, 2:14–15).

50. *Sane commoda . . . ad unum denique cuncta:* in addition to being embedded in the *Disputatio* (see note 49 above), this passage also appears in a section of Ficino's *Compendium Platonicae Theologiae* (now in his second book of *Letters*) entitled "*Deus omnibus providet. . .*" (*Opera*, p. 696.2).

51. Psalm 94[93]:9

52. *De animalibus* 12 = *De partibus animalium* 2.10.656A7 ff. Ficino thinks of Aristotle's two works — the *History of Animals* and *On Animals' Parts* —

as one continuous work with the second book of the latter as therefore the twelfth book. Even so, the reference is obscure.

53. *Platonic Theology* 13.3.1.

54. In the rest of this book Ficino will equate religion with the old Latin sense of piety and irreligion with impiety.

55. *Protagoras* 322A-C. See note 58 below.

56. *Metaphysica* 10.1–2 (ed. Lizzini-Porro, pp. 998–1019). See notes 59 and 60 below.

57. *Statesman* 271E (paraphrased), and in general 271D-272B; cf. *Laws* 4.713CD.

58. *Protagoras* 322A-D. See n. 55 above.

59. *Metaphysica* 10.2.532–533 (ed. Lizzini-Porro, pp. 1013–14). See note 56 above.

60. Ibid. 10.1–2.

61. *Enneads* 2.3 passim. Are the nods the retrograde motions of the planets?

62. Cf. *De rerum natura* 5.1161–1240.

63. Apud Proclus, *In Timaeum* 1.208.17–23 (ed. Diehl).

64. *Duas enim aetates . . . discernat quam consueverit* (i.e. this paragraph); cf. Ficino, *De Christiana religione* 3 (*Opera*, p. 3). Cf. note 46 above.

65. *Laws* 10.887C-888D.

66. Cf. Ficino's *In Philebum* 1.25 (ed. Allen, pp. 230–235).

67. Reference not identified.

68. *Second Letter* 314AB; *Phaedrus* 241AB, 279A; *Republic* 1.328D-329D; *Laws* 10.888A-D.

69. *Second Letter* 312D-314B.

70. Cf. [Pseudo-]Aristotle, *Problemata* 30.1 (the locus classicus—see *Platonic Theology* 13.2.2 at note 27, above); and Cicero, *Tusculan Disputations* 1.33.80 (i.e. just a page before the Cleombrotus anecdote—see note 79 below).

71. Avempace is Ibn Yahya or Bajja, an important Moslem philosopher and Aristotelian commentator, who flourished in Zaragoza, Spain, in the first quarter of the twelfth century. Though this is the only mention of him in Ficino, he was cited by Albertus Magnus, Aquinas and others. The source of Ficino's allusion awaits identification.

72. Cf. Diogenes Laertius, *Lives* 10.4–7; and Cicero, *De finibus*, 2, passim.

73. Ibid., 2.8.74–75, 81.

74. Cf. St. Jerome, *Chronicon* (ed. Fotheringham, p. 194).

75. For this ancient but much contested medical notion of thirsty lungs, which stems from Plato's *Timaeus* 70CD, 78C ff., 91A, and then enters into the Hippocratic corpus, see Ficino's own *Platonic Theology* 9.3.6 at note 14.

76. Not in the *Theaetetus* as such, though implied by 179D-180B.

77. *Seventh Letter* 335A-C.

78. *Gorgias* 523A-526D; *Republic* 10.614B-621B; *Laws* 10.903B-905D—i.e. the punishment myths (for "proofs not to be scorned" see 905D).

79. Cicero, *Tusculan Disputations* 1.34.84; Augustine, *City of God* 1.22.

80. There is no such story in the ancient biographical traditions regarding Plato and Demosthenes. See Riginos, pp. 134–135.

81. *Protagoras* 322A.

82. I.e. certain (baleful) planets in conjunction as distinct from planets generally in opposition.

83. Cf. 1 Corinthians 13:9.

84. Porphyry, *De abstinentia animalium* 2 (tr. Ficino, *Opera*, pp. 1936.3–1937); cf. note 48 above. Or possibly apud Proclus, *In Timaeum* 1.208.8 ff.; cf. note 63 above.

85. *Seventh Letter* 341CD, 344B. For a detailed treatment of Ficino's sources, especially Augustine and Henry of Ghent, in the following comparison of will and intellect, see James Hankins, "Lorenzo de' Medici as a student of Ficino: The *De summo bono*," in his *Humanism and Platonism* (cited in the Bibliography), vol. II, pp. 317–350.

86. *Epinomis* 989B.

87. *Phaedo* 107CD.

88. *Laws* 10.900CD, 902E-903D. Note that *Laws* 10 is very much in Ficino's mind for the rest of this chapter.

89. Orpheus, *Hymns* 10: "To Nature" (where Nature, the divine mother, is addressed in lines 13 ff. as *Dike*, as the justice that protects the air, earth and sea and provides for the universe); and 62 and 63 "To Justice" (lines 12–16 of the latter addresses Justice as goddess and universal mother).

90. Cf. Eusebius, *Praeparatio evangelica* 8.14.392 (*PG* 21, col. 665).

91. *Laws* 10.899D-900D, 904E-905C; cf. note 78 above and notes 93 and 96 below.

92. *Republic* 10.612E-613B.

93. *Laws* 10.895E-896B, 904CD and ff.; cf. notes 78 and 91 above and note 96 below.

94. Psalm 139[138]:8 (garbled).

95. *Republic* 10.612B. Note the last sentence only appears at 612B.

96. *Laws* 10.906A-D.

Bibliography

Allen, Michael J. B. *The Platonism of Marsilio Ficino: A Study of His "Phaedrus" Commentary, Its Sources and Genesis.* Berkeley & Los Angeles: University of California Press, 1984.

———. *Icastes: Marsilio Ficino's Interpretation of Plato's "Sophist".* Berkeley & Los Angeles: University of California Press, 1989. Contains studies of Ficino's ontology.

———. *Nuptial Arithmetic: Marsilio Ficino's Commentary on the Fatal Number in Book VIII of Plato's "Republic."* Berkeley and Los Angeles: University of California Press, 1994. Includes studies of Ficino's numerology and his theories of Platonic prophecy and time.

———. *Plato's Third Eye: Studies in Marsilio Ficino's Metaphysics and Its Sources.* Aldershot: Variorum, 1995. Various studies.

———. *Synoptic Art: Marsilio Ficino on the History of Platonic Interpretation.* Florence: Olschki, 1998. Includes chapters on Ficino's views on ancient theology, on Socrates, on the later history of Platonism, and on dialectic.

Allen, Michael J. B., and Valery Rees, with Martin Davies, eds. *Marsilio Ficino: His Theology, His Philosophy, His Legacy.* Leiden: E. J. Brill, 2002. A wide range of new essays.

Copenhaver, Brian P., and Charles B. Schmitt. *Renaissance Philosophy.* Oxford: Oxford University Press, 1992. Excellent introduction to the context.

Field, Arthur. *The Origins of the Platonic Academy of Florence.* Princeton: Princeton University Press, 1988. Fine, detailed study of Ficino's formative years.

Hankins, James. *Plato in the Italian Renaissance.* 2 vols. Leiden: E. J. Brill, 1990. A synoptic account of the Platonic revival.

———. *Humanism and Platonism in the Italian Renaissance.* 2 vols. Rome: Edizioni di Storia e Letteratura, 2003–2004. Includes nineteen studies on Ficino and Renaissance Platonism.

Katinis, Teodoro. "Bibliografia ficiniana: Studi ed edizioni delle opere di Marsilio Ficino dal 1986." In *Accademia* 2 (2000): 101–136. A bibliography from 1986 to 2000; updated annually.

Kristeller, Paul Oskar. *Marsilio Ficino and His Work after Five Hundred Years*. Florence: Olschki, 1987. An essential guide to the bibliography.

——. *Medieval Aspects of Renaissance Learning*, ed. and tr. Edward P. Mahoney. 2nd ed. New York: Columbia University Press, 1992.

——. *The Philosophy of Marsilio Ficino*. New York: Columbia University Press, 1943; repr. Gloucester, Mass.: Peter Lang, 1964. The authoritative study of Ficino as a formal philosopher.

——. *Renaissance Thought and Its Sources*. New York: Columbia University Press, 1979. Pays special attention to Platonism.

——. *Studies in Renaissance Thought and Letters*. Rome: Edizioni di Storia e Letteratura, 1956. Important essays on Ficino's context and influence.

——. *Studies in Renaissance Thought and Letters III*. Rome: Edizioni di Storia e Letteratura, 1993. More essays on Renaissance Platonism and on individual Platonists.

Members of the Language Department of the School of Economic Science, London, trs. *The Letters of Marsilio Ficino*. 7 vols. to date. London: Shepheard-Walwyn, 1975–.

Toussaint, Stéphane, ed. *Marcel Ficin ou les mystères platoniciens*. Les Cahiers de l'Humanisme, vol. 2. Paris: Les Belles Lettres, 2002.

Trinkaus, Charles. *In Our Image and Likeness: Humanity and Divinity in Italian Humanist Thought*. 2 vols. London: University of Chicago Press, 1970. Wide-ranging analysis of a Christian-Platonic theme.

Walker, D. P. *Spiritual and Demonic Magic: from Ficino to Campanella*. London: The Warburg Institute, 1958. A seminal study.

Wind, Edgar. *Pagan Mysteries in the Renaissance*, rev. ed. New York: Norton, 1968. A rich book on Platonism's influence on Renaissance mythography, art and culture.

Index

References are by book, chapter, and paragraph number.

Publication of this volume has been made possible by

The Myron and Sheila Gilmore Publication Fund at I Tatti
The Robert Lehman Endowment Fund
The Jean-François Malle Scholarly Programs and Publications Fund
The Andrew W. Mellon Scholarly Publications Fund
The Craig and Barbara Smyth Fund
for Scholarly Programs and Publications
The Lila Wallace–Reader's Digest Endowment Fund
The Malcolm Wiener Fund for Scholarly Programs and Publications